THE AMERICAN CONVENTION ON HUMAN RIGHTS

THE AMERICAN CONVENTION ON HUMAN RIGHTS

Cecilia MEDINA

Translated by

Peter KRUPA

intersentia
Cambridge – Antwerp – Portland

Intersentia Publishing Ltd.
Trinity House | Cambridge Business Park | Cowley Road
Cambridge | CB4 0WZ | United Kingdom
Tel.: +44 1223 393 753 | Email: mail@intersentia.co.uk

Distribution for the UK:
NBN International
Airport Business Centre, 10 Thornbury Road
Plymouth, PL6 7 PP
United Kingdom
Tel.: +44 1752 202 301 | Fax: +44 1752 202 331
Email: orders@nbninternational.com

Distribution for the USA and Canada:
International Specialized Book Services
920 NE 58th Ave. Suite 300
Portland, OR 97213
USA
Tel.: +1 800 944 6190 (toll free)
Email: info@isbs.com

Distribution for Austria:
Neuer Wissenschaftlicher Verlag
Argentinierstraße 42/6
1040 Wien
Austria
Tel.: +43 1 535 61 03 24
Email: office@nwv.at

Distribution for other countries:
Intersentia Publishing nv
Groenstraat 31
2640 Mortsel
Belgium
Tel.: +32 3 680 15 50
Email: mail@intersentia.be

The American Convention on Human Rights
Cecilia Medina

ISBN 978-1-78068-101-6
D/2014/7849/12
NUR 820

British Library Cataloguing in Publication Data. A catalogue record for this book is available from the British Library.

To Caroline, Pablo, Madeleine and María Cecilia

PREFACE

This book was originally written in Spanish and completed when I was about to start my role as a judge in the Inter-American Court of Human Rights (hereinafter "the Court"). I finished my research on 31 December 2003 and due to unfortunate circumstances the book in its Spanish version was only published later in 2005. The rights chosen for analysis (the rights to life, to personal freedom, to personal integrity, to due process of law and to a judicial remedy) are the ones about which the victims complained most often before the Court, since they represented the most common violations in the times when many of the States Parties had either just left behind a dictatorial regime or were still immersed in one. In the analysis of the Inter-American Court's jurisprudence on these rights, not only were the judgments themselves taken into consideration but also the European and the universal jurisprudence, as both the European Court of Human Rights and the Human Rights Committee of the UN had started their activities much earlier. Use was also made of the *travaux préparatoires* of the American Convention on Human Rights (hereinafter "the Convention"), although the meager professionalism shown by the drafters during the debates and the lack of information in the minutes of the Inter-American Specialized Conference on Human Rights do not help much to extract the sense of a right when the usual rules of interpretation still leave room for doubt. The book covers the first fifteen years of the Court's jurisdiction until 2003. The reader will be shown the hesitant steps of the Court in developing its position on these specific human rights with respect to states whose unseemly rules and practices regarding these rights prevailed.

In order to understand the rationale behind the application of the Convention by the Court it is necessary to consider the situation of the States in whose domestic orders the treaty was to operate. Latin America consisted of a group of countries with significant economic and social disparities, rigid class distinctions, various degrees of illiteracy, lack of health assistance for the poor, to name a few of its miseries. Aside from these flagrant violations of the essential principle of non-discrimination and of economic, social and cultural rights – very much present in the daily lives of the poor – there was in terms of civil and political rights a pervasive and perverse inclination to dictatorships with their usual sequel of assassinations, torture and whichever other means were necessary to prevent any sort of opposition to the powers they held. Furthermore even in States where the rule of law prevailed, there was no culture of human rights: torture and ill-treatment of persons who might have committed criminal offenses; blatant ill-treatment of the poor by the rest of society abounded. Authoritarianism was rampant.[1] The Inter-American Convention thus appeared as a strong response against dictatorships and the appalling situation of human rights in most of these countries. It is understandable, under these circumstances, that the Court faced an extremely difficult task: to make the rule of law in the area of human rights prevail over the whole of the continent.

While sitting in the Court I decided not to publish an update of the present work, as I thought it unwise to combine an outsider's approach – which I was until the beginning of 2004 – with that of an insider, limited, for obvious reasons, by the very nature of the position held. Later on, there was a reason not to simply update this book with the new jurisprudence, as I thought it best for readers to be able to see the development of the Court in what I consider was its initial phase. In this initial phase the Court dealt mainly with individual cases inserted in a situation of gross systematic violations, that is to say "violations instrumental to the achievement of government policies, perpetrated in such a quantity and in such a manner as to create a situation in which the rights to life, to personal integrity or to personal liberty of the population as a whole or of one or more sectors of the population of a country are continuously infringed or threatened".[2] I think this book, as it is, shows in an uncluttered manner the basic mode of reasoning with which the Court operates. I use the term uncluttered in the sense that it is not full of the necessary nuances that start to show as soon as the legal nature of the cases involved becomes more sophisticated. This mode has done much for the development of international human rights law both within and outside of the American continent. It is my conviction that this model of reasoning will only end up becoming, as has already happened,[3] more and more elaborated.

Most of the jurisprudence existing in the time covered by this book was developed on the basis of cases that occurred during periods of non-democratic regimes, and in them the Court struggled to make of the Inter-American Convention an instrument that would have a positive impact on the human rights situation of those living in the American continent. The majority of the cases it handled in those days could have been declared as violations of the Convention without further ado;[4] the facts so obviously constituted violations of a right – due

---

1 C. Medina, "The Bumpy Road to Human Rights Enjoyment", the Americas SIM lecture 2008, lecture delivered on 24 September 2008 on the occasion of the 27th anniversary of the Netherlands Institute of Human Rights (SIM), in (2008) 26(4) *Netherlands Human Rights Quarterly* 627.

2 C. Medina, *The Battle of Human Rights. Gross, Systematic Violations and the Inter-American System*, Martinus Nijhoff Publishers, Dordrecht/Boston/London, 1988, p. 16.

3 I/A Court HR, *Case of Aloeboetoe et al.*

4 On due process I allude, for example, to the criminal cases in Peru in the time of Fujimori. See I/A Court HR, *Case of Castillo Petruzzi et al.* As regards personal integrity and personal freedom, the *case of Velásquez Rodríguez*, as well as other cases on disappearances, comes to mind.

process, personal integrity or personal freedom – that the answer could have been simple, particularly since cases that had occurred during non-democratic times usually reached the Court when the dictators were gone and were not seriously contended by the States in question because the violations belonged to a former regime which they had defeated. The Court, however, took the opportunity in each case to develop the scope and content of the right, in order to start setting standards for the future. By doing so it improved the contents of its judgments through its creative interpretation, strengthening the protection of human rights far beyond the case itself. From 2004 onwards, the solid structure of the ground laid before helped to build on in cases that were a bit more legally complex. Cases then started to come before the Court that did not necessarily refer to gross violations of human rights, but to alleged violations that had occurred in states which had formerly been dictatorships and that still had remains of the past in their legal systems and administrative practices that were incompatible with the Convention.

I am hopeful that the first translation of this work into the English language will be followed by a second edition in which other aspects of the rights analyzed could be included, giving more emphasis to the interpretation of Articles 1 and 2 of the Convention that set forth the obligations of the States as regards human rights, which I believe can produce a major improvement for the system. This new period is set in a different context. What has now appeared in the inter-American arena are the inequalities of the past taking place not in the middle of a dictatorship but in States which claim to be democratic. In the first decade of the 21st century, we see the Court starting to deal with situations of what is called "structural" discrimination, that is to say, situations of social exclusion or of subjection of some groups by other groups.[5] The Court has been seized to attend to the problems of societies increasingly conscious of their heterogeneity and of their right to be treated according to their needs. The Court's task in such a situation is to develop the legal consequences of this for States regarding the measures that they should carry out in order to ensure for all persons the free and full exercise of the human rights set out in the Convention and to give effect to these. In paragraphs 166 to 168 of the 1986 judgment in the case of Velásquez Rodríguez, the basis for interpreting the word "ensure" in Article 1 was set. The interpretation was wide enough to allow the Court to impose on States the obligation to ensure human rights according to these varieties. This gave a new and deeper value to the prohibition on discrimination applied in a manner that truly answered the plea of victims to receive adequate treatment and eventually reparation. The rights of indigenous peoples and the questions of gender and particularly of women have begun to appear in full force in the analysis of the

5 R. Saba, "(Des)igualdad estructural", in D. Caicedo Tapia and A. Porras Velasco (eds.), *Igualdad y no discriminación. El reto de la diversidad*, Serie Justicia y Derechos Humanos Neoconstitucionales y Sociedad, Ministerio de Justicia, Derechos Humanos y Cultos, Argentina, p. 57, online.

obligation to ensure and that of other rights. The changes carried out in these areas are not creations of the Court. One can actually trace this back to something an Advisory Opinion of the Court had already stated as far back as 1999: the evolutionary interpretation of international instruments of protection is consistent with the general rules of treaty interpretation of the 1969 Vienna Convention on the Law of Treaties and therefore it is proper to interpret the Convention in the light of the changes that had been made over time and examine "present conditions".[6] What the Court has been doing all these years is developing the notion, on the one hand, that human rights are for "everyone", that is, for all human beings, and on the other, that a true interpretation of Article 1 on the States' obligation to ensure the free and full exercise of those rights and freedoms without any discrimination requires States to guarantee those rights according to the situation these persons are in.

The change is noticeable in the case of indigenous peoples. In the case of Aloeboetoe v. Suriname,[7] which mainly concerned the deprivation of life and violation of the right to personal integrity of a number of indigenous people or Maroons (members of the Saramaka tribe), the Court agreed to apply the Maroons' family law but did not accept the request for compensation to the Saramaka tribe as such.[8] Later on, when the right to property of indigenous peoples was invoked, for example in the case of Yakye Axa, the Court said that the essence of the protection of indigenous peoples' human rights "required consideration of their specificities and their economic and social characteristics plus their customary law, values, and customs".[9] In the case of Yatama v. Nicaragua, the Court ruled that a mechanism to elect candidates for municipal elections did not comply with the Convention if it imposed on indigenous peoples a form for electing candidates that was alien to their culture.[10] Finally, in 2012 the Court reiterated this now firm precedent when stating that "indivisibly joined by their special forms of life and identity, [indigenous peoples] exercise some of the rights recognized in the Convention *in a collective dimension*" and that the considerations of the Court in the judgment must be understood from that collective perspective.[11]

---

6 See, for example, I/A Court HR, OC-16/99 of 1 October 1999 on "the right to information on consular assistance in the framework of the guarantees of the due process of law", paras 112–114, where it quotes, *inter alia,* the advisory opinion "on the Legal Consequences for States of the Continued Presence of South Africa in Namibia (South West Africa), notwithstanding Security Council Resolution 276 (1970)" of the International Court of Justice, ICJ Reports 1971, and judgments of the European Court of Human Rights.

7 I/A Court HR, *Case of Aloeboetoe et al.*

8 I/A Court HR, *Case of Aloeboetoe et al.*, judgment on reparations, paras. 83–84.

9 *Cf. Case of the Yakye Axa Indigenous Community,* judgment of June 17 2005, para. 63. The same sentence was reiterated in the *case of Rosendo Cantú et al.*, judgment of 31 August 2010, para. 184.

10 I/A Court HR, *Case of Yatama*, judgment of 23 June 2005.

11 I/A Court HR, *Case of the Kichwa Indigenous People of Sarayacu*, judgment of 27 June 2012, para. 231.

The issue of women has also developed in a similar way. From ignoring the possible violations of particular human rights of women,[12] the Court gradually started to recognize that it was necessary to read alleged violations carefully so as to include them under the Convention. The concept of gender is present in many considerations of the judgment in the case of Castro Castro,[13] such as identifying certain actions as constituting "sexual violations".[14] In Cotton Field v. Mexico,[15] the word "gender" appears constantly and it is interesting to see how the gender perspective suddenly opens up a new vista in the area of reparations.[16] In the same fashion, the Court has approached a case involving the issue of sexual orientation.[17] I believe this is also a precedent as firm as that concerning indigenous peoples.

The developed rationale of the Court's interpretation has not only enriched the application of Articles 1 and 2; the influence has also been noted in the scope and contents of the rights this book analyzes. Article 4 on the right to life has been given new light, mainly because of cases involving indigenous peoples and children which have incorporated certain aspects of Article 4 that had formerly not been touched upon on the basis of special characteristics of certain groups, such as their particular identity and vulnerability.[18] Article 5 on personal freedom has categorized as violations actions that had not been considered as such before, especially with regard to women. Article 7 has also developed the scope of States' obligations with regard to deprivation of freedom of minors.[19] The Court has had the chance to rule on the duty of States to carry out due process as set forth in Article 8, which includes not only civil and criminal processes, but also processes regarding issues of labor, finance, or of any other nature.[20] The period starting in 2004, therefore, needs a longer explanation of certain aspects and a different approach than the book you are about to read.

This book presents the beginnings of the Inter-American Court and its hesitant steps in developing its position on certain human rights that constituted the subject of the majority of the cases that reached the Court, along with States in the background attempting to introduce the idea of human rights in a

---

12 For a novel analysis of the lack of gender perspective of the Court, see P. Palacios, "The Path to Gender Justice in the Inter American Court of Human Rights", (2007-08) 17 *Texas Journal of Women and the Law* 227.

13 I/A Court HR, *Case of the Miguel Castro-Castro Prison*, judgment of 25 November 2006.

14 *Ibidem*, paras. 306–313.

15 I/A Court HR, *Case of González et al. ("Cotton Field")*, judgment of 16 November 2009.

16 See *ibidem*, section IX, paras. 446 ff.

17 See I/A Court HR, *Case of Atala Riffo and daughters*, judgment of 24 February 2012.

18 See, for example, I/A Court HR, *Case of the Yakye Axa Indigenous Community*, judgment of 17 June 2005; and *Case of the "Juvenile Re-education Institute" (Panchito López)*, judgment of 2 September 2004.

19 See *ibidem*, *Case of Panchito López*.

20 I/A Court HR, *Case of the Constitutional Court*.

democratic society into their own legal systems. A next edition of this book will show the Court on its way towards maturity, with individuals more conscious of their human rights than States and with States that begin to realize and wonder – sometimes with agitation and distress – about the power of the Court to affect what they once thought was the private realm of their sovereign decisions.

ACKNOWLEDGMENTS

This book is a translation into English of the original Spanish version. I wish to thank Intersentia for making the publication of this book in English possible. I also wish to recognize the wonderful support that Ann-Christin Maak-Scherpe and Rebecca Pound gave me in this enterprise, along with Peter Krupa for a very conscientious and professional translation. Special thanks go to my daughter Caroline Koch Medina for her invaluable support in typing and preparing this manuscript for publication

CONTENTS

TABLE OF CASES

INTER-AMERICAN COURT OF HUMAN RIGHTS

EUROPEAN COURT OF HUMAN RIGHTS

LIST OF ABBREVIATIONS

ACHR	American Convention on Human Rights
ECHR	European Convention on Human Rights
ECtHR	European Court of Human Rights
HRC	United Nations Human Rights Council
I/A Court HR	Inter-American Court of Human Rights
IACHR	Inter-American Commission on Human Rights
OC	Opinión Consultiva (Advisory Opinion)
Specialized Conference	Inter-American Specialized Conference on Human Rights

CHAPTER 1
GENERAL LEGAL FRAMEWORK

1. THE AMERICAN CONVENTION ON HUMAN RIGHTS

1. The American Convention on Human Rights,[1] adopted in 1969 and in force since 16 July 1978, was, according to its Article 74(2), the culmination of a process that began in 1948 with the OAS's passage of the American Declaration of the Rights and Duties of Man (hereinafter "the American Declaration").[2] While 1948 was a year of rhetoric and Utopia, 1969 was the year that a number of these aspirations took form. The Convention establishes a catalogue of civil and political rights (Articles 3 to 25); a provision on the rights implicit in economic, social, educational, scientific, and cultural standards contained in the OAS Charter (Article 26);[3] general State obligations to respect the rights recognized in the Convention (principally Articles 1 and 2); regulations applicable in emergency situations (Article 27); standards for the application of the Convention in federal systems (Article 28); rules for interpretation (Article 29); references for incorporating unrecognized rights into the Convention's system of protection (Article 31); provisions on restrictions to and the relationship between rights and duties (Articles 30 and 32); and mechanisms and organs for monitoring compliance with the obligations set forth for States Parties (Articles 33 and following).

2. The system's supervisory organs are the Inter-American Commission on Human Rights – which was already in existence at the time the American Convention entered into force, as it was created in 1959 during the Fifth Meeting

---

1 The American Convention was signed in San Jose, Costa Rica, on 22 November 1969, during the Inter-American Specialized Conference on Human Rights. Currently, it has been ratified or acceded to by Argentina, Barbados, Bolivia, Brazil, Chile, Colombia, Costa Rica, Dominica, Ecuador, El Salvador, Grenada, Guatemala, Haiti, Honduras, Jamaica, Mexico, Nicaragua, Panama, Paraguay, Peru, the Dominican Republic, Suriname, Uruguay, and Venezuela. Venezuela presented a note of denunciation to the ACHR on 6 September 2012

2 The American Declaration of the Rights and Duties of Man was adopted in the Ninth International Conference of the American States, held in Bogotá, Colombia, 1948.

3 This is a reference to the OAS Charter as amended by the Protocol of Buenos Aires of 1967; however, the updated text of the OAS Charter has changed the name of the chapter to "Integral Development". See *infra* nn. 5 and 91.

of Consultation of Ministers of Foreign Affairs[4] – and the Inter-American Court of Human Rights. According to the Convention itself and the OAS Charter[5] (the Statute of the Inter-American Commission passed by the General Assembly of the OAS[6] and its own Rules of Procedure)[7] the Commission has several functions, the most important of which are: (i) promoting human rights in all OAS member countries; (ii) examining the general situation of human rights in those countries; and (iii) examining individual communications submitted against OAS member countries whether parties or not parties to the Convention.[8] For that latter function, and with regard to OAS Member States who are not party to the Convention, the Commission operates under the OAS Charter and under its statute, and the human rights it safeguards are the ones addressed in the American Declaration; with regard to States Parties to the Convention, the Commission gets its authority directly from the American Convention itself, which allows the cases examined by the Commission to be sent to the Court, whether by the Commission itself or by a State Party, as long as the processing of the case before the Commission has concluded and the State against which the case is brought recognizes or has recognized the Court's jurisdiction.[9]

3. The case law of the Inter-American Court has been generated through hearing and ruling on these individual cases. Without prejudice to this contentious jurisdiction, the Court also has advisory jurisdiction that allows it to

4 Resolution VIII of the Fifth Meeting of Consultation of Ministers of Foreign Affairs. Full text of the Fifth Meeting of Consultation of Ministers of Foreign Affairs, Santiago, Chile, 1959, Final act (OEA/Ser.C/II.5).

5 The OAS Charter was adopted during the Ninth International Conference of the American States, held in Bogotá, Colombia, 1948. As of December 2001, the Charter had been modified by the following instruments: the reform protocol of the Charter of the Organization of American States known as the "Protocol of Buenos Aires", signed on 27 February 1967, during the Third Special Inter-American Conference; the reform protocol of the Charter of the Organization of American States known as the "Protocol of Cartagena de Indias", passed on 5 December 1985, during the 14th Special Period of Sessions of the General Assembly; the reform protocol to the Charter of the Organization of American States known as the "Washington Protocol", approved on 14 December 1992, during the 16th Special Period of Sessions of the General Assembly; and the reform protocol of the Charter of the Organization of American States known as the "Protocol of Managua", adopted on 10 June 1993, in the 19th Special Period of Sessions of the General Assembly.

6 The current Statute of the Inter-American Commission was passed during the Ninth Regular General Assembly of the OAS, held in La Paz, Bolivia, from 21–23 October 1979.

7 The current Rules of Procedure of the Inter-American Commission were approved by that body during its 137th Period of Sessions held on 28 October to 13 November 2009, and modified on 2 September 2011.

8 ACHR Statute, Articles 18–20.

9 ACHR, Articles 51 and 62. Regarding the procedural aspects of the inter-American system, see H. Faúndez, *El Sistema Interamericano de Protección de los Derechos Humanos: Aspectos Institucionales y Procesales*, 2nd revised and updated edition, IIDH, San Jose, Costa Rica, 1999.

interpret the provisions of the American Convention or "other treaties"[10] on human rights protection in the States of the Americas at the request of an OAS Member State or an organ thereof.[11] Although the advisory opinion that the Court produces in these cases is not binding on States, it constitutes an authorized interpretation of the provisions of the Convention that the Court itself, as well as the Commission, use as a basis for future interpretations.

2. INTERPRETATION OF PROVISIONS THAT ESTABLISH HUMAN RIGHTS

4. The various sources of international law influence each other reciprocally. The general principles of law, customary law, the unilateral actions of States, and the resolutions of international organizations can pre- or post-date the provisions of treaties. Thus it is impossible to attempt the application of a treaty without knowledge of the general principles of law or customary law that precede or complement it, just as it is also not possible on interpreting a treaty to ignore other sources of law that may have come afterward and that clarify or complement the treaty. This, which is specific to international law, is particularly important for international human rights law, which is constantly being developed and is contained in provisions formulated in such a way as to allow their constant progress and their adaptation to the historical circumstances of the time and space in which they are applied.[12] In its Advisory Opinion 16/99, the Court supports this idea by indicating that "[t]he *corpus juris* of international human rights law comprises a set of international instruments of varied content and juridical effects (treaties, conventions, resolutions and declarations)" and proceeds to examine the subject of the opinion in "the context of the evolution of the fundamental rights of the human person in contemporary international law."[13]

Just as international sources of law influence each other, this kind of reciprocity also exists between those sources and domestic ones. From the point of view of international law, it should be remembered that general legal principles originate in the domestic law of States; this law, therefore, can be a source for international law, as well as a guiding criteria for a broader interpretation of human rights contained in international provisions. Interpretation of international provisions can also benefit from the case law generated on this point in States Parties to the system, given that the application of domestic law in individual cases can also give more precise

10 ACHR, Article 64.

11 OC-1/82, para. 52.

12 Regarding the progressive nature of international human rights law, see P. Nikken, *La Protección Internacional de los Derechos Humanos. Su Desarrollo Progresivo*, IIDH – Editorial Civitas SA, Madrid, 1987.

13 OC-16/99, para. 115.

scope and content to human rights provisions. Looking at this from another angle, when interpreting domestic human rights provisions, a domestic judge must also take international provisions and international case law into consideration.

Finally, knowledge of "judicial decisions and the teachings of the most highly qualified publicists of the various nations" is likewise relevant for interpretation, given that they and the rulings of international supervisory bodies represent auxiliary measures for determining the rules of international law, pursuant to Article 38 of the Statute of the International Court of Justice.

5. In the inter-American system, the idea of integrality is reflected and broadened in paragraphs (c) and (d) of Article 29 of the Convention. The former prohibits the interpretation of any provision of the Convention in a way "precluding other rights or guarantees that are inherent in the human personality or derived from representative democracy as a form of government". This rule clearly shows that the system is a single whole that goes beyond the mere letter of the specific treaty; it also means that the interpreter is required to consider the human being in his or her totality, keeping in mind all that a democratic system would require for the human right being interpreted to be effective. This consideration of a human being is based on his or her dignity, a concept that is perhaps difficult to define but can be clearly identified in each case in the light of an international human rights system that exists within a historical context.[14] Next, Article 29(c) reflects the position of the inter-American system that treaties do not grant human rights but simply recognize them, and that human rights can exist that have not been formally recognized by a legal body.

Article 29(d) establishes that no provision of the Convention can be interpreted as "excluding or limiting the effect that the American Declaration of the Rights and Duties of Man and other international acts of the same nature may have." In addition to supporting integrality, this provision supports the position according to which the resolutions of international bodies can have legal value even when formally and in principle they do not appear to, indicating that the interpreter cannot ignore those orders.[15]

6. All this is to emphasize that the system for the promotion and protection of human rights is – as the word "system" would indicate – a collection of rules and principles connected rationally one to another that should be viewed as a whole

14 Here we recall as an example of this position the Inter-American Court's interpretation of the expression "essential judicial guarantees" found in Article 27 of the Convention. See OC-9/87, paras. 34–37.

15 The Inter-American Court ruled on this point in Advisory Opinion No. 10, basing its opinion in part on the arguments that an interpretation of the Declaration could be necessary when interpreting the American Convention due to the provisions of the Convention's Article 29. See OC-10/89, para. 36.

when applying any of its parts. As an analogy for these ideas, we could say that national and international contributions to human rights flow into a crucible, resulting in a synergy from which human rights emerge broadened and perfected. It is there, in that crucible, where the interpreters of human rights law must step forward to do their work.

7. Rules for the interpretation of treaties are found in the Vienna Convention on the Law of Treaties. The first paragraph of Article 31 of the Vienna Convention establishes that "a treaty shall be interpreted in good faith in accordance with the ordinary meaning to be given to the terms of the treaty in their context and in the light of its object and purpose."

Toward doing so, the context of a treaty includes (i) its text, including the preamble and the annexes; (ii) all agreements relating to the treaty and that have been reached among all the parties in the conclusion of the treaty, and (iii) any instrument drawn up by one or more parties in connection with the conclusion of the treaty and accepted by the others as an instrument related to the treaty (Article 31(2)(a) and (b), Vienna Convention). Regarding the history of the adoption of the treaty (the *travaux préparatoires*), the Vienna Convention definitively gives it secondary interpretive status.[16]

The wording of the rules in Article 31 emphasizes the idea that the various elements of those rules form an interpretive system without any hierarchy: All treaty provisions must be interpreted by simultaneously taking into account good faith, the common meanings of the terms in the context of the treaty, and the treaty's objective and goal.

8. In contrast to other international treaties, human rights treaties confer rights to individuals before the State, which in turn has obligations toward those individuals. The Inter-American Court had the opportunity to rule on this point in Advisory Opinion 2/82, where it expressed the following:

> The Court must emphasize, however, that modern human rights treaties in general, and the American Convention in particular, are not multilateral treaties of the traditional type concluded to accomplish the reciprocal exchange of rights for the mutual benefit of the contracting States [...]. In concluding these human rights treaties, States can be deemed to submit themselves to a legal order within which they, for the common good, assume various obligations, not in relation to other States, but towards all individuals within their jurisdiction.[17]

---

16 Vienna Convention on the Law of Treaties (1969), A/CONF.39/27, Article 32. In this regard, the Inter-American Court has reached similar conclusions. See OC-9/87, paras. 49–50.

17 OC-2/82, para. 29. For this same reason, Article 60(5) of the Vienna Convention on the Law of Treaties establishes that the provisions of the article allowing a State to terminate or suspend a treaty by invoking a violation of the treaty by another State do not apply to treaties of a humanitarian nature.

Thus, the establishment of rights and reciprocal obligations for States Parties is not the only purpose of human rights treaties: they are also intended to establish a system for the protection of human dignity. In the above Advisory Opinion, the Court clearly stated that paragraph 2 of Article 20 of the Vienna Convention on the Law of Treaties is not applicable,[18] "among other reasons because the objective and goal of the Convention is not the reciprocal exchange of rights among a limited number of States but rather the protection of the rights of all human beings residing in the Americas, independent of their nationality."[19]

9. If we take into consideration that one of the elements for the interpretation of international law is the consideration of the object and purpose of the treaty, and that both of these are the protection of human rights, it must be concluded that the interpretation must always be to the benefit of the individual (a *pro persona* interpretation). This being the case, it follows that the content and scope of rights must be interpreted broadly, while their restriction must itself require a restrictive interpretation. This has been reiterated frequently by the Inter-American Court of Human Rights, which expressed in the first matter it heard that "the Convention be interpreted in favor of the individual, who is the object of international protection, as long as such an interpretation does not result in a modification of the system."

Pro persona interpretation is thus an important characteristic of the interpretation of human rights law, constituting the guiding principle that must govern its interpretation at all times.

10. The mention of a treaty's object and purpose as an interpretive element also confers on it a dynamic character. A treaty must be read in such a way that the law is interpreted taking into account the situation at the moment the interpretation occurs. As we have already stated, in the case of human rights, the object and purpose of treaties establishing or guaranteeing them is to protect human dignity, providing safeguards for individuals faced with the possibility of abuse from those governing them and granting those individuals the right to demand that the State organize society in such a way that the opportunity to enjoy and exercise those rights is guaranteed. The interpretation of each human right must therefore be done in such a way as to allow for protection, even from possible violations not taken into consideration at the time the provision was established. The dynamic nature of interpretation is also reflected in the broadness of the concept of the "context of the treaty", as

[18] Article 20 of the Vienna Convention on the Law of Treaties, which regulates the acceptance of and objections to reservations, indicates the following in paragraph 2: "When it appears from the limited number of the negotiating States and the object and purpose of a treaty that the application of the treaty in its entirety between all the parties is an essential condition of the consent of each one to be bound by the treaty, a reservation requires acceptance by all the parties."

[19] OC-2/82, para. 27.

instruments drawn up "for the interpretation of the treaty" necessarily post-date the treaty and, if they have been adopted by the same parties who adopted the treaty, can be understood as an interpretation of the initial agreement by those parties.[20]

The International Court of Justice recognizes this dynamism on expressing in the Advisory Opinion entitled "Legal Consequences for States of the Continued Presence of South Africa in Namibia notwithstanding Security Council Resolution 276 (1970)" that "an international instrument must be interpreted and applied within the framework of the entire legal system prevailing at the time of the interpretation".[21]

This dynamism, both in the interpretation of the content of human rights laws and in the context of treaties, is noted as well in the Inter-American Court's Advisory Opinion 10/89, whose text states as follows:

> [T]he Court finds it necessary to point out that to determine the legal status of the American Declaration it is appropriate to look to the inter-American system of today in the light of the evolution it has undergone since the adoption of the Declaration, rather than to examine the normative value and significance which that instrument was believed to have had in 1948.[22]

Finally, this form of interpretation is firmly based in the European human rights system and can be found in innumerable rulings referencing both substantive and procedural law that have been issued by the European Court of Human Rights, the international body with the fullest experience of ruling on cases of alleged human rights violations.[23]

3. STATE OBLIGATIONS IN THE AMERICAN CONVENTION

3.1. CONSIDERATIONS OF THE TERM "JURISDICTION"

11. According to Article 1(1) of the Convention, States' obligations apply to "all persons subject to their jurisdiction". Paragraph 2 of the same article clarifies

---

20 This is one of the reasons given for assigning the Universal Declaration of Human Rights the status of binding law.

21 International Court of Justice, "Legal Consequences for States of the Continued Presence of South Africa in Namibia (South West Africa) notwithstanding Security Council Resolution 276 (1970)", Advisory Opinion, ICJ Reports 1971, pp. 16–31, para. 53.

22 I/A Court HR, OC-10/89, para. 37. See also OC-16/99, paras. 113–115.

23 See, for example, ECtHR: *Dudgeon v. United Kingdom,* judgment of 22 October 1981, particularly para. 60, and *Marckx v. Belgium,* judgment of 13 June 1979, para. 41. For a general analysis on this point, see P. van Dijk, '"Positive Obligations" Implied in the European Convention on Human Rights: Are the States Still the "Masters" of the Convention?', in M. Castermans, F. van Hoof and J. Smith (eds.), *The Role of the Nation-State in the 21st Century,* Kluwer Law International, The Hague/London/Boston, 1998, pp. 17–33.

that "person" refers to "every human being". This concept of personhood reaffirms the idea of the universality of human rights and the prohibition of discrimination, as the only condition for having rights is being a "human being".[24] The position taken by the Convention does not include the protection of legal persons.[25]

12. The drafts that gave rise to the Convention included the obligation for States to respect and guarantee the human rights of persons "subject to their territory and jurisdiction".[26] However, on approval of the Convention, reference was made only to jurisdiction. On opting to delimit the Convention's scope as including all persons falling under their "jurisdiction", the States opted for a broad criterion that includes not only those actions or omissions attributable to State agents as violations of obligations under the Convention committed or omitted within State territory, but also responsibility for acts and omissions carried out outside State territory but within State jurisdiction, such as the actions of an occupying army or actions taken on diplomatic premises.[27]

Current international human rights law is beginning to address the meaning and scope of what is known as "jurisdiction". There has been an attempt to broaden the concept, for example by bringing the Bankovic case before the European Court of Human Rights. In that case, the petitioner alleged that a country that enters the air space of another State and bombs that State begins at that moment to exercise "jurisdiction" as regards its responsibility for the human rights violations presumably committed. The petition argued that the North American Treaty Organization's (NATO) control over that airspace

---

24 This has not prevented the persistence of discrimination against certain groups in the enjoyment of their rights, even subsequent to the entry into force of the Convention and other similar treaties. See Th. van Boven, *Human Rights and Rights of People*, in F. Coomans et al., *Human Rights from Exclusion to Inclusion; Principles and Practice*, Kluwer Law International, The Hague/London/Boston, 2000, pp. 282–284.

25 Although the Convention is clear on this subject, the Inter-American Commission has admitted a case for processing in which the victim is a legal person. This happened in the case pursued against Paraguay, in which the Commission determined that there had been a violation of freedom of expression to the detriment of Radio Ñandutí. Upon suffering various acts of interference, the radio station had to close as it was no longer economically sustainable, resulting in economic damage to the company and its employees (IACHR, *Radio Ñandutí v. Paraguay*, Case No. 9642, resolution 14/87 of 28 March 1987, published in IACHR, *1986–87 Annual Report*, para. 2). However, the more recent case law of the Inter-American Court has made it clear that when it comes to legal persons, the system's protection established by the Convention is aimed at protecting the human beings that form a legal person (*Case of Cantos, preliminary objections*, paras. 26–29).

26 *Inter-American Yearbook on Human Rights 1968*, General Secretariat of the Organization of American States, Washington, DC, 1973, pp. 236–418.

27 In the European system, see: ECtHR, *Cyprus v. Turkey*, judgment of 10 May 2001. A detailed analysis of this ruling can be found in: F. Hoffmeister, "*Cyprus v. Turkey*" (2002) 96(2) *American Journal of International Law* 445–452. In the universal system's sphere, see HRC, *López-Burgos v. Uruguay*, Communication 52/1979, report dated 29 July 1981, para. 12(3).

during the bombardment was "almost as complete as Turkey's control over the northern part of Cyprus", with Turkey having been found to be exercising sovereignty over that area for the purposes of attributing responsibility to it for the human rights violations committed there.[28] The case was ruled inadmissible, with the Court inclining toward the notion of "essentially territorial" jurisdiction.[29]

The Inter-American Commission ruled admissible a case containing 60 similar petitions regarding the military action carried out by the United States in Panama in December 1989 in order to arrest Manuel Noriega;[30] it also ruled admissible a case on the United States' bombardment in Grenada that destroyed Richmond Hill Insane Asylum, causing the death of 16 persons there.[31] The Commission, however, did not explicitly state the legal grounds on which it had based its ruling of admissibility, so it certainly did not cross into the concept of jurisdiction.

One of the consequences of the rise of international human rights law as a branch of international public law has been the difficulty in establishing proper concepts to define the relationships between States and relationships between States and individuals. Possibly the term "jurisdiction" should be revised in the future to adjust it to new circumstances that affect and violate human rights.

3.2. OBLIGATIONS OF FEDERAL STATES

13. In principle, the obligations established in the Convention apply equally to all States Parties. However, Article 28 of the Convention establishes that:

> 1. Where a State Party is constituted as a federal state, the national government of such State Party shall implement all the provisions of the Convention *over whose subject matter it exercises legislative and judicial jurisdiction.*
>
> 2. With respect to the provisions over whose subject matter the constituent units of the federal state have jurisdiction, the national government shall immediately

---

28 ECtHR, *Loizidou v. Turkey*, judgment of 18 December 1996, para. 52.

29 ECtHR, *Bankovic et al. v. Belgium, the Czech Republic, Denmark, France, Germany, Greece, Hungary, Iceland, Italy, Luxembourg, the Netherlands, Norway, Poland, Portugal, Spain, Turkey and the United Kingdom*, decision on admissibility of 12 December 2001, para. 62.

30 IACHR, *Case of Salas et al. v. United States*, No. 10.573, report dated 14 October 1993, published in IACHR, *1993 Annual Report*. The United States argued that the Commission did not have jurisdiction because it was an "advisory organ" without authority to rule on cases and that it could only review allegations of violations with reference to the American Declaration, "which is an agreed statement of non-binding general human rights principles" (para. 21). There is no published history on the final result of this case.

31 IACHR, *Case of Disabled Peoples' International et al. v. United States*, No. 9213, report on admissibility, published in IACHR, *1986–87 Annual Report*. This case concluded with a friendly settlement and the Commission did not prepare arguments on the problem of jurisdiction.

> take suitable measures, in accordance with its constitution and its laws, to the end that the competent authorities of the constituent units may adopt appropriate provisions for the fulfillment of this Convention.[32]

Undoubtedly these paragraphs seem less categorical than, for example, Article 50 of the International Covenant on Civil and Political Rights ("the Covenant"),[33] which establishes that its provisions "shall extend to all parts of federal States without any limitations or exceptions".

The final draft of Article 28 originated with the initiative of the United States, which was trying to keep the Convention from resulting in a centralization of power in the federal government and away from the states forming the federation.[34] The original wording of the draft ordered federal States to take the measures necessary to make the provisions of the Convention effective in all states, provinces, or federal departments, along with other territories under their jurisdiction.[35] From a legal point of view, however, the inclusion of the phrase emphasized in paragraph 1 does not succeed in liberating the federal State from its responsibility for violations of the Convention committed by states in the federation, given that paragraph 2 requires them to take immediate measures in order for the corresponding authorities to make the provisions necessary for compliance with the Convention with regard to all individuals under the jurisdiction of the State in question.

Curiously but fortunately, the rule is different when a new State is created. Paragraph 3 of Article 28 requires States that agree to integrate into a federation or other kind of association to ensure the provisions of the Convention are incorporated into the pact governing the community itself in order for the Convention to continue being effective in the new State created.[36]

3.3. OBLIGATIONS TO RESPECT AND GUARANTEE

14. Article 1 of the Convention establishes two important obligations for States Parties: the obligations to *respect* human rights and *ensure* their full and free

---

[32] Emphasis added.

[33] International Covenant on Civil and Political Rights (the Covenant), adopted and opened for signature, ratification and accession by General Assembly resolution 2200A (XXI) of 16 December 1966. Entry into force 23 March 1976.

[34] *Report of the United States Delegation to the Inter-American Conference on Protection of Human Rights*, reproduced in T. Buergenthal and R. Norris (eds.), *Human Rights. The Inter-American System,* Booklet 15, Oceana Publications, Dobbs Ferry, New York, 1984, p. 64.

[35] Specialized Conference, San José, Costa Rica, 7–22 November 1969, *Minutes and Documents*, General Secretariat, OAS, Washington, DC, 1979, p. 24.

[36] See T. Buergenthal, *The Inter-American System for the Protection of Human Rights*, and *Inter-American Juridical Yearbook 1981*, Washington, DC, 1992, pp. 80–120 (83–85) and D. Fox, "The American Convention on Human Rights and Prospects for United States Ratification", (1973) 3 *Human Rights* 243–281 (254–260).

exercise. These obligations are immediately internationally applicable and bind the State with regard to all individuals subject to its jurisdiction, without discrimination. The obligations found in Articles 1 and 2 make reference to all rights in the Convention; this notwithstanding the fact that the economic, social, and cultural rights alluded to in Chapter III of the Convention have a somewhat different regime.[37]

15. The obligation to respect requires that the State and its agents do not violate the human rights established in the Convention. It is thus an obligation to refrain.

In contrast, the obligation to ensure requires the State to take the necessary actions to ensure that all individuals subject to the State's jurisdiction are able to exercise their rights. The Inter-American Court of Human Rights exhaustively analyzed the contents of that obligation in the case of Velásquez Rodríguez, which looked at a disappearance in Honduras (in reality, one disappearance among many others that were not submitted before the Court). In its judgment, the Court found the following:

> The second obligation of the States Parties is to "ensure" the free and full exercise of the rights recognized by the Convention to every person subject to its jurisdiction. This obligation implies the duty of States Parties to organize the governmental apparatus and, in general, all the structures through which public power is exercised so that they are capable of juridically ensuring the free and full enjoyment of human rights. As a consequence of this obligation, States must prevent, investigate and punish any violation of the rights recognized by the Convention and, moreover, if possible attempt to restore the right violated and provide compensation as warranted for damages resulting from the human rights violation.[38]

This State action must not be simply formal. Regarding this, the Court added that "[t]he obligation to ensure [...] is not fulfilled by the existence of a legal system designed to make it possible to comply with this obligation – it also requires the government to conduct itself so as to effectively ensure the free and full exercise of human rights."[39]

16. In issues of human rights, therefore, the State cannot limit itself to avoiding conduct that violates those rights. Rather, it must also take the positive actions that may be necessary to make it possible for individuals subject to its jurisdiction to be able to exercise and enjoy their human rights.

From this perspective, the State's first obligation is to make sure international treaties have an effect within their jurisdiction. It falls to the State and not to international law to decide on the most appropriate method of complying with

---

37 See *infra*, section 5.
38 *Case of Velásquez Rodríguez*, para. 166.
39 *Ibidem*, para. 167.

this, whether through the incorporation of those laws directly or through the establishment of domestic laws reproducing them. In any case, once the international treaty is ratified, the State must adjust all of its domestic law to conform to it.

17. Ensuring that individuals can use and enjoy their human rights is primarily the responsibility of States, as they are in the best position to ensure this on an everyday and immediate basis; international supervision is always late and generally *ex post*. The obligation exists even when it can be concluded that, in certain legal systems, the validity of the treaties has the effect of striking down the domestic laws that are contrary to the international ones. The State's task is to facilitate the exercise of human rights and it does not do so by leaving its fate up to judicial interpretation, even when it can be stated that the tribunals themselves are required to attempt an interpretation of domestic law affecting human rights that is in harmony with the State's international obligations in this area. Therefore, it is important for guaranteeing the enjoyment of human rights that the State do a careful review of its domestic legislation for the purpose of eliminating discrepancies that may exist between domestic legislation and international law – that is, it must go through a process of adjusting domestic law to the Convention. It should be noted that the scope and content of human rights can be broadened by law, while its restrictions, as indicated in Article 30 of the Convention and the case law of the Inter-American Court, cannot be extended beyond the borders specifically provided for in the Convention and then only via a law in the formal and material sense.[40]

18. Of course, for international laws to be truly in effect, the State must also establish adequate and effective[41] remedies that individuals can exercise to denounce violations of their human rights. The Court found in a recent ruling that

> The nonexistence of an effective recourse against the violation of rights recognized under the Convention constitutes a transgression of the Convention by the State party in which the situation in question is taking place. In this sense, it should be highlighted that in order for the remedy to exist, it is not enough for it to be provided

40 OC-10/89, para. 17.

41 The standards for remedies that are "adequate and effective" are the result of extensive international case law. The Inter-American Court developed the meaning of those two words in two cases against Honduras on the obligation of those who turn to the Inter-American system to exhaust domestic remedies before doing so. *Adequate* means "that the remedies' function within the domestic legal system is suitable for addressing the infringement of a legal right" (*Case of Velásquez Rodríguez*, para. 64, and *Case of Godínez Cruz*, para. 67); while *effective* means "capable of producing the result for which it was designed" (*Case of Velásquez Rodríguez,* para. 66 and *Case of Godínez Cruz*, para. 69). The term "effective" does not imply that every remedy sought must necessarily be granted; it means that there is at least a serious possibility that the remedy will be granted (*Case of Velásquez Rodríguez*, paras. 67–68 and *Case of Godínez Cruz*, paras. 70–71). See also OC-9/87, para. 24.

for in the Constitution or the law, or for it to be formally admissible. Rather, it must be truly suitable for establishing whether a human rights violation has taken place and providing the necessary remedy.[42]

19. The existence of remedies is not enough to exhaust the State's obligation, as it must also establish the conditions necessary for the exercise of the rights. For example, in order to guarantee due process, the State must – among other things – issue procedural rules, allocate funds for the creation of the court system, ensure the existence of law schools for training attorneys, and provide free legal aid to those lacking resources, when necessary.

20. This obligation also implies the need to remove obstacles even when those obstacles arise not from domestic law but from social structure and culture. The State therefore must promote human rights in the understanding that this means not only educating the domestic community about them but also launching the campaigns necessary to create the conditions to allow them to be on the one hand exercised and on the other respected by everyone – including all State agents, who must be instructed on their international obligations and trained to be able to fulfill them. This aspect of the obligation is particularly applicable when there are groups whose human rights are constantly violated for cultural reasons. Consider, for example, the principle of non-discrimination on the basis of sex. Although each action that violates this principle can be brought before the courts, with the corresponding possibility that it will eventually be redressed, the establishment of remedies does not exhaust the State's obligation when a violation is massive and systemic. Limiting action to merely addressing each violation – which to start with implies complications of time and money, as well as evidence requirements that are sometimes impossible to meet – would constitute a tremendous injustice and failure to comply with international obligations. It would be equivalent to placing the group affected by constant violations in the situation of never having direct enjoyment of its rights and having that enjoyment constantly interrupted by the need to turn to the courts. In cases such as these, therefore, the State must do a careful review of the way in which society functions and design policies that will achieve the goal of making the enjoyment and exercise of human rights effective for all individuals.

As can be seen, the specification of the obligation to guarantee has broad scope, stretching from the promotion of rights and the removal of government or non-government obstacles, to special equal opportunity measures for groups that are at a disadvantage as compared to the rest of the community.[43]

---

42 *Case of the Mayagna (Sumo) Awas Tingni Community*, para. 113. In the same sense see: *Case of Ivcher Bronstein*, para. 136; *Case of Cantoral Benavides*, para. 164, and *Case of Durand and Ugarte*, para. 102.

43 On this point, see T. Buergenthal, 'To Respect and to Ensure: State Obligations and Permissible Derogations', in Louis Henkin (ed.), *The International Bill of Rights. The Covenant on Civil and Political Rights*, Columbia University Press, New York, 1981, pp. 72 and 77–78.

Finally, the obligation also means that those injured must have "the enjoyment of the right that was violated" re-established and the consequences of that violation redressed, as established in Article 63(1) of the Convention. The Court has recognized these obligations since its first judgment in the case of Velásquez Rodríguez.[44] This will be discussed in the following section.

3.4. OBLIGATION TO TAKE MEASURES

21. The Convention assigns such importance to persons being able to exercise and enjoy their human rights fully that it sets forth in Article 2[45] an obligation for States Parties to take the necessary measures to make the rights recognized in the Convention effective, a provision that caused real controversy at the time that its inclusion in the Convention was being discussed. The controversy concerned the relationship that would exist between it and the obligations to respect and ensure examined previously.[46]

Article 2 of the Convention establishes the following:

> Where the exercise of any of the rights or freedoms referred to in Article 1 is not already ensured by legislative or other provisions, the States Parties undertake to adopt, in accordance with their constitutional processes and the provisions of this Convention, such legislative or other measures as may be necessary to give effect to those rights or freedoms.

The provision – similar to Article 2 of the International Covenant – had been considered and rejected by a member of the Inter-American Commission, Dr Carlos A. Dunshee de Abranches,[47] because he felt it could lead those applying the Convention to interpret it to mean that States are not required to respect and guarantee the human rights enshrined therein unless they establish special laws toward doing so. Dr Dunshee de Abranches argued in his research that "under the prevailing constitutional systems in the American States, the provisions of treaties are incorporated into domestic law through ratification and following their approval by the competent legislative organ, with no need for a special law."[48]

44 *Case of Velásquez Rodríguez*, para. 166.

45 T. Buergenthal studies and provides additional comments on Article 2 of the Convention in *supra*, n. 36. Also see Donald T. Fox, *supra*, n. 36, pp. 243–281 (254–260).

46 Information on the debate over Article 2 during the San Jose Conference taken from C. Medina, *The Battle of Human Rights. Gross, Systematic Violations and the Inter-American System*, Martinus Nijhoff, Dordrecht/Boston/London, 1988, Chapter V.

47 *Comparative Study on the Covenants of the United Nations on Civil, Political, Economic, Social, and Cultural Rights and the Drafts of the Inter-American Convention on Human Rights 1968*, General Secretariat, OAS, Washington, DC, 1973, pp. 168–212.

48 *Ibidem*, p. 192.

This therefore made the passage of laws to make the treaty domestically valid unnecessary, with interested parties able to invoke the treaty directly before the courts. He also warned that it would not be advisable to include a similar provision in the Convention, arguing that "should it be included in the Convention, it would support the argument that certain States Parties would only be required to respect one or more rights defined in the Convention but not included in their domestic legislation after a special law regarding that right or those rights is passed."[49]

One opinion opposing this interpretation was that of the government of Chile. While recognizing that the provisions of treaties are generally incorporated into domestic law through their ratification, it argued that the purpose of a provision of this kind was to create a clear obligation for States Parties to establish new law *where it may be necessary* due to a lack of specificity in the Convention's provisions. As examples of this, the Chilean delegate cited Articles 16(5) of the draft (currently Article 17(5) of the Convention)[50] and Article 17(2) of the draft (the current Article 18 of the Convention).[51] He also argued that the danger seen by Dr Dunshee de Abranches on the inclusion of this provision was not real, as the terms of the draft could not in any way lead to an interpretation of this kind, adding finally that this could be ensured by explicitly establishing the meaning and purpose of the provision during the Conference.[52] Chile's position was backed by several representatives and the inclusion of Article 2 in terms that were similar but not identical to the Chilean proposal was approved.[53]

22. The interpretation of Article 2 of the Convention in the sense that it does not affect the immediate applicability of the obligations established in Article 1 from the moment the Convention enters into force for each State is on our understanding derived clearly from Article 1 of the Convention and, in addition, from the debate that took place during the treaty's gestation. This same position was reaffirmed in a concurrent vote by Judge Gross Espiell in the Inter-American Court's Advisory Opinion 7/86 requested by the government of Costa Rica. Therein, Judge Gross Espiell indicated that the obligation found in Article 2 is

> an obligation additional to that imposed by Article 1 of the Convention. It is intended to make respect for the rights and freedoms recognized by the Convention more

---

49 *Ibidem.*

50 Article 17(5) ACHR establishes that: "The law shall recognize equal rights for children born out of wedlock and those born in wedlock."

51 Article 18 ACHR establishes that: "Every person has the right to a given name and to the surnames of his parents or that of one of them. The law shall regulate the manner in which this right shall be ensured for all, by the use of assumed names if necessary."

52 Specialized Conference, *supra*, n. 35, p. 38. The arguments of the Chilean delegate were based on the text that had been proposed by the Chilean delegation whose language more clearly expressed the objectives sought (see the text of the Chilean proposal, *ibidem*).

53 See *ibidem*, pp. 55, 104, 107 and 145.

> definite and certain. The obligation derived from Article 2 thus complements, but in no way substitutes or replaces, the general unconditional obligation imposed by Article 1 [...] It was originally thought, understandably, that a commitment of the type referred to in the current Article 2 exists naturally under International Law, as the logical consequence of the obligations derived from an international treaty. For that reason, when Article 2 was proposed, it was explained that its only purpose was to emphasize and clarify that the requirement to comply with that obligation was immediate, direct and obligatory, and not to signify a change or ignore the special obligation that results from Article 1 [... Another interpretation] would lead to the irrational and absurd result that Article 1 would be inapplicable if the measures referred to in Article 2 had not been promulgated. This conclusion is inadmissible because it would paralyze the functioning of the system established by the Convention and it would practically eliminate [Article 1's] essential obligations to protect human beings.[54]

It seems evident that Article 2 does not annul the obligations of Article 1(1), which are immediately applicable; it is likely that given that a State party to a treaty has the obligation to adapt its domestic legislation to the provisions of the treaty and to comply with its provisions fully, Article 2 was not really necessary and should be considered only as a provision in application of the maxim *abundans cautela non nocet* (abundant caution does no harm). Subsequently, in the countries in which treaties take on the force of domestic law upon being ratified or upon the completion of certain proceedings established in those countries' legal systems, Article 2 of the Convention cannot be used to block the domestic application of the treaty's provisions.

23. One consequence of Article 2 of the Convention is that the State is required to develop within its domestic legislation those rights whose international expression lacks the precision necessary for their application by State organs and, especially, in order to be invoked before courts of law. In other words, for the rights worded in such a way that the organ applying the provision domestically does not have a clear option in the treaty's text for resolving a particular case, the State is required to make them operative. A second consequence is the State duty to take all necessary non-legislative measures to allow for the full exercise and enjoyment of human rights.[55] The separate opinion of Judge Piza in the previously cited Advisory Opinion argues for this meaning, which, over the years and the development of the inter-American system, has come to be understood to be included in the verb "ensure" used in Article 1(1) of the Convention.[56]

---

54 OC-7/86, separate opinion of Judge Héctor Gros Espiell, para. 6.

55 *Case of "The Last Temptation of Christ" (Olmedo Bustos et al.)*, para. 87.

56 Judge Piza argues that Article 2 is not a repetition of Article 1(1) – because that would be equivalent to emptying the latter of meaning – nor is it equivalent to a simple generic duty of making a treaty effective domestically, as in that case it would not perhaps have been necessary. On the contrary, Article 2 operates "in the event that Article 1(1) is ineffective, or at least insufficient, not due to limitations of domestic law which would imply violations of

24. The Inter-American Court's judgment in the case of the Street Children is perhaps the clearest explanation of Article 2;[57] In it the Court declared that even if a violation of Article 2 has not been found, it is a State's obligation to adopt such legislative or other measures as may be necessary to give effect to the rights therein recognized, "merely because it has ratified this legal instrument". The interpretation of the (in)significance of Article 2 remains the same.[58]

3.5. OBLIGATION TO COOPERATE

25. In addition to the obligations examined in the preceding sections, States have a third obligation: the obligation to cooperate with the international organs monitoring them. This obligation is derived generally from their status as parties to the treaty and from the existence of a principle of international law that requires States to comply with treaties in good faith. This obligation appears specifically in the American Convention.

Article 41(d) of the American Convention grants the Inter-American Commission on Human Rights the authority to ask OAS Member States to submit reports on the measures taken on the subject of human rights. In addition, Article 48, which regulates the processing of individual communications before the Commission, establishes that the State shall send the information requested by the Commission within a reasonable period of time and that, in the event that the Commission should decide to carry out an investigation, "the States concerned shall furnish to it [...] all necessary facilities".

The obligation to cooperate is thus clear and includes providing information that is timely, pertinent, and truthful with regard to the general situation of human rights in the State or with regard to a specific fact that the international body is weighing. On this subject, the consistent position of oversight organs has been that the States are the only ones in a position to provide them with the information necessary for evaluation of whether States are complying with or violating international law.[59]

Article 1(1) itself, but because certain rights – not all – themselves need complementary domestic provisions or measures in order to be immediately and unconditionally applicable" (OC-7/86, separate opinion of Judge Rodolfo E. Piza Escalante, para. 27). To explain this, he uses Article 23, which sets forth political rights that cannot be effective "without a detailed set of regulations and without a complex institutional, economic, and human apparatus to provide effectiveness for those making claims" (*ibidem*). This would include, for example, the need to create electoral registries, voting centers, and electoral councils, and the need to establish voting dates and deadlines.

57 *Case of the Street Children (Villagrán Morales et al.), judgment on reparations*, para 98. The judgment quotes the *case of Garrido and Baigorria, judgment on reparations*, para. 68.

58 *Case of Forneron and daughter*, para 130; *Case of Suárez Rosero*, para. 98; *Case of Barrios Altos*, para. 42; and *Case of Hilaire, Constantine and Benjamin, et al.*, paras. 116–118.

59 See, for example, HRC, *Santullo v. Uruguay*, Communication 9/1977, ruling of 26 October 1979, paras. 7 and 10, and *García Lanza, Weismann de Lanza and Lanza Perdomo v. Uruguay*, Communication 8/1977, ruling of 3 April 1980, para. 15.

26. As a consequence of this position, the Inter-American Commission on Human Rights has adopted a provision in Article 39 of its Rules of Procedure according to which, "[t]he facts alleged in the petition, the pertinent parts of which have been transmitted to the State in question, shall be presumed to be true if the State has not provided responsive information during the period set by the Commission under the provisions of Article 38 of these Rules of Procedure, as long as other evidence does not lead to a different conclusion."

The Inter-American Court has ruled in favor of this evidentiary measure on establishing that "the silence of the accused or elusive or ambiguous answers on its part may be interpreted as an acknowledgment of the truth of the facts set forth in the application, so long as it is not contradicted by the record or is not compelled as a matter of law."[60] It has also repeatedly indicated that the State "cannot rely on the plaintiff's inability to present evidence in the proceedings since, in such cases, it is the State that controls the means to clarify the facts that have occurred in its jurisdiction and, therefore, in practice, it is necessary to rely on the cooperation of the State itself in order to obtain the required evidence."[61]

Although this statement was made with regard to cases of disappearance, it is valid for all those cases in which the State is in possession of the evidence of a violation of any human rights.

4. ATTRIBUTION OF STATE RESPONSIBILITY

27. The failure to comply with an international obligation through State action or omission results in State responsibility. This translates into the obligation to provide full reparations,[62] both pecuniary and nonpecuniary, for any damage the violation may have caused. The obligation to provide reparations thus does not arise autonomously but is rather the consequence of a substantive violation.[63] In international human rights law, a wrongful act that results in responsibility consists of the violation of one of the obligations established in the Convention to the detriment of an individual who is subject to the jurisdiction of the State responsible.[64]

28. The provisions regulating State responsibility are part of international law, not domestic law.[65] The International Law Commission has been working on

60 *Case of Velásquez Rodríguez*, para. 138.

61 *Case of Bámaca Velásquez*, para. 152.

62 International Court of Permanent Justice, *Usine de Chorzów, judgment on merits*, 1928, Series A No. 17, para. 13.

63 *Case of Caballero Delgado and Santana*, dissenting vote of Judge Nieto Navia, pp. 48–49.

64 The obligation to provide reparations will be examined in more detail with regard to the rights to life and personal integrity. See *infra*, Chapters 2 and 3.

65 *Case of Las Palmeras, judgment on reparations*, para. 38; *Case of the Caracazo, judgment on reparations*, para. 77; *Case of Juan Humberto Sánchez*, para. 149.

drawing them up for years with a document titled Draft Articles on Responsibility of States for Internationally Wrongful Acts.[66] Article 2 of that draft established that an internationally wrongful act exists when an action or omission (i) is attributable to the State according to international law and (ii) constitutes a violation of one of the State's international obligations.

Any agent of the State can incur this international responsibility, either through action or omission.[67]

The draft does not mention fault or malice as elements of responsibility.[68] In general, this position is supported by internationalists who indicate that international responsibility is objective and determined by the causal relationship between the agent and the wrongful act.[69]

29. The Inter-American Court has ruled on State responsibility in several of its judgments. It has followed the theory of objective responsibility from its first ruling, in which it insists that it is not necessary to take into account "elements of a psychological nature intended to categorize the individual guilt of the perpetrators".[70] It has also established that State responsibility can exist for acts presumably committed by private individuals, concluding that the State can incur international responsibility directly, as a result of the actions of its agents, and indirectly, for failing to act in response to the actions of private individuals that infringe rights established in the Convention.

Regarding direct responsibility, the Court has said that "[a]ccording to Article 1(1) [of the Convention], any exercise of public power that violates the rights recognized by the Convention is unlawful. Whenever a State organ, official or public entity violates one of those rights, this constitutes a failure of the duty to respect the rights and freedoms set forth in the Convention."[71]

Regarding indirect responsibility, the Court has expressed that "[a] wrongful act which violates human rights and which is initially not directly imputable to a State (for example, because it is the act of a private person or because the person responsible has not been identified) can lead to international responsibility of the State, not because of the act itself, but because of the lack of due diligence to prevent the violation or to respond to it as required by the Convention."[72]

Applying this general provision to a specific case, the Court found that although it had been proven that the disappearance of Velásquez Rodríguez was

---

66 International Law Commission, *Draft Articles on Responsibility of States for Internationally Wrongful Acts,* A/56/10, ch. IV.E.1, 2001.

67 *Ibidem,* Articles 4 and following.

68 On fault and malice, see I. Brownlie, *Principles of Public International Law,* 4th edn, Clarendon Press, Oxford, p. 440.

69 *Ibidem,* pp. 437–440.

70 *Case of Velásquez Rodríguez,* para. 173.

71 *Ibidem,* para. 169.

72 *Ibidem,* para. 172.

clearly attributable to State agents, the attribution of responsibility could equally be made given that it was proven that the State did not act, this being "a failure on the part of Honduras to fulfill the duties it assumed under Article 1(1) of the Convention, which obligated it to ensure Manfredo Velásquez the free and full exercise of his human rights."[73]

30. When responsibility arises indirectly, so the problem also arises of determining which exact obligations the State must comply with to guarantee the exercise and enjoyment of the right in question – that is, what is the content and scope of the obligation to guarantee each right? It is impossible to give a general and abstract rule for this; the decision must be made case by case, establishing whether according to the circumstances, the State's conduct constitutes a violation of the Convention. Without prejudice to this, it is useful for the supervisory organs to be able to determine the standard of conduct required in order to guide interpretation and guide the State in complying with its obligations.

The Court has done this, but in my opinion it would be very advisable for it to be particularly careful in establishing this standard. According to the considering paragraph quoted earlier, for example, in order to assign responsibility the Court requires "lack of due diligence to prevent the violation or to respond to it as required by the Convention"; however, in an earlier considering paragraph, it replaces this phrase with a different one:

> What is decisive is whether a violation of the rights recognized by the Convention has occurred with the support or the acquiescence of the government, or whether the government has acted in such a way as to allow the violation to take place in impunity or in the absence of any preventative action. Thus, the Court's task is to determine whether the human rights violation is the result of a State's failure to fulfill its duty to respect and ensure those rights, as required by Article 1(1) of the Convention.[74]

With this, assigning indirect responsibility to a state for "lack of due diligence" becomes more difficult, as what the Court requires is for the act to have been perpetrated "without taking any measures to prevent" it or "in impunity".

Another example of a lack of precision in defining this standard can be found in the case of Caballero Delgado and Santana. In this judgment, the Court rules it proven that the detention and disappearance of the two victims was carried out by members of the Colombian military and by civilians acting as soldiers, and that the State "has undertaken a prolonged judicial investigation, not free of defects, to find and sanction those responsible", an investigation that as of that moment was still ongoing. Although it grants that the obligation to investigate is an obligation of means or behaviour, it concludes that "it is not sufficient that the Government undertake an investigation and try to sanction those guilty; rather

73 *Ibidem*, para. 182.
74 *Ibidem*, para. 173.

it is also necessary that all this Government activity culminate in the reparation of the injured party, which in this case has not occurred." Taking this into consideration, the Court finds that a violation has taken place of Articles 7 and 4 with regard to Article 1(1) of the Convention. Curiously, although it does not find that Articles 25 and 8 have been violated, it finds that the reparation "should consist of the continuation of the judicial proceedings inquiring into the disappearance of Isidro Caballero Delgado and María del Carmen Santana and punishment of those responsible in conformance with Colombian domestic law".

In this case, the Court's wording is such that it seems to require in reality that the investigation not only be carried out but that it be successful.[75]

31. Another interesting point on international responsibility has to do with its nature. In the case of Velásquez Rodríguez, the Court found categorically that "international protection of human rights must not be confused with criminal justice. States do not appear before the Court as criminal defendants. The purpose of international human rights law is not to punish the persons guilty of the violations but to protect the victims and provide reparations for the damages that have been caused by the States responsible for the actions in question."[76]

It can be deduced from this statement that international State responsibility is not criminal, and that as a consequence, the obligation to provide reparations is merely to compensate the damage caused by the failure to comply and should not be understood as a punishment inflicted on the State. This idea was reiterated in the judgment on reparations in the Velásquez case, in which the Court insisted that "under the current state of international law",[77] indemnities cannot be used to make an example or as a deterrent.

32. In the case of Myrna Mack Chang, this position of the Court was directly challenged by Judge Cançado Trindade, who argues that "a State's international responsibility includes elements of both civil and criminal nature in international law's current developmental stage",[78] a statement intended to advocate for the need for reparations established by the Court to eventually take on the status of penalties or deterrents.[79] Cançado Trindade argues that even when one acknowledges that State responsibility is objective, this does not mean "that responsibility based on the infraction or guilt is totally dismissed in any and all hypothesis or circumstance. There are cases – such as this case, Myrna

75 *Case of Caballero Delgado and Santana*, paras. 54, 57, 58 and 69.

76 *Case of Velásquez Rodríguez*, para. 134.

77 *Case of Velásquez Rodríguez, judgment on reparations*, para. 38.

78 *Case of Myrna Mack Chang*, concurring opinion of Judge A.A. Cançado Trindade, para. 36.

79 *Ibidem*, para. 38. In para. 46, he argues that "reparations can perfectly function as both compensation and penalty, with the purpose of putting an end to impunity and ensuring that justice be carried out."

Mack Chang v. Guatemala – in which the State's intention to cause damage or its negligence in preventing it can be demonstrated; the infraction or guilt here rests on the indispensable foundation of State responsibility, *aggravated* by this circumstance."[80]

The concurring opinion calls this aggravated responsibility a "State crime", attributing consequences to these crimes that do not include reparations that are "necessarily pecuniary", but rather obligations intended to "set an example or establish a deterrent in the sense of preserving the memory of the violations that took place, providing satisfaction (a sense justice has been done) to the relatives of the victim, and contributing to guaranteeing the non-repetition of those violations (including through human rights education and training)"[81] giving examples from the case law of the Court itself.[82]

33. In that same case, the concurring opinion of Judge García Ramírez takes a position with some shades of difference. The judge admits that in the case of Myrna Mack Chang, "an objective aggravation of the facts" can be observed because it was not an isolated crime. Rather, it was the product of a plan prepared to deprive the victim of life, in which "both operatives and security officials presumably took part". Meanwhile, the investigation of those individuals and their criminal prosecution were subjected to numerous obstacles.[83] Despite this admission, his opinion argues that "the Inter-American Court does not operate in the area of criminal justice, which corresponds to domestic jurisdictions".[84] Therefore, the consequences of aggravation are not related to changes in the nature of responsibility enforced by the Court. Without prejudice to this, the opinion finds that the greater gravity of the facts should be taken into account in the wording of the reproach and can be reflected in the reparations ordered by the Court, having an influence, for example, "in acts of nonpecuniary compensation, circulation of the judgment, expression of guilt and the requirement for an official apology, and the exaltation of the memory of the victim".[85] What the opinion does not accept is an influence on monetary reparations through "the establishment of 'punitive damages', a category that the case law of this Tribunal has not established, which corresponds more to the notion of a fine than to the reparation of damage and that in any case represents a burden that would rest on the treasury. This obviously implies an additional burden for taxpayers and a reduction in funds that should be used for social programs."[86]

---

80 *Ibidem*, para. 40.

81 *Ibidem*, paras. 49–50.

82 *Ibidem*, paras. 51–52.

83 *Case of Myrna Mack Chang*, concurring opinion of Judge Sergio García Ramírez, paras. 44–45.

84 *Ibidem*, para. 44.

85 *Ibidem*, para. 47.

86 *Ibidem*, paras. 46–47.

34. An examination of the case law of the Court will find that it does not require evidence for nonpecuniary damages.[87] This being the case, it could be argued that if one form of reparation is satisfaction, it is possible to argue that satisfying the victim of a violation of human rights committed with clear malice by a State agent will require greater reparations than when the violation is the result of an oversight, as the resulting lack of safety and fear is greater in the former case. In fact, in the judgment in the case of Sánchez, the Court found that due to "the grave circumstances in this case", one of which was the prevailing impunity attributable to the State, it must order the payment, in equity, of compensation for nonpecuniary damages.[88] In its considerations for establishing reparations in the case of Myrna Mack Chang, the Court took into account the poor handling of the judicial proceedings, their lateness, and the obstructions that prevented all those responsible from being punished. All these factors had caused the relatives of the victims "feelings of insecurity, defenselessness, and anguish".[89] As can be seen, in both cases the Court took the gravity of the conduct into account when establishing pecuniary indemnity.

Whatever the ruling on the nature of responsibility and the effect of an "aggravated" violation, what seems to be clear is that proving intention on the part of the State agents who committed the violation facilitates the attribution of responsibility and can influence the determination of reparations. It seems that the Court must reflect on this point and debate it further in order to reach consensus on an issue that could be very important.

5. PROTECTED RIGHTS

35. The American Convention sets forth civil and political rights, found in Articles 3 to 25. The Convention's catalogue of civil and political rights differs in some aspects from the ones in other general human rights treaties. Possibly this is the result of being the most recent treaty. The drafters of the Convention were able to use not only the textual models of the International Covenants and the European Convention on Human Rights but were also able to examine the practice of the European system, which began functioning in 1953. Also, the rights are drafted in such a way that from time to time they allow for the traditions and idiosyncrasies of OAS Member States to be seen. The main focus of this book is the scope and content of certain civil and political rights. Thus in this introductory chapter, I only want to address the general provisions that

---

87 *Case of Bámaca Velásquez, judgment on reparations*, para. 62; *Case of Trujillo Oroza, judgment on reparations*, para. 85; and *Case of Juan Humberto Sánchez*, para. 175.

88 *Case of Juan Humberto Sánchez*, para. 172 and 176.

89 *Case of Myrna Mack Chang*, para. 271.

allow for the restriction or suspension of State obligations regarding those rights. All this notwithstanding, this seems a good time to say something about economic, social, and cultural rights in the context of the American Convention.

36. Article 26 of the Convention does not mention individual economic, social, and cultural rights. On the contrary, it makes reference to the rights "implicit in the economic, social, educational, scientific, and cultural standards set forth in the Charter of the Organization of American States as amended by the Protocol of Buenos Aires", which today correspond to the standards on "Integral Development" in the rewritten text of the OAS Charter and changes introduced by the Protocols of Cartagena de Indias, Washington and Managua, making reference to achieving compliance through progressive development.[90]

It cannot be denied that treaties and practice have given less emphasis to these rights. After the Inter-American Commission made great efforts to give these rights more relevance, the OAS adopted an additional protocol to the Convention on economic, social, and cultural rights (known as the "Protocol of San Salvador") which entered into force on 16 November 1999, almost 11 years after its adoption.[91] The Protocol contains some of these rights and defines State obligations with regard to them in a way that suggests, in principle, an approach that is different and not as effective as the approach used with civil and political rights.[92]

The Court faced an Article 26 pleading in a contentious case in which the Inter-American Commission argued that the State had violated Article 26 on establishing a decree law that constituted "an unjustified reverse in the level of

---

90 The reference is to chapters VII, VIII, and IX of the OAS Charter (Articles 45–50), which was changed by the Protocol of Buenos Aires; however, subsequent amendments to the Charter, especially those introduced by the Protocols of Cartagena de Indias, Washington, and Managua, have developed the same principles under the heading of "Integral Development". In his concurring opinion in Advisory Opinion 4, Judge Piza states as follows: "the difference between civil and political rights and economic, social and cultural rights is due merely to historical reasons and not to juridical differences among them [...] This is why the principles of 'progressive development' contained in Article 26 of the Convention, although they refer literally to the economic, social, educational, scientific, and cultural standards contained in the Charter of the Organization of American States, should in my judgment be understood to be applicable to any of the 'civil and political' rights established in the American Convention to the extent and in the ways in which they are not reasonably requirable in themselves, and vice versa, that the standards of the Convention itself may be understood to be applicable to the so-called 'economic, social and cultural rights,' to the degree and in the ways in which they are reasonably requirable in themselves (as occurs, e.g., with the right to strike)", OC-4/84, concurring opinion of Judge Rodolfo E. Piza Escalante, para. 6.

91 As of October 2004, the Protocol of San Salvador had been acceded to or ratified by 13 States (Argentina, Brazil, Colombia, Costa Rica, Ecuador, El Salvador, Guatemala, Mexico, Panama, Paraguay, Peru, Suriname and Uruguay).

92 Protocol of San Salvador, Articles 1 and 19. Article 19(6) allows for the submission of individual communications before the Commission and for the possibility of the intervention of the Court only with regard to the right to education and union rights as autonomous claims.

development of the right to social security that the victims had achieved" under a previous decree law.[93]

The Commission argued that Article 26 prevents States from taking regressive measures in this area without justification.[94] The victims were in agreement and asked the Court to determine "the contents of the clause on the progressive development of economic, social, and cultural rights and establish parameters and criteria that show States how to comply with their legal obligations, as well as criteria for determining the way in which regressive measures violate obligations under the Convention."[95]

Addressing this point, the Court found that these rights have both an individual and a collective dimension and that their progressive development "should be measured in function of the growing coverage of economic, social and cultural rights in general, and of the right to social security and to a pension in particular, of the entire population, bearing in mind the imperatives of social equity, and not in function of the circumstances of a very limited group of pensioners, who do not necessarily represent the prevailing situation."[96] Considering that the case was not representative of the general situation, the Court dismissed the request for a ruling on the aforementioned pleadings,[97] such that the questions raised were not resolved.

This allows for the conclusion that the Court seems willing to rule on a possible violation of Article 26 in a case it considers more appropriate. It would have been useful had the judgment said something with regard to the possibility of examining this provision in the individual communications proceedings, particularly because in its Article 19(6), the Protocol of San Salvador grants very limited jurisdiction to this organ.

Nevertheless, there is no doubt that in applying the civil and political rights found in the Convention, the system's oversight organs can and should take their economic and social aspects into consideration. The United Nations Human Rights Committee has taken this route, primarily based on the fact that States must guarantee the human rights established in the Covenant without discrimination. Some examples demonstrate the broad scope that civil and political rights can have should they be applied in this way. In its 1982 General Comment on the right to life, the Committee was critical of restrictive interpretations of this right, noting that in taking positive measures to guarantee it, the State must, among other things, take all possible measures to decrease infant mortality rates.[98] In General Comment 25 on Article 25, entitled "The right to participate in public affairs, voting rights and the right of equal access to public

93 *Case of the "Five Pensioners"*.
94 *Ibidem*, para. 142(b).
95 *Ibidem*, para. 143(f).
96 *Ibidem*, para. 147.
97 *Ibidem*, para. 148.
98 HRC, General Comment 6, Article 6 (16th Period of Sessions), 30 April 1982, para. 5.

service", it held that "[f]reedom of expression, assembly and association are essential conditions for the effective exercise of the right to vote and must be fully protected. Positive measures should be taken to overcome specific difficulties, such as illiteracy, language barriers, poverty, or impediments to freedom of movement which prevent persons entitled to vote from exercising their rights effectively."[99]

It has also taken this route in its concluding observations to States Parties on the reports they submit. For example, in observations to Canada on compliance with its obligations with regard to the right to life, the committee stated that "[t]he Committee is concerned that homelessness has led to serious health problems and even to death. The Committee recommends that the State party take positive measures required by Article 6 to address this serious problem."[100]

As can be seen, the combination of the obligation to guarantee and the prohibition of discrimination allows civil and political rights a broadness that helps to diminish the artificial breach between them and economic, social, and cultural rights.

6. RESTRICTIONS

37. The catalogues of rights contained in the treaties not only formulate human rights but also regulate the possibility of State restrictions of them. Given that the rights of others form the principal limit to human rights – that is, all rights of all persons should be able to coexist – international law allows the State to restrict them in order to harmonize them. The authority to restrict, however, is not left up to State discretion. Rather, it is limited by international law, which requires compliance with certain conditions that, when lacking, make the restriction illegitimate and therefore in violation of the State's international obligations.

38. The first limit on all restrictions is that the general conditions and circumstances allowing a restriction of the exercise of a human right must be established by law.[101] Article 30 of the Convention indicates that "The restrictions that, pursuant to this Convention, may be placed on the enjoyment or exercise of the rights or freedoms recognized herein may not be applied except in accordance with laws enacted for reasons of general interest and in accordance with the purpose for which such restrictions have been established."

The requirement that a law be put in place in order to be able to regulate rights is a safeguard against potential government arbitrariness, as the

[99] HRC, General Comment 25, Article 25 (57th Period of Sessions), 12 July 1996, para. 12.

[100] HRC, *Concluding Observations of the Rights Committee: Canada* (65th Period of Sessions), 7 April 1999, para. 12.

[101] For examples, see Articles 6, 9, 12, 19 and 22 of the International Covenant, and Articles 4, 7, 12, 13, 16 and 30 of the American Convention.

expression "law" implies both formal[102] and material requirements. Interpreting the word "law" as meaning a formal law is reasonable, as instruments coming from the legislature are submitted to proceedings that are carefully designed to reflect the points of view of the majority and of minorities and are, at least formally, representative of the wishes of the majority. In light of the political reality on the American continent, it seems quite clear that the purpose of the safeguard is to prevent the imposition of restrictions by mere executive decrees. Secondly, it is also reasonable to argue that the word "law" incorporates the requirement of "generality" – that is, of law in a material sense. Any other interpretation of the word would be contrary to Article 1(1) of the Convention, which establishes the general principle of nondiscrimination.[103]

An Advisory Opinion of the Inter-American Court issued at the request of the government of Uruguay has found that the word "law" in the Convention must be understood in this way upon establishing that "the word 'laws' in Article 30 of the Convention means a general legal norm tied to the general welfare, passed by democratically elected legislative bodies established by the Constitution, and formulated according to the procedures set forth by the constitutions of the States Parties for that purpose."[104]

Naturally, the Court will have to revise this case law to adjust it to common law countries, which have a different legal system that allows for the creation of law through custom and legal precedent.

Article 30 also establishes that laws imposing restrictions on human rights must be issued "for reasons of general interest". There is nothing in the preparatory work to clarify the meaning of that sentence. The sentence can be considered a safeguard against the arbitrary imposition of limitations and a reinforcement of provisions establishing specific causes which can be invoked in order to restrict rights. In an advisory opinion already mentioned, the Inter-American Court interpreted "the general interest" as being "the common good", which is "a basic element of public order in democratic States". In the words of

102 The word "law" has a clear meaning in the legal systems of the majority of the Latin American States that participated in the drafting of the Convention. In the majority of those States, the word is used to mean an instrument created by the legislature through the observance of specific procedural steps provided for in the Constitution (R. Medina and C. Medina Quiroga, *Nomenclature of Primary Legal Sources*, Library of Congress, Washington, DC, 1979, pp. 2, 8, 16, 22, 38, 48, 65–66, 90, 95–96, 102, 112 and 120–121). The majority of the other States define "law" as the content of the instrument created by the legislature in accordance with specific proceedings, while the instrument itself is called a "decree" (*ibidem*, pp. 54–55, 59–60, 72, 84–85 and 107–108). Mexico uses both words – "law" or "decree" – to indicate a decision of the Congress (*ibidem*, p. 77). Therefore, they are all in agreement that "law" can only be the result of the action of legislators (this being understood as one or two assemblies of representatives of the people plus, in general, the president of the Republic), carried out in accordance with a proceeding provided for at the highest level of law: the Constitution.

103 C. Medina, *supra* n. 46, pp. 102–103.

104 OC-6/86, para. 27 and conclusion.

the American Declaration, its principal aim is "the protection of the essential rights of man and the creation of circumstances that will permit him to achieve spiritual and material progress and attain happiness".[105] This notion will probably be developed and solidified through the practice of States, supervised by the work carried out by the Commission and the Court.

39. The second limit on all restrictions is that the cause invoked to justify the restriction be one of those established in the Convention, whether through a general or, for certain rights, specific provision. These are generally in the interest of national security, public order or security, or the protection of health and public morals and the freedoms of others.[106] One provision allows the restriction of the right to property for reasons of social interest.[107] All these grounds are currently semi-empty containers which legislators, domestic legal authorities, the Commission, and the Court must provide with concrete content on a regional level. Some of them will surely be subject to controversy. For example, national security is a concept that has been used broadly by dictators in the Americas to justify extremely serious limitations that resulted in massive and systematic human rights violations.[108] Regarding this, although it has accepted the right of societies to defend themselves from attacks on them – for example through terrorist acts – the case law of the Court has been restrictive as regards accepting measures that may violate human rights in the name of national security.[109] Another point of disagreement would probably be the limitations imposed in defense of "the rights and liberties of others" or for "social interests", as the decisions taken in this regard will often reflect an ideological position.

40. There is a third limitation in the inter-American system: only restrictions that are "necessary in a democratic society" are permitted. This requirement was established explicitly for the rights of peaceful assembly, freedom of association, and freedom of movement.[110] However, its application as a limit on the restrictions of each of the rights of the Convention can be deduced from the context of the Convention itself, especially in light of its object and purpose[111] - both established in the preamble – and of Article 29(c) of the Convention. In the preamble, the American States reaffirmed their intention "to consolidate in this hemisphere, within the framework of democratic institutions, a system of

105 *Ibidem*, para. 29.

106 ACHR, Articles 15 and 16.

107 *Ibidem*, Article 21.

108 C. Medina, *The impact of domestic and international legal systems on human rights in Latin America*, Stichting Rechtshulp Chili, Utrecht, the Netherlands, 1982.

109 See, in particular: *Case of Loayza Tamayo*, para. 44 and *Case of Castillo Petruzzi et al.*, paras. 89 and 204.

110 ACHR, Articles 15, 16 and 22.

111 In this sense, see the Vienna Convention on the Law of Treaties (1969), A/CONF.39/27, Article 31(1) and (2).

personal liberty and social justice based on respect for the essential rights of man." For its part, Article 29 establishes that no provision in the Convention can be interpreted in the sense of "(c) excluding or limiting the effect that the American Declaration of the Rights and Duties of Man and other international acts of the same nature may have".[112]

The expression "necessary in a democratic society" has been interpreted at great length by the European Court of Human Rights, and the Inter-American Court of Human Rights has offered a similar interpretation which, in its Advisory Opinion 5/85, draws comparisons with European case law and incorporates it into the system. The Inter-American Court found that in the inter-American system, (i) restrictions must be in response to the "existence of an urgent social need" – that is, it must be oriented towards "satisfying an imperative public interest"; (ii) of the various options for achieving this objective, "the one must be chosen that restricts the protected right the least"; and (iii) the restriction must be "proportional to the interest justifying it and closely aligned with the achievement of this legitimate objective".[113] This settled interpretation of the expression can be summarized by saying that (i) the restriction must be intended to protect the value that can be protected through the restriction of this particular right; (ii) the restriction must be proportional, that is to say, involving only the measures that are strictly necessary to achieve the intended purpose; and (iii) there must be no other alternative to restricting this right in order to achieve the intended aim, meaning that if an alternative does exist, it must be used in place of the greater restriction.

7. TEMPORARY SUSPENSION OF OBLIGATIONS

41. In Article 27, the Convention allows States Parties to temporarily suspend their obligations in the event of war, public danger, or other emergency that threatens the independence or security of the State Party. In these cases, States generally tend to declare the existence of a situation they often describe as "emergency" or "martial law" or other similar nomenclature. This provision was key for many Latin American States. Effectively, according to a study prepared for the Commission, during the decade between 1950 and 1960 there were more than 100 occasions on which a situation like this was declared or extended in Latin America.[114] In its 1981–82 Annual Report, the Commission indicated that "the declaration of states of emergencies was one of the most frequent human rights violations".[115]

---

112 See P. van Dijk and G.J.H. van Hoof, *Theory and Practice of the European Convention on Human Rights*, 2nd edn, Kluwer, Deventer/Boston, 1990, pp. 583–606.

113 OC-5/85, para. 46.

114 IACHR, Doc. OEA/Ser.L/V/II.8, No. 6.

115 IACHR, *1981–82 Annual Report*, p. 133.

42. For this reason, and following the general trend, the Convention sets forth the guidelines according to which a State can declare a state of emergency. The guidelines establish (i) the grounds on which certain treaty obligations can be suspended; (ii) the rights for which the State cannot suspend any obligation; (iii) a requirement of proportionality for the duration and kind of suspensions ordered; (iv) a requirement that the measures cannot be discriminatory; and (v) the prohibition on suspending obligations when the suspension is not compatible with a State's other international obligations – this because the State, as noted previously, must apply the rule that most favours individuals. Finally, the Convention requires that the other States Parties be informed of the declaration of a situation of emergency.

7.1. GROUNDS FOR AUTHORIZING SUSPENSION

43. Article 27 of the Convention establishes that suspension is authorized in time of war, public danger, or other emergency that threatens the independence or security of a State Party. The drafting history of the provision does not clarify the specific meaning of the phrase "in time of war, public danger, or other emergency that threatens the independence or security of a State Party". It is evident that this part of the provision originated in the European Convention on Human Rights, meaning that the precedents established in the European system with regard to Article 15 of its Convention can be useful for its interpretation. However, the American Convention differs from Article 15 of the European Convention on Human Rights by replacing the European expression "the life of the nation" with "the independence or security of a State Party". This wording must be interpreted and developed in terms of the inter-American system. We should take into consideration the fact that these concepts are dangerously vague, particularly in view of the various interpretations – some rather extreme – of "national security" that have prevailed at certain times and in certain States on the American continent. This has made the supervision of regional organs crucial in every case in which the authority to suspend the observance of human rights is invoked.[116]

The Court has been especially strict in limiting States' authority to take measures that can affect the rights of persons, and particularly those rights whose obligations, according to the Convention, cannot be suspended.[117]

---

116 See R.E. Norris and P.D. Reiton, "The Suspension of Guarantees: A comparative analysis of the American Convention on Human Rights and the Constitutions of the States Parties", (1980) 30 *American University Law Review* 189–223 (191–199).

117 *Case of Loayza Tamayo*, para. 57; *Case of Cantoral Benavides*, para. 96; *Case of Bámaca Velásquez*, para. 155.

7.2. OBLIGATIONS NOT SUSCEPTIBLE TO SUSPENSION

44. As far as the obligations not susceptible to suspension are concerned, Article 27 itself prohibits suspending rights emerging from the following Articles: 3 (right to recognition of juridical personality); 4 (right to life); 5 (right to humane treatment); 6 (freedom from slavery and servitude); 9 (principle of legality and retroactivity); 12 (freedom of conscience and religion); 17 (protection of the family); 18 (right to a name); 19 (rights of the child); 20 (right to nationality); and 23 (right to participate in government), adding that neither are "the judicial guarantees essential for the protection of such rights" subject to suspension.

The wording of the Commission's draft, which prevailed in this Article of the Convention, was the result of the idea that the list of rights whose obligations were susceptible to suspension should be kept to a minimum. It is not possible to deduce from the drafting history of the Convention the criteria used for selecting these rights; the list seems to include either rights that are very basic, such as the right to life and the right to not be tortured, or rights whose restriction could not be relevant for dealing effectively with an emergency situation, such as for example the right to a name set forth in Article 18 of the Convention.

45. The long history of threats to political participation on the American continent, in which the suspension of constitutional guarantees under emergency situations has frequently resulted in the suspension of all political rights for long periods of time, is reflected in the provision that obligations with respect to political rights are not susceptible to suspension in emergency situations. It has been argued that the non-susceptibility of these obligations to suspension can in practice be highly difficult to abide by, especially in times of war.[118] However, if the inclusion of Article 23 in Article 27(2) is interpreted reasonably, and if its goal and purpose are taken into account, one can reach a different conclusion. Sections (a) and (c) of the provision, which address the right to participate in the conduct of public affairs and equal access to public services, respectively, present no problems. Both of them establish rights whose exercise should be possible under any circumstances. Furthermore, section (c) is only addressing an aspect of the general principle of equal protection, which obviously cannot be suspended. Only section (b), which sets forth the right to vote and to be elected, could present a problem, as it could be said that there are many circumstances in the life of the nation in which the organization of an election can be difficult or even impossible – for example, a natural disaster or a war. When analysing this point, it should be taken into consideration that it refers to the temporary suspension of a right due to a decision to do so, meaning that the right could be materially

[118] T. Buergenthal, "The American Convention on Human Rights: Illusion and Hopes", (1971–2) 21 *Buffalo Law Review* 121–136.

exercised if it were not for the suspension. It could be argued that in the case of a natural disaster or a war, it would be impossible to exercise the right to vote due to events that are beyond the control of the authorities, not due to a suspension. The inclusion of Article 27(2) in Article 23 seems to have the clear goal of preventing measures such as the dissolving of the parliament or congress or the prohibition of political parties on the grounds of an emergency, or the suspension of the right to vote for reasons other than the material impossibility of holding an election.

46. Article 27 also prohibits the suspension of the judicial guarantees that are indispensable for the protection of rights whose obligations cannot be suspended. This provision has been elaborated upon in two opinions of the Inter-American Court. The first of those[119] identifies Articles 7(6) and 25 of the Convention as guarantees that cannot be suspended, arguing that an emergency situation should not affect representative democracy, should not entail "a temporary suspension of the rule of law",[120] and should not authorize governments to acquire "absolute powers that go beyond the circumstances justifying the grant of such exceptional legal measures" given that "there exists an inseparable bond between the principle of legality, democratic institutions and the rule of law".[121] For this reason, independent and impartial judicial authorities suitable for determining the legality of actions taken during a state of emergency must be able to have oversight of the measures.[122]

In the second opinion, the Court reiterates its arguments and position with regard to Article 25. However, it pauses to examine Article 8 – which sets forth legal due process – noting that it "does not contain a specific judicial remedy, but rather the procedural requirements that should be observed in order to be able to speak of effective and appropriate judicial guarantees under the Convention".[123] It concludes that the concept of legal due process "should be understood as applicable, in the main, to all the judicial guarantees referred to in the American Convention, even during a suspension governed by Article 27 of the Convention".[124] The Court then states that, in addition to the guarantees already mentioned, there are other guarantees that arise from Article 29(c)[125] of the Convention that "imply not only a particular political system against which it is unlawful to rebel (Ibid., para. 20), but the need that it be supported by the judicial guarantees essential to ensure the legality of the measures taken in a state of emergency, in order to preserve the rule

119 OC-8/87, para. 20.

120 On this, see *infra,* Chapters 4 and 6.

121 OC-8/87, para. 24.

122 *Ibidem*, para. 30.

123 OC-9/87, para. 27.

124 *Ibidem*, para. 29.

125 Article 29, entitled "restrictions regarding interpretation", establishes that: "No provision of this Convention shall be interpreted as: [...] precluding other rights or guarantees that are inherent in the human personality or derived from representative democracy as a form of government."

of law (Ibid., para. 40)".[126] The Court reiterates once more that the rule of law, representative democracy, and the regime of personal freedom are innate characteristics of the Inter-American system and, in particular, of the system for the protection of the human rights set forth in the Convention."[127]

The final conclusion of this opinion is as follows:

1. That the "essential" judicial guarantees which are not subject to derogation [...] include *habeas corpus* (Art. 7(6)), *amparo*, and any other remedy effective before judges or competent tribunals (Art. 25(1)) designed to guarantee the respect of the rights and freedoms whose suspension is not authorized by the Convention
2. That the essential judicial guarantees which are not subject to suspension include those judicial procedures, inherent to representative democracy as a form of government (Art. 29(c)), provided for in the laws of the States Parties as suitable for guaranteeing the full exercise of the rights referred to in Article 27(2) of the Convention and whose suppression or restriction entails the lack of protection of such rights.
3. That the above judicial guarantees should be exercised within the framework and the principles of due process of law, expressed in Article 8 of the Convention.[128]

In sum, both the American Convention and the Court emphasize that the general rule is that rights should be respected and ensured; the suspension of States' international obligations to respect and ensure the exercise and enjoyment of rights when merited by very special circumstances is the exception. However, the guarantee of rights for which there is no possibility of suspension of obligations cannot be suspended, nor can any suspension result in the invalidation of the principle of legality.

7.3. PROPORTIONALITY OF MEASURES OF SUSPENSION

47. The requirement of proportionality is expressed in Article 27 of the Convention, which allows suspension "to the extent and for the period of time strictly required by the exigencies of the situation". If the exigency of the situation is what justifies the measures, international law requires that in addition to being proportional in duration and form, the measures taken must contribute to the objective of overcoming the emergency causing the situation. This requirement is applicable both to the general measure of restriction of a right as well as to every specific measure taken by the authorities in the application of the general measure.[129] The principle of proportionality, which

126 OC-9/87, para. 37.

127 *Ibidem*, paras. 34 and 35. Here the Court repeats what it had expressed in Advisory Opinions 5, 6 and, naturally, 8.

128 OC-9/87, para. 41.

129 OC-8/87, para. 39.

originates in the principle of necessity,[130] is thus linked with the idea that the necessary measures taken must also be adequate, requiring a relationship between the danger facing the community and the measures for counteracting it;[131] the actions taken by the authorities to limit fundamental rights and freedoms must never exceed the particular rational limit of any restrictive measure.[132]

For its part, the Inter-American Court has indicated that "it is clear that what might be permissible in one type of emergency would not be lawful in another. The lawfulness of the measures taken to deal with each of the special situations referred to in Article 27(1) will depend, moreover, upon the character, intensity, pervasiveness, and particular context of the emergency and upon the corresponding proportionality and reasonableness of the measures."[133]

The limits alluded to address two aspects of the issue: the form in which rights are affected and the persons who will be affected by the measures. As regards the first, the authorities cannot under any circumstances be excessive in the severity of the measures taken, as they must constitute only those measures that are suitable for re-establishing normality. As regards the persons affected, the authorities must limit themselves to suspending the exercise of the rights of persons who are directly involved in the emergency situation, without affecting the rights of others.[134]

7.4. PROHIBITION ON AFFECTING OBLIGATIONS NOT SUBJECT TO SUSPENSION IN OTHER INTERNATIONAL LAW

48. Article 27 of the Convention sets forth the principle that the human rights enshrined therein and the State obligations regarding them are not exclusive of the content of other laws, ordering that measures suspending obligations during emergency cannot be incompatible with other obligations imposed by international law. This provision is repeated in Article 4 of the International Covenant and in Article 15 of the European Convention on Human Rights, both

130 F. Meléndez, *La Suspensión de los Derechos Fundamentales en los Estados de Excepción Según el Derecho Internacional de los Derechos Humanos*, IIDH, San José, Costa Rica, 1999, p. 106.

131 *Ibidem*, pp. 95–97.

132 "This principle, like its justification – legitimate defence – presupposes the existence of an imminent threat and requires a proportional relationship between that threat and the measures used to avert it. These measures in turn, to be legitimate, must be proportional to the severity of the threat. Thus any excess in the use of the measures makes the 'defence' illegitimate and thus transforms it into aggression." (Report of the Special Rapporteur of the Human Rights Subcommission on the Question of Human Rights and States of Emergency. E/CN.4/Sub.2/1997/19 of 23 June 1997, para. 84).

133 OC-8/87, para. 22.

134 See H. Faúndez, *supra* n. 9, p. 115.

of which refer to the provisions of treaties, including humanitarian law treaties, and customary law.[135]

7.5. PROHIBITION ON DISCRIMINATION

49. The measures of suspension that the State can take during an emergency situation cannot entail any discrimination based on race, color, sex, language, religion or social origin. It must be noted that this provision repeats the wording of Article 4 of the International Covenant and does not mention political or other opinions, nationality, economic status or birth as possible bases for prohibited discrimination, nor does it mention the clause that allows for the incorporation of other grounds of discrimination not specified under the category of "any other social condition", all present in Article 1 of the Convention. There is nothing in the preparatory work that would help explain the absence of these grounds; it has been said that in the International Covenant, the exclusion of the grounds of "national origin" was due to the idea that in a war, foreign enemies would have to be treated differently than the citizens of the country in question,[136] but Nowak argues that the elimination of the grounds of discrimination based on "national origin" and "political opinion" was done with the purpose of allowing differentiated treatment of the members of a certain race or certain ethnic, religious or linguistic minorities as long as it does not "intentionally aim at these population groups".[137] There does not appear to be any explanation for the other missing grounds. Professor Meléndez refers only to political motivations to argue that although they have not been included in the grounds, they should be understood to be included because Article 1(1) of the Convention mentions them and because Article 27(2) of the Convention prohibits the suspension of obligations connected with political rights.[138] This opinion seems doubtful, given that Article 27 expressly mentions the grounds of discrimination, and the non-suspension of political rights does not necessarily lead to the conclusion reached by Professor Meléndez. However, it should be taken into account that the application of the principles of necessity and proportionality, as well as the principle that all difference in treatment must be objective and reasonable, constitutes a powerful barrier to differences in treatment based on political opinions or other possible reasons as well.[139]

---

135 J. Fitzpatrick, *The International System for Protecting Rights During States of Emergency*, Procedural Aspects of International Law Series, Vol. 19, University of Pennsylvania Press, Philadelphia, 1994, pp. 59–60.

136 *Ibidem*, p. 62.

137 M. Nowak, *UN Covenant on Civil and Political Rights. CCPR Commentary*, N.P. Engel Publisher, Kehl/Strasbourg/Arlington, 1993, p. 86.

138 F. Meléndez, *supra* n. 130, pp. 94–95.

139 Paragraph 8 of General Comment 29 of the United Nations Human Rights Committee (CCPR/C/21/Rev.1/Add.11, 31 August 2001) is an interesting addition to the obligations that cannot be suspended pursuant to the Covenant on Civil and Political Rights.

7.6. NOTIFICATION OF OTHER STATES PARTIES AND INTERNATIONAL OVERSIGHT

50. The Convention indicates that "[the State declaring an emergency] shall immediately inform the other States Parties, through the Secretary General of the Organization of American States" of the contents of the declaration, its motives and its duration. This is an evident reduction of the scope of domestic jurisdiction, as it means that a fact that is imminently domestic and closely linked with the idea of statehood gives rise to an obligation to notify the international community. The notification requirement is a clear signal that the suspension of obligations is in the joint interest of States Parties to the Convention, and that they have the right to act upon the declaration of an emergency.

International monitoring organs also have authority to monitor whether the declaration of emergency and the specific measures taken based on that declaration violate the Convention, given that Article 27 is a provision that is binding for States Parties and the Commission and the Court are organs charged with overseeing States' observance of the provisions of the Convention.[140] A contrary interpretation would have the result of annulling the meaning of Article 27 and several other articles of the Convention, significantly diminishing the beneficial effect that the Convention can have for human rights in the Americas. It is likely that in the exercise of their jurisdiction, regional oversight organs take into consideration the fact that governments could have more information available to them than the oversight organs possess about the problems the States face and will take care to carry out their oversight in a reasonable manner. This also leads to the conclusion that – given that the decision on the justifiableness of the human rights suspensions imposed by State is always in the end brought before the international organ supervising it[141] and that this international supervision is subsidiary – domestic courts must also have oversight of the decision, both in its reasonableness and its legality.

Professor Fitzpatrick wondered in her excellent book on the topic of human rights during states of emergency whether the inclusion of the prohibition on taking measures that affect other international obligations means that the oversight organs, in this case the Commission and the Court, have jurisdiction to hear the substance of these other obligations.[142] She argues that on supervising

140 *Case of Neira Alegría et al.*, para. 77.

141 The authorities of those organs are established in the corresponding treaties. Articles 44 and 45 of the American Convention give the Inter-American Commission the authority to hear petitions or complaints of any and all violations of the Convention; Article 62 gives the Inter-American Court authority to hear, under certain conditions, "all cases concerning the interpretation and application" of the Convention.

142 J. Fitzpatrick, *supra* n. 135, p. 60.

the application of Article 27, the Commission and the Court will be obligated to review whether the State has other obligations, the content and scope of those obligations, and whether the State is violating them on making use of Article 27. Finally, it could be concluded that should the State be found to be in breach of those obligations, it is also violating Article 27 of the Convention.

CHAPTER 2
RIGHT TO LIFE

Article 4. Right to Life

1. *Every person has the right to have his life respected. This right shall be protected by law and, in general, from the moment of conception. No one shall be arbitrarily deprived of his life.*
2. *In countries that have not abolished the death penalty, it may be imposed only for the most serious crimes and pursuant to a final judgment rendered by a competent court and in accordance with a law establishing such punishment, enacted prior to the commission of the crime. The application of such punishment shall not be extended to crimes to which it does not presently apply.*
3. *The death penalty shall not be reestablished in states that have abolished it.*
4. *In no case shall capital punishment be inflicted for political offenses or related common crimes.*
5. *Capital punishment shall not be imposed upon persons who, at the time the crime was committed, were under 18 years of age or over 70 years of age; nor shall it be applied to pregnant women.*
6. *Every person condemned to death shall have the right to apply for amnesty, pardon, or commutation of sentence, which may be granted in all cases. Capital punishment shall not be imposed while such a petition is pending decision by the competent authority.*

1. INTRODUCTION

1. Determining the scope and content of the protection of the right to life is, in general, a complex task. This is principally due to the fact that the debate on how and to what degree this right is guaranteed is strongly affected by philosophical and religious positions and beliefs that are at times difficult to reconcile.

For example, there is consensus in the human rights world that the right to assembly does not force anyone to assemble, and that the right to religion does not force anyone to have one;[1] however, with regard to the right to life, there is

[1] For the universal system, M. Nowak, *UN Covenant on Civil and Political Rights. CCPR Commentary*, N.P. Engel Publisher, Kehl/Strasbourg/Arlington, 1993, pp. 389–390 and 315–316.

debate over whether it is only a right, or if remaining alive also constitutes an obligation for persons, with which the State must attempt to ensure compliance.

2. Interpretation of Article 4 of the American Convention does not escape this complexity. Initially, on examination of the article's first clause, it could be said that the right consists exclusively of not being deprived of life arbitrarily. This interpretation seems to be confirmed in the reading of the five subsequent clauses, which refer to the death penalty. Some of the drafters of the Convention held the conviction that the death penalty should be prohibited by international law, but the States could not reach a consensus that this provision should be established absolutely. Thus one can argue that what the drafters of Article 4 had in mind was to reduce as much as possible a State's opportunity to arbitrarily deprive a person of life by means of a death sentence that was not the result of rigorous due process. Without prejudice to this, an interpretation limited to understanding the right as a mere State obligation to comply with the requirements established in Article 4 regarding the imposition of the death penalty would be mistaken. We cannot read this provision without taking into consideration that Article 1 of the Convention establishes State obligations regarding this right, and that among them the obligation to respect imposes upon the States the duty to refrain from committing human rights violations, while the obligation to ensure requires action to be taken to allow for the effective enjoyment of the right.

Article 4 of the Convention also presents another complexity on including in its first clause the State obligation to protect the right to life "in general, from the moment of conception", as there is dispute over whether this wording broadens the concept of rights holders to include fetuses.

These issues will be the subject of this study of Article 4.

2. RIGHT TO LIFE: A RIGHT, OR ALSO AN OBLIGATION?

3. The question of the possibility of the State having authority to force a person to preserve his or her life and on the unlawfulness of ending one's life or putting one's own life at risk is generally raised with regard to failed suicide attempts and certain decisions that necessarily imply putting an end to life, such as euthanasia, and the decisions of members of certain religions to not allow blood transfusions or vaccination against illness. None of these questions has been submitted before the Inter-American Court for its review, neither in requests for an advisory opinion nor through the submission of a case. However, there

---

For the European system, D.J. Harris, M. O'Boyle and C. Warbrick, *Law of the European Convention on Human Rights*, Butterworths, London/Dublin/Edinburgh, 1995, pp. 421 and 361–362.

have been domestic cases – in Chile,[2] at least – and there is a possibility that international oversight bodies will face the need to resolve these problems in the future.

4. In initially approaching this interpretation, we must remember that even though human life is fundamentally important for society and, therefore, a decision on its voluntary ending must be made by taking into consideration the profound respect that it deserves, it is difficult to argue that this decision should not, in the end, belong to the person whose life is in question. It can also be argued that human rights are exercised or cease to be exercised at the will of the rights holder, for which reason a decision to put an end to one's own life should not constitute a violation. In general, although they do not necessarily share the same argumentation, this position is reflected in the Penal Codes of the States Parties to the Convention, which generally do not bring criminal charges for unsuccessful suicides.[3]

Suicide assisted by a third party, on the other hand, is a different matter. One could reasonably assume that an individual who wants to commit suicide possibly suffers from an emotional disorder, perhaps combined with objective life situations that lead to desperation. Therefore, the expected conduct of a third party is to dissuade the potential suicide victim as best as possible, not to collaborate in the victim's suicide. Based on this, it seems possible to argue that a State that does not prohibit the assisting of a suicide would be violating Article 4 of the Convention. This is reflected in the domestic legislation that frequently punishes such actions.

However, a problem arises with euthanasia, a situation in which an individual suffering from a terminal illness is helped to die. Undoubtedly, humanitarian considerations come into play here that cannot be easily dismissed.[4] An argument in favor of allowing euthanasia could be based on the absolute prohibition of subjecting a person to torture or to cruel, inhuman or degrading

---

2 Relevant cases have included those on the refusal of members of the Jehovah's Witnesses to practice blood transfusions. For examples, see Santiago Court of Appeals, *remedy of protection roll 5.844-91*; Copiapó Court of Appeals, *remedy of protection roll 3.569-92*; San Miguel Court of Appeals, *remedy of protection roll 20-95*; Rancagua Court of Appeals, *remedy of protection roll 1030-95*; Santiago Court of Appeals, *remedy of protection roll 3996-95*; San Miguel Court of Appeals, *remedy of protection roll 77-2001*; Coyhaique Court of Appeals, *remedy of protection roll 39-2002*. A study of these cases can be found at A. Retamales, "Lecciones que dejan los pacientes adultos que rechazan transfusiones de sangre a partir de la doctrina de nuestros tribunales", in *La Semana Jurídica*, LexisNexis No. 122, published at www.bibilioteca.uandes.cl/doc/IP2003_11p75.pdf (visited on 24 July 2003).

3 This is the case for example in the penal codes of Argentina, Colombia, Chile, Brazil and Venezuela. For its part, Costa Rica's penal code imposes a security measure on individuals who have tried and failed to commit suicide consisting of "adequate psychiatric treatment" (Article 114).

4 For interpretation of the subject with regard to the European Convention on Human Rights, M. Nowak, *supra* n. 1, pp. 124–125.

treatment, as it is possible to argue that, in compliance with this prohibition, it would not be justifiable to criminalize without exception a humanitarian action intended to end serious and incurable suffering that is carried out in compliance with the wishes of the sick person. In examining this problem, the Human Rights Committee has not found that euthanasia is incompatible with the right to life and that the State must therefore prohibit it without exception. However, it has highlighted the necessity of carefully regulating euthanasia and ensuring that the necessary oversight is established in order to ensure that legal safeguards are complied with in each case.[5]

As regards a person's refusal to accept a specific kind of medical care, I think that a distinction must be made between situations involving adults and situations involving children or adolescents. In cases involving adults, I do not believe it can be argued that the State has the authority to force an individual to accept unwanted medical treatment. The motives of the denial could be religious, but they could also be based on the conviction that certain forms of medicine are not effective. There is a significant debate, for example, on homeopathic versus allopathic medicine, and it does not seem legitimate to argue that the State, through its doctors or its courts, is the one with the authority to make the decision. To this it should be added that, even from a strict right to health perspective starting from a holistic approach to human rights, the Committee on Economic, Social, and Cultural Rights has highlighted that States' specific legal obligation to respect health implies, *inter alia*, that they refrain from applying medical treatments coercively, except in the treatment of persons with mental illnesses or in cases of prevention and control of illnesses or infectious diseases.[6] In the case of children and adolescents, over whom the State has greater authority to intervene due to their stage of development, the Convention imposes upon the State an additional obligation to protect. This could perhaps be invoked in order for the State to be able to decide – overriding the parents and to the best of its knowledge – on the measures of medical care that should be provided to the children in situations in which it finds that the parents' decision to refuse medical treatment puts the life or health of a child in real danger.

---

5 The Netherlands allows euthanasia, regulating it carefully. In comments on the Netherlands' periodic report submitted in 2001, the Human Rights Committee recommended that the State implement *ex ante* oversight and expressed concern at the fact that under Dutch law, adolescents between the ages of 16 and 18 that are in compliance with the strict requirements of the law are allowed to make the decision by themselves. HRC, *Concluding Observations of the Rights Committee: The Netherlands* (72nd Period of Sessions), 19 and 23 July 2001.

6 Committee on Economic, Social, and Cultural Rights, General Comment 14, "The right to the highest attainable standard of health" (Article 12), para. 34. Thanks to Carlos Rafael Urquilla Bonilla for having brought this General Comment to my attention.

3. PROTECTION OF LIFE FROM THE MOMENT OF CONCEPTION

5. In contrast to the International Covenant[7] and the European Convention on Human Rights,[8] in the right to life, the American Convention introduces an obligation to protect, in general, as of the moment of conception. This provision requires interpretation, as it is necessary to establish the contents of the obligation of Article 4(1) and who can demand that the State apply it. So far, the debate over this provision on our continent has been limited mainly to examining the criminalization or decriminalization of abortion, although it is possible that, in the future, scientific and technological progress will present new challenges for the right to life. This section will concentrate only on the subject on which the discussion is currently focused. It will fall to others subsequently to move forward in the interpretation of the provision or to properly modify it in order to adjust it to the changes that have already begun to take place in the field of human reproduction.

6. The effects of this interpretation are not trivial. The high rates of maternal mortality resulting from backalley abortions on this continent and throughout the world[9] is concerning, as are the varied and difficult consequences a woman faces for various reasons when carrying an unwanted pregnancy to term. Because of this, international supervisory bodies, whose area of supervision includes the rights of women, have advocated for, at least, the elimination of the total criminalization of abortion[10] with the purpose of protecting the rights to life and humane treatment, specifically of women. The Human Rights Committee has repeatedly indicated that both when a pregnancy puts the life of the mother in danger and when it is the result of rape, States that criminalize abortion are violating their obligations under Articles 6 and 7 of the Covenant by failing to protect the life of the mother or failing to abide by the absolute ban on torture and cruel, inhuman or degrading treatment or punishment.[11]

---

7 Article 6 of the ICCPR, adopted on 16 December 1966; it entered into force internationally on 23 March 1976.

8 Article 2 of the ECHR, adopted on 4 November 1950; it entered into force internationally on 3 September 1953.

9 See R. Cook, "Human Rights Dynamic of Abortion Law Reform" (2003) 25 *Human Rights Quarterly* 1–59, with abundant information based principally on the research of the World Health Organization.

10 Committee on the Elimination of Discrimination against Women (CEDAW), General Recommendation No. 24: Woman and Health (1999), para. 31(c); and HRC, General Comment No. 28, Article 3 (The equality of rights between men and women) (2000), paras. 10 and 11. See also *Bringing Rights to Bear: An Analysis of the Work of UN Treaty Monitoring Bodies on Reproductive and Sexual Rights,* The Center for Reproductive Law and Policy and U. of Toronto International Programme on Reproductive and Sexual Health Law, 2002, Chapter III E.

11 HRC, *Concluding Observations: Ecuador,* 18 August 1998, para. 11; *Concluding Observations: Chile,* 30 March 1999, para. 15; *Concluding Observations: Peru,* 15 November 2000, para. 20.

7. The reality on the American continent has not prevented Spanish- and Portuguese-speaking States Parties to the Convention from deciding to criminalize all types of abortion[12] or to decriminalize some types, normally those performed to protect the life of the mother or end a pregnancy resulting from rape. In this latter case, in practice States often allow innumerable obstacles to be raised that women have to deal with, thus generally creating a clear risk to the life and personal integrity of women. An important factor in the imposition of these rules and practices is the fact that the Convention covers a continent where the Catholic Church holds great power, power which it has used to advance the struggle against abortion and, often, against all forms of family planning – a subject that is a priority in its activities domestically and internationally. Generally, the continent has a conservative perspective on a woman's place in society and her role in the family.[13]

8. These circumstances make the issue of abortion a particularly difficult one; it is not simply a problem of law and human rights. Rather, what is at issue is a subject in which the position taken on it is intimately linked with religious ideas that attempt to impose themselves as legal rules. There is no other explanation for the extremes to which the prohibition of abortion goes. A case presented before the Inter-American Commission on Human Rights is illustrative. In that case, the victim was a girl who was raped, and one of the consequences of that rape was pregnancy; although the legislation in the State involved allowed abortion under those circumstances, the public health service doctors refused to perform one.[14] In 2003, a news item appeared in Latin American newspapers about a nine-year-old girl who had been raped and impregnated, and was prevented from having an abortion with such zeal that authorities even wanted to prevent her from leaving the country to have the abortion elsewhere.[15] In addition, in early 2003, Chilean newspapers recounted two cases in which immense suffering was caused to two pregnant women. In one, a woman was forced to carry for six months a fetus that had not developed past the second month, while in another, a woman was forced to prolong a molar pregnancy,

12 Chile and El Salvador are in this situation.

13 See Encyclical Letter *Evangelium Vitae*, John Paul II, 25 March 1995; Encyclical Letter *Redemptoris Mater*, John Paul II, 25 March 1987; Apostolic Letter *Mulieris Dignitatem*, John Paul II, 15 August 1988.

14 See L. Cabal, J. Lemaitre and M. I Roa (eds.) *Cuerpo y Derecho. Legislación y Jurisprudencia en América Latina*, Legal Center for Reproductive Rights and Public Policy, Facultad de Derecho, Universidad de los Andes, Editorial Temis, Bogotá, Colombia, 2001, p. 383.

15 The tragic story of this girl and the reaction of different members of the community, among them the Episcopal Conference that "made a call for respect for life" stating that "a baby cannot be killed, not even to save the life of the mother", can be read in successive stories in the Costa Rican newspaper *La Nación* from the year 2003, published on 31 January; 5, 14, 20, 21, 22, 23 and 27 February; 1 and 4 March; and 15 May (www.nacion.co.cr).

putting her life in serious danger.[16] It goes without saying that both the victims were economically disadvantaged.[17]

Religious convictions also had a bearing on the drafting of Article 4(1) of the Convention. The original draft included a State obligation to protect the right to life from the moment of conception, and it was the Inter-American Commission[18] that suggested adding the expression "in general", explaining that this addition was due to the need to reconcile different points of view on the subject, as objections had arisen from the Conference of Bogotá based on the argument that the legislation of several American States allowed abortion, *inter alia* to save the life of the mother and in cases of the rape of a minor.[19] The Commission's proposal for the Convention was reviewed by a rapporteur in order to examine whether it met the standards of the International Covenant. The rapporteur recommended that the phrase "and, in general, from the moment of conception" be eliminated both to reconcile the text with the legislation of many American States[20] and "to avoid any possibility of conflict with article 6, paragraph 1, of the Covenant of the United Nations on Civil and Political Rights, which establishes this right only generally". The Commission decided "on principle" to keep the provision.[21] During the Specialized Conference of 1969, Brazil and the Dominican Republic submitted amendments to remove the phrase, as the rapporteur had suggested, and the delegation from the United States supported Brazil's position, arguing that the clause was "vague" and not effective for preventing States Parties to the future Convention from not criminalizing under domestic law abortions carried out for different reasons.[22] Ecuador's delegation requested – without success – that the expression "in general" be removed. In

---

16 On that occasion, the doctors finally moved to operate on the woman, who was likely to need treatment for an extended period of time due to the physical problems resulting from the situation. See *Diario la Nación,* 20 January 2003 (www.lanacion.cl); also see www.argumentos.cem.cl/ediciones/argu58.htm.

17 The information given covers only what appears in public documents; no further information is given in order to respect what remains of the victims' privacy.

18 "Report of the Inter-American Commission on Human Rights regarding the draft Convention on Human Rights approved by the Inter-American Council of Legal Consultants", in the *Inter-American Yearbook on Human Rights 1968*, General Secretariat, OAS, Washington, DC, 1973, p. 320.

19 IACHR, *Baby Boy v. United States*, Case No. 2141, Report No. 23/81 of 6 March 1981, published in the *1980–1981 Annual Report*, para. 25.

20 Abortions to save the life of the mother were already decriminalized in Uruguay in 1889 and in Colombia in 1890. Article 640 of the Colombian Code decriminalized abortion performed "as a measure absolutely necessary to save the life of the woman" or indispensable "according to the principles of medical science". The 1938 Uruguayan Penal Code considered abortions performed for therapeutic, ethical or social reasons as not criminal. See *Silencios Públicos Muertes Privadas. Estudio comparativo de la regulación jurídica del aborto en América Latina y el Caribe*, CLADES, Lima, Perú, 1998, pp. 26, 125 and 146.

21 *Inter-American Yearbook 1968*, *supra* n. 18, p. 97.

22 Specialized Conference, San José, Costa Rica, 7–22 November 1969, *Minutes and Documents*, General Secretariat, OAS, Washington, DC, 1978, pp. 57, 121 and 160.

the end, the Conference approved the paragraph in the wording proposed by the Commission.[23] When it ratified the Convention, Mexico made an interpretive declaration, saying that it did not consider the expression "in general" found in paragraph 1 of Article 4 to constitute an obligation to adopt or maintain in force legislation protecting life "from the moment of conception".[24] No other State seems to have found it necessary to make a declaration or reservation as regards this point.

As can be seen, one can deduce from the drafting of the treaty that the expression "in general" was added to the original text with the specific purpose of reconciling the possibility that domestic legislation would allow abortion and that the proposal to eliminate it would not be accepted, for which reason, basing an interpretation of this unclear provision on the preparatory works, one would have to conclude that paragraph 1 of Article 4 does not block a State's authority to allow abortion under the circumstances it determines.

The American Declaration does not include the phrase in question, expressing briefly in its Article I that all humans have the right to life. In a case related to an abortion (case of Baby Boy) brought before the Inter-American Commission against the United States, the petitioners argued that this provision protects the right to life from the moment of conception and asked the Commission to find that the United States had violated the right to life of the fetus with the abortion performed on the mother. The communication holds that the right to life in the Declaration should be understood to be "clarified by the definition and description of 'right to life' found in the American Convention", even though the United States was not a party to the Convention.[25]

The United States used three different arguments to respond to the communication. First, it rejected the possibility of using the Convention to clarify the content of Article I of the Declaration. Next, it argued that there had already been an attempt to insert this language into the first draft of the Declaration prepared by the Inter-American Juridical Committee, and that attempt had been rejected.[26] Finally, it argued that the *travaux préparatoires* of Article 4 makes it clear that States were left with the option of not criminalizing abortion and that, in any case, in order to decide whether an abortion violates Article 4, one would have to examine whether or not it constitutes an arbitrary act in light of the circumstances of the case.[27]

---

23 *Ibidem*, pp. 160 and 481.

24 Interpretive Declaration of Mexico in IACHR, Basic Documents Pertaining to Human Rights in the Inter-American System (up-to-date through May 2001), General Secretariat, OAS, Washington, DC, 2001, pp. 58–59.

25 IACHR, *Baby Boy, supra* n. 19, pp. 187–209, para. 2.

26 The United States cited the Ninth International Conference of the American States, *Minutes and Documents*, Vol. V, p. 449 (1948) (see *ibidem*, para. 14(a)).

27 *Ibidem*, para. 14.

In its report, the Commission spent time examining the *travaux préparatoires* of the Declaration, arriving at the conclusion that as the United States had indicated, the drafting of Article I, which expressly left out any mention of the right to life from the moment of conception, constituted "an agreement reached in order to resolve problems raised by the delegations from Argentina, Brazil, Cuba, the United States, Mexico, Peru, Uruguay and Venezuela",[28] as the draft provided by the Inter-American Juridical Committee was incompatible with laws on abortion in the majority of American States, which by 1948 permitted abortion: "A) when necessary to save the life of the mother; B) to end the pregnancy of a victim of child rape; C) to protect the honor of an honorable woman; D) to prevent the transmission of a hereditary or contagious disease to the fetus; and E) in cases of economic distress."[29]

The Commission also examined the *travaux préparatoires* of Article 4 of the American Convention with the purpose of clarifying the expression "in general" used in that provision, reaching a conclusion similar to the one expressed in the prior section, that is, that the expression had been added in order to allow for the possibility of abortion.[30]

Taking this into consideration, the Commission did not accept the argument of the petitioners and concluded that the United States had not violated Article I of the American Declaration.[31]

The Commission's resolution included two dissenting opinions based on a different interpretation of the *travaux préparatoires* of Article I of the Declaration, one on medical opinions on the problem of when human life begins, and the other on religious arguments.[32]

9. Whatever the drafters of Article 4(1) of the Convention were thinking – and if we do not wish to turn to its preparatory work – the provision must be interpreted in accordance with the rules of treaty hermeneutics, which require a *pro persona* and dynamic standard.[33] In addition, interpreting human rights provisions in a way that would imply a complete distortion of the system is not permissible, as the task of the interpreter is to harmonize the different human rights set forth in the treaty. I will therefore attempt herein to give an interpretation of the expression "in general, from the moment of conception" that is faithful to human rights theory and the system based on it.

---

28 *Ibidem*, para. 19(d).

29 *Ibidem*, para. 19(e) and (f).

30 *Ibidem*, para. 30.

31 *Ibidem*, para. 1 of the operative paragraphs.

32 See *ibidem*, dissenting votes of Marco Monroy Cabra and Luis Tinoco Ramírez. Commissioner Monroy Cabra states in para. 8 of his opinion that "[t]he maternal womb in which the flame of life is lighted is sacred and may not be profaned to extinguish what God has created in his image and in his likeness."

33 *Matter of Viviana Gallardo et al.*, para. 16; see also OC-10/89, para. 37.

10. For the interpretation of this provision, I will start with two basic ideas. The first is that a mother is a person both in the legal systems of States Parties to the Convention and under the Convention itself. She is therefore the holder of all the human rights set forth in the Convention. The second is that a fetus that has not been removed from the mother's womb is dependent on her, is not a person, and therefore cannot have its own rights, but rather has rights through the mother.

The fact that the mother is a person both in the legal systems of States Parties to the Convention and under the Convention itself, and that she is therefore the holder of all the human rights set forth in the Convention, need be neither demonstrated nor reasoned out. In addition, it is clear that human rights constitute a limit on State action, meaning that any State action taken with regard to a woman's body has to take her rights into consideration.

The rights that can be affected by decisions made by the State regarding a woman's pregnancy come from various sources: the rights to a woman's life and personal integrity come from the Convention itself and from Article 6 and 7 of the Covenant; subsumed within them is the right to health, which is also set forth in Article 10 of the Protocol of San Salvador and Article 12 of the International Covenant on Economic, Social and Cultural Rights;[34] the right of a woman to decide the number of children she wants, on the basis of equality with the man, is derived from Article 10(h) and Article 12(1) of the Convention on the Elimination of All Forms of Discrimination against Women;[35] and also the right to privacy, which allows for decisions to be made freely as to one's own person, is established in Article 11(2) of the American Convention and Article 17 of the International Covenant.

11. In contrast, the American Convention sets forth a different rule for the fetus. To start with, if it had been considered a person and, as a consequence, a bearer of rights established in the Convention the same as other human beings, the mention of it made in Article 4(1) of the Convention would not have been necessary. Furthermore, a summary examination of the protection and regulation of human rights in the Convention leads necessarily to the conclusion that it is impossible to argue that the fetus bears all the rights found in the Convention.

In reality, neither does the fetus have the rights indicated in Article 4(1) of the Convention. Rather, this provision places an obligation to protect on the

---

34 The International Covenant on Economic, Social, and Cultural Rights, adopted by the United Nations General Assembly on 16 December 1966, entered into force on 3 January 1976. Its States Parties include, among others, all the States Parties to the Convention, with the exception of Haiti.

35 The Convention on the Elimination of All Forms of Discrimination against Women (CEDAW), adopted by the United Nations General Assembly on December 18, 1979, entered into force on 3 September 1981. Its States Parties include, among others, all the States Parties to the American Convention, with the exception of Paraguay, which has only signed it.

State. The reason for this protection has to do with the respect that a legal system owes to a woman embarking on the important task – both for her and for society – of bringing a child into the world. Therefore, the direct subject of the protection is the pregnant mother. The protection of the fetus is carried out indirectly through the protection of the mother, as established in the provisions of Article 15(3)(a) of the Protocol of San Salvador, which requires States Parties to "provide special care and assistance to mothers during a reasonable period before and after childbirth", and Article VII of the American Declaration, which establishes the right of a pregnant woman to protection, care and special aid.

The Convention imposes on the State not only an obligation to allow the woman to carry out the task of procreation on which she has embarked; it must also help the pregnancy to reach full term in different ways. The protection should consist of any measure required by the mother to reach this objective. This could include medical assistance, the provision of basic foodstuffs necessary during the pregnancy, or other measures of this nature.[36] These measures give content to the obligation found in Article 4(1) of the American Convention.

The obligation to protect can only be demanded by the mother: it cannot be invoked by third parties should the mother wish to terminate her pregnancy. This is because State action in these cases affects the rights of the woman. Not protecting the rights of women in this regard – rights which impose limitations on the States – brings about, aside from the probable violation of the rights, particularly serious consequences for the future, as bringing a child into the world constitutes a commitment that includes obligations that the woman can never excuse herself from except were she to renounce her motherhood completely. The State cannot impose this obligation on any human being. Furthermore, with the purpose of protecting the mother, and taking into consideration that the circumstances in which a pregnancy is terminated can present a high degree of risk to the life of the mother, the State must regulate those circumstances in order to protect her health.

12. The situation is different when the fetus ceases to be completely dependent on the mother and one could assume with a degree of certainty that it would survive upon being removed from the mother's womb. In that case, the State must establish rules for regulating the extraction of a fetus that has reached that level of development, given that, when separated from the mother, the fetus legally becomes a human being to whom the right to life established in Article 4(1) of the Convention applies. In this case, the State has the obligation to protect it from any arbitrary action against it. Here it seems appropriate to make reference to the solution provided by the Supreme Court of the United States to the effect that, should a pregnancy be terminated at a stage in which the fetus has

[36] This is the sense in which Article 15(3)(a) of the Protocol of San Salvador, among others, should be interpreted.

no chance of surviving outside the mother's body (theory of viability), the act would be permissible, as it would be subject to the mother's freedom to decide what happens to her body. However, at the stage at which the fetus's viability is possible, it takes on a degree of autonomy, and in this case the State has an interest and a duty to intervene.[37]

Without prejudice to this, there are circumstances that make it necessary to extract a viable fetus if it will injure the mother by remaining in her womb. This case presents a situation in which the goal is to protect the life or health of the mother, not to eliminate the fetus. Cases like this can result in a collision of rights, a collision that must be resolved through the application of the general rules of international human rights law. The conflict normally arises between the risk to the life or health of the mother and whether the viable fetus can remain in her uterus. I have no doubt that given a choice between the right to life or health of the mother and potential risk to the life of the fetus, the decision should be to terminate the pregnancy, as the State cannot cease to protect the right to life of someone who is at the time of the conflict already a person – and therefore a full individual – in order to diminish the risk to a potential life. Starting with the assumption that the woman has had a chance to resolve possible conflicts with other human rights in stages prior to viability, it could be considered reasonable to limit the legality of late-term abortion to these two cases, which are justified on the grounds of their supervening nature.

13. In sum, arguing that the American Convention requires the State to criminalize abortion altogether is profoundly erroneous. In my opinion, which is supported by arguments based on the interpretation of both its text and *travaux préparatoires,* the Convention absolutely does not establish this obligation. In my opinion, even the most conservative interpretation has no basis to argue that a prohibition on abortion must be applied in all cases. On the contrary, in certain cases – such as a pregnancy that puts the life or health of the mother in danger or that was the result of rape – the criminalization of abortion implies a violation of the State's obligation to protect the life of the mother. In all other cases, the criminalization of abortion would be a violation of the rights referred to in paragraph 10 of this section – unless, of course, the fetus is viable, as in that situation the State has an interest in intervening. In addition, as the State must protect the life of the mother just as it protects the lives of others – without discrimination – it must provide her with access to health services such that any termination of a pregnancy that falls within the guidelines that have been set forth can be performed without putting her life in danger.

---

[37] Supreme Court of the United States, *Roe v. Wade*, 410 U.S. 113 (1973). See, on the position of the European system, European Commission of Human Rights, *Bruggemann and Scheuten v. Federal Republic of Germany*, No. 6959/75.

4. SCOPE AND FORMS OF PROTECTION

14. Paragraph 1 of Article 4 of the Convention sets forth the right of all persons to have their lives respected, according to which no person can have his or her life taken arbitrarily. This means that except for in certain circumstances, the State is prohibited from taking a person's life. The right to life, therefore, is not absolute, as situations exist in which it is possible to take the life of a person without violating Article 4(1) of the Convention. A possible way to do so is through the imposition of the death penalty by a court. Another possibility would include a private individual taking a life in legitimate self-defense or defense of a third party. A third possibility would be the undesired taking of a life by law enforcement personnel as the result of licit use of force in pursuit of a legitimate aim.

This paragraph adds that the right to life "shall be protected by law", thus establishing a positive obligation for the State to broaden its area of concern, given that it includes actions that can affect the conduct both of State agents and private individuals. By virtue of this positive obligation, the State must take the necessary measures – legislative or otherwise – to prevent violations of the right to life or mete out punishment when violations do take place, guided by the American Convention and the development of its provisions through case law. In several rulings, the Inter-American Court has established that:

> Active protection of the right to life and of the other rights enshrined in the American Convention is set within the framework of the duty of the State to ensure free and full exercise of the rights of all persons under the jurisdiction of a State, and it requires that the latter take such steps as may be necessary to punish deprivation of the right to life and other human rights violations, as well as to prevent abridgment of any of these rights by its own security forces or by third parties acting with its acquiescence.[38]

4.1. THE DEATH PENALTY

15. Even though the imposition of the death penalty clearly constitutes cruel and inhuman treatment of a human being and conflicts directly with the provisions of Article 5(6) of the American Convention, which establishes that "[p]unishments consisting of deprivation of liberty shall have as an essential aim the reform and social readaptation of the prisoners", Article 4 of the Convention allows it, reflecting the lack of consensus among the States that drafted the treaty to abolish it. However, its acceptance has a clear abolitionist slant: paragraph 3 of Article 4 establishes that "the death penalty shall not be reestablished in states

---

[38] *Case of Bulacio*, para. 111. In the same sense see: *Case of Juan Humberto Sánchez*, para. 110; *Case of Bámaca Velásquez*, para. 172; and *Case of the Street Children (Villagrán Morales et al.)*, paras. 144–145.

that have abolished it" and paragraph 2 says that nor "shall capital punishment be inflicted for political offenses or related common crimes".

As the Inter-American Court ruled in Advisory Opinion 3/83, the second provision establishes a true freeze on the death penalty as of the moment the Convention enters into force for a particular State. This Advisory Opinion was requested by the Commission with regard to a reservation made by Guatemala on ratifying the Convention according to which the death penalty could be imposed for new common crimes related to a political crime, in contradiction to the provisions of Article 4(2). The Court expressed at that time that the article cited "imposes a definite prohibition on the death penalty for all categories of offenses as far as the future is concerned".[39]

The *travaux préparatoires* only confirm this abolitionist slant, which in any case is part of a global trend.[40] In the same Advisory Opinion noted above, the Court references the drafting history of the Convention to argue that although the proposal to abolish the death penalty did not achieve majority support as required under the rules of procedure, neither was there any vote against it, while 14 of the 19 delegations participating in the Plenary Closure Session of the Specialized Conference where the Convention was drafted made a solemn declaration of their "firm hope of seeing the application of the death penalty eradicated from the American environment" and their intention to sign an additional protocol enshrining that abolition.[41] In compliance with this aspiration, in 1990 the Protocol to Abolish the Death Penalty was approved.[42]

16. Article 4 of the Convention establishes strict conditions for States to be able to impose the death penalty, meaning that not all crimes punishable by the death penalty at the moment the Convention entered into force for a State are compatible with it. If the rules regulating its application do not meet all the conditions, there will have been a violation of the provision that could leave the State internationally responsible, unless, of course, a State makes a reservation to Article 4(2).[43]

---

39 OC-3/83, paras. 56 and 68. Also see *Case of Hilaire, Constantine and Benjamin, et al.*, para. 99.

40 The European Convention on Human Rights, which was drafted in 1950 and also allows the death penalty, was amended with a Protocol (number 6) on the abolition of the death penalty, adopted on 28 April 1983. As of October of 2004, 44 States were party to it. The International Covenant on Civil and Political Rights also has a Protocol (number 2) for the abolition of the death penalty, adopted on 15 December 1989, and as of October 2004, ratified or adhered to by 46 States.

41 OC-3/83, para. 58.

42 Protocol to the American Convention on Human Rights to Abolish the Death Penalty, approved on 8 June 1990, entered into force on 28 August 1991. As of June 2013, thirteen States have ratified or adhered to the Protocol.

43 OC-3/83, paras. 70 and 71.

Based on the text of Article 4 of the Convention, the Inter-American Commission has grouped the limitations on the death penalty in countries that have not abolished it into three categories: (i) the first is substantive, as "its scope of application must be reduced to the most serious of crimes", understanding that political crimes and common crimes connected with political crimes cannot be included in that category; (ii) the second is related to certain conditions of persons, as death sentences cannot be applied to minors under the age of 18, those over the age of 70, or pregnant women; and (iii) the third constitutes a procedural limitation: the State must comply with certain procedural rules, "respect for which must be strictly guarded and required".[44]

The determination of what are considered "the most serious crimes" is made according to the fact that the death penalty is only acceptable "under truly exceptional conditions";[45] it is not enough for a crime to be serious for the death penalty to be applied: the crime must be "among the most serious". The United Nations Human Rights Committee has addressed the subject both in its reports on individual cases and in its examination of the reports that States submit pursuant to Article 40 of the Covenant. Its members have stated that crimes against property,[46] economic crimes,[47] political crimes, and in general crimes in which force has not been used[48] cannot be punished with the death penalty.[49] More recently, the Committee has not only urged States to restrict the application of the death penalty to the "most serious crimes", but has also invited States to take measures to abolish it completely.[50]

The case law of the inter-American system has not addressed the point of how to tell when one is in the presence of "one of the most serious crimes", but the Court has indicated in a case against Trinidad and Tobago that it is crucial that on recognizing and contemplating the intentional and unlawful taking of a person's life in its criminal legislation, the State must do so "under the various categories (classes of criminal offenses) corresponding to the wide range of seriousness of the surrounding facts, taking into account the different facets that can come into play",[51] mentioning, among other things, the relationship between the facts and the victim, motive, circumstances and methods used, all to

---

44 IACHR, *Roach and Pinkerton v. United States*, Case No. 9647, Report 3/87, resolution of 27 March 1987, published in *1986–1987 Annual Report*, para. 55.

45 *Ibidem*, para. 54. In the same sense see HRC, General Recommendation 6 (on Article 6 of the Covenant), of 12 July 1996, para. 7.

46 HRC, *Concluding Observations: Republic of Korea*, A/47/40 (1992) 113, para. 517.

47 HRC, *Concluding Observations: Algeria*, A/47/40 (1992) 61, para. 297.

48 HRC, *Concluding Observations: Iran,* A/48/40 vol. I (1993) 44, para. 255; HRC, *Concluding Observations: Iraq,* A/53/40 vol. I (1998) 18, para. 99.

49 M. Nowak, *supra* n. 1, p 118.

50 HRC, *Concluding Observations: Republic of Korea*, A/47/40 vol. I (2001) 98, para. 86.13; HRC, *Concluding Observations: Guatemala*, A/47/40 vol. I (2001) 93, para. 85.17.

51 *Case of Hilaire, Constantine and Benjamin, et al.*, concurring opinion of Judge Sergio García Ramírez, paras. 7–12.

conclude that legislation cannot order that the death penalty be applied automatically.[52]

17. Stated thus, the limitation on the State applies not only to legislators, requiring that they establish the death penalty only with regard to certain crimes: it also applies to judges intending to issue the death penalty in a particular case, requiring them to weigh the results of the unlawful action, the odiousness of the crime, and its perversity, among other circumstances of any specific case.

Consequently, any provision that makes the death penalty obligatory without allowing any alternative sentence does not seem to be compatible with the Convention. The Inter-American Commission has found that rulings issuing the death penalty must, among other requirements, be "individualized",[53] meaning that they "may include some factors as the offender's character and record, subjective factors that might have motivated his or her conduct, the designed and manner of execution of the particular offense, and the possibility of reform and social re-adaptations of the offender".[54] In the case of rulings where a death sentence is the only punishment allowed, the judge cannot take any of these factors into consideration, making this ruling arbitrary and thus in violation of Article 4(1) of the Convention.[55] The Inter-American Court has ruled similarly, basing its ruling on the fact that the application of a mandatory death penalty does not allow for establishing the personal circumstances of the convict.[56] Mandatory application of the death penalty therefore would not necessarily correspond only to the most serious crimes[57] and, as a consequence, violates Article 4(2) of the Convention.

18. Neither is there any case law defining political crimes, nor criteria for establishing when a common crime is linked to a political one. In fact, there was intense debate over this provision: during the discussion of the text, the Dominican Republic indicated that in order to keep this provision, a definition of "political crimes" was indispensable.[58] Brazil suggested the provision be eliminated, arguing that the provision could not be separated from a definition of the concept of political crime, "regarding which no positive international law text or jurist of the inter-American system has been able to reach a consensus";[59]

---

52 *Case of Hilaire, Constantine and Benjamin, et al.*, paras. 102–103 and 106.

53 The problem is addressed in IACHR, *McKenzie et al. v. Jamaica*, Case Nos. 12023, 12044, 12107, 12126, 12146, Report No. 41/00 of 13 April 2000, published in the *1999 Annual Report*, para. 208; and IACHR, *Joseph Thomas v. Jamaica,* Case No. 12183, Report No. 127/01 of 3 December 2001, published in the *2001 Annual Report*, para. 104.

54 *Mackenzie et al.*, paras. 208, 209 and 212; and *Joseph Thomas*, para. 104. Both *supra* n. 53.

55 *Mackenzie et al.*, para. 238.

56 *Case of Hilaire, Constantine and Benjamin, et al.*, paras. 103 and 104.

57 *Ibidem*, para. 106.

58 Specialized Conference, *supra* n. 22, p. 57.

59 *Ibidem*, p. 121.

the United States agreed with Brazil, adding that if the provision was not removed, an effort would have to be made to define the term.[60] El Salvador attempted a definition that was not taken up,[61] while Uruguay stated that political crimes are defined and codified in domestic legislation and that "everyone knows what a political crime is".[62] In the end, the paragraph in question was approved and the concept of political crimes was left undefined.

To this day, there is still debate over what criteria should serve as a basis for deciding whether a crime is political, as well as which crimes can be classified as "related" to political crimes. The Inter-American Court will have to rule on whether it is faced with a political crime or other crimes connected therewith on a case-by-case basis.

19. Certain personal circumstances can exempt one from being a candidate for the death penalty: in keeping with Article 4(5) of the American Convention, those older than 70 years old and pregnant women cannot be subjected to the death penalty, nor can those younger than 18 years old. This provision, like others in the Convention, can be subject to reservations by those States that do not wish to be bound by it. However, a *jus cogens* provision of international law is recognized that prohibits the execution of minors based on the prohibition established in the Convention on the Rights of the Child, ratified by practically all States in the international community;[63] a similar provision is found in the International Covenant, also ratified by a considerable number of States;[64] and the elimination of the death penalty for minors is established in a significant number of domestic legal systems. All this prevents States from making reservations with regard to paragraph 5 of Article 4 in order to subject minors to the death penalty. In a 1986 case against the United States, the Inter-American Commission – in addition to arguing for the existence of a *jus cogens* provision prohibiting sentencing a minor to death – accepted the United States' argument that, as of that date, there was no customary international law norm establishing the age of 18 as the minimum age for the imposition of the death sentence. However, it noted that the norm was emerging in light of the growing number of countries that have ratified the American Convention and the International Covenant,[65] and that as a consequence of ratification, those countries had

---

60 *Ibidem*, p. 164.

61 *Ibidem*, p. 165.

62 *Ibidem*, p. 166.

63 Only Somalia and the United States have not ratified this Convention.

64 As of June 2013, the International Covenant had been ratified by 167 States.

65 The International Covenant on Civil and Political Rights includes a provision similar to that of the Convention prohibiting imposition of the death penalty for crimes committed by minors under the age of 18 (Article 3(5)). The United States issued a reservation with regard to the prohibition of the execution of minors, and Thailand has issued a statement to the effect that it will not subject those under the age of 17 to the death penalty, in keeping with its domestic laws. For its part, the American Convention on Human Rights has been ratified by

modified their domestic legislation in order for it to conform to those instruments.[66] In 1995, during the examination of the first report of the United States to the Human Rights Committee and in response to several members of the Committee who objected to the reservation it had made with regard to the prohibition on the death penalty for minors, the delegation was in agreement that "[i]t was generally accepted that children below a certain age should not suffer the death penalty no matter how terrible the crime", and that in the United States, that age had been set at 16.[67] This could mean that the United States recognized the *jus cogens* norm, but was arguing that there was no customary international legal provision with regard to the age limit separating minors from adults.[68]

In a similar case, also against the United States, the Inter-American Commission concluded, based on the Convention on the Rights of the Child, the International Covenant, the Fourth Geneva Convention,[69] other provisions or resolutions of the United Nations, domestic practice of States, and the domestic practice of the United States itself, that by 2002, a clear international definition existed establishing for the purposes of the death penalty the age of an adult as 18.[70]

20. The third condition that the State must meet in order to avoid violating the Convention in its application of the death penalty is strict respect for certain proceedings during the criminal trial. The trial must be carried out by a competent court and in accordance with a law establishing such punishment, enacted prior to the commission of the crime. The wording of this requirement is not the most fortunate, as the provision does not make the need for the trial to be carried out with strict respect for due process explicit; rather, it simply accentuates certain elements of due process, failing even to mention that the principles of non-retroactivity of criminal law and interpretation of the law most favorable to the accused cannot be violated.[71]

25 States Parties. Of them, only one State – Barbados – has issued a reservation with regard to the ban on the death penalty for minors under the age of 18.

66 IACHR, *Roach and Pinkerton v. United States, supra* n. 44, para. 60.

67 "It was generally accepted that children below a certain age should not suffer the death penalty no matter how terrible the crime. In the United States that age had been set at 16." (Summary record of the 1405th meeting (CCPR/C/SR.O405, 24 April 1995), paras. 13 and 14).

68 In its concluding observations on the United States, the Committee itself expressed its concern over the application of the death penalty to those under the age of 18 and urged the United States to take all necessary measures to address the situation; see HRC, *Concluding Observations: United States*, A/50/40 vol. I (1995) 52, paras. 281 and 296.

69 As of the date of the Commission's report, the Fourth Geneva Convention had 189 States Parties.

70 IACHR, *Michael Domínguez v. United States*, Case No. 12285, Report No. 62/02, of 22 October 2002, published in *2002 Annual Report.*

71 Regarding Article 9, see *infra*, Chapter 6.

Although it may seem superfluous to point this out, the fact that Article 4(2) of the Convention accentuates only certain aspects out of all these guarantees, and not all of them, does not help convey the idea of the strictness with which procedural requirements must be met in order to apply the death penalty in a manner that is compatible with the Convention.[72] The inescapable need to rigorously comply with all procedural requirements has led the Human Rights Committee to find that if certain requirements are not met, not only has the due process provision, Article 14 of the International Covenant, been violated, but so has the provision on the right to life, Article 6 of the Covenant.[73]

The Inter-American Court took the same position in Advisory Opinion 16/99, which originated in a question from Mexico on whether failing to inform the accused of his or her right to be put in contact with legal counsel in his or her country in proceedings that could – and in fact did – lead to a death sentence constituted a violation of due process of the law and therefore a violation of Article 4 of the Convention. The Court ruled therein that:

> Because execution of the death penalty is irreversible, the strictest and most rigorous enforcement of judicial guarantees is required of the State so that those guarantees are not violated and a human life not arbitrarily taken as a result. [...] For the foregoing reasons, the Court concludes that nonobservance of a detained foreign national's right to information, recognized in Article 36(1)(b) of the Vienna Convention on Consular Relations, is prejudicial to the guarantees [...] of the due process of law; in such circumstances, imposition of the death penalty is a violation of the right not to be "arbitrarily" deprived of one's life, in the terms of the relevant provisions of the human rights treaties (eg the American Convention on Human Rights, Article 4; the International Covenant on Civil and Political Rights, Article 6) with the juridical consequences inherent to a violation of this nature, i.e., those pertaining to the international responsibility of the State and the duty to make reparations.[74]

21. The Convention's abolitionist leaning and the care it takes in regulating the imposition of the death penalty extend even beyond conviction and sentencing. Article 4(6) of the Convention provides that every person condemned to death shall have the right to apply for amnesty, pardon or commutation of sentence, noting that any of these may be granted in all cases.

---

72 From a legal point of view, it is not necessary to specify some elements explicitly as Article 8 of the Convention clearly states that no punishment can be applied absent all the requirements established therein. For a full list of the elements of due process, see *infra*, Chapter 5.

73 HRC, *Mbenge v. Zaire*, Communication 016/1977, report dated 25 March 1983, para. 17; see also *Wright v. Jamaica*, Communication 349/1989, report dated 18 August 1992, para. 8.7.

74 OC-16/99, paras. 136 and 137.

4.2. PROTECTION THROUGH PREVENTATIVE MEASURES

22. Placing the different forms of protection in categories is not easy, as the actions that States take in the area of human rights are often attempting to achieve several objectives. An action such as a trial in the case of a homicide can be considered dissuasive and thus preventative, or it can contribute to providing satisfaction to the relatives of the victim and thus be a measure of reparation.

23. The Court has had many opportunities to rule on the subject of prevention as regards the right to life, as until recently petitions before the Inter-American Commission on the violation of this right, together with petitions on the right to humane treatment, made up a significant majority of the cases being processed before the Commission.[75] In reality, almost the entirety of the Court's development of the obligation to ensure human rights found in Article 1 of the Convention has been done through cases of deprivation of life by law enforcement and military, the majority of those being intentional deprivation of life consisting in disappearances or summary executions.

In a dozen of these cases, the Court ruled on the forced disappearance of persons. Given that among other characteristics, these disappearances imply "secret execution without trial, followed by concealment of the body to eliminate any material evidence of the crime and to ensure the impunity of those responsible"[76] – that is, a State attitude of denial of its actions and indifference toward the actions of others – the Court's main task has been precisely the construction of an interpretation of the obligations set forth in the Convention that provides a legal basis for declaring this kind of violation.[77] In doing so, it has developed in depth the State's positive obligations to protect the right to life and specified their scope and content.

24. In its judgment on the merits in the first case it heard – the case of Velásquez Rodríguez – the Court found that the State has an obligation to prevent violations of the right to life and that a State must act on this obligation in order for its conduct to be compatible with its international obligations. However, the contents of the obligation to prevent has not been defined univocally, or perhaps the use of terminology has not been consistent; the concept of "prevent" has at times been used broadly and at other times narrowly. In the judgment handed down in the aforementioned case, the Court found the following:

---

75 C. Grossman, "Palabras del Presidente de la Comisión Intera-Americana de Derechos Humanos, decano Claudio Grossman, en la sesión inaugural del 95° Período Ordinario de Sesiones de la CIDH", in J. E. Méndez and F. Cox (eds.), *El futuro del sistema interamericano de protección de los derechos humanos*, IIDH, Costa Rica, 1988, pp. 155–166 (157).

76 *Case of Velásquez Rodríguez,* para. 157.

77 On the phenomenon of disappearances, see *infra,* section 6 of this chapter.

> This duty to prevent includes all those means of a legal, political, administrative and cultural nature that promote the protection of human rights and ensure that any violations are considered and treated as illegal acts, which, as such, may lead to the punishment of those responsible and the obligation to indemnify the victims for damages.[78]

However, three paragraphs earlier in its consideration, the Court had found that the State must "prevent [a verb obviously used narrowly], investigate and punish" human rights violations, adding that "[a]n illegal act which violates human rights and which is initially not directly imputable to a State (for example, because it is the act of a private person or because the person responsible has not been identified)" can lead to international responsibility for the State "because of the lack of due diligence to prevent the violation or to respond to it as required by the Convention".[79]

The duty to prevent was used in its broad sense in the dissenting opinion of Judge Cançado Trindade in the judgment handed down in the case of El Amparo. Therein, the Judge disagreed with the majority which had decided not to rule on the compatibility of a Venezuelan legal provision because it had not yet been applied, indicating that "[i]f it were necessary to wait for the effective application of a law causing a damage, the duty of prevention [and the duty to provide reparations][80] could hardly be sustained".[81]

From all this, it is possible to conclude that, for the Court, "preventing" is equivalent to "ensuring".

25. The State has a variety of obligations when it comes to prevention. The first that can be mentioned is the establishment of deterrents for private individuals regarding life. These generally will consist of establishing as a crime a variety of forms of homicide, should it be necessary,[82] as well as the strict statutory regulation of legitimate self defense and the establishment of pertinent procedural provisions in order for courts of law to be able to hear cases of deprivation of life at the hands of private individuals.

26. The State is also required to prevent possible violations of the right to life by its own agents. Given that the State has a monopoly on violence, the provisions regulating its use must be drafted carefully in order to prevent any abuse that could lead to the death of a person, whether intentionally or as a result of negligence. Not all deaths resulting from the use of force by State agents constitute a violation of the Convention; it is possible for State agents with

---

78 *Case of Velásquez Rodríguez,* para. 175.

79 *Ibidem*, para. 172.

80 *Case of El Amparo, judgment on reparations*, dissenting opinion of Judge A.A. Cançado Trindade, para. 6.

81 *Ibidem*, para. 3.

82 *Case of Caballero Delgado and Santana, judgment on reparations,* para. 56.

authority to use force to take a human being's life through actions outside the imposition of the death penalty and for these actions to be attributed to the State without generating international responsibility because there has been no violation of the American Convention.

Even though it can mean taking a life, the legitimacy of the State's right to use force was acknowledged by the Inter-American Court in the case of Neira Alegría, in which it ruled that the death of individuals as a result of actions carried out in order to maintain the public order can be legitimate as long as they meet certain conditions,[83] some of which are typically preventative in nature.

27. The Court has found that "States have the obligation to ensure creation of the conditions required to avoid violations of this inalienable right and, specifically, the duty of avoiding violations of this right by its agents".[84] This active protection "does not only involve legislators, but all State institutions and those who must protect security, both its police forces and its armed forces",[85] for which reason "States must take all necessary measures not only to prevent and punish deprivation of life as a consequence of criminal acts, but also to prevent arbitrary executions by its own security forces".[86]

Therefore, States have the important task of establishing rules regulating the conduct of their agents in the use of force and of informing both those agents and the rest of society of those rules. The rules must be established according to the standards of absolute necessity and proportionality that every infraction of a human right requires in order to not become a violation. There is no provision in the inter-American system indicating generally or specifically what the content of these rules should be. However, the universal system created in the framework of the United Nations includes a series of instruments for specifying State obligations in this area, addressing both the use of firearms and the treatment of persons subjected to detention or prison, rules that protect both individuals' right to life and their right to humane treatment.[87]

28. The State must also train its agents on the content of rules governing the use of force and the obligations imposed on security forces by the right to life. Psychological training to prevent agents from responding emotionally in a way that exceeds the limits established by the rules also seems indispensable.

83 *Case of Neira Alegría et al.*, para. 74.

84 *Case of Juan Humberto Sánchez*, para. 110. In a similar sense: *Case of the Street Children (Villagrán Morales et al.)*, para. 145.

85 *Ibidem*. Also: *Case of Myrna Mack Chang*, para. 153.

86 *Ibidem*.

87 See, for example, Basic Principles on the Use of Force and Firearms by Law Enforcement Officials, adopted by the Eighth Congress of the United Nations Congress on the Prevention of Crime and the Treatment of Offenders, held in Havana, Cuba, from 27 August to 7 September 1990.

The obligation to train personnel is made explicit in Article VIII of the Inter-American Convention on Forced Disappearance of Persons, which holds that "[t]he States Parties shall ensure that the training of public law-enforcement personnel or officials includes the necessary education on the offense of forced disappearance of persons". In the case of Bámaca Velasquez, the Inter-American Court ordered Guatemala to comply with this obligation.[88] In the case of Suárez Rosero, the petitioner asked the Court to order the State to "adopt measures to avoid a repetition of the violations in the future, including provision of human rights training to the officials in charge of applying the law".[89] In response to the petition, the Court reiterated its judgment on the merits handed down in the same case in the sense that Ecuador is required to "adopt such measures as may be necessary to ensure that violations such as those established in the instant case never again occur in its jurisdiction",[90] by which one can conclude that the Court finds training of law enforcement personnel to be necessary and obligatory.[91] Recently, the Court reiterated and detailed this obligation in a judgment handed down in the case of the Caracazo, ordering the State to at all costs prevent the situation from being repeated by making provisions

> for education and training of all members of its armed forces and its security agencies on principles and provisions of human rights protection and regarding the limits to which the use of weapons by law enforcement officials is subject, even in a state of emergency;[92]

adding that:

> The State must also adjust operational plans regarding public disturbances to the requirements of respect and protection of those rights, adopting to this end, among other measures, those geared toward control of actions by all members of the security forces in the very field of action to avoid excess.[93]

29. In principle, it could be argued that when the State prevents the commission of acts that violate Article 4, it does so not to the benefit of one particular subject but of the population in general. There could be a situation in which people's lives are in danger because of a general situation of insecurity in a

88 *Case of Bámaca Velásquez, judgment on reparations*, para. 86.

89 *Case of Suárez Rosero, judgment on reparations*, para. 84.

90 *Ibidem*, para. 87.

91 The Human Rights Committee reminds all States almost uniformly of their obligation to train law enforcement personnel on their obligations regarding human rights in general. See, for example, *Concluding Observations: Bolivia* (CCPR/C/79/Add.74, 5 May 1997, para. 33); *Concluding Observations: Brazil* (CCPR/C/79/Add.66, 24 July 1996, para. 19), *Concluding Observations: Cyprus* (CCPR/C/79/Add.39, 3 August 1994, para. 22), *Concluding Observations: Kyrgyz Republic* (CCPR/CO/69/KGZ, 24 July 2000, para. 6).

92 *Case of the Caracazo, judgment on reparations*, para. 127.

93 *Ibidem*.

particular State.[94] However, it seems evident that the State cannot be held responsible for this because it is impossible to require it to protect life such that there is no possibility that it will be taken by third parties; all individuals who live in society run the risk of losing their lives unnaturally.

Still, it is a possibility that the State must eventually grant more personalized protection of the right to life in order to prevent potential violations of it aimed at specific individuals whose lives are apparently being threatened, so long as the danger of death is clear and individualized. This is not a hypothetical problem on our continent: there have been situations in many countries in which people who are part of a group have seen their lives threatened simply because they belonged to that group, as was the case, for example, with political and union leaders during the time of dictatorships, or with human rights defenders in situations of mass violations; it is also possible for a specific person to face a threat to his or her life in connection with some specific event, such as for example having witnessed a massacre or other grave human rights violation.

The American Convention contains a provision that provides a basis for arguing that the State has obligations toward individual persons in specific circumstances. Article 63(2) of the American Convention holds that "[i]n cases of extreme gravity and urgency, and when necessary to avoid irreparable damage to persons, the Court shall adopt such provisional measures as it deems pertinent in matters it has under consideration." Provisional measures can be granted by the Court in any matter that it is hearing or they can be requested by the Inter-American Commission in matters that have not been submitted before the Court.[95] The central purpose of this provision is probably not to require the State to protect specific lives but rather to prevent international justice from being frustrated. Without prejudice to this, the Court's application of this authority has led it – with argumentation that supports the State's obligation – to require the State to protect the life of specific persons under certain circumstances by taking special protective measures to the benefit of one or many persons, singled out by name or according to their membership of some group, even when the purpose is not to ensure that the objective sought in a case before the system is not frustrated. The request for and granting of provisional measures in the case of the Miguel Agustín Pro Juárez Human Rights Center *et al.*, before the Inter-American Commission, is a good example. The Commission cited the murder of a human rights lawyer as background in its petition and asked the Court to order provisional measures for all members of the aforementioned Human Rights Center without naming them individually. One of the arguments used to request

---

94 The European system was faced with this problem in Communication 9348/81, *W. v. United Kingdom*, D&R 32 (1983) and Communication 9829/82, *X. v. United Kingdom and Ireland* (not published) on the general situation of security in Northern Ireland (cited by P. van Dijk, F. van Hoof, A. van Rijn and L. Zwaak, (eds.), *Theory and Practice of the European Convention on Human Rights*, 4th edn, Intersentia, Antwerp/Oxford, 2006, p. 353, n. 6).

95 ACHR, Article 63(2).

the measure was that "the State is responsible for taking all necessary measures to guarantee the safety of all citizens, in particular the safety of those who dedicate themselves to defending and promoting human rights". In addressing these issues, the Court has raised two important considerations on this point. In the first, it held

> that the purpose of provisional measures in international human rights law is to effectively protect fundamental rights, insofar as they seek to prevent irreparable damages to persons;[96]

while in the second it expressed

> that Article 1(1) of the American Convention sets forth the general obligations of States Parties to respect the rights and liberties enshrined in the Convention and to guarantee the free and full exercise of these rights for all individuals subject to their jurisdiction, implying a duty to take those security measures that are necessary for their protection. These obligations become even more evident with respect to individuals linked to proceedings before the supervisory organs of the American Convention.[97]

Thus the Inter-American Court made it clear that the responsibility to take these measures does not exist solely with regard to individuals whose cases are being heard before the Court or by the Commission.

In the judgment handed down in the case of Juan Humberto Sánchez, the Court found that "the State must include effective procedures to investigate, seriously and in depth, the circumstances in which a violation of the right to life may have occurred"[98] and cites the Fourth Principle of the Principles on the Effective Prevention and Investigation of Extra-legal, Arbitrary and Summary Executions[99] which "provides that effective protection must be ensured, by means of judicial or other remedies, to persons who are in danger of being executed in an extra-legal, arbitrary, or summary manner".[100]

It is thus possible to conclude that the Commission and the Court have laid the groundwork for developing a State obligation to protect the right to life of specific persons if the threat to their lives is clear and imminent, and that failure to comply with that obligation would constitute a violation of Article 4 of the Convention.[101]

---

96 *Matter of Miguel Agustín Pro Juárez, Human Rights Center, et al.*, Provisional Measures requested by the Inter-American Commission on Human Rights with regard to the United Mexican States, decision of the I/A Court HR of 30 November 2001, para. 8.

97 *Matter of the Urso Branco Prison*, Provisional Measures requested by the Inter-American Commission on Human Rights regarding the Federal Republic of Brazil, decision of the I/A Court HR of 18 June 2002, para 5.

98 *Case of Juan Humberto Sánchez,* para. 133.

99 Principles on the Effective Prevention and Investigation of Extra-legal, Arbitrary and Summary Executions (UN, ECOSOC, Resolution 1989/65 of 24 May 1989).

100 *Case of Juan Humberto Sánchez,* para. 133.

101 In this sense, see Chapter 6 on the interpretation of the right to personal safety.

4.3. PROTECTION THROUGH SUPERVISION OF COMPLIANCE WITH PREVENTATIVE REGULATION

4.3.1. Obligation to investigate, try and punish

30. The obligation to protect is not fulfilled through the existence of provisions that could become useless if not applied consistently and without discrimination. Therefore, a new area for State action is opened up related to the establishment of adequate procedural regulation for supervising its agents, the establishment of an independent and impartial organ to carry out that supervision, and the consistent application of that supervision, without discrimination, in order to deter potential offenders. It is crucial that all taking of life due to the actions of third parties that is not the result of a death sentence handed down with absolute respect for the guidelines indicated in the Convention be investigated, that the accused be brought to trial, and that those found guilty for the facts be punished.[102]

31. The investigation, trial and punishment must naturally be undertaken "in a serious manner and not as a mere formality preordained to be ineffective".[103] The examination of Article 8 of the Convention will show that basic principles exist for ensuring due process. Among them should be highlighted the existence of an independent and impartial organ with enough authority to be able to carry out an efficient investigation, along with the requirement that such investigations be carried out within a reasonable period of time.[104] Even when these guarantees are established for judicial organs, it is clear that the need for serious investigation prior to the judicial proceedings to determine the circumstances surrounding a death at the hands of third parties in order to decide whether there is a basis for the State to exercise its punitive authority, requires guarantees of independence and impartiality to extend to the non-judicial organs that carry out the initial investigative work. The Court does not seem to have ruled on this. However, the Human Rights Committee has insisted on this point both with regard to the taking of life by security forces and to violence that infringes on the prohibition of torture and cruel, inhumane and degrading punishment,[105] and it

---

102 See, *inter alia*, *Case of Velásquez Rodríguez*, para. 174; *Case of Godínez Cruz*, para. 184; *Case of El Amparo, judgment on reparations*, para. 61 and operative para. 4; *Case of Castillo Páez*, para. 90; *Case of Suárez Rosero*, para. 107 and operative para.; *Case of Blake*, para. 121 and operative para. 3; *Case of the "White Van" (Paniagua Morales et al.)*, para. 178 and operative para. 6.

103 *Case of Velásquez Rodríguez*, para. 177.

104 *Case of Myrna Mack Chang*, concurring opinion of Judge Sergio García Ramírez, para. 35.

105 See, for example, HRC, *Concluding Observations: Bolivia* (CCPR/C/79/Add.74, 5 May 1997, para. 28); *Concluding Observations: Azerbaijan* (CCPR/CO/73/AZE, 12 November 2001, paras. 9 and 10); *Concluding Observations: Cameroon* (CCPOR/C/79/Add.116, 4 November 1999, paras. 15 and 20).

seems sensible to conclude that this position should be shared in the interpretation of the American Convention.

32. The judgment handed down in the case of Garrido and Baigorria clearly established that "Argentina has a legal obligation to investigate the facts leading to the disappearance of [...] and to bring to trial and punish the authors, accomplices, accessories after the fact, and all those who may have played some role in the events that transpired."[106] It also clarified that the obligation to ensure is different from the obligation to provide reparations, indicating that the victim of a human rights violation can decline the indemnity due and the State will not have to pay it, whereas if the person in question pardons the perpetrator of the violation, this does not exempt the State from its obligation to punish that perpetrator except for in the case of crimes prosecuted at the request of an individual.[107]

The Court's ruling implies that the State must take *ex officio* action to investigate, try and punish perpetrators of an act of this nature. The obligation is a "legal duty" that must be fulfilled "regardless of what agent is eventually found responsible for the violation. Where the acts of private parties that violate the Convention are not seriously investigated, those parties are aided in a sense by the government, thereby making the State responsible on the international plane."[108] Therefore, the obligation must be fulfilled consistently, unavoidably and without discrimination.

33. Without prejudice to this clear and categorical contention, the Court's judgment in the case of Las Palmeras raises a question. The judgment weighs an argument presented by the Inter-American Commission to the effect that "because the State had not conducted a serious investigation of the events that transpired, it had to assume responsibility for the death of Lizcano Jacanamejoy", one of the alleged victims in the case.[109] The Commission based this argument on the case law of the European Court of Human Rights and could have also based it on the Court's judgment in the case of Velásquez Rodríguez. In answer to the Commission, the judgment indicates that "while in some cases, the failure to investigate may be construed as an attempt to protect the authors of the crime of murder, this reasoning cannot be postulated as a generic rule applicable across the board",[110] thus introducing the requirement that the purpose of the lack of investigation must be to protect the perpetrators of the illegitimate taking of a life in order to constitute a violation. Although the Court established here that

106 *Case of Garrido and Baigorria, judgment on reparations*, para. 74. Para. 73 of the same judgment cites settled case law on these obligations.

107 *Ibidem*, para. 72.

108 *Case of Velásquez Rodríguez*, para. 177. In this sense, see *Case of Myrna Mack Chang*, para. 156.

109 *Case of Las Palmeras*, para. 42.

110 *Ibidem*, para. 42.

Colombia did carry out a serious investigation and the ruling does not take a route similar to the one taken in Velásquez, the generalness of the wording allows for the conclusion – in my judgment erroneous – that if the lack of a serious investigation is attributable, for example, to neglect, then there has been no violation of the obligation to investigate, even when the result of the lack of investigation is precisely that the act remains in impunity.

34. Further case law has specified even more certain aspects of this obligation. In the case of Juan Humberto Sánchez, the Court specified State obligations in the event of an extrajudicial execution, ruling that it must follow the basic guidelines of the United Nations Model Protocol for a legal investigation of extra-legal arbitrary and summary executions (the "Minnesota Protocol"),[111] which include, *inter alia*, the identification of the victim, collection and preservation of evidence, and the determination of the cause, manner, place and time of death.[112]

4.3.2. Impunity

35. From all this, it is evident that a consequence of the obligation to investigate, try and punish those responsible is that the phenomenon of impunity is not compatible with the Convention. The Court has defined impunity as the "total lack of investigation, prosecution, capture, trial and conviction of those responsible for violations of the rights protected by the American Convention"[113] and has firmly repeated that "if a violation goes unpunished in a State, in such a way that the victim's full enjoyment of such rights is not restored as soon as possible, the State has failed to comply with its obligation to ensure the free and full exercise of those rights to the persons within its jurisdiction."[114]

36. The most frequent form of impunity results from the passivity of the court responsible for hearing a case of an alleged violation of the right to life,[115] although the most obvious impunity is the consequence of the passage of amnesty laws. The problem of these laws and their compatibility with human rights treaties has been debated in other forums, but there is agreement in the end that they are not compatible.[116] In the inter-American system, it was the Commission that first addressed this subject. It raised the alarm in 1985 about

111 United Nations Model Protocol for a legal investigation of extra-legal arbitrary and summary executions ("Minnesota Protocol"), UN Doc E/ST/CSDHA/.12 (1991).

112 *Case of Juan Humberto Sánchez*, paras. 127–128.

113 *Case of Paniagua Morales et al.*, para. 173.

114 *Case of Garrido and Baigorria, judgment on reparations*, para. 73.

115 *Case of Bulacio*, para. 119; *Case of Myrna Mack Chang*, para. 210.

116 See, for example, HRC, *Concluding Observations: Argentina* (CCPR/C/79/Add.46, para. 144); *Concluding Observations: Chile* (CCPR/C/79/Add.104, para. 7); *Concluding Observations: Peru* (CCPR/CO/70/PER, para. 9).

an amnesty decree in Guatemala, arguing that it could hinder and make courts ineffective in their work of investigating the crimes and punishing the guilty parties.[117] However, it was in response to amnesties in Uruguay and Argentina that the Commission developed a detailed basis for concluding that these laws were in violation of Article XVIII (right to justice) of the American Declaration and of Articles 1, 8, and 25 of the American Convention.[118]

37. The Inter-American Court has ruled similarly, adding, in addition to amnesty laws, other forms of impunity that would not be compatible with the Convention. The judgment handed down in the case of Barrios Altos, which ruled that Peru's amnesty laws that were at issue in that case had violated Article 8(1), Article 25, Article 1(1) and Article 2 of the Convention, is categorical where it states that:

> This Court considers that all amnesty provisions, provisions on prescription and the establishment of measures designed to eliminate responsibility are inadmissible because they are intended to prevent the investigation and punishment of those responsible for serious human rights violations such as [...] extrajudicial, summary or arbitrary execution and forced disappearance, all of which are prohibited because they violate non-derogable rights recognized by international human rights law.[119]

38. In the case of Bulacio, the Court advanced even further on this route – in my opinion in the wrong case – by ruling that:

> In accordance with the obligations undertaken by the States pursuant to the Convention, no domestic legal provision or institution, including extinguishment, can oppose compliance with the judgments of the Court regarding investigation and punishment of those responsible for human rights violations. If that were not the case, the rights enshrined in the American Convention would be devoid of effective protection. This understanding of the Court is in accordance with the language and the spirit of the Convention, as well as the general principles of law; one of these principles is that of *pacta sunt servanda*, which requires ensuring effective application of the provisions of a treaty in the domestic legal system of the States Party.[120]

The Court made use of this case law during the compliance proceedings in the judgment handed down in the case of Benavides Cevallos.[121]

---

117 IACHR, *1985–1986 Annual Report*.

118 IACHR, *Case on the expiry of the State's punitive intention (Uruguay)*, Nos. 10029, 10036, 10145, 10305, 10372, 10373, 10374, 10375, resolution 29/92, 2 October 1992 (IACHR, *1992–93 Annual Report*) and Cases Nos. 10147, 10181, 10240, 10262, 10309 and 10311 (Argentina) resolution 28/92, 2 October 1992 (IACHR, *1992–93 Annual Report*).

119 *Case of Barrios Altos*, para. 41–43.

120 *Case of Bulacio*, para. 117.

121 *Case of Benavides Cevallos*, order on compliance with judgment of 9 September 2003. See the interesting concurring opinion of Judge Sergio García.

39. All this raises the interesting question of how it can be reconciled with the discretion generally granted to prosecutors to decide whether to proceed to a criminal trial. This point has not been ruled on by the Court, but it could be suggested that in the case of the taking of a life, a right that cannot be suspended even under martial law, this discretion must be reduced to a minimum and can only be exercised to dismiss the possibility of bringing charges against someone who, based on the investigation, is not clearly involved in the facts. The discretion cannot be exercised to decide not to investigate the facts at all.

40. The Court's rulings have been issued in addressing situations of political violence carried out by the State or at least tolerated by it; these are the types of cases that have been brought before the Court to date. Nevertheless, these principles developed in its case law can be applied to other situations. Phenomena such as, for example, lynchings,[122] "social cleansing",[123] so-called "honor crimes",[124] domestic violence against women resulting in the death of the victim or a serious threat to her life,[125] and others, also require the State to comply with its obligation to investigate, try and punish the guilty parties.

4.3.3. Situations in which an obligation applies

41. The obligation to investigate applies both when the death has been sought intentionally, as the result of a voluntary action of the perpetrator, and when it seems to have been the not necessarily desired result of the use of force. The obligation to investigate is particularly important in that first case.[126] As has been noted, the Court's case law in this field is abundant, and fortunately, its rulings have been able to define this aspect of the obligation to ensure in detail. Still, certain aspects of it remain unclear, and they must be resolved upon examination at the proper time.

The importance of compliance with the obligation has been highlighted by the Court in several rulings where it holds that "[statute of limitations] provisions or any other domestic legal obstacle that attempts to impede the

---

122 IACHR, *Report on the human rights situation in Guatemala* (OEA/Ser.L/V/II.111, Doc. 21 rev., 6 April 2001), pp. 89–95.

123 *Ibidem*, pp. 95–98.

124 The uxoricides committed by men against their partners in response to alleged infidelity are known as "honor crimes". There are countries in which these crimes are not punished because courts have found that the motive exempts perpetrators from criminal responsibility. See IACHR, *Report on the human rights situation in Brazil* (OEA/Ser.L/V/II.97, Doc. 29 rev. 1, 29 September 1997), p. 140.

125 For a pioneering case on domestic violence, see *Maria da Penha Maia Fernández v. Brazil*, Case No. 12,051, Report 54/01, resolution of 16 April 2001 (IACHR, *2000 Annual Report*).

126 *Case of Myrna Mack Chang*, para. 156.

investigation and punishment of those responsible for human rights violations are inadmissible".[127]

42. When a death is the not necessarily intentional result of the use of force, it is the responsibility of the supervisory agency to examine the facts in light of the framework established in the Convention for deciding whether affecting a human right is compatible with the obligations of the Convention. It must first examine whether there is a provision authorizing the agent in question to use force; second, whether the force was used in order to achieve an aim permitted by the law and, naturally, the Convention as well; and finally, if the measure itself that resulted in the taking of a life is "necessary in a democratic society", for which it is necessary to examine whether the measure is appropriate and proportional and whether there is any alternative for achieving the objective.[128]

This standard has been applied by the Court on more than one occasion. The case of Neira Alegría weighed the legitimacy of the death of 118 prisoners in a cell block of the San Juan Bautista Prison as a result of an order given by the Peruvian Navy to demolish the cell block after the prisoners, who had been rioting, had surrendered. The considering paragraphs of the judgment indicate that Peru had the right and duty to put down the riot, which had apparently been planned beforehand and had already resulted in the capture of three security guards as hostages, injuries to another four security guards, and a shootout that resulted in the deaths of several members of the security forces attempting to end the uprising; that is, the Court found that the aim for which force was used was compatible with the American Convention. The Court then introduced the standard of "necessity in a democratic society" by adding that Peru's right does not allow for the exercise of unlimited power.[129] Based on abundant evidence, including reports from the Peruvian Congress, the Court concluded that the elements of the case did not justify the degree to which force was used.[130]

The case of Durand and Ugarte posed a similar situation. Therein, the Court ruled that it had been proven "that Cell Block Blue had been demolished by forces of the Peruvian Navy, who used force disproportionate to the danger presented by the uprising (*supra* para. 59(j)). This resulted in many of the inmates being crushed to death."[131] It added that "the corresponding authorities were not interested in rescuing the inmates who were still alive after the demolition" and

---

127 *Case of Bulacio*, para. 116. In the same sense, *Case of Trujillo Oroza, judgment on reparations*, para. 106; *Case of Barrios Altos*, para. 41.

128 *Case of Neira Alegría et al.*, para. 74.

129 *Ibidem*, paras. 61 and 75.

130 *Ibidem*, para.74.

131 *Case of Durand and Ugarte*, para. 68. Translator's own English version. The official English version reads: "the Blue Pavilion was demolished by the Peruvian Navy forces. They resorted to a disproportionate use of force in relation to the supposedly danger that riot represented (*supra* para. 59. j), said situation caused the deaths of many of the detainees by crushing."

"there was a lack of diligence in identifying the bodies, as only a small number of bodies were identified in the days following the end of the conflict, and the process of recovering the bodies lasted around nine months."[132] Responding to one of the State's pleadings, the Court added:

> While accepting that the inmates in Cell Block Blue in El Frontón prison could have been armed and guilty of very serious crimes, these facts are far from [...] sufficient to justify the amount of force used in this and in other prison uprisings and the understanding of those uprisings as political confrontations between the Government and real or alleged Shining Path terrorists. [...] This understanding likely led to the demolition of the block and all the resulting consequences, including the deaths of inmates who would have eventually ended up surrendering and the clear negligence in the search for survivors and subsequent recovery of bodies.[133]

4.3.4. Identification of the rights violated and entitlement to demand compliance with the obligation

43. What has been said up to this point represents the consistent position of the Court and its logic is clear. However, there are other aspects of the obligation to investigate that have not been clarified. One of these relates to the identification of the rights violated in the event that the obligation to investigate, try and punish the guilty party is not fulfilled, along with the identification of those who could be considered victims of the failure to comply with the obligation. In principle, it could be argued first that the obligation corresponds to the right to life (or the right to humane treatment if the facts of the case indicate torture or cruel, inhuman or degrading treatment) interpreted in connection with Article 1(1) of the Convention, such that if it is not complied with, that right is violated given that the obligation forms part of that right; and second, that the victim of the failure to comply is the same as the victim of the violation of the right to life. This is derived from the judgment in the case of Velásquez Rodríguez, where the Court finds that "Honduras has violated, in the case of Angel Manfredo Velásquez Rodríguez, its obligation to ensure the right

---

[132] *Ibidem.* Translator's own English version. The official English version reads: "there was no interest by the corresponding authorities to rescue. [*sic*] the detainees who were alive after the demolition" and "a lack of arrangements to identify the corpses taking into consideration that only a few of them were identified in the following days after the conflict was concluded, and the corpses recovering process lasted around nine months".

[133] *Ibidem*, para. 70. Translator's own English version. The official English version reads: "In spite of accepting the possible detainees' responsibility for committing serious crimes besides and being armed, while in the Blue Pavilion of El Frontón prison, these facts are far from constituting [...] sufficient elements to justify the amount of force used in this and in other rioted prisons and that it was understood like a political clash between the Government and Sendero Luminoso true or alleged terrorists [...] which probably led to Pavilion demolition, with all of its consequences, including the deaths of detainees who eventually had ended up surrendering and a clear disregard to look for survivors and afterwards rescuing corpses."

to life set forth in Article 4 of the Convention, read in conjunction with Article 1(1) thereof."[134]

44. Despite this ruling, the Commission introduced in a later case the idea that there was a "right to truth and information" without specifying a provision of the Convention on which it would be based.[135] The Court responded to this pleading by arguing that the right "does not exist in the American Convention, although it may correspond to a concept that is being developed in doctrine and case law",[136] ruling in the judgment it handed down in the case that the State had the obligation to investigate "in connection with the above-mentioned violations of the American Convention",[137] without identifying the right violated. One can infer from a reading of the judgment that the obligation to investigate does not arise specifically from the right to life,[138] nor from Article 8 of the Convention,[139] nor from Article 25 of the Convention,[140] given that the examination of those rights in the judgment does not contain any reference to the lack of investigation. Thus, it seems to be vaguely derived from all the violations found in the case.

45. In the case of Blake, the Court clearly adjusted the position it had taken in Velásquez Rodríguez. In Blake, a case on a disappearance, the Court declared itself without jurisdiction to weigh the issue of a violation to the right to life because the victim's body had been found, and witness testimony and the death certificate indicated that Mr Blake's death – and thus his kidnapping – took place prior to the date on which the State of Guatemala recognized the contentious jurisdiction of the Court.[141] In the judgment handed down in the case, the Court weighed the problem of the lack of investigation in connection with the potential rights of the relatives of Mr Blake and reached the conclusion, citing in support of its position the UN Declaration on the Forced Disappearance of Persons, that Article 8(1) of the Convention includes the right of relatives of the victim to judicial guarantees, and that as a consequence, the article "recognizes the right of Mr Nicholas Blake's relatives to have his disappearance and death effectively investigated by the Guatemalan authorities; to have those responsible prosecuted for committing said unlawful acts; to have the relevant punishment, where appropriate, meted out; and to be compensated for the damages and injuries they sustained."[142]

---

[134] *Case of Velásquez Rodríguez*, para. 194, point 4.
[135] *Case of Castillo Páez*, para. 85.
[136] *Ibidem*, para. 86.
[137] *Ibidem*, para. 90.
[138] *Ibidem*, paras. 68–74.
[139] *Ibidem*, paras. 75–79.
[140] *Ibidem*, paras. 80–84.
[141] *Case of Blake*, paras. 85–86.
[142] *Ibidem*, para. 97.

Thus in that judgment, the Court ruled that the obligation to investigate, try and punish was derived from the right to due process, and that the relatives of the victim of a violation of the right to life were the holders of this right.[143]

46. One could understand the Court to have seen itself in a difficult position in the Blake case due to the problem of its lack of jurisdiction to examine the death of the victim, such that it had to change the identity of the victim from the person who was kidnapped, disappeared and murdered to that of the person's relatives, invoking the violation of their right to have the incidents leading to Blake's death investigated.

However, the problem of the lack of jurisdiction does not explain this interpretation being extended to other cases in which the Court did have jurisdiction to rule with regard to Article 4 of the Convention, abandoning the idea that the obligation to investigate also came from that substantive right. In the case of Paniagua Morales *et al.*, the judgment found that the victims' right to life had been violated on ruling it proven that State agents were the ones who took the lives of those individuals. However, it examined the lack of a serious investigation into the facts of the case, as alleged by the Commission, in the framework of Article 8 of the Convention.[144] It is not clear from the ruling if this lack of investigation was the basis for the ruling that Article 8(1) had been violated or if it was only mentioned in passing, as the judgment includes other justifications – for example, that the proceedings had extended far beyond a reasonable period of time and that, in the case of one of the victims, there was no evidence that the pertinent proceedings had even been started, both arguments that in and of themselves could have served as sufficient justification for the Court's ruling as regards Article 8.[145]

Nevertheless, there is no doubt that the Court placed Article 8, along with Article 25 of the Convention,[146] as the source of the obligation to investigate when it issued its judgment in the case of Durand and Ugarte. Therein, it uses the wording put forward by the Commission in the case of Castillo Páez and speaks of the "right to truth", explaining that "Article 8(1) of the American Convention, in connection with Article 25(1) thereof, confers on victims' relatives the right to investigate their disappearance and death by State authorities, to carry out a process against the liable parties of unlawful acts, to impose the corresponding sanctions, and to compensate damages suffered by their relatives."[147]

---

143 The subject will be addressed again in Chapter 5, section 2.1 of this book.

144 *Case of the "White Van" (Paniagua Morales et al.)*, para. 139.

145 *Ibidem*, para. 152.

146 As regards Article 25, this point will be addressed once more in Chapter 7.

147 *Case of Durand and Ugarte*, para. 130. This same position appears in several of the Court's judgments; see *Case of Bámaca Velásquez*, para. 201; *Case of Barrios Altos*, para. 48; and *Case of Juan Humberto Sánchez*, para. 136.

This positions the right to truth as a positive aspect of the obligation to investigate, whose rights holders are the victim and, in the case of the violation of a right to life, the victim's relatives as well, all derived from the rights recognized in Articles 8 and 25 of the Convention.[148]

47. Perhaps unintentionally, in my opinion the Court's judgment in Paniagua Morales and Durand and Ugarte considerably diminished the contents of the obligation to ensure the right to life and, in turn, other rights. All the argumentation in the Court's first judgment, valued for its development of the obligation to ensure, makes no sense unless this obligation is linked with the corresponding right that it protects.[149]

48. Another interesting aspect of this "right to truth" and the obligation to investigate, try and punish is that the Court has found that a failure to comply with this obligation hurts society as a whole, which seems to be in harmony with the idea that the American Convention creates a code of conduct for States that is in the interest of the whole community. The Court established this position in its judgment in the case of Juan Humberto Sánchez, in which it ordered the State to release to the public the results of a judicial inquiry into the extrajudicial execution of the victim, "for Honduran society to know the truth".[150]

4.3.5. Nature of the obligation to investigate, try and punish

49. One thing that must still be clarified relates to the nature of the obligation to investigate. It was previously noted how difficult it is to identify the nature of the various measures that a State must take to comply with the Convention, but sometimes this identification is necessary. Even though the obligation to investigate and the closely related right to the truth are normally identified by the Court with the duty to prevent, the Court has ruled on at least two occasions that "the possibility of the victim's next of kin knowing what happened to the victim and, if that be the case, the whereabouts of the victim's mortal remains, is a means of reparation, and therefore an expectation regarding which the State must satisfy the next of kin of the victims and society as a whole."[151]

---

148 The distinction that should be drawn between Article 8 and Article 25 as sources of this right will be observed in the corresponding chapters.

149 This was the position that Judge Cançado Trindade took in his concurring opinion in the judgment in the *Case of Las Palmeras* in which he stated that "[w]e find it crucial to link *expressis verbis* – in operative paragraph 1 of this Judgment – the violation of Article 4 of the Convention to the general obligation set forth in Article 1(1) of the Convention in keeping with the *settled case law* of this Tribunal."

150 *Case of Juan Humberto Sánchez*, para. 186.

151 *Case of Bámaca Velásquez, judgment on reparations*, para. 76. Also see *Case of Trujillo Oroza, judgment on reparations*, para. 114.

I think that anyone who has had any experience with the phenomenon of disappearances would agree that knowing the truth is a very important part of reparations. However, conceiving of the right for the State to investigate as a form of reparation has consequences that the Court has perhaps not noticed. In its judgment in the case of Garrido and Baigorria, the Court found that the obligation to ensure, which includes the obligation to investigate, is not a form of reparation, given that the victim of a human rights violation can decline a reparation (in this case the reparation being identified as pecuniary indemnity), while the victim's forgiveness cannot excuse the State from its obligation to mete out punishment in connection with the facts and therefore investigate them beforehand.[152] This is a point that must be re-examined to bring it to its logical conclusion. Perhaps it would be possible to reconcile this by adopting the position expressed by Judge Cançado Trindade in a dissenting opinion in the case of El Amparo in which he argues that reparations include – along with *restitutio in integrum* – indemnity, rehabilitation, satisfaction and "significantly – the guarantee of non-repetition of the acts in violation of human rights (the duty of prevention)",[153] which can be reinforced by the obligation to investigate as a measure of prevention. Thus, the obligation to investigate serves two purposes: prevention, and satisfaction through prevention. Naturally, the idea that a victim can release the State from an obligation cannot be applied to this for two reasons: in addition to being a form of reparation, it is a State obligation derived from the right violated as interpreted in light of Article 1(1) and, as the Court has said, the so-called "right to truth" is established not only for the benefit of the victim and the victim's relatives but for society as a whole: "[p]reventive measures and those against recidivism begin by revealing and recognizing the atrocities of the past, as was ordered by the Court in its judgment on the merits. Society has the right to know the truth regarding such crimes, so as to be capable of preventing them in the future."[154]

4.4. OBLIGATION TO PROVIDE REPARATIONS

50. Finally, if a violation has taken place, has been detected, and the conclusion is that it is attributable to the State, it seems indispensable that any guarantee of the right include reparations. The right to life thus requires the State to have mechanisms and measures of reparation available should that right be violated. Reparations normally consist of a pecuniary indemnity, but other measures can be ordered, particularly when the violation of the right to life is preceded by the disappearance of the person, and consequently of the victim's body.

152 *Case of Garrido and Baigorria*, para. 72.

153 *Case of El Amparo, judgment on reparations*, dissenting opinion of Judge Cançado Trindade, para. 6.

154 *Case of Bámaca Velásquez, judgment on reparations*, para. 77. In the same sense, see *Case of the Caracazo, judgment on reparations*, para. 117 and 118.

51. The Court has always ordered monetary reparations for the relatives of the deceased victim. The amount is normally set in a procedural stage subsequent to the judgment on the merits. The problem of how to set the indemnity arose in the case of Velásquez Rodríguez, the first case before the Court. The majority vote assigned the task of determining the amount of the indemnity to the Commission and the State, without including the victim. This led to a dissenting opinion from Judge Piza.[155] A change to the Rules of Procedure, which entered into force on 1 January 1997, allowed for the autonomous participation of the victim, his or her relatives, or his or her representatives in the stage establishing the amount of the reparation.[156] Should the parties not be able to reach an agreement, it falls to the Court to set the amount,[157] decide who the beneficiaries are, and establish how the indemnity will be distributed.

52. Aside from the indemnity, the Court can establish other possible reparations. For example, in the case of Trujillo Oroza, it ordered Bolivia to establish the crime of forced disappearance of persons in its domestic legal system within a reasonable period of time, adding that the reparation would only be considered to have been complied with once the bill in question became a law of the Republic and entered into force.[158] In the case of Bámaca Velásquez, it found that the State had the duty to locate the remains of Efraín Bámaca Velásquez and turn them over to his relatives "to be buried in accordance with their customs and religious beliefs", adding that the exhumation should be done in the presence of the relatives and the remains should be turned over to them, ensuring their transportation to the place chosen by the relatives without any cost to them. All this was to take into consideration that Mr Bámaca belonged to a Mayan religion that teaches that funeral rites ensure that the living, the deceased person and deceased ancestors will be reunited. The Court also "considers that the State must implement [...] a national exhumations program, as the State itself mentioned in its brief with observations on the reparations", something that the State itself had offered in its response regarding reparations.[159] This latter measure clearly shows an attempt to resolve an aspect of the problems arising from situations of massive and systematic violations

---

155 *Case of Velásquez Rodríguez*, dissenting opinion of Judge Piza Escalante.

156 Inter-American Court, *Rules of Procedure*, Article 23, approved in its XXXIV Regular Period of Sessions, held on 9–20 September 1996. The Rules of Procedure of the Court have been amended so that they currently allow the victim and his or her relatives to act autonomously in the process (see Article 23, Rules of Procedure of the Court, approved by the Court in November 2000, and entered into force on 1 June 2001).

157 *Case of Velásquez Rodríguez*, para. 191. With the exception of the *Case of Neira Alegría et al.*, where the Court ruled that the indemnity must be set by the Commission and the State (operative para. 4), the trend subsequent to the *Case of Caballero Delgado and Santana* has been to set it directly.

158 *Case of Trujillo Oroza, judgment on reparations*, paras. 94–97.

159 *Case of Bámaca Velásquez, judgment on reparations*, paras. 79–83.

using reparations. In the case of Juan Humberto Sánchez, the judgment orders the State to carry out "a public act of acknowledgment of its responsibility in connection with the facts in this case and of amends to the victims" and to "publish in the official gazette (*Diario Oficial*) and in another national-circulation daily, once only, the operative part of this Judgment and the chapter on proven facts in this same Judgment".[160]

As has already been noted, the Court also includes the State obligation to carry out a serious investigation into the facts, bring those allegedly responsible to trial and punish those it finds guilty to be a form of reparation.

Finally, another form of reparation is the turning over of mortal remains in cases of disappearances. This is categorized by the Court as an act of justice and reparation in itself, with the possibility of providing victims with dignity by treating the remains with respect and allowing a proper burial as constituting the reparation.[161]

53. In sum, we can say that the obligation to protect the right to life requires the State to carry out a collection of dissuasive actions, preventative actions, control of the taking of lives by third parties, and finally, reparation of violations of the right. These actions cannot be described in detail for each case, but they must respond to the central purpose of the obligation to guarantee, that is, to attempt in the best way possible to diminish the possibility of violations of the right to life, and when one occurs, to take the necessary measures to ensure that the infraction does not remain in impunity and redress the moral and material damages suffered by the victims.

5. OTHER ASPECTS OF THE RIGHT TO LIFE

54. The extent of the right to life is not exhausted by what we have examined thus far. Like other rights, it has economic and social aspects which the bodies applying it in specific cases have no reason not to consider. Thus, a measure of prevention that is completely different from those examined thus far involves keeping people alive by providing an economic and social situation to prevent death by starvation or lack of medical care.

It should not be forgotten that the State must guarantee human rights to all persons, without discrimination, and that one possible basis for discrimination is economic status or "any other social condition". Almost from the beginning, the Human Rights Committee has been considering the State obligation in this area, expressing in General Comment No. 6 that the right to life cannot be understood in a restrictive manner and that "the protection of this right requires that States

160 *Case of Juan Humberto Sánchez*, para. 188.

161 *Case of Trujillo Oroza, judgment on reparations*, para. 115.

adopt positive measures", recommending that States take "all possible measures to reduce infant mortality and to increase life expectancy, especially in adopting measures to eliminate malnutrition and epidemics".[162] This initial approach has been reaffirmed and refined over time as the Committee and States have gained experience regarding compliance with the obligations under the Covenant. The Committee uses the right to life together with the prohibition of discrimination to give this right the social and economic content it should always have had.[163]

Given that the American Convention has provisions that are similar to those found in the Covenant, it is possible to expect this obligation to continue to develop similarly. Perhaps the most significant judgment on this point is that of the case of Villagrán Morales, or the case of the Street Children, in which the Court found that, "[o]wing to the fundamental nature of the right to life, restrictive approaches to it are inadmissible. In essence, the fundamental right to life includes, not only the right of every human being not to be deprived of his life arbitrarily, but also the right that he will not be prevented from having access to the conditions that guarantee a dignified existence."[164] The concurring opinion of judges Cançado Trindade and Abreu Burelli in the same ruling goes even further:

> 3. The right to life cannot continue to be interpreted restrictively – as it was in the past – as addressing only the prohibition of the arbitrary taking of physical life. We believe that there are different ways to take a person's life arbitrarily: when that person's death is caused directly by the unlawful act of homicide, as well as when circumstances are not avoided which likewise *lead* to the death of persons as in the *cas d'espèce*. In this case – Villagrán Morales versus Guatemala (Merits), pertaining to the death of children at the hands of State police officers – the fact that the lives of the children were already devoid of any meaning stands as an aggravating circumstance; that is, the victimized children were already prevented from creating and developing a life project and even from seeking out a meaning for their own existence.
> 4. [...] The arbitrary taking of life is thus not limited to the illicit act of homicide; it extends itself likewise to the taking of the right to live with dignity. This perspective conceptualizes the right to life as belonging to the domain of civil and political rights while at the same time it belongs to the domain of economic, social and cultural rights, thus illustrating the interrelation and indivisibility of all human rights.[165]

The signatories of the opinion recall the Court's case law to the effect that international instruments must be interpreted according to the evolution of the

---

162 HRC, General Comment No. 6, 1982, in A/37/40 (1982) Annex V (pp. 93–94), para. 5.

163 HRC, *Concluding Observations: United States*, A/50/40 vol. I (1995) 52, paras. 291 and 302; *Concluding Observations: Guatemala*, A/51/40 vol. I (1996) 33, para. 221; *Concluding Observations: Israel*, A/53/40 vol. I (1998) 45, paras. 308 and 310; *Concluding Observations: Canada*, A/54/40 vol. I (1999) 48, para. 242.

164 *Case of Villagrán Morales*, para. 144.

165 *Ibidem*, paras. 3–6 of the concurring opinion.

times and indicate that this concept of life is a manifestation of that evolutionary interpretation, particularly because an abstraction cannot be made of the deterioration of living conditions in broad sectors of the population in the States Parties to the American Convention, especially in the case of children in situations of risk.

55. The opinion also mentions a concept that had already appeared in the judgment on reparations in the case of Loayaza Tamayo, that of life's project as distinct from "special damages" and "loss of earnings", concepts used to calculate reparations for human rights violation, as it "deals with the full self-actualization of the person concerned and takes account of her calling in life, her particular circumstances, her potential, and her ambitions, thus permitting her to set for herself, in a reasonable manner, specific goals, and to attain those goals."[166] A life plan, which is associated with the concept of self-actualization, is based on the options that people might have for living their lives and achieving the goals that they set for themselves, options that in themselves have "important existential value" and whose "elimination or curtailment objectively abridges freedom and constitutes the loss of a valuable asset, a loss that this Court cannot disregard."[167] The Court extends the concept by stating that

> damage to the "life plan", understood as an expectation that is both reasonable and attainable in practice, implies the loss or severe diminution, in a manner that is irreparable or reparable only with great difficulty, of a person's prospects of self-development. Thus, a person's life is altered by factors that, although extraneous to him, are unfairly and arbitrarily thrust upon him, in violation of laws in effect and in a breach of the trust that the person had in government organs duty-bound to protect him and to provide him with the security needed to exercise his rights and to satisfy his legitimate interests.[168]

The signatories of the concurring opinion use the judgment and their opinion to argue that "project of life is consubstantial of the right to existence, and requires, for its development, conditions of life with dignity, of segurity [*sic*] and integrity of the human person",[169] adding later that:

> A person who in his or her childhood lives, as in so many countries of Latin America, in the humiliation of misery, without even the minimum conditions for creating his or her life plan, experiences a state of suffering which amounts to a spiritual death; the physical death which follows in these circumstances is the culmination of the total destruction of the human being. In addition to making victims out of those who suffer from them directly in body and soul, these offenses also project themselves painfully into the persons dear to them, in particular into their mothers, who usually also suffer from abandonment.[170]

---

166 *Case of Loayza Tamayo, judgment on reparations*, para. 147.

167 *Ibidem*, para. 148.

168 *Ibidem*, para. 150.

169 *Case of the Street Children (Villagrán Morales et al.)*, para. 8 of the concurring opinion.

170 *Ibidem*, para. 9.

Curiously, in the judgment on reparations in Loayza Tamayo, although the Court recognized the existence of serious damage to the life project of the victim derived from the violation of her human rights, it concluded that the development of case law and doctrine to date did not allow this recognition to be translated into financial terms, and the Court therefore declined to quantify it. However, it also noted that the victim's access to international courts and the issuing of the corresponding judgment imply a measure of satisfaction with regard to these considerations.[171] Something similar took place in the case of Villagrán Morales, as the judgment does not mention the life's project, and the mention of that concept by the signatories of the concurring opinion does not lead them to conclude that in the case of these children, the damage should be reflected at the reparations stage.

These judgments are indications that it is possible that the path toward broadening the scope and content of Article 4 – a path also incipiently taken by the Human Rights Committee – could continue.

56. In the case of Bulacio, relatives of the victim argued that although Bulacio was working as a golf caddy at the time of his death, it had to be taken into consideration that this was not a job that would last all his life because he was planning to become a lawyer. They called this loss of opportunity a "chance lost" for which reparations should be fully provided.[172] The Court found it "likely and reasonable to assume that young Bulacio would not have worked in that position for the rest of his life, but there are no clear facts allowing for the activity or profession he would have carried out in the future to be known". Consequently, it turns to equity for establishing a sum for loss of income.[173] The judgment does not say whether this "chance lost" is related with the life project or if it is only a different way of determining the amount of income lost by a victim whose life has been taken.

6. DISAPPEARANCES AND THE RIGHT TO LIFE[174]

57. The first time the Court had to hear cases on disappearances – the three cases against Honduras brought before the Court by the Inter-American

---

171 *Case of Loayza Tamayo, judgment on reparations*, para. 153.

172 *Case of Bulacio*, para. 81(c).

173 *Ibidem*, para. 84. Translator's own English version. The official English version reads: "that it is reasonable to assume that youth Bulacio would not have carried out this activity the rest of his life, but there is no certain fact that makes it possible to ascertain the activity or profession that he would have exercised in the future."

174 The phenomenon of forced disappearance goes beyond the scope of the right to life, for which reason this chapter will address it only partially.

Commission[175] – there was no basis for them under the Convention; the phenomenon of disappearance was not set forth specifically in the American Convention as a human rights violation, and the violation therefore had to be constructed, determining whether forced disappearance was a specific violation of the Convention – as is "torture" for example – or if the phenomenon of disappearance violates specific human rights found in the Convention. In the latter case, it had to be decided which rights it violated. Likewise, it was crucial to decide whether disappearance broke down into isolated specific human rights violations set forth in the Convention or if the violations formed part of a single phenomenon, which must therefore be treated as a single violation. Finally, due to possible problems with jurisdiction, it was also necessary to establish the time at which the phenomenon took place and at which it concluded. Underlying these issues is the problem of deciding the identity of the victim who could file complaints in connection with these actions, or in whose name the complaints could be filed.

58. In the three cases indicated, the Court chose to define disappearance in terms of the violations of human rights found in the Convention that it entailed, but without specifying whether those violations should be treated jointly. Regarding the rights violated, the Court found that disappearance "constitutes a multiple and continuous violation of numerous rights under the Convention", naming the rights found in Articles 5 and 7 of the Convention and adding that the "practice of disappearances often involves secret execution without trial, followed by concealment of the body to eliminate any material evidence of the crime and to ensure the impunity of those responsible. This is a flagrant violation of the right to life, recognized in Article 4 of the Convention."[176]

In this way, disappearance was described as a violation of three rights found in the Convention in relation to the person who was disappeared, who became the subject of the protection; the three rights violated were identified as the right to humane treatment of Article 5, the right to personal freedom of Article 7, and of course the right to life of Article 4. The operative paragraphs of the judgment in Velásquez state as much, adding that these three rights have been violated "in conjunction with Article 1(1)", which establishes the State's obligation to respect and ensure the free and full exercise of the rights found in the Convention.[177]

59. As regards the right to life, the definition formulated as such allows for the Court to rule that the right to life has been violated every time that there has been a disappearance, whether or not the death was proven during the

175 *Case of Velásquez Rodríguez*; *Case of Godínez Cruz*; and *Case of Fairén Garbi and Solís Corrales*.

176 *Case of Velásquez Rodríguez*, paras. 155–157.

177 *Ibidem*, para. 194.

proceedings. This is what happened in the case of Velásquez Rodríguez, in which the body of the victim was not found. The Court ruled that "the context in which the disappearance of Manfredo Velásquez occurred and the lack of knowledge seven years later about his fate create a reasonable presumption that he was killed."[178] However, the judgment in question opened another possibility for the violation of Article 4 on reasoning that even if there existed the slightest chance that Manfredo Velásquez was still alive, "his fate was decided by authorities who systematically executed detainees without trial and concealed their bodies in order to avoid punishment", and this, in addition to the lack of investigation of the facts, constituted a violation of the duty to guarantee found in Article 1(1) of the Convention, with regard to Article 4(1) of the Convention. Along with that, a violation of Article 4 could have taken place based on the sole fact that Manfredo Velásquez's life was put in danger when he was placed in the hands of authorities with a reputation for murdering those they detain – that is, the mere clear and imminent threat to life is enough to find a violation of that right.

60. In 1992, after the three cases against Honduras but prior to the subsequent cases on disappearances, the Declaration on the Protection of All Persons from Enforced Disappearances was approved.[179] This Declaration establishes in its Article 1(2) that forced disappearance "violates or constitutes a grave threat to the right to life".[180] With this Declaration in place and after the cases against Honduras, the Court heard two more cases before there was a Convention in the inter-American system defining and addressing the phenomenon of forced disappearance. Of these two cases, in one the judgment again assumed death,[181] while in the other the State accepted the facts, which included the fact that the whereabouts of the victims were unknown. Although in contrast to its findings in the other cases, the Court did not explicitly establish the rights that had been violated,[182] one can derive from its ruling during the reparations stage that it began with the assumption that the two victims were dead.[183]

61. In March 1996, the Inter-American Convention on Forced Disappearance of Persons (the "Convention on Disappearance") entered into force.[184] In contrast to what the United Nations Declaration establishes, the definition of

---

[178] *Ibidem*, para. 188.

[179] The Declaration on the Protection of All Persons from Enforced Disappearances was approved by the General Assembly of the United Nations by Resolution 47/133, of 18 December 1992.

[180] It is also interesting to note that the same article of the Declaration considers disappearance to violate the right of the disappeared to recognition as a person before the law.

[181] *Case of Caballero Delgado and Santana*, para. 53(b).

[182] *Case of Garrido and Baigorria*, para. 24.

[183] *Case of Garrido and Baigorria, judgment on reparations.*

[184] The Inter-American Convention on Forced Disappearance of Persons was adopted on 9 June 1994, and entered into force on 29 March 1996. As of January 2003, it has ten States Parties.

forced disappearance given in Article II of the Convention establishes that "forced disappearance is considered to be the act of depriving a person or persons of his or their freedom, in whatever way [...], followed by an absence of information or a refusal to acknowledge that deprivation of freedom or to give information on the whereabouts of that person".

As can be seen, the Convention on Disappearance does not definitively link disappearance with a violation of the right to life;[185] on the contrary, Article III allows States to establish mitigating circumstances for those responsible "when they help to cause the victim to reappear alive or provide information that sheds light on the forced disappearance of a person", allowing for the possibility of a Disappearance without the taking of a life, something that in fact occurs very rarely and that has never appeared in a case brought before the Court.

The Convention's definition establishes disappearance as a specific unlawful act, makes it a crime, and requires States to include this criminal offense in domestic criminal legislation. In addition, Article VIII of the Convention on Disappearance explicitly states that the Commission and the Inter-American Court can be turned to in the case of a disappearance, for which reason as of the entry into force of the Convention and with regard to the States that are party to it, the Court must consider disappearance as a specific type of violation of an obligation under that Convention and will not need to break down disappearance into a violation of particular rights.

62. This situation raises two questions: (i) in the case of a disappearance regulated by the Convention on Disappearance, could the Court rule that there has been a violation of the right to life even though that right is not addressed in that Convention; and (ii) in the case of a disappearance in a State not party to the aforementioned Convention, could the Court treat the phenomenon of disappearance holistically instead of breaking it down into violations of rights set forth in the American Convention? The reader will note how strange it is that the Court would address the same phenomenon in different ways, for which reason it would be advisable for the Court to find some sort of reasoning to harmonize them.

63. With regard to the first question – the problem of a possible violation of the right to life in the definition in the Convention on Disappearance – there does not seem to be any obstacle to adding a violation of the right to life in these cases through an application of the American Convention itself, as most probably, in the case of forced disappearance, the Court will use both Conventions as part of its legal framework; up until now, violations of other rights set forth in the

[185] On the subject of presuming death and disappearances, see N. Rodley, *The Treatment of Prisoners under International Law*, 2nd edn, Oxford University Press, Oxford/New York, 2002, pp. 246–247 and 261–264.

American Convention on Human Rights have always been found along with disappearance, such as for example the right to due process or the rights set forth in Articles 8 and 25. A violation of the Convention on Disappearance cannot preclude the possibility of other related violations.

64. As regards the second question, it seems unlikely that the Court would rule in a case in which it applies only the American Convention that a State has violated the prohibition on disappearing a person, given that this prohibition is not made explicit in the text; it seems unavoidable that it must formulate that violation in the terms of the provisions of the Convention applicable to the case. However, it does not seem impossible to me that even proceeding in this way, it would address the phenomenon as a whole, basing its ruling precisely on the Court's first and fortunate reaction describing disappearance as "a multiple and ongoing violation", suggesting a unified violation. It seems reasonable to argue that in the event of an arbitrary (and generally also illegal) detention for which the State can be assigned responsibility, followed by a lack of information on that detention and the elimination of any opportunity for the detainee to appear before a judge to contest it, there has been an immediate violation of Article 5 (for prolonged detention and forced lack of communication),[186] Article 7 (for arbitrary detention and prevention from exercising the rights set forth therein),[187] and Article 4 (not necessarily because experience indicates that people kidnapped this way generally die, but because the State has placed a person in a situation of grave threat to his or her right to life).[188]

It is also sensible to argue that the violation of these rights continues until the State redresses it – that is, the violations persist as long as the State has not admitted what took place, providing information on what happened to the individual disappeared and, if he or she is dead, reporting where the remains are located; has not investigated, brought to trial and punished the guilty parties; and has not provided satisfaction and/or monetary compensation to the relatives of the victim should the victim not be found. Looking at the phenomenon of disappearance in this way, the fact that a death took place, the date on which it took place, and the need to seek a reason to assume it took place all become irrelevant. If the Court continues thus and acts consistently in all cases of disappearance, this case law will be settled in the manner that seems most correct.

65. An example of this could be the case of Trujillo Oroza, which naturally has its own particular circumstance: specifically, that the State recognized its responsibility. In that case, the Court addressed the phenomenon of

---

186 *Case of Velásquez Rodríguez*, para. 156.

187 *Ibidem*, para. 155.

188 *Ibidem*, para. 188.

disappearance as comprising a single violation. José Carlos Trujillo Oroza disappeared in Bolivia in February of 1972, and only in January of 1999 was an *ex officio* investigation into the facts launched.[189] Bolivia ratified the American Convention on 19 July 1979 – that is, seven years after the disappearance – and recognized the jurisdiction of Article 62 of the Convention on 27 July 1993, 21 years after the facts took place. The case before the Commission was launched in September 1992 and on 14 June 1994, the State accepted its responsibility for the facts alleged and reported on actions taken to investigate the fate of the disappeared individual and to find the perpetrators.[190] Without prejudice to this, a friendly settlement was not reached because Bolivia alleged that the relatives had never sought a remedy aimed at punishing the guilty or reimbursing moral damages even though the country's democracy had been developing since 1982 and, since that date, legal due process had been in place.[191] The Commission submitted the case before the Court and the State did not raise any preliminary objections, acquiescing to the application.[192] In the event of acquiescence, normally the facts are considered to have been acknowledged and the ruling establishes the specific violations that have been committed by the State as a result. In this case, however, the Court found that Bolivia had violated Articles 3 (right to juridical personality), 4, 5, 7, 8(1) and 25 of the American Convention, to the detriment of both the disappeared individual and his relatives.[193] Here I do not wish to address the problem of the Court's jurisdiction but rather place the emphasis on its reasoning to arrive at this conclusion. The judgment on reparations, which is the part of the proceedings in which the specific consequences of a violation are determined, reads as follows:

> The Court bears in mind that some of the facts in the case occurred prior to the dates of the State's ratification of the American Convention and acknowledgement of the Court's obligatory jurisdiction. However, the Court also observes that the defendant State did not raise any objection to the facts of the case being considered as a whole, and with regard to the entire period from 1971 to the date of this judgment. It is also worth recalling that the Constitutional Court of Bolivia indicated (*infra* para. 107) that "unlawful deprivation of freedom or unlawful detention [...] is a permanent crime", that "the extinguishment of permanent crimes should begin to be calculated from the day on which the execution of the crime ceases" and "that the victim has still not recovered his freedom; consequently, the extinguishment has not yet begun to be calculated." In view of the foregoing, the Court will examine and decide on the continued situation of forced disappearance of José Carlos Trujillo Oroza and the consequences of this situation.[194]

---

189 *Case of Trujillo Oroza*, para. 2.
190 *Ibidem*, paras. 4–6.
191 *Ibidem*, para. 8.
192 *Ibidem*, paras. 36–37.
193 *Ibidem*, para. 41.
194 *Case of Trujillo Oroza, judgment on reparations*, para. 72.

In this way, the Court ruled on "the facts of the case considered as a whole" based on the fact that the State had not objected and proceeded to set reparations by, it appears, taking into consideration the date on which the victim disappeared.[195]

66. In the cases of disappearance in which it has applied the American Convention and in which the victims' bodies were not found (except for the Blake case), the Court has found that there had been a violation of the right to life.[196] The case of Blake, in which Guatemala raised a *ratione temporis* objection to the Court's jurisdiction, was different and led the Court to change this position. Blake's disappearance took place on 28 March 1985, and the whereabouts of the victim were not known until 14 June 1992, the date on which, thanks to the strenuous efforts of Blake's relatives, he was found dead, appearing to confirm[197] that his death took place at the end of March 1985. While the American Convention was in force for Guatemala, the State did not recognize the Court's jurisdiction until 9 March 1987. It recognized jurisdiction "with the reservation that cases in which the competence of the Court is recognized are exclusively those that shall have taken place after the date that this declaration is presented to the Secretary General of the Organization of American States." Based on this background, Guatemala objected to the Court's jurisdiction to hear the case because the kidnapping, subsequent disappearance and taking of life predated recognition of that jurisdiction.

67. The Court accepted the fact that the kidnapping and death of Mr Blake took place on the date indicated and declared itself without jurisdiction over the violation of the victim's right to life.[198] However, considering that the victim's whereabouts were not known by the family until 14 June 1992, the Court denied the objection of lack of jurisdiction with regard to possible violations arising from "effects and

---

195 *Ibidem*, paras. 73 ff.

196 However, in the *Case of Caballero Delgado and Santana*, the judgment found that the disappearance of the victims had not violated Article 5 "as […] according to [the Court's] judgment, there is not sufficient evidence that the detainees were tortured or subjected to mistreatment" (para. 65). Yet as previously examined in the *case of Velásquez Rodríguez*, the Court had found that "prolonged isolation and coerced lack of communication" were violations of Article 5 and would therefore be so in all disappearances. This departure from the case law goes against the idea of the unity of the violation.

197 The supposed agreement between the State and the Commission as regards the date of death, accepted by the Court as fact, was objected to by Judge Cançado Trindade, who stated in his separate opinion that it was not demonstrated that the Commission had accepted that the disappearance and death of Mr Blake had taken place on the date indicated by the State (*Case of Blake, judgment on preliminary objections*, dissenting opinion of Judge Cançado Trindade, para. 7).

198 This is despite the fact that the Commission insisted consistently all throughout the proceedings that the disappearance and death of Mr Blake "should be considered to be a continuous crime since it was only discovered on 14 June 1992" (*Case of Blake, judgment on preliminary objections*, para. 32).

conduct subsequent" to that date.[199] In arriving at this decision, it argued that the victim's deprivation of liberty and his death cannot be considered "*per se* to be continuous", meaning that the Court did not have jurisdiction with regard to these facts.[200] Without prejudice to this, it ruled that principles of international law recognized by Guatemala establish that forced disappearance involves the violation of several rights and that the effects of the violations, even when they are committed previously, "may be prolonged continuously or permanently until such time as the victim's fate or whereabouts are established".[201] However, when it explains what these effects are, the Court is in reality making reference to new actions carried out by State agents subsequent to the date on which the Court's jurisdiction was accepted and up to and including June 1992, consisting of complicity with and concealment of the detention and death of Mr Blake, denial of the victim's death to his parents, and attempts to make the body disappear.[202] In sum, in the Blake case, the Court found that the consequences of disappearance include the violation of several rights independent of one another and that the date of the kidnapping was decisive for establishing the Court's jurisdiction. For this reason, because it did not have jurisdiction to rule on violations committed against the personhood of the disappeared individual resulting from the fact of his disappearance, potential violations of the rights to life, humane treatment and personal liberty of the disappeared individual were outside of the Court's jurisdiction.

68. Judge Cançado Trindade issued a separate opinion in which he advanced the argument that the violations in a case of forced disappearance should be unified, though he did not argue that the Court should have declared itself to have had jurisdiction over the violations of Mr Blake's rights given that his opinion is not a dissenting one. First, he argued that "the characterization of the present case as one of disappearance, requires that this latter be understood in an integral manner, comprising its multiple aspects";[203] he noted next that the Commission did not ask for the Court to rule on the violation of a particular right but rather on the alleged multiple violations "taken as a whole";[204] and concluded by lamenting that the Court's acceptance of the preliminary objection will have the effect of "returning or abandoning issues related to the investigation of the detention and death of a person, along with the punishment of those responsible, to domestic jurisdiction after international jurisdiction was turned to specifically because of the failings of domestic jurisdiction in this regard."[205]

---

199 *Ibidem*, para. 40.
200 *Ibidem*, para. 33.
201 *Ibidem*, para. 39.
202 *Ibidem*, para. 34.
203 *Ibidem*, separate opinion, para. 4.
204 *Ibidem*, separate opinion, para. 10.
205 *Ibidem*, separate opinion, para. 14. Translator's own English version. The official English version reads: "*renvoi* or abandonment to the national jurisdiction of the issues of the

69. Consistent with its initial ruling, in the judgment on the merits in the Blake case, the Court found that Guatemala had violated Article 5 of the Convention to the detriment of the mental and moral integrity of the relatives of Mr Blake,[206] along with Article 8 of the same Convention, given that the Convention grants to his "relatives [the right] to have his disappearance and death [...] effectively investigated by the Guatemalan authorities; to have those responsible prosecuted for committing said unlawful acts; to have the relevant punishment, where appropriate, meted out; and to be compensated for the damages and injuries they sustained."[207]

70. As can be observed, the Blake case shows that the Court does not consider the phenomenon of disappearance as a whole, since in its judgment it breaks it down. In addition, it ruled that the date on which the kidnapping took place was the decisive date for establishing jurisdiction, failing to consider that the crime remained in progress and was therefore a "continuous violation" up until the moment in which the body turned up on a date subsequent to Guatemala's recognition of the Court's jurisdiction. In doing so, it did not follow the Inter-American Convention on Forced Disappearance, which establishes in Article III that the crime "shall be deemed continuous or permanent as long as the fate or whereabouts of the victim has not been determined."

This position contrasts with the situation of a disappearance in which the body is not found. In this case, as the phenomenon of disappearance has not concluded, there is nothing to prevent the Court from ruling on the violation of the right to life, the right to personal freedom, and the right to humane treatment of the disappeared individual, as it did in Velásquez.

71. The judgment in Blake leads one to ask why disappearance is referred to as a "continuous" violation if the Court's jurisdiction is determined by when the disappearance first took place and that moment also defines whether the victim in the case is the disappeared person or the disappeared person's relatives. It could perhaps be argued that if the violation is continuous, the Court must rule that it has jurisdiction to hear pleadings in relation to violations of the rights of Mr Blake given that the violation – the result of negligence or perhaps simply the State's refusal to look for the body and investigate the disappearance of Mr Blake – have continued until a date subsequent to the date on which Guatemala recognized the contentious jurisdiction of Article 62 of the Convention.

Judge Cançado Trindade returned to all of this in a separate opinion annexed to the judgment on the merits in the Blake case. He salvaged from the judgment

---

investigation of the detention and death of a person, and the punishment of those responsible for them, after resorting to the international jurisdiction precisely in view of the shortcomings or insufficiencies of national jurisdiction to this effect."

[206] *Case of Blake*, para. 124(2).

[207] *Ibidem*, paras. 124(1) and 97.

the fact that for the first time, the Court had found that disappearance violates the rights of the relatives, something that was not a part of rulings in previous cases,[208] though obviously he could not reach a conclusion different from what had already been ruled in the judgment on preliminary objections.[209] The separate opinion tries in some ways to diminish the effects of the Court's ruling, arguing that as with the substantive human rights obligations generated for Guatemala upon its ratification of the American Convention, it was clear that the State must take into consideration the recommendations of the Inter-American Commission regarding the facts that the Court had declined to hear.[210] When this case is compared against the Trujillo Oroza case, it gives the impression that the Court has not been as precise as it should have been in order to resolve this point, and that it should be examined more closely given that it seems to be indispensable for reconciling the Court's position on disappearance with, on the one hand, the provisions of the pertinent Convention, now in force, and on the other, its own case law.

208 The Court reiterated this position in the *case of Bámaca Velásquez*, para. 165.

209 *Case of Blake*, separate opinion of Judge Cançado Trindade, para. 37.

210 *Ibidem*, para. 36.

CHAPTER 3
RIGHT TO HUMANE TREATMENT

Article 5. Right to Humane Treatment

1. *Every person has the right to have his physical, mental, and moral integrity respected.*
2. *No one shall be subjected to torture or to cruel, inhuman, or degrading punishment or treatment. All persons deprived of their liberty shall be treated with respect for the inherent dignity of the human person.*
3. *Punishment shall not be extended to any person other than the criminal.*
4. *Accused persons shall, save in exceptional circumstances, be segregated from convicted persons, and shall be subject to separate treatment appropriate to their status as unconvicted persons.*
5. *Minors while subject to criminal proceedings shall be separated from adults and brought before specialized tribunals, as speedily as possible, so that they may be treated in accordance with their status as minors.*
6. *Punishments consisting of deprivation of liberty shall have as an essential aim the reform and social readaptation of the prisoners.*

1. INTRODUCTION

1. In contrast to Article 7 of the International Covenant and Article 3 of the European Convention on Human Rights, which only enshrine the prohibition on torture and cruel, inhuman or degrading treatment, Article 5 of the Convention establishes in its first clause the right of all people to have their physical, mental and moral integrity respected, while its second clause establishes a prohibition on certain types of conduct. This suggests that the provision's content goes beyond merely providing protection from torture and other prohibited conduct. Thus, taking this into consideration, Article 5 presents a challenge in the determination of its scope and content. The American Convention's *travaux préparatoires*, which is very slight, says nothing on this, and nor has the Inter-American Court elaborated on the concept in any cases that have come before it.

It can be argued that this enshrining of a *right* to humane treatment reveals two aspects of this provision: first, it generates an obligation for the State to refrain from any of the acts or omissions prohibited by Article 5 of the Convention and to ensure others refrain from them as well; and second, it alludes to the status of every individual as a being deserving of respect, with no one allowed in principle to interfere with that individual or that individual's personal decisions. This thereby suggests that the individual is the owner of him- or herself, is personally autonomous, and therefore has the authority to make decisions in that regard, while the State does not in principle have authority to prevent him or her from doing so. Approaching the right in this way, it is closely related to the right to private life, which is no surprise given that the rights established in the Convention seek jointly to protect the dignity of persons from many different angles.[1]

If we accept this approach, analysis of the right should deviate from the usual conclusions, as we can argue that conduct that does not reach the level of severity or meet the other requirements necessary for it to be understood as prohibited could nevertheless constitute a rights violation if it does not pass the test of being necessary in a democratic society. Should this be the case, Article 5 of the Convention, in the part in which it grants a right to personal integrity, would not have the same characteristics as the prohibition on certain conduct, such as – for example – its absolute character.

This chapter will follow a traditional analytical approach, but my position as regards this dichotomy in Article 5 of the Convention will be evident throughout.

2. Article 5 includes in the right to humane treatment several provisions on conditions that must be provided for persons deprived of liberty and sets forth the purposes that sentences of deprivation of liberty must serve. Despite this, it is clear that the prohibition of torture and cruel, inhuman or degrading punishment is at its core. The fundamental role played by the prohibition of this conduct, not only in the American Convention but also in all other international law, reflects the existence of numerous instruments intended specifically to prohibit the conduct and special provisions applicable to those who practice it.

In 1975, the Declaration on the Protection of All Persons from Being Subjected to Torture and Other Cruel, Inhuman or Degrading Treatment or Punishment was adopted in the framework of the United Nations;[2] subsequently, also in the framework of the United Nations, the Convention against Torture and Other Cruel, Inhuman, or Degrading Punishment was adopted;[3] and in the

1 For a similar position, see IACHR, *Martín de Mejía v. Peru*, Case No. 10.970, Report No. 5/96, of 1 March 1996, published in IACHR, *1995 Annual Report*, pp. 168–214 (200–201).

2 Declaration on the Protection of All Persons from Being Subjected to Torture and Other Cruel, Inhuman or Degrading Treatment or Punishment, approved by the General Assembly of the United Nations on 9 December 1975 (Resolution 3452 (XXX)).

3 Convention against Torture and Other Cruel, Inhuman, or Degrading Punishment (CAT), approved on 10 December 1984 (Resolution 39/46) UN Doc. A/39/51 (1984). The Convention entered into force on 26 June 1987, and as of November 2003 it had 133 States Parties.

framework of the OAS, the Inter-American Convention to Prevent and Punish Torture (hereinafter the "Inter-American Convention on Torture")[4] was adopted. There is also a European Convention for the Prevention of Torture and Inhuman or Degrading Treatment or Punishment.[5] In addition, this conduct constitutes a severe violation of the Geneva Conventions of 1949, where the need for humane treatment of all is established along with the prohibition of torture and similar acts,[6] and which could also be the basis for the crime of apartheid.[7] Another series of international instruments regulates different aspects of this phenomenon.[8]

The gravity of this conduct[9] is illustrated not only by the number of international instruments that regulate it separately, but also by the fact, *inter alia*, that some of this conduct can result in international criminal responsibility for the perpetrators;[10] that it is covered by universal jurisdiction;[11] that it is, in

4 Inter-American Convention to Prevent and Punish Torture, approved on 9 December 1985. The Convention entered into force on 28 February 1987.

5 European Convention for the Prevention of Torture and Inhuman or Degrading Treatment or Punishment, approved in the framework of the Council of Europe on 26 November 1987. The Convention entered into force on 1 February 1989.

6 Also see Additional Protocol II to the Geneva Conventions, dated 12 August 1949, relating to the Protection of Victims of Non-International Armed Conflicts, approved on 8 June 1977. The Protocol entered into force on 7 December 1978.

7 Convention on the Suppression and Punishment of the Crime of Apartheid, approved on 30 November 1973; entered into force on 18 July 1970.

8 Other instruments referencing torture include: Standard Minimum Rules for the Treatment of Prisoners, adopted by the First United Nations Congress on the Prevention of Crime and the Treatment of Offenders, held at Geneva in 1955, and approved by the Economic and Social Council by its resolutions 663 C (XXIV) of 31 July 1957 and 2076 (LXII) of 13 May 1977; Body of Principles for the Protection of All Persons under Any Form of Detention or Imprisonment, adopted by the General Assembly in its Resolution 43/173, of 9 December 1988; Principles of Medical Ethics relevant to the Role of Health Personnel, particularly Physicians, in the Protection of Prisoners and Detainees against Torture and Other Cruel, Inhuman or Degrading Treatment or Punishment, adopted by the General Assembly in its Resolution 37/194 of 18 December 1982; Declaration on the Protection of All Persons from Being Subjected to Torture and Other Cruel, Inhuman or Degrading Treatment or Punishment, adopted by the General Assembly in its Resolution 3452 (XXX), of 9 December 1975; Basic Principles on the Use of Force and Firearms by Law Enforcement Officials, adopted by the Eighth United Nations Congress on the Prevention of Crime and the Treatment of Offenders, held in Havana, Cuba, from 27 August to 7 September 1990.

9 The word "conduct" denotes an action or omission attributable to an individual. On this, see M. Novak, *UN Covenant on Civil and Political Rights. CCPR Commentary*, N.P. Engel Publisher, Kehl/Strasbourg/Arlington, 1993, p. 128.

10 See, among others, Article 6 Of the Charter of the Nuremberg Tribunal; Article 50 of Convention I, Article 51 of Convention II, Article 13 of Convention III, Article 147 of Convention IV, Article 75 of Protocol I, Article 4 of Protocol II, Article 3(1)(a) of the four Geneva Conventions; Article 7(1)(f) of the Statute of the International Criminal Court.

11 Article 5.1 UN Convention against Torture; Principles of international co-operation in the detection, arrest, extradition and punishment of persons guilty of war crimes and crimes against humanity (Resolution 3074 (XXVIII) of the General Assembly, dated 3 December 1973); United States Court of Appeal for the Second Circuit: *Filartiga v. Peña-Irala,* 630 F 2d 876 (2nd Cir. 1980).

principle, not subject to the statute of limitations;[12] and that its prohibition constitutes a *jus cogens*[13] norm, that is, a peremptory norm of international law from which a State cannot exempt itself by, for example, making a reservation upon committing itself to a human rights treaty.[14] In addition, in contrast to others, this character of this right is absolute, that is, it cannot be restricted or suspended under any circumstances.[15] There are no grounds that would allow for a State to restrict this right in the way that grounds can be found – public order, public health – for authorizing restrictions of other human rights. Finally, nor does the Convention allow this prohibition to be suspended during emergency situations. This has been reiterated by the Inter-American Court, which has found that circumstances in which a State is faced by a situation of terrorism must not lead to restrictions on the protection of the physical integrity of persons.[16]

3. The existence of an Inter-American Convention on Torture and an Inter-American Convention on the Prevention, Punishment and Eradication of Violence against Women (hereinafter the "Belem do Pará Convention"),[17] and the fact that Article 5 of the American Convention contains such broad provisions, complicate the approach to the article. Out of a variety of different options, I have selected the following structure for this chapter: it will first examine the substantive aspect related to the concept of prohibited conduct and the elements that can be used to distinguish between prohibited conduct and permitted conduct; next, the chapter analyzes the Inter-American Court's case law on the determination of prohibited conduct; following that, the chapter

12 Convention on the Non-Applicability of Statutory Limitations to War Crimes and Crimes Against Humanity. Adopted and opened for signing, ratification and adherence by the General Assembly in its Resolution 2391 (XXIII); entered into force on 11 November 1970, and as of July 2003, it had 45 States Parties.

13 ICJ, *East Timor (Portugal v. Australia)*, Reports 1995, p. 90, at p. 102, para. 29; ILC, *Report of the International Law Commission on the work of its fifty-third session*, United Nations, Geneva, 2001, pp. 208 and 284 (commentaries on Articles 26 and 40); C. Villán Durán, "La Convención contra la Tortura y su contribución a la definición del derecho a la integridad física y moral en el derecho internacional", *Revista Española de Derecho Internacional*, Vol. XXXVII N° 2, 1985, pp. 381–384. See also *Case of Maritza Urrutia*, para. 92.

14 E. Schwelb, "Some aspects of international *jus* cogens as formulated by the International Law Commission", (1967) 61 *American Journal of International Law* 946–975; A. Cebada Romero, "Los conceptos de obligaciones *erga omnes, ius cogens* y violación grave, a la luz del nuevo proyecto de la CDI sobre responsabilidad de los Estados por hechos ilícitos", (2002) *Revista Electrónica de Estudios Internacionales* 2–10, accessed at www.reei.org/reei4/reei.4.htm.

15 Regarding torture, see *Case of Maritza Urrutia*, para. 89.

16 *Case of Cantoral Benavides*, para. 96, reiterating what had already been found in the *case of Castillo Petruzzi et al.*, para. 197, and the *case of Loayza Tamayo*, para. 57.

17 Inter-American Convention on the Prevention, Punishment and Eradication of Violence against Women ("Convention of Belem do Pará"), adopted in Belém do Pará, Brazil, on 9 June 1994, at the Twenty-Fourth Regular Session of the General Assembly; entered into force on 5 March 1995.

addresses the Inter-American Convention on Torture and its consequences with regard to the Inter-American Court's jurisdiction for addressing violations of personal integrity, which then allows for an examination of the protection of personal integrity according to the Inter-American Convention on Torture and Article 5 of the American Convention; the chapter concludes with an examination of the Belem do Pará Convention, which brings up a relatively new subject. Paragraphs 4, 5 and 6 of Article 5 of the Convention will be examined separately at the end, as they are in some ways outside the core of the Article in question.

2. DIFFERENT KINDS OF PROHIBITED CONDUCT

4. The American Convention does not define the different types of conduct prohibited by Article 5(2), nor does it give any elements to guide an interpreter towards determining when we are in the presence of such conduct, except for establishing that the conduct that can constitute a violation is that which endangers the physical, mental or moral integrity of a person. Rather, it leaves it up to the interpreter to determine whether the specific facts constituting the basis of a complaint form a violation of this provision. Nor are these terms defined in Article 7 of the International Covenant or in Article 3 of the European Convention on Human Rights.

The supervisory body applying the treaty must decide which elements allow, first, to differentiate between prohibited conducts, and second, to determine whether a particular instance of conduct is among that expressly prohibited by Article 5(2) of the Convention. The first is a relative problem, as whatever the prohibited conduct committed, there is a violation of the corresponding provision, and from that point of view, there is no need to make a distinction unless the supervisory body is applying a treaty in which the prohibited conduct is already defined, as with torture, and where there are provisions making reference solely to that conduct. The distinction can be important from the point of view of a State's image before the international community: torture has a greater sense of infamy associated with it than do other actions; also in addition, the distinction can serve for the purposes of determining reparations for the victim, although it is possible to make this determination according to the specific circumstances of each case without the need to give a specific name to the conduct. That second issue is significant and complex, but the case law has not developed enough to allow one to reach firm conclusions.

5. It is often said that a distinction between different types of conduct must be made in order particularly to highlight torture, as the term torture has a greater stigma associated with it that must be expressed. This probably has to do with the fact that the history of the prohibition of torture is related to its use by State agents as a means of obtaining information.[18] It is, as a consequence, a response to the intentional actions of State agents towards a subject who necessarily is under their power and who is made to suffer severely. Torture viewed in this way becomes more serious because the State uses its power on a defenseless subject, and naturally the approach that it deserves should be in accordance with these circumstances.

It is no wonder then that of all the conduct mentioned in Article 5(2) of the Convention, torture is the one that has been defined by international instruments. Universally, this is done by both the Declaration on the Protection of All Persons from Being Subjected to Torture and Other Cruel, Inhuman or Degrading Treatment or Punishment, and the Convention against Torture and Other Cruel, Inhuman, or Degrading Punishment.[19] Both definitions, which are relatively similar, take into consideration the following: (i) the agent, a public official, that causes or instigates it (according to the Declaration), or a public official or other person in the exercise of public authority who, in addition to causing it or instigating it, tolerates it or is aware of it (in the Convention); (ii) intent; (iii) the conduct's effects on the victim: severe pain or suffering, physical or mental (in the Declaration), or serious pain or suffering, physical or mental (in the Convention); and (iv) the purpose of the conduct: obtaining information or a confession from the victim or a third party, punishment or intimidation (in the Declaration) or, in addition to these purposes, coercion or discrimination (in the Convention).[20]

The Committee against Torture, a body established by the United Nations Convention, has not analyzed the elements of torture on applying the Convention to a particular case.

6. In the Inter-American system, Article 2 of the Inter-American Convention on Torture offers the following definition:

> For the purposes of this Convention, torture shall be understood to be any act intentionally performed whereby physical or mental pain or suffering is inflicted on a person for purposes of criminal investigation, as a means of intimidation, as personal punishment, as a preventive measure, as a penalty, or for any other purpose. Torture shall also be understood to be the use of methods upon a person intended to obliterate the personality of the victim or to diminish his physical or mental capacities, even if they do not cause physical pain or mental anguish.

---

18 N. Rodley, *The Treatment of Prisoners under International Law,* 2nd edn, Oxford University Press, 2002, pp. 7–11.

19 On the scope of the Convention, see C. Villán Durán, *supra* n. 13, pp. 386–398.

20 For detailed analysis of these elements, see N. Rodley, *supra* n. 18, pp. 75–106.

The definition's failure to identify the perpetrator of the conduct is remedied in Article 3 of the Convention, which states the following:

> The following shall be held guilty of the crime of torture:
> a. A public servant or employee who acting in that capacity orders, instigates or induces the use of torture, or who directly commits it or who, being able to prevent it, fails to do so.
> b. A person who at the instigation of a public servant or employee mentioned in subparagraph (a) orders, instigates or induces the use of torture, directly commits it or is an accomplice thereto.

7. This definition differs somewhat from the universal system definitions already mentioned. One difference is that it identifies as perpetrators both public officials and private parties who commit, instigate or induce; the Inter-American Convention on Torture does maintain the need for there to exist a link between the private party and the public official, but a tenuous one. In addition, the Inter-American Convention on Torture qualifies certain acts as torture without requiring as an essential element that they have a specific purpose, given that its Article 2 uses the all-inclusive wording "any other purpose". This seems sensible, as in the end, the purpose of torture is to subject a person to the will of the torturer. What the torturer would do with that person once the person's will is broken can be more varied than one might think and is surely irrelevant for deciding whether the conduct is reproachable and should be prohibited by international law. Finally, it establishes that the act must cause physical or mental suffering to the victim, without specifying any requirements for severity, adding the possibility that if the purpose of the torture is to "obliterate the personality of the victim or to diminish his physical or mental capacities", the suffering of physical pain or mental anguish is not required as part of the definition. This gives the definition of torture considerable breadth that frees it from the restrictions imposed by the classic concept of torture.[21]

8. The International Covenant does not define torture or other prohibited conduct. The Human Rights Committee of the United Nations, which supervises the application of this international instrument, has generally tried not to distinguish among the conduct prohibited by its Article 7, perhaps to emphasize

---

21 This idea coincides with the concerns expressed by a judge of the European Court of Human Rights in the case of *Ireland v. United Kingdom* in the sense that on requiring the existence of suffering in the victim, and a significant level of suffering, the European Court of Human Rights could be excluding new forms of suffering from the definition of torture that have little to do with the physical suffering of traditional torments but aim "at inducing even temporarily the disintegration of the human personality, the destruction of man's mental and psychological balance and the annihilation of his will" (cited in D.J. Harris, M. O'Boyle and C. Warbrick, *Law of the European Convention on Human Rights*, Butterworths, London/Dublin/Edinburgh, 1995, p. 61, n. 2).

that all such conduct is prohibited. In General Comment No. 20, which replaces General Comment No. 7, the Committee indicates that:

> 4. The Covenant does not contain any definition of the concepts covered by Article 7, nor does the Committee consider it necessary to draw up a list of prohibited acts or to establish sharp distinctions between the different kinds of punishment or treatment; the distinctions depend on the nature, purpose and severity of the treatment applied.[22]

As a result of this position, when the Committee finds that there has been a violation of Article 7 of the International Covenant, it rules as much, without specifying whether the facts constitute torture or another form of prohibited conduct.[23]

9. In contrast, in the European system, which also does not provide normative definitions, the distinction has generally been made in order to develop the concept of torture as an aggravated form of inhuman treatment, with this latter expression often appearing as a generic concept. The now-defunct European Commission of Human Rights conceptualized each conduct, finding that:

> The notion of inhuman treatment covers at least such treatment as deliberately causes severe suffering, mental or physical, which, in the particular situation, is unjustifiable. The word "torture" is often used to describe inhuman treatment, which has a purpose, such as the obtaining of information or confessions, or the infliction of punishment, and it is generally an aggravated form of inhuman treatment. Treatment or punishment of an individual may be said to be degrading if it grossly humiliates him before others or drives him to act against his will or conscience.[24]

Thus, the Commission addresses the severity of the treatment and the purpose it pursues to distinguish between torture and inhuman treatment.[25] As far as degrading treatment, it is defined by the humiliation it causes to the one receiving it.[26]

Nothing in the European Commission's opinion indicates the parameters to be used for measuring when suffering is severe or humiliation is serious. The European Court of Human Rights found in the judgment handed down in the

---

22 HRC, General Comment No. 20, Article 7, A/47/40 (1992), Annex VI, pp. 193–195, para. 4.

23 HRC, *Boodlal Sooklal v. Trinidad and Tobago,* Communication 928/2000, ruling of 25 October 2001, A/57/40, Vol. II (2002), Annex IX, sec. EE, (pp. 264–269), para. 4.6; *Michael Freemantle v. Jamaica*, Communication 625/1995, ruling of 24 March 2000, A/55/40, Vol. II (2000), Annex IX, sec. A., (pp. 11–21), para. 7.2.

24 European Commission of Human Rights, *Denmark v. Greece*, Yearbook XII (1969), p. 186; cited in P. van Dijk, F. van Hoof, A. van Rijn and L. Zwaak (eds.), *Theory and Practice of the European Convention on Human Rights*, 4th edn, Intersentia, Antwerp/Oxford, 2006, p. 406.

25 The European Convention on Human Rights does not make any mention of cruel treatment, but its case law is considered to include it under the term inhuman (D.J. Harris et al., *supra* n. 21, p. 58).

26 This concept of degrading treatment was also used by the European Court of Human Rights in the case of *Tyrer v. United Kingdom*, judgment of 25 April 1978, para. 30 (1978).

case of Ireland v. United Kingdom that degrading treatment is treatment capable of "arous[ing] in [the] victims feelings of fear, anguish and inferiority capable of humiliating and debasing them and possibly breaking their physical or moral resistance".[27] The explanation seems to place emphasis on the victim's reaction to the treatment in question, but does not make reference to the fact that there must be at least a prevailing social standard in the international community to be taken into consideration when determining whether conduct is prohibited and which could be used as a threshold not to be crossed. However, both the reaction of the victim and the social standard must be used with extreme caution. If not, it could lead to reasoning – in my opinion unacceptable – like that of the European Commission in the Greek case, where it found that:

> A certain roughness of treatment by both the police and military authorities is tolerated by most detainees and even taken for granted. Such roughness may take the form of slaps or blows of the hand on the head or face. This underlines the fact that the point up to which prisoners and the public may accept physical violence as being neither cruel nor excessive varies between different societies and even between different sections of them.[28]

A look at the case law of the European Court of Human Rights shows that it is difficult to find the criteria taken into consideration in deciding whether conduct is sufficiently severe and cruel to be classified as torture. It is possible that the victim's circumstances play a role in a ruling, as do the consequences of the acts performed on the person being subjected to torture. Nor is it simple to differentiate by examining the purpose sought by the act, because according to the ruling of the European Court of Human Rights in the case of Ireland v. United Kingdom, inhuman or degrading treatment can have the same intent as torture. In this case, for example, that Court found that the five techniques used in Northern Ireland – consisting of keeping individuals on tiptoe for long hours, covering heads with hoods, subjecting detainees to intense and constant noise, and depriving them of sufficient sleep, food and drink – do not reach the level of torture but rather inhuman treatment, as the term torture attach a special stigma denoting "deliberate inhuman treatment causing very serious and cruel suffering".[29]

---

27 ECtHR, *Ireland v. United Kingdom,* judgment of 18 January 1978, p. 167; cited by J. Barquin Sanz, *Los delitos de tortura y tratos inhumanos o degradantes*, EDERSA, Madrid, 1992, p. 89.

28 *Denmark v. Greece*, ruling of 5 November 1969, Yearbook XII, 1969; cited in P. van Dijk and G.J.H. van Hoof, *Theory and Practice of the European Convention on Human Rights,* 3rd edn, SIM, Kluwer Law International, The Hague/London/Boston, 1998, p. 812.

29 The fact that the European Commission of Human Rights, in the proceedings prior to the Court's hearing of the case, had classified these techniques as "torture" reflects the difficulty and subjectivity of the distinction (report of 25 January 1976, B.23-I, 1980), p. 411, cited in P. van Dijk and G.J.H. van Hoof, *supra* n. 28, p. 309.

In the case of Aksoy v. Turkey, the European Court of Human Rights ruled that conduct consisting of undressing an individual and hanging him by the arms, which were tied behind his body, constituted torture because it had to have been inflicted deliberately and apparently with the purpose of getting the subject to admit a fact or give information and had caused temporary paralysis in both arms. The cruel and severe nature of the action could only be classified as torture.[30]

10. Up to this point, we have looked only at treatment that can be considered torture or as cruel, inhuman or degrading. However, punishments with these characteristics are prohibited as well. Normally, the punishments most apt to being considered as belonging to one of these categories are corporal in nature. In contrast to treatment, punishments are institutionalized, accepted by legislation, ordered by a court and applied by an agent of the State. The European Court of Human Rights indicated as much in the case of Tyrer by ruling that:

> The very nature of judicial corporal punishment is that it involves one human being inflicting physical violence on another human being. Furthermore, it is institutionalised violence that is in the present case violence permitted by the law, ordered by the judicial authorities of the State and carried out by the police authorities of the State. Thus, although the applicant did not suffer any severe or long-lasting physical effects, his punishment – whereby he was treated as an object in the power of the authorities – constituted an assault on precisely that which it is one of the main purposes of Article 3 (art. 3) to protect, namely a person's dignity and physical integrity.[31]

This leads Barquin to deduce from the judgment of the European Court of Human Rights that all institutionalized violence is by nature intrinsically degrading.[32] However, the European Court of Human Rights has not gone so far as to find that all corporal punishment is *per se* degrading. Rather, it indicates that it depends on the degree of humiliation or debasement caused, given that all punishments can have this effect. The European Court of Human Rights finds that this interpretation is, "in the nature of things, relative: it depends on all the circumstances of the case and, in particular, on the nature and context of the punishment itself and the manner and method of its execution." An attack on decency or shame can be a factor that aggravates the punishment and makes it degrading.[33]

---

30 ECtHR, *Ireland v. United Kingdom*, judgment of 18 January 1978, pp. 66–67, and *Akzoy v. Turkey*, judgment of 18 December 1996, Reports 1996-VI, Vol. 26, para. 64, both cited in P. van Dijk and G.J.H. van Hoof, *supra* n. 28, p. 310.

31 ECtHR, *Tyrer v. United Kingdom*, *supra* n. 26, para. 33.

32 *Ibidem*. Cited in Barquin, *supra* n. 27, p. 92.

33 *Ibidem*, para. 30. It should be noted that the punishment in the Tyrer case consisted of being struck on the naked buttocks with a rod.

Without ruling on what kind of conduct is prohibited, the Human Rights Committee has taken the same position, finding that whippings violate Article 7 of the International Covenant.[34]

11. From this, it could be concluded that while there have been attempts to distinguish between the different forms of prohibited conduct, the distinctions have not been consistent. In addition, it should be recalled that with regard to personal integrity, as well as with regard to other rights, what is monitored internationally is State compliance with all obligations found in Article 5(2) of the Convention; it is not the responsibility of the international body to determine individual criminal guilt. Should it exist, the criminal offense must be carefully described and the court must be convinced that all aspects of the crime have been proven before finding an individual guilty. Should this not be the case, as a logical consequence and as has already been stated, the distinction between one conduct and another is not, in principle, relevant for establishing a violation and can only be significant in weighing reparations or for the reputation of the State against which the supervisory body is ruling.

12. The attempts to differentiate between types of prohibited conduct have failed not only to do so, but to assist efficiently in deciding when conduct meets the minimum standards for inclusion in the expression "torture or other cruel, inhuman or degrading treatment or punishment". Nevertheless, this determination is crucial, as although the ban on prohibited conduct cannot be restricted or suspended, it is possible to conceive of treatments that affect personal integrity without violating the prohibition. To start with, we can admit that if legitimate self-defense is allowed as a justification for the taking of a life, a similar approach could be used to justify acts affecting personal integrity;[35] if punishments that include deprivation of liberty are allowed – which can very likely cause mental and moral suffering, as well as physical suffering at times – the circumstances that transform a deprivation of liberty into a violation of Article 5(2) of the Convention must be defined.

13. If we allow ourselves to be guided by the aforementioned definitions and by case law, we note that torture and inhuman treatment require premeditated action that results in a degree of suffering that must be very severe for the former and severe for the latter; in the case of degrading treatment, the action must result in severe humiliation or must lead the victim to act against his or her will

---

34 HRC, *Boodlal v. Trinidad and Tobago*, Communication 928/2000, ruling of 8 November 2000, A/57/40, Vol. II (2002), Annex IX, sec. EE, (pp. 264–269), para. 4.6; *Osbourne v. Jamaica*, Communication 759/1997, ruling of 13 March 1999, A/55/40, Vol. II (2000), Annex IX, sec. L (pp. 133–139), para. 9.1.

35 In the sense, see the separate opinion of Judge Fawcett in *Ireland v. United Kingdom*, B 23-I, p. 502, Com Rep (1976), cited by D.J. Harris et al., *supra* n. 21, p. 56.

or conscience, in the opinion of the European Commission. Even leaving aside premeditation, it must be concluded that degrading treatment also requires intent to cause a particular effect.

14. I suggest examining these types of conduct by using the elements of severity of suffering and intention to cause harm or suffering or to bend the will of the victim, but I would add an element: the absence of a legitimate purpose for such actions. This last element implies an understanding that the definition of prohibited conduct includes the implicit requirement, not sufficient in and of itself, that violations of integrity do not have a legitimate aim under the Convention but rather respond to other aims, those being to cause suffering in order to achieve certain illegitimate ends (in the case of torture and cruel or inhuman treatment) or to cause humiliation (in the case of degrading treatment). Conduct that has no set purpose but that was the result of grave negligence can be equated with intentional conduct.[36]

The lack of intent to achieve an illegitimate end through suffering could in principle justify certain conduct: legitimate self-defense that causes suffering to others would not constitute prohibited conduct given that the actor's intent is not to cause harm but rather to defend him- or herself. A prison sentence or certain forms of confinement can also be justified for the same reason: they do not seek to cause suffering but to protect social values and rehabilitate the prisoner. The same reasoning protects medical treatments carried out with the patient's authorization.

It should be noted, however, that the absence of legitimate purpose is only one of the two elements, for which reason even if the purpose is acceptable, the conduct must be examined according to the first element – that is, the severity of the suffering. Article 2 of the Inter-American Convention on Torture perhaps tries to indicate this – in my opinion unsuccessfully – by stating that:

> The concept of torture shall not include physical or mental pain or suffering that is inherent in or solely the consequence of lawful measures, provided that they do not include the performance of the acts or use of the methods referred to in this article.

This provision does not help to draw the line between prohibited and permitted conduct, as it limits itself to indicating that conduct resulting from legal measures or inherent to them does not constitute torture or other prohibited conduct, as long as those measures are not torture or other prohibited conduct, which seems unintelligible.

15. Drawing the dividing line based on the harmlessness or severity of the conduct is not easy. The European Court of Human Rights in the case of Ireland

[36] Here I take the example cited by Nowak of an Austrian case in which an individual detained by the authorities was forgotten by the authorities in his place of detention and survived 20 days without food or water. See M. Nowak, *supra* n. 9, p. 130.

v. the United Kingdom found that the treatment of a person must reach a minimum level of severity in order to be classified as prohibited conduct.[37] In one recent case, the European Court of Human Rights issued more explicit criteria on this point on finding that:

> As regards the types of "treatment" which fall within the scope of Article 3 of the Convention, the Court's case-law refers to "ill-treatment" that attains a minimum level of severity and involves actual bodily injury or intense physical or mental suffering [...]. Where treatment humiliates or debases an individual, showing a lack of respect for, or diminishing, his or her human dignity, or arouses feelings of fear, anguish or inferiority capable of breaking an individual's moral and physical resistance, it may be characterised as degrading and also fall within the prohibition of Article 3. [...] The suffering which flows from naturally occurring illness, physical or mental, may be covered by Article 3, where it is, or risks being, exacerbated by treatment, whether flowing from conditions of detention, expulsion or other measures, for which the authorities can be held responsible.[38]

This element of the severity or intensity of suffering must be weighed with particular care, and it is possible that this will continue to be done on a case-by-case basis, making it impossible to draw from it standards that can be transformed into an abstract norm; in any case, this point will surely continue to evolve over the coming years. This may be what the European Court of Human Rights is referring to when it admits a gradation in severity between torture and other kinds of treatment by ruling

> that certain acts which were classified in the past as "inhuman and degrading treatment" as opposed to "torture" could be classified differently in the future, given that the increasingly high standard being required in the area of the protection of human rights and fundamental liberties correspondingly and inevitably requires greater firmness in assessing breaches of the fundamental values of democratic societies.[39]

This reasoning could be applied, *mutatis mutandi*, to the differentiation of conduct that falls under one of the classifications indicated in Article 5 of the Convention.

While these two criteria help, robust case law is needed to be able to draw elements from it and establish the dividing line more precisely.

16. Thus far, our reasoning has only taken into consideration the first part of paragraph 2 of Article 5 of the Convention – that is, the provision establishing prohibited conduct. However, it was noted at the start of this chapter that

---

37 ECtHR, *Ireland v. United Kingdom*, judgment of 18 January 1978, cited in D.J. Harris et al., *supra* n. 21, p. 61.

38 ECtHR, *Pretty v. United Kingdom*, judgment of 29 April 2002, para. 52.

39 ECtHR, *Selmouni v. France*, judgment of 28 July 1999, para. 101, cited in *Case of Cantoral Benavides*, para. 99.

Article 5 has an added plus point because it enshrines the right to personal integrity. This added plus point can make a difference in the reasoning. If every person has the right for the State or private parties to not interfere with them or their decisions with regard to themselves, it can be argued that any interference that is not reasonably justified would constitute a violation of that provision, independent of whether the State's conduct falls under the classification of prohibited conduct. Towards this, it will be necessary to examine the State's conduct in terms of its suitability and proportionality, and to confirm the absence of an alternative for achieving its aim. As noted, this is the test to which all violations of human rights are subjected to determine whether they are justified or whether they constitute a violation, a test to which prohibited conduct is not subjected. I believe that the Inter-American Court is insinuating this when it finds that "any use of force that is not strictly necessary to ensure proper behavior on the part of the detainee constitutes an assault on the dignity of the person [...] in violation of Article 5 of the American Convention."[40] As can be noted, the Court does not indicate here any requirement for a purpose or a specific level of severity and implicitly contradicts the idea that if the conduct of a State or private parties enjoying the State's acquiescence or tolerance does not include the elements of purpose, severity or others discussed, the conduct will be legitimate. If one accepts this interpretation, which seems to me to be correct, one could only conclude that while the conduct is not prohibited under Article 5(2) of the Convention absent these requirements, that does not necessarily mean that the conduct is compatible with Article 5(1) of the Convention.

3. PROHIBITED CONDUCT IN THE CASE LAW OF THE INTER-AMERICAN COURT

3.1. CONCEPTS AND ELEMENTS OF DIFFERENTIATION

17. Differentiating between one type of prohibited conduct and another is not an exercise that the Inter-American Court engages in frequently, and when it does so it is not easy to figure out which elements it uses to differentiate. This is despite the fact that its case law contains a significant number of examples of actions or omissions that violate Article 5 of the Convention. Nor does it seem to have felt compelled to develop its own concept of one or more types of prohibited conduct, nor to use the definition found in the Inter-American Convention in any particular case. Frequently, on classifying an action or omission as torture, the Court does so based on the elements of all the previously examined

[40] *Case of Loayza Tamayo*, para. 57.

definitions. However, the variety of cases that the Court has heard on violations of that provision allow us to take note of a variety of different kinds of facts that, in the Court's opinion, violate Article 5(2) of the Convention, and thus we can identify some elements of these types of conduct.

18. There is one case, that of the forced disappearance of Mr Bámaca Velásquez, in which the Inter-American Court took a clear path toward defining the conduct as torture. In examining a possible violation of Article 5 of the Convention on Torture, it used Article 1 of the United Nations Convention against Torture and Other Cruel, Inhuman or Degrading Punishment and Article 2 of the Inter-American Convention, concluding from the case file that the acts alleged, namely serious acts of physical and psychological violence, caused severe anguish and intense suffering for the victim and were perpetrated over a long period of time, deliberately, with the purpose of obtaining information that was relevant for the Army, and thus constituted physical and psychological torture and the violation of Article 5 of the American Convention.[41] Here one can note the presence of the elements of severity and the deliberateness of the act, the effect on the victim, and the perpetration of the acts over a long period of time (an addition that perhaps is not decisive).

19. In the case of Loayza Tamayo, the Inter-American Court followed the position of the European Court of Human Rights that uses the severity of the conduct as an element of differentiation. It began by drawing distinctions between different levels of severity by finding that:

> The violation of the right to physical and psychological integrity of persons is a category of violation that has several gradations and embraces treatment ranging from torture to other types of humiliation or cruel, inhuman or degrading treatment with varying degrees of physical and psychological effects caused by endogenous and exogenous factors which must be proven in each specific situation.[42]

It also put forward the concept of degrading treatment on finding that "the degrading character [of other types of conduct] is expressed through feelings of fear, anxiety and inferiority in order to humiliate, degrade and breakdown the physical and moral resistance of the victim."[43]

Nevertheless, when it ruled on the specifics of the case, the Court did not distinguish between different types of prohibited conduct, finding that solitary confinement during detention, public display in humiliating clothing, isolation in a small cell with neither ventilation nor natural light, beatings, simulated drowning, intimidation, the threat of other violent acts, and restrictions on

41 *Case of Bámaca Velásquez*, paras. 156–158.

42 *Case of Loayza Tamayo*, para. 57.

43 *Ibidem*, citing the judgment of the European Court of Human Rights in the case of *Ireland v. United Kingdom*, judgment of 18 January 1978, para. 167.

visits, "constitute torture, cruel, inhuman and degrading treatment, or both, in violation of Article 5(2) of the American Convention".[44]

20. In the case of Cantoral Benavides, the Inter-American Court found that it must determine whether the acts under examination constituted torture, or cruel, inhuman or degrading treatment, or both, without prejudice to which it hastened to note that "regardless of the nature of the acts referred to, they are strictly prohibited under international human rights law".[45] In that judgment, the Inter-American Court found guidance in the case law of the European Court of Human Rights, the definition found in Article 2 of the Inter-American Convention on Torture, and the definition found in Article 1 of the United Nations Convention, all of which make reference to intent towards obtaining certain ends, finding that the proceedings had proven a deliberate willingness to commit these prohibited acts in order to achieve certain purposes.[46]

Likewise, the Inter-American Court set aside a number of paragraphs in this ruling to reaffirm the idea that torture "can be inflicted not only via physical violence, but also through acts that produce severe physical, psychological or moral suffering in the victim", introducing a new element into the definition with the adjective "severe".[47] Finally, taking up the position of the European Court of Human Rights, the Inter-American Court includes a caveat to the effect that the definition of what constitutes torture can change, noting that the passage of time can broaden the range of conduct included therein.[48]

However, subsequent to these reflections, the Inter-American Court stated that "at least some of the acts of aggression examined in this case can be classified as physical and psychological torture",[49] without specifying which ones, adding that the acts sought on one hand "to wear down his psychological resistance and force him to incriminate himself or to confess to certain illegal activities", and on the other "to subject him to other types of punishment, in addition to imprisonment".[50] With this, the Inter-American Court introduced that final element, which we have mentioned already, yet does not truly clarify when a certain type of conduct can be understood to constitute torture.

21. In the case of Myrna Mack Chang, one of the last of a series of cases in which the Inter-American Court developed the idea that the personal integrity of the relatives of a victim of a violation of the right to life can be violated when the

---

44 *Ibidem*, para. 58.

45 *Case of Cantoral Benavides*, para. 95.

46 The Court cited the European Court of Human Rights in the case of *Mahmut Kaya v. Turkey*, judgment of 28 March 2000, para. 117. See *ibidem*, para. 97.

47 *Ibidem*, para. 100.

48 *Ibidem*, para. 99.

49 *Ibidem*, para. 104.

50 *Ibidem*.

State has not fulfilled its obligation to investigate, try and punish those responsible, the Inter-American Court broadened the array of possible violations, indicating the following as conduct constituting inhuman or cruel treatment: threats and harassment suffered by the relatives from the start of the investigation into the extrajudicial execution of Myrna Mack Chang, aggravated "by the pattern of obstruction of the aforementioned investigations, the murder of a police investigator, the threats and harassment suffered by some of the legal operators, policemen, and witnesses, which forced them into exile". It adds one other element: that the obstructions took place over a considerable period of time.

These acts caused the relatives of the victims to experience constant anguish, feelings of frustration and impotence, and profound fear of being exposed to the same pattern of violence imposed by the State, constituting a violation of their mental and moral integrity.[51]

22. In the case of Maritza Urrutia, the Inter-American Court found a violation of Article 5 of the Convention for a variety of types of conduct by State agents, including "hooding" of the victim, the use of noise to prevent the victim from sleeping, and the threatening of the victim with physical torture and with death for her and members of her family.[52] However, later on it used the same facts to weigh up whether Article 2 of Inter-American Convention on Torture, which defines torture, had also been violated, concluding that "the acts alleged in this case were prepared and inflicted deliberately to obliterate the victim's personality and demoralize her, which constitutes a form of mental torture", in violation of Articles 5(1) and 5(2) of the American Convention on Human Rights and Articles 1 and 6 of the Inter-American Convention on Torture.[53]

23. In the case of Velásquez Rodríguez, its first contentious case, the Inter-American Court made a contribution to the extension of the interpretation of Article 5(2) of the Convention by introducing the idea that subjecting a person to the danger of being mistreated constitutes in and of itself a violation of Article 5 of the Convention, as it violates the obligation to ensure found in Article 1(1) of the Convention because

> although it has not been directly shown that Manfredo Velásquez was physically tortured, his kidnapping and imprisonment by governmental authorities, who have been shown to subject detainees to indignities, cruelty and torture, constitute a

---

51 *Case of Myrna Mack Chang*, para. 232. The Court cited therein the cases of *Juan Humberto Sánchez*, para. 101, *Bámaca Velásquez*, paras. 160 and 162, and *Blake*, para. 114. It also cited a judgment of the European Court of Human Rights, *Kurt v. Turkey*, judgment of 25 May 1998, in *Reports of Judgments and Decisions 1998-III*, paras. 130–134.

52 *Case of Maritza Urrutia*, paras. 85–88.

53 *Ibidem*, paras. 89–98.

> failure of Honduras to fulfill the duty imposed by Article 1(1) to ensure the rights under Article 5(1) and 5(2) of the Convention.[54]

This position of the Court coincides with what it has found with regard to disappearances, and is complemented by what it found later in the case of Cantoral Benavides, where, using European case law and the case law of the Human Rights Committee, it found that the mere danger of being subjected to any of the conduct prohibited by Article 3 of the European Convention on Human Rights can constitute torture, as long as the risk at issue is real and immediate.[55] It also held that "to threaten someone with torture" can also constitute torture.[56]

24. As can be noted, the case law is not clear on whether the Court finds it advisable to differentiate between different types of conduct, nor on the precise elements it considers in arriving at its conclusions when it does in fact differentiate. For this reason, the Court's definitive position is expressed in its judgment in Cantoral Benavides: "regardless of the nature of the acts referred to, they are strictly prohibited under international human rights law". This seems to be the most appropriate position.

3.2. PROHIBITED CONDUCT AND THE RIGHT TO LIFE

25. Based on the principle of specialization, the Court has found that a violation of the right to life does not in and of itself entail a violation of personal integrity, as the taking of any life inevitably involves physical suffering and anguish.[57] However, in the case of Villagrán Morales *et al.*, the Court ruled that a violation of Article 5 of the Convention can be assumed due to the fact that the young victims of the illegal detention "were isolated from the external world and certainly aware that their lives were in danger. It is reasonable to infer that, merely owing to this circumstance, they experienced extreme psychological and moral suffering during those hours."[58]

This is a different way of approaching the effects of illegal detention with regard to Article 5 of the Convention, linking it this time to the idea of impending death. However, it does not appear to be settled case law of the Inter-American Court.[59]

---

54 *Case of Velásquez Rodríguez*, para. 187.

55 See Chapter 2.

56 *Case of Cantoral Benavides*, para. 102.

57 *Case of Neira Alegría et al.*, para. 86; *Case of Durand and Ugarte*, paras. 78–80.

58 *Case of Villagrán Morales et al.*, paras. 163–164.

59 See *Case of Neira Alegría et al.*, para. 86, and *Case of Durand and Ugarte*, paras. 75–80, the latter including a dissenting opinion from Judge de Roux Rengifo.

3.3. PROHIBITED CONDUCT AND PERSONAL FREEDOM

26. The Inter-American Court has also linked the right to humane treatment with another right in the Convention, that of Article 7, given that Article 5 and its paragraphs 2 and 4 include the effects of deprivation of liberty as possible infractions to the detriment of personal integrity, introducing the right of all persons deprived of liberty tobe treated "with respect for the inherent dignity of the human person". It should be noted that the Convention uses the expression "deprived of liberty" and not the word "detention".

This implies that whatever form deprivation of liberty takes, whether detention (according to the meaning given to the word in the criminal procedural law of many of the countries on the continent), internment in a psychiatric hospital, or deprivation of liberty of any other kind, the rule found in paragraph 2 of Article 5 of the Convention is always applicable.

If a person deprived of liberty has the right to be treated with respect for his or her dignity, it follows that the person has, in principle, the right to exercise and enjoy all human rights, unless some of them are limited as the inevitable result of that person's situation. Thus, deprivation of liberty does not necessarily bring with it absolute restrictions on the right to, for example, maintain correspondence with people on the outside, have one's privacy respected, or be able to express one's religion. Certainly the right not to be discriminated against is also in force for those deprived of liberty.[60]

27. The deprivation of a person's liberty generates obligations for the State as regards the protection of that person's integrity. In a number of judgments, the Inter-American Court has found that the State has a responsibility and duty to guarantee the personal integrity of the individual while that individual is being held in custody.[61] In the case of Juan Humberto Sánchez, the victim was detained, and his body appeared later bearing clear indications of torture. In the judgment handed down in that case, the Inter-American Court established that if a person is in normal physical condition when detained, it is up to the State to provide a reasonable explanation for why marks of torture are found on the person's body following the detention.[62] In the case of Bulacio, it was the State

60 See in this sense, *Case of Hilaire, Constantine and Benjamin, et al.*, concurring opinion of Judge Sergio García Ramírez, para. 18, in which, based on the position of the Court to the effect that the State is the guarantor of the rights of the detained (*Case of Neira Alegría et al.*, para. 60), he argues that this function implies "omitting everything that could inflict deprivations beyond what is strictly necessary for the purposes of detention or the serving of the sentence"; and the concurring opinion of the same judge, para. 24, in the *Case of Bulacio.*

61 *Case of Neira Alegría et al.*, para. 60; *Case of Cantoral Benavides*, para. 87; *Case of Hilaire, Constantine and Benjamin, et al.*, para. 165.

62 *Case of Juan Humberto Sánchez,* para. 100. A similar position is taken in the *Case of Bulacio*, both in the judgment, para. 138, and in paras. 22–25 of the separate concurring opinion of Judge Sergio García Ramírez.

itself that recognized its responsibility for having failed to "appropriately exercise the duty of custody".[63]

28. The Inter-American Court has scrutinized detention conditions when ruling on their compatibility with Article 5 of the Convention. In the case of Loayza Tamayo, the Court lists treatment that should be prohibited, including public display in humiliating clothing via the media, restrictions on visitation, and isolation in a small cell without ventilation or natural light.[64] In contrast, the Court did not consider refusing to allow a detainee to be attended by a physician of his or her choice and requiring the detainee to receive medical attention in a military hospital, based on a decision of the authorities, to be a violation of Article 5(2) of the Convention.[65] This is not the case when what is alleged is deficient medical care, as that would indeed be a violation of the article in question.[66]

The Inter-American Court had already ruled in its first judgment on the merits – the case of Velásquez Rodríguez – that "the mere subjection of an individual to prolonged isolation and deprivation of communication is in itself cruel and inhuman treatment which harms the psychological and moral integrity of the person, and violates the right of every detainee [...] to treatment respectful of his dignity."[67] Other cases in which forms of solitary confinement in inhuman conditions and/or for prolonged periods of time are found to constitute a violation are those of Suárez Rosero, Castillo Petruzzi, and Hilaire, Constantine and Benjamin, *et al.*[68] In Suárez Rosero, another form of suffering emerged provoked by this kind of solitary confinement: that of being prevented from seeking a lawyer or communicating with family.[69]

In Hilaire *et al.*, the Inter-American Court found that the fact that the detainees were under constant threat of being hung at any moment constituted a violation of Article 5 of the Convention. The Court cited the case law of the European Court of Human Rights on "death row".[70]

---

63 *Case of Bulacio*, paras. 32–33 and 38(c).

64 *Case of Loayza Tamayo*, para. 58.

65 *Case of Cesti Hurtado*, paras. 153–160.

66 *Case of Bulacio*, para. 131.

67 *Case of Velásquez Rodríguez*, para. 187. Other rulings of the Court in which it finds likewise include: *Case of Suárez Rosero*, para. 91; *Case of Loayza Tamayo*, para. 57; *Case of Castillo Petruzzi et al.*, paras. 192–194; *Case of the Street Children (Villagrán Morales et al.)*, paras. 163–164; and *Case of Cantoral Benavides*, paras. 180–191. The Court departed from this ruling only in the *case of Caballero Delgado and Santana* – also on a disappearance – in which it found that Article 5 had not been violated "as in its judgment there is not sufficient evidence that the detainees were tortured or subjected to mistreatment" (*Case of Caballero Delgado and Santana*, para. 65).

68 *Case of Suárez Rosero*, paras. 90–91; *Case of Castillo Petruzzi et al.*, paras. 192–194; *Case of Hilaire, Constantine and Benjamin, et al.*, para. 164.

69 *Case of Suárez Rosero*, para. 91.

70 *Case of Hilaire, Constantine and Benjamin, et al.*, paras. 167–169.

29. In addition to treatment related to detention conditions, the Court has put forward the idea that subjecting a person to an illegal detention places that person in an "exacerbated situation of vulnerability creating a real risk that his other rights, such as the right to humane treatment and to be treated with dignity, will be violated",[71] constituting a violation of Article 5 of the Convention. It could thus be understood from this that if a detention is illegal, other cruel or inhuman treatment is not necessary for the Court to conclude that this article has been violated. This interpretation is honed by the recent position of the Inter-American Court in the case of Juan Humberto Sánchez. That judgment establishes that a short period of time in illegal detention is enough for a violation of the mental and moral integrity of the victim to have taken place.[72] The judgment in this case modifies the ruling handed down in the case of Gangaram Panday, in which the Inter-American Court did not assign responsibility to the State for the violation of his personal integrity despite having established a violation of Article 7 of the Convention on the illegality of Gangaram Panday's detention.[73]

The Court has not had the opportunity to rule on other ways of violating this provision that have a direct relationship with other rights found in the Convention. It is possible that when faced with a case of this kind, it would use the general rules designed for the universal system, such as the Body of Principles for the Protection of All Persons under Any Form of Detention or Imprisonment.[74]

3.4. PROHIBITED CONDUCT AND RELATIVES OF CERTAIN HUMAN RIGHTS VICTIMS

30. The prohibition on violating the right to life and/or physical and moral integrity of persons has also led the Inter-American Court to develop in its case law the status of victim for relatives of victims of certain kinds of human rights violations, although this classification has not been applied in all cases. The first judgment recognizing this was in the case of Blake, where the Court found that Guatemala had violated Article 5 of the Convention with regard to the relatives of Mr Blake, whose lives had been seriously altered by the disappearance of their relative.

This fact had caused them "suffering and anguish, in addition to a sense of insecurity, frustration and impotence in the face of the public authorities' failure to investigate".[75] The Court also found that incineration of Mr Blake's mortal

---

71 *Case of the Street Children (Villagrán Morales et al.)*, para. 166; *Case of Bulacio*, para. 127.
72 *Case of Juan Humberto Sánchez*, para. 98.
73 *Case of Gangaram Panday*, paras. 51 and 57–62.
74 This instrument was adopted by the General Assembly in Resolution 43/173, 9 December 1988.
75 *Case of Blake*, paras. 113–114.

remains, done in order to destroy any trace of them, was an attack on Guatemalan society's prevailing cultural values and had likewise contributed to an intensification of the family's suffering.[76]

In the case of Villagrán Morales *et al.*, the facts constituting a violation of Article 5 of the Convention to the detriment of the relatives of the victim were: lack of provisions for establishing the victims' identities; the negligence of the authorities in locating the immediate family of the victims in order to notify them of their deaths, turn over the remains, and keep them informed of any developments in the investigations (which in reality were never carried out); and the abandonment of the bodies in an uninhabited area, leaving them exposed to the elements and the activities of animals.[77]

In the case of Cantoral Benavides, the Commission alleged that Mr Cantoral's mother "suffered cruel, inhumane and degrading treatment from the Peruvian authorities, and alluded to the 'pain, humiliation, helplessness, uncertainty and frustration she felt as a result of the deceit and mistreatment' she was subjected to when she asked about her detained sons and when she visited them in jail". It also argued that the victim's brother had been directly subjected to torture and cruel, inhuman and degrading treatment. As a consequence of this, the Commission asked the Court to find Peru to have violated Article 5(2) of the Convention to the detriment of Mrs Benavides de Cantoral and of Luis Fernando Cantoral Benavides.[78] The Court recognized in paragraph 105 of the judgment that the detention and imprisonment of the victim had caused suffering and severe anguish for these relatives and that this would be taken into account when determining the corresponding reparation. Despite having recognized them as beneficiaries of the reparation, and in contrast to what it had ruled in the case of Villagrán Morales and in other cases, the Court did not rule that Peru had violated Article 5 of the Convention with regard to these two people, but rather solely with regard to the victim in the case, Luis Alberto Cantoral Benavides.[79]

In the case of Bámaca Velásquez, it found that the lack of respect for the mortal remains of the family member constituted a failure to comply with the obligation to respect the human dignity of next of kin, aggravated by the fact that the treatment of those remains violated the Mayan culture to which the victim belonged.[80]

In this last case, and in the context of a forced disappearance, the Court delved more deeply into the circumstances under which the relatives of a person whose human rights have been violated could be considered for their own part as victims of a violation of Article 5 of the Convention. Using the case

---

76 *Ibidem*, paras. 115.

77 *Case of the Street Children (Villagrán Morales et al.)*, paras. 173–174.

78 *Case of Cantoral Benavides*, para. 78(e).

79 *Ibidem*, paras. 106 and 198, point 1.

80 *Case of Bámaca Velásquez, judgment on reparations*, para. 81.

law of the European Court of Human Rights, it found that when a person's fundamental rights are violated, including the right to life or the right to physical integrity, those closest to that person also become victims, adding that in order to decide who should be considered to belong in that category, it was necessary to examine "the closeness of the family relationship, the particular circumstances of the relationship with the victim, the degree to which the family member was a witness of the events related to the disappearance, the way in which the family member was involved in attempts to obtain information about the disappearance of the victim and the State's response to the steps undertaken."[81]

In the case of Myrna Mack Chang, the Inter-American Court reiterated its position that the relatives of the victims of human rights violations can for their own part be considered victims,[82] even when the violation of Article 5 of the Convention found in that case was based also on actions directly aimed at the relatives, including threats, surveillance, harassment and intimidation.[83]

In the case of Maritza Urrutia, the representatives of the alleged victim argued in their brief of final arguments that the victim's son had himself been the victim of a violation of Article 19 of the Convention and connected this violation with the suffering that he had experienced as a result of what happened to his mother. Although the Inter-American Court found that the allegation was time-barred, it recognized that the kidnapping and detention of his mother caused the son suffering and anguish, which would be taken into account when establishing the pertinent reparations.[84] With this, he was not considered a victim but the beneficiary of reparations.

Thus the Court has established case law to the effect that third parties can be victims of a violation of Article 5 of the Convention as a consequence of a violation of the rights of another person, although the specific characteristics of these situations are difficult to pin down based only on the judgments reviewed. I think it is important to indicate, however, that these victims are in reality direct victims and not indirect victims, as what is examined is the effect that a violation of another person's rights has on their personal integrity. Case law has settled on the standards for deciding which third parties can be considered victims of a violation of the rights of a person, whom we could consider the principal victim. As far as the reasoning that these third parties can invoke for the basis of a violation of Article 5 of the Convention with regard to them, the case law seems settled that when the Court finds a violation of that article, it does so with regard

---

81 *Case of Bámaca Velásquez*, paras. 162–163. The European case law cited by the Court is: ECtHR, *Kurt v. Turkey*, judgment of 25 May 1998, Reports of Judgments and Decisions 1998-III, paras. 130–134; *Timurtas v. Turkey*, judgment of 13 June 2000, para. 95; and *Cakici v. Turkey*, judgment of 8 July 1999, para. 98.

82 *Case of Myrna Mack Chang*, para. 225.

83 *Ibidem*, paras. 226–233.

84 *Case of Maritza Urrutia*, paras. 140 and 145.

to those closest in cases of disappearance[85] and summary execution. An unequivocal standard has not yet been defined allowing for the clear identification of violations that can result in a level of suffering sufficient for the Court to find that these third parties have been subjected to treatment prohibited by Article 5 of the Convention, although one can infer that the violation with regard to the principal victim must always be related to Articles 4 and 5 of the American Convention. In addition, it should be noted that, in a juridical construct that is difficult to understand, a situation has been created in which the Court names relatives who are not considered victims of a violation of a right set forth in the Convention as beneficiaries of reparations.

3.5. SUMMARY

31. An examination of the Inter-American Court's case law illustrates, on one hand, the wide gamut of conduct that violates the prohibition found in Article 5(2) of the Convention and, on the other, the impossibility of finding elements to differentiate among the different types of prohibited conduct. In reality, attempts to make these distinctions do not seem necessary, as reparations – which is where the distinction could make a difference – are decided on by the Court based on a diligent examination of the facts of the case and their consequences for the victims.

4. THE INTER-AMERICAN CONVENTION ON TORTURE AND THE COURT

4.1. THE INTER-AMERICAN CONVENTION ON TORTURE

32. The American Convention on Human Rights is not the only inter-American treaty establishing a prohibition on torture and cruel, inhuman or degrading punishment or treatment. As mentioned previously, subsequent to the American Convention, in 1985 the Inter-American Convention on Torture was adopted. Despite its name, this Convention contains provisions that address other prohibited conduct. As there are two treaties addressing the same subject and it is difficult to imagine that they are not related to each other and cannot reciprocally influence each other, it is necessary to examine the relationship that could exist between them, both to see whether the Inter-American Court should or could apply the definition of torture found in Article 2 of the Inter-American Convention on Torture to cases of torture brought before its jurisdiction and in

[85] See, in the same sense see, the ruling of the HRC in *Quinteros v. Uruguay*, of 21 July 1983, Communication No. 107/1981, also cited in the judgment in the *case of Bámaca Velásquez*.

the cases in which the violation of Article 5 of the American Convention on Human Rights is invoked, as well as to analyze whether the obligations of States Parties to the American Convention are affected by other provisions, such as those of Articles 6 and 8 of the Inter-American Convention on Torture

Another reason for this examination is that despite the fact that this Convention does not contain a clear and explicit provision granting jurisdiction to the Inter-American Court to hear cases in which a violation has been alleged, the Court has applied it in some of the cases brought before its jurisdiction. An analysis of this application can help the reader answer a number of questions that arise on the relationship between the Inter-American Convention on Torture and the American Convention: (i) does the Court have jurisdiction to apply the Inter-American Convention on Torture in the cases before it; (ii) does the application of this treaty depend on whether the State being accused is also party to this treaty; and (iii) may the Court use the Inter-American Convention on Torture as an element for interpreting State obligations under Article 5(2) of the American Convention on Human Rights even when the State against which the case has been presented is not part of the former Convention?

33. To start with, it should be noted that the Inter-American Convention on Torture does not replace Article 5 of the American Convention on Human Rights but rather complements it, given that in its Article 16 it establishes that "[t]his Convention shall not limit the provisions of the American Convention on Human Rights, other conventions on the subject, or the Statutes of the Inter-American Commission on Human Rights, with respect to the crime of torture." In addition, in its Preamble it establishes a link with the American Convention on Human Rights by indicating that States that adopt the Convention are "[a]ware of the provision of the American Convention on Human Rights that no one shall be subjected to torture or to cruel, inhuman, or degrading punishment or treatment." This link also extends to the OAS Charter, the United Nations Charter, the American Declaration of the Rights and Duties of Man and the Universal Declaration of Human Rights. The States also indicate that "in order for the pertinent rules contained in the aforementioned global and regional instruments to take effect, it is necessary to draft an Inter-American Convention that prevents and punishes torture." It thus appears evident that the intent of the States that approved this Convention was to use this new treaty to make the provisions on torture established in the American Convention on Human Rights – among other instruments – more effective.

34. The State obligations to prevent and punish torture and other cruel, inhuman or degrading treatment or punishment are established in Article 1 of the Inter-American Convention on Torture and developed in several provisions, the majority of which only make reference to torture.[86] Torture must be a criminal offense and States must take other measures with regard to other prohibited conduct (Article 6); police officers and others responsible for the custody of persons deprived of liberty must receive training in order to ensure proper treatment (Article 7); State authorities must, either on the petition of a party or *ex officio*, carry out an investigation and launch the corresponding criminal proceedings where appropriate (Article 8); domestic regulations on reparations must be in place (Article 9); extradition of an alleged or demonstrated torturer must be granted (Article 11), or, failing that, the State must investigate the torturer and, where appropriate, launch the corresponding criminal proceeding (Article 14); and States must establish their jurisdiction over the crime in accordance with specific rules (Article 12).

35. Once domestic remedies have been exhausted, the Inter-American Convention on Torture also authorizes a case of torture to be brought before "the international fora whose competence has been recognized by that State" (Article 8(3)). In addition, it establishes explicitly that nothing in the Convention can be interpreted in a way that limits the right to asylum or modifies the obligations of States parties with regard to extradition (Article 15).

The Inter-American Commission on Human Rights is empowered to monitor compliance with the Convention by studying the reports that States must send it on the legislative, judicial, administrative and other measures they have adopted in applying the provisions of the Convention and will examine the situation of torture not only in States parties to the Convention but also in all OAS Member States (Article 17).

4.2. APPLICATION OF THIS CONVENTION BY THE INTER-AMERICAN COURT

36. The Court has applied the Inter-American Convention on Torture in only some of the cases brought before it. In the case of Loayza Tamayo, for example, it did not apply it even though Peru has been party to the Convention since 1991 and even though the proven facts of the case demonstrated that in addition to being subjected to detention conditions not compatible with international rules, the victim was subjected to beatings and "maltreatment, including total immersion in water, intimidation with threats of further violence".[87]

37. The Court applied the Inter-American Convention on Torture for the first time in the case of Paniagua Morales *et al.* The Commission asked the Court to

86 The provisions of the Inter-American Convention on Torture that regulate aspects of cruel, inhuman or degrading treatment or punishment are contained in Articles 6, 7, 13, 14, 15 and 17.

87 Regarding extradition, also see the provisions of Article 13 of the Convention on Torture.

find that Guatemala had violated Article 5 of the American Convention on Human Rights as well as the obligations established in Articles 1, 6 and 8 of the Inter-American Convention on Torture. It argued on one hand that Guatemala had not investigated the torture inflicted on the victims as required by Article 8 of the latter Convention,[88] while on the other hand it indicated that almost all the victims have been subjected to "intentional acts that produced pain and physical and mental suffering in order to intimidate and punish them",[89] fitting the definition of torture found in Article 2 of that Convention.

The Court examined possible violations of Articles 1, 6 and 8 as raised by the Commission in the section on the violation of Article 5 of the American Convention on Human Rights, mentioning only this latter provision in the section's heading. This could indicate either a certain reticence toward applying it directly or the idea that it is complementary to Article 5 of the American Convention on Human Rights. The Court did not use the definition of torture found in Article 2 of the Inter-American Convention on Torture, and nor did it invoke that article in ruling that the torture of the victims who later had their lives taken had been proven irrefutably, with that torture including being tied up, beatings, and "stab wounds to the neck and thorax, which increased their suffering [... I]n some cases they were even decapitated."[90] The Court concluded that Guatemala had violated Articles 5(1) and 5(2) of the American Convention on Human Rights and the obligations found in Articles 1, 6 and 8 of the Inter-American Convention on Torture;[91] that is, the judgment directly applied the obligations derived from the latter Convention, but not its definition of torture. Curiously, it also applied Article 8, which refers only to torture, to both victims of the conduct classified by the Court as torture and to two of the victims of violations classified in the judgment as cruel, inhuman or degrading treatment.[92]

38. In the second case, Villagrán Morales *et al.*, the Court decided to go one step further. Along with explicitly affirming its jurisdiction to apply the Inter-American Convention on Torture, it dedicated a section exclusively to examining possible violations of Articles 1, 6 and 8 of that Convention and concluded that the State (Guatemala) had violated these provisions with actions that were subject to international adjudication.[93] As regards its jurisdiction, based on the Report of the Committee on Political and Juridical Affairs on the draft Convention, it held that:

> As some member countries of the Organization of American States were still not parties to the American Convention and had not accepted the jurisdiction of the

[88] *Case of Loayza Tamayo,* paras. 57–58.

[89] *Case of the "White Van" (Paniagua Morales et al.),* paras. 126 and 130.

[90] *Ibidem*, para. 129.

[91] *Ibidem*, para. 134.

[92] *Ibidem*, para. 136.

[93] From a substantive point of view, the Court could also have turned to its general case law on the obligation to ensure to reach the same conclusion that the State must investigate, try and punish.

> Court, the drafters of the Convention against Torture decided not to include in it an article that made express and exclusive reference to the Inter-American Court in order not to indirectly bind them to the former Convention and the aforementioned jurisdictional organ.[94]

At this time, it added that what was important was to attribute jurisdiction or the application of the Inter-American Convention on Torture to an international body, present or future, and that as this case was before the Inter-American Court, it was the Court's responsibility to exercise jurisdiction.[95] It would have helped to clarify this point if the Court had explicitly stated the legal basis for this position, which surely is Article 8 of the Inter-American Convention on Torture, where it establishes that once domestic remedies are exhausted, the case can be submitted to "the international fora whose competence has been recognized by that State". The Inter-American Court should have then interpreted this provision to find a basis in the Convention for exercising this jurisdiction. In order to do so, a plausible argument could have perhaps been that through this provision, the States Parties were granting broad rather than specific jurisdiction to hear violations of compliance with the Inter-American Convention on Torture.

39. In the case of Cantoral Benavides, the Court again dedicated a special section to examining compliance with the Inter-American Convention on Torture, concluding that Peru had violated Articles 2, 6 and 8 of that Convention by having failed to carry out an investigation into the acts of torture proven during the trial.[96] In that judgment, the Court directly established a violation of Article 2, which defines torture, despite the fact that when it examined the State's conduct according to Article 5(2) of the American Convention on Human Rights, it is not guided exclusively by that definition.[97] This means that the Court analyzes the facts under Article 5(2) of the American Convention on Human Rights, where the definition of Article 2 of the Inter-American Convention on Torture is but one of several that it uses to conclude that torture was committed and limits itself in section XVI to finding a violation of only this latter provision. This solution does not appear to be the most appropriate and may present an obstacle to more extensive use of the Inter-American Convention on Torture in the future.

40. In the judgment handed down in the case of Bámaca Velásquez, the Court again examined the existence of torture, turning to the two conventions that are in force on the subject – the United Nations Convention on Torture and the Inter-American Convention on Torture – and dedicates another section, section XVIII, to examining possible violations of Articles 1, 2, 6 and 8 of the Inter-

---

94 *Case of the Street Children (Villagrán Morales et al.)*, paras. 239–252.

95 *Ibidem*, paras. 247–248.

96 *Case of Cantoral Benavides*, paras. 180–191.

97 *Ibidem*, paras. 95–106.

American Convention. This latter section reproduces the Inter-American Commission's argument according to which that Convention "develops the principles contained in Article 5 of the American Convention in greater detail and, therefore, constitutes an auxiliary instrument to the Convention", noting that Guatemala had ratified that Convention in 1989, that is, on a date prior to the date on which the facts of the case took place.[98] The Inter-American Court did not rule on this argument, but concluded that as torture had been proven and Guatemala had not immediately moved *ex officio* to carry out an investigation and punish those guilty, the State had failed to comply with its obligation to prevent and punish torture, under the terms of Articles 1, 2, 6 and 8 of the Inter-American Convention on Torture.[99]

41. A joint analysis of this case law leads to several conclusions. First, one can argue that the Court has applied Articles 1, 6 and 8 of the Inter-American Convention on Torture directly to those States party to it. Although there is no indication that this is because the States in question were parties to that Convention, it is clear that there is no other implicit reason that would allow the Court to rule that a State has violated the obligations of a treaty which does not concern it. This being the case, it seems strange that the Court does not, along with finding States responsible for failing to comply with their obligations under that Convention, base its ruling on the facts of the case that constitute torture under the terms of Article 2 of that Convention. The Court has not been clear on the role that Convention plays in its judgments. It is perfectly possible that it used it as an auxiliary means of interpreting Article 5 of the American Convention on Human Rights, but in that case the wording of its considering paragraphs and conclusions should have been different.[100] It is also possible that even when that Convention is not invoked in a case, whether by the victim or during the proceedings before the Commission, the Court can invoke it by applying the principle of *iura novit curiæ*.[101]

42. With regard to the States that are not party to the Inter-American Convention on Torture, it is also possible to think that insofar as its provisions align with the provisions of the American Convention on Human Rights, and lines of interpretation are made explicit that have begun to be developed through

98 *Case of Bámaca Velásquez*, para. 215(a).

99 *Ibidem*, paras. 220–223.

100 The Court makes this criteria explicit in another judgment where it states that: "Although the Court has broad authority to hear human rights violations, they must address the rights protected by the Convention, except for cases in which an international instrument ratified by the State grants jurisdiction to weigh violations of rights protected by that same instrument", mentioning that it has acted thusly in the cases of *Bámaca Velásquez*, *Cantoral Benavides*, *Villagrán Morales et al.*, and *Paniagua Morales et al.* (all cited in the *case of Baena Ricardo et al.*, para. 97).

101 *Case of the "Five Pensioners"*, paras. 153–155; *Case of Myrna Mack Chang*, para. 224.

case law, the Court will use the former Convention as an auxiliary means of interpretation.[102] The Court's reaction in the case of Bámaca Velásquez (in which, without directly taking up the Commission's argument to the effect that the Inter-American Convention on Torture was an auxiliary instrument for the interpretation of Article 5 of the American Convention on Human Rights, the Court used the facts invoked by the Commission along with this argument to rule that the Inter-American Convention on Torture was not complied with in that particular case) can lead to the conclusion that when faced with a case against a State that is not party to the Inter-American Convention on Torture, the Court would be willing to use not only the definition but also the obligations established therein for the interpretation of provisions on torture and other cruel, inhuman or degrading punishment or treatments established in the American Convention on Human Rights. This action could be based on the fact that the system for the protection of human rights is an integrated whole that allows for the use of the development of the corresponding human rights in any other international treaty or any other case law, whether domestic or international, for the interpretation of any of its rules.[103]

43. Without prejudice to these conclusions, the Inter-American Court has yet to further refine its analysis in its cases in order to put an end to these incongruities and advance regulation of this State duty, a duty that is so essential that the Court itself has found that currently, "a true international system prohibiting all forms of torture has been put in place".[104]

5. SCOPE AND CONTENT OF PROTECTION FROM PROHIBITED CONDUCT

44. The obligations derived from the prohibition on torture found in Article 5(2) of the American Convention on Human Rights can be deduced from a careful reading of that article, together with a reading of Article 1(1) of the Convention, all in light of the development of the inter-American system's case law. The States Parties to the American Convention must respect and ensure the right of all persons to not be subjected to torture or cruel, inhuman or degrading treatment or punishment at the hands of both agents of the State and private parties. The obligation to guarantee implies the existence of positive State

[102] For example, see the considering paragraphs in the judgment handed down in the *case of Villagrán Morales* in relation to the Convention on the Rights of the Child; see *Case of the Street Children (Villagrán Morales et al.)*, paras. 192–196.

[103] On this idea, see C. Medina and C. Nash, "Manual de Derecho Internacional de los Derechos Humanos para Defensores Públicos. Sección doctrina", in *Documentos Oficiales*, Centro de Documentación Defensoría Penal Pública, no. 1, December 2003, pp. 40–41.

[104] *Case of Cantoral Benavides*, para. 103.

obligations – to prevent, to regulate (that is, investigate, try and punish), and to provide reparations for violations that have taken place – that are similar to the ones the State has with regard to the right to life and are based on the same case law examined in the previous chapter. This case law has often been repeated for both types of violations, and when it has referred only to the right to life, it can be applicable *mutatis mutandi* to the prohibition of certain conduct that infringes on the right to humane treatment.

This chapter will only analyze aspects of these obligations that are specific to this latter right and particularly the contribution made by the Inter-American Convention on Torture to the interpretation of these obligations, as, according to what we have looked at so far, it can be concluded that the obligations on torture under Article 5(2) of the American Convention on Human Rights are clarified and made more specific and precise by some of the provisions of the former Convention. These more comprehensive formulations can be applied directly to States Parties to that Convention, or to States that are not party to the Convention, by using Article 1(1) of the American Convention on Human Rights as a means for interpreting it, read jointly with the prohibition on torture and other cruel, inhuman or degrading punishments or treatments found in Article 5.

5.1. PROTECTION THROUGH PREVENTATIVE MEASURES

45. The State must prevent the perpetration of conduct prohibited by Article 5(2) of the American Convention on Human Rights committed by both State agents and private parties. In order to prevent the acts of private parties, the State must establish deterrents, which in the case of torture would consist of its being qualified as a crime. Article 6 of the Inter-American Convention on Torture requires this by instructing States that they must ensure that all acts of torture and attempts to commit those acts constitute a crime under criminal law, with punishments whose severity matches the gravity of these acts. As indicated previously, the Court has applied this obligation in its case law.[105]

Regarding cruel, inhuman or degrading treatment, it is possible that not all of it can be classified as criminal, although in any case it must be prohibited by law. In addition, just as it is necessary to strictly regulate statutes on legitimate self-defense in order to prevent violations of the right to life, here also it is necessary to consider the requirements of proportionality and necessity demanded for conduct affecting personal integrity in order for it to not constitute a violation. Classification as a criminal offense, as well as the prohibition of the conduct, must be accompanied by pertinent procedural regulations that allow for court supervision of compliance with the obligations.

105 See section 5, *supra*.

46. It seems clear that as with the right to life, it is the responsibility of the State to prevent possible violations of the right to humane treatment at the hands of its own agents, and that this implies establishing regulations for the use of force, the teaching of these regulations to the officials authorized to exercise force, and existence of mechanisms for overseeing compliance with these regulations. The Inter-American Court has also ruled on these points.[106]

The State must take particular care to train the officials in charge of persons who are deprived of liberty, who for that sole reason are in a situation of great vulnerability. Initially, the Inter-American Court did not assign to States the responsibility for the integrity of those detained: in the case of Gangaram Panday, the violation of Article 5 of the American Convention on Human Rights because of the victim's having committed suicide while being subjected to an illegal detention was only mentioned by three judges who, in a dissenting opinion, argued that a State that has carried out an illegal detention must be responsible for its consequences.[107] However in later cases, the Court has followed the European Court of Human Rights by presuming that the State is responsible "for ill-treatment exhibited by a person who has been in the custody of State agents, if the authorities are incapable of demonstrating that those agents did not incur in such behavior."[108]

In the case of Suárez Rosero, the victim asked the Court during the reparations stage to order the State to adopt measures to prevent the repetition of the violations in the future, including human rights training for law enforcement officials. For its part, the Inter-American Commission said that "the promulgation of laws, regulations, instructions or orders for preventing prolonged detention under conditions of isolation is necessary, as is the adoption of measures necessary for respecting judicial guarantees."[109] In answering these petitions, the Court reiterated what it had found in its judgment on the merits, in the sense that Ecuador was required to ensure the non-repetition of violations by virtue of the general duties to respect rights and adopt domestic legal provisions, obligations established in Articles 1(1) and 2 of the American Convention on Human Rights.[110] Although Ecuador was not party to the Inter-American Convention on Torture as of the time of the facts, the Court could have based its argument for constructing the obligations emerging from Article 5, read jointly with Article 1(1) of the American Convention on Human Rights, on Article 7 of

106 See Chapter 2; specifically, see *Case of Suárez Rosero, judgment on reparations*, para. 84.

107 *Case of Gangaram Panday*, dissenting opinion of Judges Picado Sotela, Aguilar-Aranguren and Cançado Trindade, para. 2.

108 *Case of the Street Children (Villagrán Morales et al.)*, para. 170. The case law of the European Court of Human Rights cited in this judgment is: ECtHR, *Aksoy v. Turkey*, judgment of 18 December 1996, p. 2278, §61; ECtHR, *Ribitsch v. Austria*, judgment of 4 December 1995, Series A, no. 336, p. 26 ff, §34; and ECtHR, *Tomasi v. France*, judgment of 27 August 1992, Series A, no. 241-A, pp. 40–41, §§108–111.

109 *Case of Suárez Rosero*, para. 84.

110 *Ibidem*, para. 87.

the Inter-American Convention on Torture, which obliges States to take measures to emphasize prohibiting the use of torture when training police agents and other public officials responsible for the custody of individuals deprived of liberty.

47. The punishments imposed on inmates must follow certain minimum principles established by the United Nations for the treatment of persons subjected to detention.[111] First of all, the following must be set forth by law or regulation in every country: the conduct that constitutes a disciplinary infraction; the type and length of disciplinary punishments that can be applied; and the authority with competence to rule on these sanctions.[112]

The principles on minimum standards establish the following: an inmate can only be punished in keeping with the requirements of the law or regulations and can never be punished twice for the same infraction; no inmate can be punished without having been informed of the infraction of which he or she is accused and without allowing the inmate to submit a defense beforehand; the competent authority will proceed to carry out a full examination of the case; and should it be necessary and viable, the inmate will be allowed to present his or her defense through an interpreter.[113] Finally, with regard to the punishments that can be applied to inmates, it establishes that the following punishments shall be completely prohibited: corporal punishment and imprisonment in a dark cell, as well as all cruel, inhuman or degrading punishments; punishments of isolation and reductions in rations shall be applied only when a physician has certified that an inmate can bear them after having examined that inmate; this is also applicable to all other punishments that can endanger the physical or mental health of the inmate: the physician will visit the inmates to whom those disciplinary punishments are being applied every day and will report to the director should he or she find it necessary to end or change the punishment for reasons of physical or mental health; measures of coercion such as handcuffs, chains, shackles and straitjackets shall never be applied as punishment.[114]

All this indicates that the State must comply with requirements both procedural and regarding the merits in establishing and applying punishments for individuals deprived of liberty. Among those requirements, I would highlight the need for a State body and proceedings to enforce compliance with the regulations established, as well as for a judge for the execution of punishments. In addition, it is possible that as the concept of torture or cruel, inhuman

---

111 Standard minimum rules for the treatment of prisoners. Adopted by the Economic and Social Council by its Resolutions 663C (XXIV) of 31 July 1957 and 2076 (LXII) of 13 May 1977.

112 *Ibidem*, para. 29.

113 *Ibidem*, para. 30. However, this minimum standard is subordinate to the standards of due process, which can in principle be applied to proceedings for the punishment of prisoners.

114 *Ibidem*, paras. 31–33.

or degrading treatment or punishment may change, so some of these basic principles that today establish the limits of what is permissible may also change.

48. A related subject is the need for authorities to establish effective mechanisms for supervising the physical and mental integrity of prisoners in those cases in which situations of violence or aggression among them arise. In relation to this, the Court has handed down provisional measures to Brazil,[115] instructing the State to take measures of protection with regard to the inmates of the Urso Branco prison, as some of the individuals under detention there were being subjected to serious attacks on their lives and personal integrity by groups inside the prison, and as the State has the

> responsibility to take security measures to protect the persons subject to its jurisdiction [...] This duty is more evident when it comes to individuals held in a State detention center, in which case the State is presumed to be responsible for what happens to persons in its custody.[116]

5.2. PROTECTION THROUGH MONITORING COMPLIANCE: THE OBLIGATION TO INVESTIGATE, TRY AND PUNISH

49. The obligation to investigate, try and punish those involved in actions prohibited under Article 5(2) of the American Convention on Human Rights has been developed by the Inter-American Court jointly with the obligations to guarantee the right to life. For this reason, the content of the previous chapter is applicable with regard to the right to humane treatment, without any changes. As noted therein, the obligation to investigate, try and punish the guilty parties should be exercised, according to the Court, *ex officio*; it constitutes a legal duty of the State, derived from the obligation to ensure, and does not depend on the activity of the victim or the victim's relatives for its compliance.[117] There was one older case in which the Court did not take this position: the case of Gangaram Panday. In its judgment in this case, the Court rejected the allegations that the victim had been subjected to torture and mistreatment, which petitioners attempted to prove through a video and expert witness reports, because the evidence was insufficient. It did so without informing the State that it was its duty to carry out a serious investigation into the facts as soon as the allegations were raised.[118]

---

115 I/A Court HR, *Case of the Urso Branco Prison*, Provisional Measures requested by the Inter-American Commission on Human Rights regarding the Federal Republic of Brazil, order of 18 June 2001.

116 *Ibidem*, para. 8.

117 See Chapter 2.

118 *Case of Gangaram Panday*, paras. 52–56.

50. In the cases in which the Court has used the Inter-American Convention on Torture, it has applied Article 8 of that Convention to develop the obligation to investigate, try and punish. In its pertinent part, Article 8 establishes for the State: (i) the obligation to ensure for the alleged victims their right for their case to be heard impartially; and (ii) the obligation to ensure that, given a complaint or well-founded reason to believe that an act of torture has been committed, its authorities must proceed *ex officio* to carry out an investigation and launch, where pertinent, the corresponding criminal proceedings.

In the case of Villagrán Morales *et al.*, the Court found that given that despite having collected "a great deal of concurring evidence [...] on the cruel treatment and torture of the victims when the homicides were investigated", the Guatemalan authorities had not taken "any formal decision to initiate a criminal investigation into the alleged perpetration of the crime of torture, neither did they investigate it in the practice", Guatemala had violated the aforementioned Article 8.[119] The case of Cantoral Benavides included similar reasoning.[120] In the case of Bámaca Velásquez, the Court employed the same reasoning, but it added an obligation for the State to disclose the investigation publicly.[121] Future cases will probably develop and/or confirm the jurisprudence on this matter.

5.3. IMPUNITY

51. Everything said about impunity with regard to violations of the right to life also applies to impunity of conduct prohibited by Article 5(2) of the American Convention on Human Rights.[122]

5.4. OBLIGATION TO PROVIDE REPARATIONS

52. The violation of the right to humane treatment generates an obligation for the State to provide reparations. As in the case of the right to life, money always forms part of the reparation. In the case of Cantoral Benavides, the Court established an amount of money that included, among other things, the payment of the victim's future medical expenses, expenses for transporting the family to visit him in prison, and medical expenses for treating the physical and psychological problems experienced by the mother and the brother of the victim.[123]

---

119 *Case of the Street Children (Villagrán Morales et al.),* paras. 250–252.

120 *Case of Cantoral Benavides*, paras. 188–190.

121 *Case of Bámaca Velásquez, judgment on reparations*, paras. 77 and 87.

122 See Chapter 2.

123 *Case of Cantoral Benavides, judgment on reparations*, para. 51.

In the case of Bámaca Velásquez, the Court established a joint reparation for all violations, and in setting its amount, took into consideration the need to ensure that the violations that took place do not happen again. The Court ruled that:

> Regarding the violation of the right to life and other rights (personal liberty and humane treatment, right to fair trial and to judicial protection), if *restitutio in integrum* is not possible and given the nature of the right infringed, reparation is made, *inter alia*, according to international case law and by means of just indemnification or monetary compensation, to which positive measures on the part of the State must be added to ensure that damaging acts such as the ones in this instant case do not take place again.[124]

The Court ordered the torture suffered by the victim and the effects of this treatment on his closest family member to be compensated monetarily. It issued the same order as regards the feelings of vulnerability and state of defenselessness these relatives faced due to the impunity that prevailed in the case. The wife, siblings and father of the victim benefited from this compensation.[125] The positive measures that can be included in the category of "satisfaction" must constitute, for example, the carrying out of acts or projects with public scope or impact to restore the memory of the victims, re-establish their dignity and comfort their next of kin, or the broadcasting of an official message expressing disapproval of the human rights violations that took place and commitment to make efforts toward ensuring they do not happen again.

6. THE BELÉM DO PARÁ CONVENTION AND ARTICLE 5 OF THE AMERICAN CONVENTION ON HUMAN RIGHTS

53. As can be noted, the violations of personal integrity examined by the Court have so far been the result of political violence and been executed with the clear participation of State agents. However, this does not mean that what was said in the above sections is valid only for those types of cases. According to the case law on the obligation to ensure, ever since the case of Velásquez Rodríguez it can be argued that the way the obligation has been developed also makes it applicable when the violence is perpetrated by private actors. This was discussed previously, where it was noted that in general, it is the responsibility of the State to prohibit illicit conduct that can be committed by private parties and to regulate compliance with that prohibition, incurring international responsibility should it not carry out these actions. It should be recalled that the Inter-American Court established in the judgment handed down in the case of Velásquez Rodríguez that:

---

124 *Case of Bámaca Velásquez*, para. 40.

125 *Ibidem*, paras. 56 and 62–65.

> An illegal act which violates human rights and which is initially not directly imputable to a State (for example, because it is the act of a private person or because the person responsible has not been identified) can lead to international responsibility of the State, not because of the act itself, but because of the lack of due diligence to prevent the violation or to respond to it as required by the Convention.[126]

54. These words are pertinent for the introduction of the subject of unpunished violence against women, which undoubtedly affects (apart from other rights) their right to humane treatment. In principle, it would not be necessary to examine this problem separately, as the protection of these rights is covered by the provisions of the American Convention. However, as a result of State negligence (fortunately in decline) in the application of the system for the protection of women's human rights, for many years they have not enjoyed this protection.[127] One need not delve too deeply into the past to find evidence of this negligence. Domestically, in Latin America's traditional legal codes, provisions against rape, which is normally considered a criminal infraction, did not have the protection of the woman's physical integrity or her personal freedom as their principal purpose, but rather generally protected the honor of the woman's husband or family.[128] In addition, the punishment of these crimes in some countries increased in line with the "honesty" or "chastity" of the woman, with punishments also increasing if the woman was married. Rape within a marriage, another type of conduct that violates personal integrity, is in many countries only just now considered as such. Until very recently, mistreatment of women by their husbands or parents and brothers was also not a subject of State concern, and nor was the harassment that many women suffer from their superiors in their workplaces. All these different expressions of violence are understood to fall within the realm of the private, and the distinction between public and private – the latter being the area in which the State must refrain from acting – was applied rigorously.[129]

---

126 *Case of Velásquez Rodríguez*, para. 172.

127 Paragraph 5 of the preamble of the Declaration on the Elimination of Violence against Women of the United Nations states that the General Assembly is "concerned about the long-standing failure to protect and promote those rights and freedoms in the case of violence against women". Text of the Declaration in document A/RES/48/104, dated 23 February 1994.

128 In the Chilean Criminal Code, in force as of June 2002, abortion, rape, rape of a minor and incest, among other things, are crimes "against family order and public morality".

129 See C. Medina, "Women's Rights as Human Rights: Latin American Countries and the Organization of American States", in M. Díaz-Diocaretz and I.M. Zavala (eds.), *Women, Feminist Identity and Society in the 1980's*, John Benjamins Publishing Company, Amsterdam, 1985; C. Medina, "Toward a More Effective Guarantee of the Enjoyment of Human Rights by Women in the Inter-American Systems", in R.J. Cook (ed.), *Human Rights of Women*, University of Pennsylvania Press, Philadelphia, 1994, Chapter 10, pp. 257–284; and C. Medina, "The Inter-American Commission on Human Rights and Women, with Particular Reference to Violence", in M. Castermans, F. van Hoof and J. Smith, *The Role of the Nation-State in the 21st Century*, Kluwer Law International, the Netherlands, 1998, pp. 117–134.

55. The causes behind the phenomenon of violence against women are complex, as they are intimately linked to the subordination of women to men and women's position in society, these being the manifestations of a culture whose change will necessarily be slow. A clear sign of the difficulty in changing people's attitudes can be found in what happens in the case of murders of women by their husbands in Brazil, where the "husband's honor" defense regularly works to excuse the perpetrators of responsibility despite repeated judgments from the Supreme Court finding that this defense lacks all legal value.[130] Another sign was the judgment of the Supreme Court of the Netherlands in which in addressing a criminal complaint of rape from a woman against her ex-lover, there was no inquiry into whether violence against the woman had been effectively exercised in carrying out the sexual acts; rather, the Court examined whether the accused "was aware" that the stable relationship that he had had with the victim had concluded,[131] as the crime of rape can only be committed when the victim and offender are not united by marriage or a comparable stable relationship. As that Court found that this point was not clearly proven, it acquitted the accused.[132] This does not take place only in Brazil and the Netherlands: it has also taken place in Maryland, in the United States, as recently as the 1990s. In October 1994, in a Baltimore County court, a judge ruled to convict a husband who had murdered his wife several hours after finding her apparently lying with another man, sentencing him to the minimum punishment established by law: three years in prison. The judge also suspended half of the sentence. When handing down his ruling, the judge stated: "I seriously wonder how many married men [...] would have the strength to walk away [...] without inflicting some corporal punishment, whatever that punishment might be. I shudder to think what I would do."[133]

56. Until recently, international supervisory bodies had kept their distance from the problem. The curious thing about this is that from its beginning, international human rights law has offered a legal instrument appropriate for addressing the subject of violence against women.[134] From the perspective of

---

130 A documentary report on this can be found in *Americas Watch, Criminal Injustice, Human Rights Watch*, New York, 1991. See also IACHR, *Report on the Human Rights Situation in Brazil (1997)*, OEA/Ser.L/V/II.97, Doc. 29 rev. 1, 29 September 1997, Chapter VIII, para. 27.

131 It was proven during the trial that the woman had told the accused that the relationship had ended, but the Court had doubts as to whether he understood her clearly.

132 Judgment of 16 June 1987, handed down in a cassation proceeding against the judgment of the Court of Amsterdam dated 11 February 1986, in the criminal trial of Leslie Luciano A., reproduced in *Nederlandse Jurisprudentie 1988*, No. 156, pp. 667–673. The judgment caused a stir in the Netherlands legal community, which reacted strongly against the Court (NJD, 1 June 1988, no. 23, pp. 819–820).

133 The information was provided by Igualdad Ya, *Acción Mujeres 7.1*, December 1994.

134 See in this sense, J. Fitzpatrick, "Utilización de las normas internacionales sobre derechos humanos para combatir la violencia contra la mujer", in R.J. Cook (ed.), *supra* n. 129, pp. 530-567.

rights affected, it is clear that violence against women violates, at the least, their right to physical and mental integrity, their personal security, and at times their right to life, all of which are set forth in all international human rights treaties.[135] This means that, in principle, it is possible to argue that violence against women can and should be a subject of international concern, given that it can affect and violate three rights found in lists of international rights that are obligatory for very many States.

57. This background was the driving force on the Latin American continent behind the drafting of a special treaty on violence against women, the Inter-American Convention on the Prevention, Punishment and Eradication of Violence against Women,[136] which constitutes, according to those who drafted it, "a positive contribution to protecting the rights of women and eliminating violence against them".[137]

Although this Convention refers to all the human rights found in the American Convention on Human Rights, it is clear that the purpose of its protection is to prevent attacks on the physical, psychological and mental integrity of women, and that the extension of the Convention's content to other rights is a result of the fact that violence against women is nothing but a culmination – the most serious manifestation of the situation of subordination faced by women – and in order to diminish it in a meaningful way, women's position in society must be improved, requiring action to be taken for them to be able to exercise all their human rights in full freedom.

Because of this, the Convention of Belém do Pará does not replace general treaties but rather complements them, playing the role of specifying the State obligations derived from Article 5 of the American Convention with the purpose of protecting the personal integrity of women. From this point of view, it plays a role similar to that of the Inter-American Convention to Prevent and Punish Torture.

58. The definition of violence given by the Convention of Belém do Pará places us directly in the field of Articles 4 and 5 of the American Convention on Human Rights. Article 1 establishes that violence against women is understood to be "any act or conduct, based on gender, which causes death or physical, sexual or psychological harm or suffering to women, whether in the public or the private sphere".

---

135 ICCPR, Articles 6, 7 and 9; ACHR, Articles 4, 5 and 7.

136 The Inter-American Convention on the Prevention, Punishment and Eradication of Violence against Women, the "Convention of Belém do Pará", was adopted by the General Assembly of the OAS in a resolution dated 9 June 1994. Text at OAS/Ser.P, AG/Doc. 3115/94 rev. 2, 9 June 1994.

137 *Ibidem,* Preamble.

Article 2 of the Convention of Belém do Pará complements this definition by clarifying that for the purposes of the international instruments application, it applies to violence against women:

a) that occurs within the family or domestic unit or within any other interpersonal relationship, whether or not the perpetrator shares or has shared the same residence with the woman, including, among others, rape, battery and sexual abuse;
b) that occurs in the community and is perpetrated by any person, including, among others, rape, sexual abuse, torture, trafficking in persons, forced prostitution, kidnapping and sexual harassment in the workplace, as well as in educational institutions, health facilities or any other place; and
c) that is perpetrated or condoned by the state or its agents regardless of where it occurs.

The definition is not ideal from a legal point of view because it inadequately mixes the elements of place with the elements of the type of personal relationship and the specific form the violence can take. Despite these problems, it constitutes a valuable contribution to the determination of these State obligations on giving clear indications as to what they must "prevent", "punish" and "eradicate" in order to protect the personal integrity of women.

59. From the point of view of the protected rights at issue for the examination of Article 5 of the American Convention, the Convention of Belém do Pará sets forth in Article 3 a woman's right to live a life free of violence, both in her public and private life. Article 6 of this instrument precisely specifies the content of this right, establishing that it includes the right to not be discriminated against and to be assessed and educated free from stereotypical patterns of social and cultural behavior and practices that are based on concepts of inferiority or subordination.[138]

60. The Convention of Belém do Pará establishes two types of obligations for States. One kind, indicated in Article 7, is to be complied with immediately and allow complaints regarding these obligations to be made before the Inter-American Commission on Human Rights. The others, found in Article 8, are obligations whose content is progressive, and complaints cannot be made over failures to comply with them, although they will at least be supervised by the Inter-American Commission of Women through the examination of the reports that States submit to it.[139]

---

[138] See HRC, General Comment No. 28 (Article 3 equality of rights between men and women), of 29 March 2000. CCPR/C/21/Rev.1/Add.10, para. 5. In the same sense see: *Concluding Observations: Chile*, CCPR/C/79/Add.104, 30 March 1999, para. 3.

[139] The Inter-American Commission of Women is a specialized body of the OAS made up of 34 Permanent Delegates, one for each Member State, designated by their respective governments. Its mission is to promote and protect the rights of women and support Member States in their efforts to ensure full access to civil, political, economic, social and cultural rights, allowing women and men to participate under equal conditions in all areas of social life.

Article 7 of the Convention of Belém do Pará reiterates the obligation to respect the physical integrity of women and expands on the obligation to guarantee personal integrity. Paragraphs (a), (b) and (c) of the article repeat obligations that have already been indicated previously: prohibition on violating rights contained in the Convention (para. (a)), and obligation to act with due diligence to prevent, investigate and punish violence against women (para. (b)), through both legislative and administrative actions (para. (c)). The following specify other measures: preventative measures to warn aggressors to refrain from harassing, intimidating, threatening, damaging or putting in danger the life of a woman (para. (d)); and the establishment of just and effective procedures so that women can have effective access to protective measures and a fair trial (para. (f)) and to reparations (para. (i)). Finally, paragraph (h) contains the all-encompassing obligation to "adopt such legislative or other measures as may be necessary to give effect to this Convention".[140]

The obligations of Article 8 of the Convention of Belém do Pará are a step backwards with regard to the protection derived from Article 5 of the American Convention, such as it has been developed by the case law of the Inter-American Court, as among the obligations that States must comply with progressively are some that should be complied with immediately, including the obligations to educate justice, police and other law enforcement officials, as well as the personnel in charge of policy in this area (para. (c)); to establish services for attending to women subjected to violence (para. (d)) to rehabilitate and train them (para. (f)); and to inform the public about the violence, the legal remedies available for filing complaints against it and the methods for obtaining reparations (para. (e)). It would be up to supervisory bodies to make the pertinent adjustments when examining a specific case, a task that is not difficult because, in addition to the content of the general obligations, the Court can resort to paragraph (h) of Article 7 of the Convention of Belém do Pará which, in reality, allows for the inclusion of all the measures found in the cited Article 8 should it be necessary and compatible with the Inter-American Court's development of the article's provisions thus far.

61. The obligations of Article 7 of the Convention of Belém do Pará can be monitored by the Inter-American Commission "in accordance with the norms and procedures established by the American Convention on Human Rights and the Statutes and Regulations of the Inter-American Commission on Human Rights for lodging and considering petitions." It is unfortunate that this provision does not explicitly include the possibility that communication of this kind can reach the Inter-American Court in search of a ruling on these issues that is legally binding for States. Nevertheless, I would argue that as the provision makes reference to the petitions set forth in the American Convention – these

---

140 It should be recognized that in previous writings I had not approached it in this way.

being the only ones that can lead to the presentation of the case before the Inter-American Court – Article 7 allows the Court to base its *ratione materiæ* jurisdiction on this. In addition, there is no doubt that women can make use of Article 5 of the American Convention and the development of the case law of the Inter-American Court in any case in which they allege a violation of that provision, meaning that the situation can eventually reach the Court, and that the Court could use the Convention of Belém do Pará to interpret and apply Article 5 of the American Convention in the specific case.

At the time of writing, the Court had not yet heard any cases of violence against women based solely on the Convention of Belém do Pará. Should such a case reach the Inter-American Commission, it would be highly appropriate for it to include in its examination the pertinent provisions of the American Convention – to which there would be no obstacle – and to examine the case based on the provisions of both treaties. This would allow the victim to have prior certainty with regard to the Court's jurisdiction.[141] Should the Court affirm its jurisdiction, the problem would disappear for the future.

62. At the time of writing, the inter-American system had heard one individual case on violence against a woman: the case of Maria da Penha Maia Fernándes v. Brazil. It was dealt with by the Inter-American Commission on Human Rights. The victim identified in the case suffered for many years from domestic violence at the hands of her husband, culminating in a murder attempt in May 1984. She became a paraplegic as a result, along with other injuries that continually affect her health. The victim filed a domestic criminal complaint over the incident and waited 15 years for it to be investigated seriously and for her husband to be brought to trial and convicted. Before the Inter-American Commission, she argued that Brazil had violated Articles 1(1), 8, 24 and 25 of the American Convention, with regard to a Articles II and XVIII of the American Declaration of the Rights and Duties of Man, as well as Articles 3, 4(a)–(g), 5 and 7 of the Convention of Belém do Pará. Her reason for invoking these different instruments was probably the fact that Brazil could be monitored by the Inter-American Commission under its obligations set forth in the American

[141] However, the Court has explicit authority to give advisory opinions on the interpretation of the Convention, as Article 11 authorizes States Parties and the Inter-American Commission of Women to ask the Court for them. In reality, this provision is not necessary given that all OAS Member States already have authority to request advisory opinions, as does, among other OAS bodies, the Inter-American Commission of Women. The authority comes from Article 64 of the American Convention on Human Rights, its content specified by Advisory Opinion No. 1 of the Court, which reached the conclusion that the "advisory jurisdiction of the Court can be exercised, in general, with regard to any provision dealing with the protection of human rights set forth in any international treaty applicable in the American States, regardless of whether it be bilateral or multilateral, whatever be the principal purpose of such a treaty, and whether or not non-Member States of the inter-American system are or have the right to become parties thereto." (OC-1/82, para. 1 of the operative section).

Declaration as an OAS Member State since the creation of the Commission. However, it only acceded to the American Convention on Human Rights on 25 September 1992, and ratified the Convention of Belém do Pará on 27 November 1995, meaning that in principle, the petitioner could not have clarity with regard to the Commission's jurisdiction to monitor those treaties.[142]

The Commission found the communication admissible under Articles 46(2)(c) and 47 of the American Convention, which regulates the processing of individual communications alleging violations of that Convention, but also under Article 12 of the Convention of Belém do Pará. On the merits, it found that Brazil had violated Articles 8 and 25 of the American Convention and Articles II and XVIII of the American Declaration,[143] as well as Article 7 of the Convention of Belém do Pará. The Commission's jurisdiction to apply the American Convention was correctly based on the fact that an ongoing violation of obligations was alleged, as the State had failed to provide due process.[144] Its jurisdiction to examine the facts under the Convention of Belém do Pará was based on two arguments: one, that the Commission had "general jurisdiction" over that Convention because it is "an inter-American human rights instrument"; and two, the content of Article 12 of that Convention, to which Brazil was party.[145]

The important part of this report from the Commission is the content of its recommendations. Therein, the Commission made explicit the measures that the Brazilian State must take in order to comply with its obligation to guarantee the physical integrity of the victim, indicating that the State must: rapidly and effectively complete the criminal processing of the man responsible for the facts; carry out a serious, impartial and exhaustive investigation to determine the responsibility of the judiciary for the violation of Articles 8 and 25 of the American Convention and to take the corresponding administrative, legislative and judicial measures; to adopt, without prejudice to eventual actions regarding civil liability in the attack, the measures necessary for the State to provide the victim with adequate material and symbolic reparation for the violations established, including reparation for the fact that the delay eliminated an

---

142 The American Declaration of the Rights and Duties of Man, adopted in the Ninth International Conference of the American States, Bogotá, Colombia, 1948.

143 I would note without examining the point that a procedural problem could arise when the Commission uses the American Declaration and the American Convention at the same time, as the processing of cases in which a violation of one is alleged that is not exactly the same as the alleged violation of the other.

144 IACHR, *Maria da Penha Maia Fernández v. Brazil*, Case No. 12.051, Report No. 54/01 of 16 April 2001, in IACHR, *2000 Annual Report* (OEA/Ser.L/V/II.111 Doc. 20 rev., 16 April 2001), para. 27.

145 *Ibidem*, para. 28. The Commission does not clearly establish whether its general jurisdiction authorizes it to apply the Convention directly or to use it as a supplementary instrument for interpreting State obligations with regard to Article 5 or other articles of the American Convention.

opportunity to bring an action for civil reparation and indemnity. Additionally, the Commission made general recommendations for compliance with the State's obligations with regard to women, namely: to continue deepening the process of reforms aimed at preventing State tolerance for and discriminatory treatment of domestic violence against women in Brazil, in particular recommending measures for training and sensitizing specialized judicial and police officials; to simplify criminal court proceedings in order to reduce their length; to establish rapid and effective nonjudicial alternatives for resolving intra-family conflict, as well as increasing sensitivity to their seriousness and criminal consequences; to increase the number of special police delegations on the rights of women and provide them with the special resources necessary for effective work; and finally, to ensure that its pedagogical plans include curricular units on understanding the importance of respecting women and their rights recognized in the Convention of Belém do Pará, as well as on the handling of intra-family conflict.

Unfortunately, and despite the fact that Brazil recognized the contentious jurisdiction of the Inter-American Court in 1995, the Commission did not send the case to the Court, preventing the possibility that a legally binding judgment would be issued on this subject that is so important for the continent.

7. PLACES OF DETENTION AND HUMANE TREATMENT: OTHER ISSUES

63. Paragraphs 4 and 5 of Article 5 of the American Convention establish rules related with certain requirements for detention: the accused must be separated from the convicted and minors must be separated from adults; in addition, the accused must be treated in a way that is appropriate to their status as individuals who have not been convicted. It is difficult to understand the relationship between these provisions and the right to humane treatment unless it is understood in the case of the accused and the condemned that mixing the former with the latter is detrimental to the dignity of the accused and that, in the case of children and adolescents, their separation from adults is in order to avoid placing them at risk of violations of their personal integrity. This latter point was made by the Court in a recent case.[146]

64. During discussion of the American Convention, the Government of Chile made an observation to the effect that this article intended "to regulate a subject that seems more appropriate to entrust exclusively to the corresponding domestic criminal legal systems than to an International Convention on Human Rights",

146 *Case of Bulacio*, para. 136.

and suggested it be deleted.[147] It shared this position with the Dominican Republic, the United States and Mexico,[148] but the proposal was struck down.[149]

Without being in agreement with the argument that the provision ordering the separation of the accused and the convicted (granting the right to different treatment to the former) and the separation of children and adolescents from adults should not be international, I think that this provision should have been included in other rights or as another right, because it does not seem to have its most fundamental and unique connection with the right to humane treatment.

65. In order to be able to decide on whether the rules have been complied with properly in a particular case, the specific circumstances of the separation must be examined. The Human Rights Committee, for example, opined in one case that the fact that the accused and the convicted were in the same building, but in separate sections, with the accused having contact with the convicted because some of the convicted served the food or cleaned the sections where the accused were being held, did not constitute a violation of Article 10(2)(a) of the International Covenant, whose content is similar to that of Article 5(4) of the American Convention.

At the time of writing the Court had no case law on the separation of the accused from the convicted. The Inter-American Commission has expressed particular concern on this subject.[150] Its interest is reflected in the establishment of a Work Group on Detention Conditions in the Americas,[151] assigned with monitoring of States' compliance with their international obligations in this area.

66. The American Convention also requires that the accused be subjected to "separate treatment appropriate to their status as unconvicted persons". It seems evident that an individual who is only accused enjoys the presumption of innocence established in Article 8(2) of the American Convention, and that this

---

147 Specialized Conference, *Minutes and Documents*, San Jose, Costa Rica, 7–22 November 1969, (OEA/Ser.K/XVI/1.2), p. 39.

148 *Ibidem*, pp. 59, 94 and 175, respectively.

149 HRC, *Larry James Pinkney v. Canada*, Communication 27/1978, Report of 25 November 1977 (UN Doc. Supp. no. 40 (A/37/40), 1982, p. 101).

150 See, for example, IACHR, *Fifth Report on the human rights situation in Guatemala (2001)*, OEA/Ser.L/V/II.111 Doc. 21 rev., 6 April 2001, Chapter VIII, paras. 34–45. This report details detention conditions with special reference to separation of the prison population, establishing criteria for separating the condemned from the accused and minors from adults, as well as for separating prisoners according to the seriousness of the crime. It also examines requirements regarding the physical and mental health of the prisoners and their sexual orientation. In addition, it highlights the lack of oversight of the physical condition of the individuals entering the penitentiary system and the lack of registry of inmates to allow for them to be properly separated.

151 The Work Group was established during the 85th and 86th Periods of Sessions of the IACHR (see IACHR, *1996 Annual Report* (OEA/Ser.L/V/II.95 Doc. 7 rev., 4 March 1997), p. 785).

should have consequences for that person's treatment, consequences that thus far have not been subjected to an examination by the Court. The content of the provision of Article 5(4) of the American Convention will acquire greater precision on this issue with future case law.

67. The American Convention says nothing on the separation of men from women, but it seems obvious that in order to protect the personal integrity of women, they should be separated from the men and guarded by personnel of their own sex. In this sense, in its report on the human rights situation in Mexico, published in 1998, the Inter-American Commission stated:

> Likewise, Article 18 of the Constitution indicates that the women's prison must be separated from that of the men. However, this has not been effectively put into practice, with the presence of women in several male facilities having been confirmed. As alleged, this is a source of abuse and undesirable consequences.[152]

8. SPECIAL PROVISIONS FOR CHILDREN AND ADOLESCENTS

68. Article 5(5) of the American Convention regulates not only the separation of children and adolescents from adults, but also delves into their rights during legal proceedings, establishing that special juvenile courts are required before which the minors must be brought "as speedily as possible, so that they may be treated in accordance with their status as minors". The wording must be understood as requiring that the time period for ruling on the situation of children be less than the reasonable period of time mentioned in Article 8(1) of the American Convention.

The wording of this paragraph could be incorrect. What does "treated" mean? A Uruguayan proposal during the Specialized Conference used the word "tried", which gave a more clear idea in the sense that speediness would refer to the definitive conclusion of the trial. However, this amendment was rejected and it is impossible to know the reasons why, if there are any, because they are not found in the text.[153] The term treatment is reminiscent of the way in which children and adolescents were, or in some cases still are, "handled" in the penitentiary system. Applied to a case, one would have to conclude that for them, it is possible for cases to be handled without judicial processing or judgment. This interpretation is, of course unacceptable because it is incompatible with the fact that children and adolescents must be treated as subjects of law and must, therefore, have the opportunity to exercise and enjoy all their human rights, among which are the

---

152 IACHR, *Report on the human rights situation in Mexico (1998).* OEA/Ser.L/V/II.100 Doc. 7 rev. 1, 24 September 1998, para. 259.

153 Specialized Conference, *supra* n. 147, p. 176.

principle of legality, the presumption of innocence, the right to legal counsel, and the right to appeal a conviction, when the proceedings and conviction are allowed according to the age of the accused.[154] In this sense, the provisions of the American Convention and the provisions of the Convention on the Rights of the Child constitute a minimum to which States are bound, and as a consequence, neither regulations nor proceedings can be applied that do not at least guarantee the basic institutions of due process established in those instruments.

69. The American Convention requires the establishment of special courts for processing children and adolescents. With the entry into force of the Convention on the Rights of the Child and scientific progress in the field of psychology, it is possible to argue that children and adolescents need not only special courts but also specialized laws, and to apply them, specialized personnel who have been trained to communicate with children and adolescents, as the proceedings for a criminal infraction must conclude with punishments and/or measures that promote the reintegration of the child and allow the child to "assum[e...] a constructive role in society".[155] The American Convention does not contain any provision regarding these points, possibly because it was drafted near the end of the 1960s, when the legal status of members of this age group as rights holders still had yet to be explicitly recognized or even discussed.

70. The Inter-American Court plays an important role in integrating the provisions of the Convention on the Rights of the Child with the provisions of Article 5(5) of the American Convention and the interpretation of Article 19 of the same American Convention.[156]

9. INDIVIDUALISATION AND THE PURPOSE OF A SENTENCE

71. Given that no one can be convicted and sentenced without due process that has led to a ruling issued on the basis of unequivocal evidence that a person is guilty of a specific crime, it is clear that the sentence cannot transcend the criminal him- or herself, as set forth in Article 5(3) of the American Convention. At the time of writing, the Inter-American Court had not yet had an opportunity

---

[154] See Article 40 of the Convention on the Rights of the Child, United Nations, adopted on 20 November 1989. The Convention entered into force on 2 December 1990, and only two States in the world are not parties to it: the United States and Somalia. Also see the United Nations Standard Minimum Rules for the Administration of Juvenile Justice ("The Beijing Rules"), adopted by resolution 40/33 of the General Assembly of the United Nations on 28 November 1985, Article 7.

[155] Convention on the Rights of the Child, Article 40.

[156] *Case of the Street Children (Villagrán Morales et al.),* paras. 192–196.

to examine cases in which a failure to comply with this provision has been alleged. The Commission ruled very tangentially on this in the case of Alan García v. Peru. Alan García's house was searched by the Peruvian military and the former Peruvian president's wife and young children were subjected to house arrest by the military. This was not a punishment, but rather a human rights violation on the part of State agents. However, the Commission expressed that it wished to recall that "there is a special prohibition in the Convention that proscribes extending punishment to the family of the person alleged to be guilty of a crime". Without prejudice to this, the Commission did not find that Article 5(6) of the American Convention had been violated.[157]

72. Article 5(6) of the American Convention establishes peremptorily that punishments consisting of deprivation of liberty "shall have as an essential aim the reform and social readaptation of the prisoners". The Convention does not give any guidance as to how convicts must be treated in order to achieve this aim. It is highly probable that firstly, there are many ways to do so, and secondly, that they will change as the fields of criminal sociology and criminology develop.

73. The Human Rights Committee has instructed States on this point, as there is a similar provision in the International Covenant, indicating that States must report to the Committee with "specific information concerning the measures taken to provide teaching, education and re-education, vocational guidance and training and also concerning work programmes for prisoners inside the penitentiary establishment as well as outside." The Committee also requires information on the existence or nonexistence of a post-incarceration support system.[158]

74. It is up to States to decide which measures to use to achieve the goal established by the American Convention, and the supervisory bodies must supervise compliance with this provision by necessarily taking into consideration the range of possibilities. At the time of writing, the Inter-American Court had no case law on this.

---

[157] IACHR, *Alan García v. Peru*, Case No. 11.006, Report No. 1/95, published in the *1994 Annual Report.*

[158] HRC, General Comment No. 21, Article 10 (44th Period of Sessions), 1992, paras. 10 and 11, reproduced in HRI/GEN/1/Rev. 4, 7 February 2000, p. 133.

CHAPTER 4
RIGHT TO PERSONAL LIBERTY

Article 7. Right to Personal Liberty

1. *Every person has the right to personal liberty and security.*
2. *No one shall be deprived of his physical liberty except for the reasons and under the conditions established beforehand by the constitution of the State Party concerned or by a law established pursuant thereto.*
3. *No one shall be subject to arbitrary arrest or imprisonment.*
4. *Anyone who is detained shall be informed of the reasons for his detention and shall be promptly notified of the charge or charges against him.*
5. *Any person detained shall be brought promptly before a judge or other officer authorized by law to exercise judicial power and shall be entitled to trial within a reasonable time or to be released without prejudice to the continuation of the proceedings. His release may be subject to guarantees to assure his appearance for trial.*
6. *Anyone who is deprived of his liberty shall be entitled to recourse to a competent court, in order that the court may decide without delay on the lawfulness of his arrest or detention and order his release if the arrest or detention is unlawful. In States Parties whose laws provide that anyone who believes himself to be threatened with deprivation of his liberty is entitled to recourse to a competent court in order that it may decide on the lawfulness of such threat, this remedy may not be restricted or abolished. The interested party or another person in his behalf is entitled to seek these remedies.*
7. *No one shall be detained for debt. This principle shall not limit the orders of a competent judicial authority issued for nonfulfillment of duties of support.*

1. INTRODUCTION

1. The American Convention titles this right as the "right to personal liberty," but in its first paragraph it enshrines the right "to personal liberty *and security*". The concepts of both "liberty" and "security" can be understood more broadly than in the way that Article 7 of the Convention seems to suggest.

2. Speaking broadly, liberty is associated with the opportunity for self-determination, that is, for a person to live his or her life as he or she wishes, obviously as long as that person's actions do not affect the rights of others. Liberty thus conceived is the foundation of human rights, with the catalogue of human rights constituting specific protection of certain aspects of liberty such as for example the freedom to associate, to meet and to express oneself.

In Article 7 of the American Convention, the liberty that is protected is also an aspect of human liberty, but only as regards the ability to move spatially without any limitations. Looking at it this way, the personal liberty found in Article 7 overlaps with the right enshrined in Article 22 of the Convention, that being the right to move about the territory of a State in which one is legally present, as well as the right to freely leave any country, including one's own. There is no background that would help draw the line between one right and the other, but due to the fact that Article 7 of the Convention puts practically all its emphasis on deprivation of liberty understood as imprisonment, one could conclude that the right protected in this provision is principally the right to not be confined to a relatively small space, like a prison.[1]

3. That said, we must immediately note the caveat that the fact of its emphasis on prison does not mean that Article 7 of the Convention only protects from that type of deprivation of liberty: any deprivation of liberty that involves the detention of a person in a small space falls within the realm of this right. In interpreting any human right, it is essential to look at its essence, the core that it protects, and not the conduct mentioned as possibly being in violation of that right, as that conduct is only a reflection of what seemed likely to be in violation of the right at the time the catalogue was written. The interpretation of rights is dynamic. This position is reaffirmed with the wording of paragraph 2 of Article 7, which separates the right from the notion of "detention" or "imprisonment".

The deprivations of liberty to which Article 7 would apply thus include every kind of confinement, whether for medical reasons, disciplinary reasons (including discipline within the armed forces), or others. Article 9 of the International Covenant, which is a similar provision whose range of application was discussed during its drafting, has been interpreted in the same way, an interpretation that was later established by the Human Rights Committee. The Committee found that Article 9 protects from "all deprivations of liberty, whether in criminal cases or in other cases such as, for example, mental illness, vagrancy, drug addiction, educational purposes, immigration control, etc."[2] As a consequence of this

---

1 Manfred Nowak arrived at the same conclusion in his study on the rights found in the International Covenant on Civil and Political Rights. See M. Nowak, *UN Covenant on Civil and Political Rights. CCPR Commentary*, N.P. Engel Publisher, Kehl/Strasbourg/Arlington, 1993, p. 160.

2 HRC, General Comment No. 8, 16th Period of Sessions (1982), HRI/GEN/1/Rev.5, 26 April 2001, para. 1. Also see *ibidem*, p. 176.

position, the Committee has also recognized that the confinement of women to their homes and prevention of them from leaving without the permission of their husbands, authorized by customary law in certain Muslim countries, falls under the auspices of Article 9 of the International Covenant.[3]

4. The concept of security raises other problems. To be "secure" means to be free from danger, free from risk; this meaning seems to place the right to security more in the area of humane treatment and life than that of personal liberty. The American Declaration, Article I, establishes that "all humans have right to life, liberty and the security of his person". This could be understood as the enshrinement of different rights, but seems to have been understood differently when reproduced in the American Convention.[4]

Despite any issues with regard to its location, the right to personal security is set forth in Article 7 of the Convention together with the right to personal liberty, raising the question of whether it is a right that is distinct from the right to personal liberty, and if so, if it is inevitably linked thereto, that is, if it should be understood only with regard to personal liberty. On the former question, rules of interpretation indicate that the interpreter must try to give an *effet utile* to a provision's content, for which reason one must conclude that the right to personal security should be separate from the right to personal liberty.

5. As regards the latter, the European Court of Human Rights holds that the right to personal security must be understood "in the context of physical liberty".[5] In the words of Fawcett, "liberty and security are the two sides of the same coin; if personal liberty spells actual freedom of the movement of the person, security is the condition of being protected by law in that freedom".[6] This latter point has also been made by the European Court of Human Rights – although not in reference to legality but rather to arbitrariness – when it has ruled that the right to personal security translates into a State obligation to prohibit arbitrary detentions and arrests.[7]

---

3 HRC, General Comment No. 28 (Article 3: Equality of rights between men and women), 68th Period of Sessions (2000), HRI/GEN/1/Rev.5, 26 April 2001, para. 14; *Concluding Observations: Sudan*, CCPR A/53/40 (1998), para. 125.

4 Article 5 of the European Convention on Human Rights, adopted in 1950, likewise establishes that everyone has the right to liberty and personal security, and Article 9 of the International Covenant on Civil and Political Rights, adopted in 1966, repeats that same wording. However, the source of both of these is Article 3 of the Universal Declaration of Human Rights, which also makes reference to three rights: life, liberty and security.

5 D.J. Harris, M. O'Boyle and C. Warbrick, *Law of the European Convention on Human Rights*, Butterworths, London/Dublin/Edinburgh, 1995, p. 103, citing the European Commission and the Committee of Ministers in *East African Asians v. UK* [1973] 3 EHRR 76, 89.

6 J.E. Fawcett, *The Application of the European Convention on Human Rights*, Clarendon Press, Oxford, 1987, p. 70.

7 D.J. Harris et al., *supra* n. 5, p. 103, citing *Bozano v. France*, judgment of 18 December 1986, paras. 54 and 60.

In contrast, the Human Rights Committee has taken a different position. In the case of Delgado Páez v. Colombia, in which the victim alleged having been dismissed from his job due to his religious beliefs, and who later was subjected to death threats that forced him to leave the country, the Committee found that Colombia had violated the petitioner's right to personal security, rejecting the idea that the fact that the right to personal security was in the same paragraph as the right to personal liberty necessarily meant that the right "arises only in the context of arrest and detention". The Committee added that:

> It cannot be the case that, as a matter of law, States can ignore known threats to the life of persons under their jurisdiction, just because he or she is not arrested or otherwise detained. Given that States parties are under an obligation to take reasonable and appropriate measures to protect them, an interpretation of article 9 which would allow a State party to ignore threats to the personal security of non-detained persons within its jurisdiction would render totally ineffective the guarantees of the Covenant.[8]

In the inter-American system, the Convention's preparatory work does not shed any additional light on this question. In the Specialized Conference, the original text of this article only protected physical liberty.[9] In the discussion in Commission I, the delegate from Ecuador introduce the current wording, with no additional justification for it appearing in the minutes. That wording was approved without debate.[10] Later, as revealed the final report on Commission I, a work group was formed that repeated Ecuador's idea in the sense that the right enshrined was a right to liberty and personal security.[11] This text remained in place until the end of the conference.

The Inter-American Court has connected personal security with personal liberty in the cases of Villagrán Morales *et al.* and Bámaca Velásquez, where it indicated that "by protecting personal liberty, a safeguard is also provided for both the physical liberty of the individual and his personal safety".[12] From this, one could perhaps infer that when speaking of personal security in the context of an absence of guarantees, that term is used only in reference to the physical

---

8 *W. Delgado Páez v. Colombia*, Communication 195/1985, decision of 12 July 1990, in *Report of the Human Rights Committee*, A/45/40, Vol. II, para. 5.5. This case law of the Committee has been repeated in several other cases: see HRC, *Peter Chiiko Bwalya v. Zambia*, Communication 314/1988, decision of 14 July 1993, A/48/40, Vol. II, 1993; *Angel N. Olo Bahamonde v. Equatorial Guinea*, Communication 468/1991, decision of 20 October 1993, A/49/40, Vol. II, 1994; *Agnes N'Goya, on behalf of her husband, Katombe L. Eshishimbi v. Zaire*, Communication 542/1993, decision of 25 March 1996, A/51/40, Vol. I, 1997; *Carlos Dias and Carolina de Fatima da Silva v. Angola*, Communication 711/ 1996, decision of 20 March 2000, A/55/40, Vol. II, 2000; and *Rodger Chongwe v. Zambia*, Communication 821/1998, decision of 25 October 2000, A/56/40, Vol. II, 2001.

9 See Specialized Conference, *Minutes and Documents*, San Jose, Costa Rica, 7–22 November 1969, (OEA/Ser.K/XVI/1.2), p. 16.

10 *Ibidem*, pp. 180 and 185.

11 *Ibidem*, p. 297.

12 *Case of the Street Children (Villagrán Morales et al.)*, para. 135; and *Case of Bámaca Velásquez*, para. 141.

integrity of those deprived of liberty. However, there is nothing conclusive one way or the other.

Whatever the interpretation of the Court of this part of Article 7 of the Convention – and in my opinion there is no textual obstacle to the Court following the position of the Human Rights Committee – from an imminent and real threat to the right to life, the right to humane treatment and also the right to personal liberty, a State obligation to protect threatened individuals arises, via the application of Article 1(1) of the American Convention.[13] I would argue that a very broad concept of "safety" can be derived from the obligation to ensure, a concept that goes beyond the rights mentioned[14] and that makes the existence of an autonomous right to security irrelevant.

2. GENERAL REQUIREMENTS FOR ALL DEPRIVATIONS OF LIBERTY

6. After laying out the rights that it enshrines, Article 7 of the American Convention establishes in paragraph 2 a general provision to the effect that no one shall be deprived of physical liberty except for the causes and conditions established beforehand by State constitutions or by laws put in place under those constitutions. The following paragraph stipulates that no one shall be subjected to arbitrary arrest or imprisonment.

Thus from one paragraph to the next, the terminology changes. Paragraph 2 uses a broad expression ("deprived of [...] physical liberty") that indicates that any type of physical deprivation of liberty committed by any agent is covered by the provision; in contrast, paragraph 3 refers to "arrest or imprisonment". The minutes do not provide an explanation, but it is highly probable that the difference does not correspond to any fundamental reason but is simply stylistic. Obviously, it seems impossible to draw from that the conclusion that all physical deprivations of liberty require a basis in law, but that only arrest or imprisonment[15] are required to be carried out non-arbitrarily; no restriction on human rights – and the deprivation of liberty is a restriction – can be made arbitrarily. It must therefore be understood that the prohibition on arbitrariness applies to all forms of deprivation of liberty.

---

13 See Chapter 2, section 4.2 on the State's obligation to protect persons that have been subjected to real and imminent threats to their lives.

14 The idea of a broad definition of security is reinforced historically with Article 8 of the Constitution of the Republic of France of 24 June 1793, cited by Nowak: "La sûreté consiste dans la protection, acordée par la société à chacun de ses membres pour la conservation de sa personne, de ses droits et de ses propriétés." He argues that in the French Revolution, law had a horizontal effect, that is, the State was required to protect citizens from third-party interference in their rights (M. Nowak, *supra* n. 1, p. 162).

15 Nor are there elements for clarifying what is meant by "detention" and by "imprisonment". See *infra*, para. 13.

2.1. LEGALITY

7. The requirements of legality imply the need for States to have regulations with the status of law[16] governing everything that has to do with deprivation of liberty, from the grounds permitting a deprivation of liberty, to the proceedings to which the action of depriving a person of liberty must be subjected. The Court has clearly indicated that Article 7 has both a material and a formal aspect. The material aspect means that "no one shall be deprived of his physical liberty, except for reasons, cases or circumstances specifically established by law", while according to the formal aspect, this deprivation can only be carried out "under strict conditions established beforehand by law".[17] Naturally, the content of both aspects will vary if the deprivation of liberty takes place within the context of a possible judicial proceedings – which is undoubtedly what the Convention regulates in detail – or in the context of a medical or some other kind of procedure. The legal provisions are to be domestic and will be ruled on in general by each country's legal system, without prejudice to which they must be adjusted to meet the requirements established in other paragraphs of Article 7 of the Convention.

8. As international supervisory bodies do not in general have jurisdiction to interpret domestic laws, with this being a task normally left to domestic courts, the decision on whether a detention is legal is first handed down by those courts. This does not prevent an international body from deciding in the case of a flagrant violation of domestic regulations that a detention was "illegal" – that is, that it did not take place in accordance with the regulations of the State in which it was carried out. The Court carried out this type of oversight in, for example, the case of Castillo Páez, in which it found that:

> it is proven that the victim was detained by members of the National Police of Peru without application of the causes and conditions set forth in the Political Constitution of July 12, 1979, [...] inasmuch as that fundamental law provided that no one may be arrested except by written order issued by a judicial authority, which did not occur in this Case.[18]

In the case of Juan Humberto Sánchez, the Inter-American Court found that Article 7(2) of the Convention had been violated on the State's having failed to comply with the provisions of the Honduran Constitution in the arrest of the

---

16 Article 7 refers to the law both in its formal sense and its material sense, which agrees with the meaning that the Inter-American Court attributes the expression "law" in Advisory Opinion 6, interpreting Article 30 of the American Convention. The Court found that law means "a general legal norm tied to the general welfare, passed by democratically elected legislative bodies established by the Constitution, and formulated according to the procedures set forth by the constitutions of the States Parties for that purpose" (OC-6/86, operative paragraphs).

17 *Case of Gangaram Panday*, para. 47; *Case of Bámaca Velásquez*, para. 139; *Case of Durand and Ugarte*, para. 85; *Case of Juan Humberto Sánchez*, para. 78, *Case of Maritza Urrutia*, para. 65.

18 *Case of Castillo Páez*, para. 56. Also see *Case of Suárez Rosero*, para. 44, and *Case of the Street Children (Villagrán Morales et al.)*, para. 132.

victim, who had been detained by military personnel without being found *in flagrante delicto* during a time of day when arrests were prohibited by the Constitution, and who had not been informed of his rights and the reasons for the arrest.[19]

In the case of Cesti Hurtado, the Court found a violation of the legality required by Article 7 of the Convention based on the military authorities' having proceeded to detain the petitioner, failing to execute an order to release him issued by the Specialized Chamber of Public Law of the Superior Court of Justice of Lima after it granted a writ of *habeas corpus*.[20]

If a victim alleges that a detention was unlawful, it falls to the State, being accused by a private party of having violated its own law, to demonstrate before the international body that such a violation has not occurred and to prove that in contrast to what the alleged victim says, the person who carried out the detention was authorized by law to do so, or that the standard procedures for depriving someone of liberty were followed. Should the State fail to do so, it will be assumed that the action was not legal. This was what the Inter-American Court ruled in the case of Gangaram Panday in response to the State's failure to provide the Court with the official texts of the Constitution and substantive and criminal procedural laws applicable to the cases of detention, documents that the Court requested based on the petitioner's complaint that those provisions had not been complied with in this case.[21]

2.2. ABSENCE OF ARBITRARINESS

9. Deprivation of liberty not only requires that the principle of legality be adhered to but also demands an absence of arbitrariness, both in the law regulating deprivation of liberty and in the conduct of the agents applying it.

The concept of arbitrariness is assessed not only according to domestic law or considerations adapted solely to the national perception of "what is arbitrary", but also to the interpretation of the international supervisory body. The discussion of this condition during the drafting of the International Covenant, which contains a similar provision, led some of the drafters to equip arbitrariness with elements of injustice, unpredictability, lack of reasonability, capriciousness and lack of proportionality.[22] In the case of Van Alphen v. the Netherlands, the Committee found that a detention following a legal arrest must be reasonable and necessary under all circumstances, a condition not met in this case. It therefore declared that the Netherlands had violated Article 9 of the International Covenant.[23]

---

19 *Case of Juan Humberto Sánchez,* para. 79.
20 *Case of Cesti Hurtado,* paras. 140–143.
21 *Case of Gangaram Panday,* paras. 50 and 51.
22 M. Nowak, *supra* n. 1, p. 172.
23 HRC, *Alphen v. the Netherlands*, Case No. 305/1988, cited by Nowak, *supra* n. 1, p. 173.

10. The Inter-American Court addressed arbitrariness in Gangaram Panday, ruling that the provision preventing arbitrary detention or imprisonment implies that no one can be subjected to them "for reasons and by methods which, although classified as legal, could be deemed to be incompatible with the respect for the fundamental rights of the individual because, among other things, they are *unreasonable, unforeseeable or lacking in proportionality*."[24]

In the case of Cantoral Benavides, the Court ruled that Article 7 of the American Convention had been violated because of the State's having subjected the victim to arbitrary imprisonment. It based this ruling on the fact that the victim remained in prison on the orders of military judges – after the Special Tribunal of the Supreme Council of Military Justice had acquitted him definitively – in order for the petitioner to be brought to trial for the same facts, this time in civilian court.[25] In the case of Juan Humberto Sánchez, the arbitrariness was derived from the fact that the detentions to which he had been subjected "come within the framework of abuse of power" corresponding to a pattern of human rights violations taking place at that time.[26]

The adjectives used by the Court in that case, and also the position of the Human Rights Committee in the Van Alphen case, allow for the argument that the concept of "arbitrariness" is intimately connected with the requirements to which all restrictions of human rights must be subjected: deprivation of liberty must seek to achieve an objective that is permitted by the Convention and must be "necessary in a democratic society". That is, it must be conducive to achieving the objective sought and be proportional, and there must not exist any measure for achieving the objective other than the deprivation of liberty. A lack of any of these elements would make a deprivation of liberty arbitrary.

According to all this, mass detentions do not satisfy the requirement of reasonability, necessity and proportionality, for which reason they must be considered arbitrary in principle unless each individual detention can be independently justified.[27]

3. DEPRIVATION OF LIBERTY IN THE CONTEXT OF POSSIBLE CRIMINAL PROCEEDINGS

11. The beginning of this chapter noted that Article 7 of the Convention protects individuals from all illegal or arbitrary deprivations of liberty, but that without prejudice to this, the provision regulates in detail the deprivations of liberty carried out by State agents in the context of possible criminal proceedings.

24 *Case of Gangaram Panday*, para. 47 (emphasis added).
25 *Case of Cantoral Benavides*, para. 75. A similar case is that of *Loayza Tamayo*, para. 54.
26 *Case of Juan Humberto Sánchez*, para. 80.
27 *Case of Bulacio*, concurring and separate opinion of Judge Sergio García Ramírez, para. 20.

This is what will be examined next. Without prejudice to this, it should be recalled that Article 7 also protects personal liberty, which can be affected for causes not related to a criminal trial. Therefore, those who interpret Article 7 and apply it to one of those circumstances should use the rules analyzed next as a guide for the procedure.[28]

3.1. GROUNDS ALLOWING FOR THE APPREHENSION OF A PERSON

12. Paragraph 2 of Article 7 of the Convention requires that the grounds for which one can be deprived of liberty be established in the Constitution of each State or in laws enacted in accordance with the Constitution, meaning that the grounds are determined by the State. The Convention thus chose a method that is different from that of the European Convention on Human Rights, which in its Article 5 establishes exhaustively the reasons for or grounds on which a person can be detained.[29]

However, domestic law cannot establish these grounds as it wishes. It cannot be forgotten that deprivation of liberty cannot be arbitrary, for which reason the grounds for detaining someone are also subject to this requirement.[30] As already discussed, given that deprivation of liberty is a restriction on a human right, it must meet the same requirements as all restrictions, that is, the grounds must ultimately require that a detention be "necessary in a democratic society". This means that, for example, the law can allow a person to be arrested when caught *in flagrante delicto* even without meeting the other conditions for the procedure, such as a requirement for an arrest warrant issued by a competent authority. In addition, when an arrest warrant is required, it must be based on reasonable suspicion that the individual has participated in the crime, and it thus also corresponds to the law to establish and determine which criminal offenses can justify an arrest and which cannot.

---

[28] In the European system, see ECtHR, *Van der Leer v. the Netherlands*, judgment of 21 February 1990, para. 27, cited by D.J. Harris, M. O'Boyle and C. Warbrick, *supra* n. 5, p. 129. On the system of the International Covenant on Civil and Political Rights, see M. Nowak, *supra* n. 1, p. 174.

[29] One attempt to specifically establish in the Convention the cases in which one could be deprived of liberty, put forward by the Brazilian delegation, did not receive support, with the more generic wording being preferred (see Specialized Conference, *supra* n. 9, pp. 122–123 and 189–185).

[30] For example, from this point of view, the so-called "detention for being suspicious" – that is, the detention of someone who without committing a crime and without an arrest warrant is detained because a police officer believes that the person may, in the words of article 260 of the Chilean Criminal Procedural Code prior to its reform, have "bad intentions" – is not compatible with the Convention.

3.2. PROCEDURAL REQUIREMENTS FOR AN ARREST

13. Paragraphs 4 and 5 of Article 7 of the Convention establish the procedural requirements for carrying out a detention or a "retention" (*retención*). The *travaux préparatoires* do not explain the possible differences between these two forms of deprivation of liberty; they only mention that the word "retained" (*retenida*) was added to paragraphs 4 and 5 of Articles 7 during the first full session of the Conference, but do not indicate the origin of the amendment or the reasons for it.[31] This means that one can only speculate as to the meaning of each of these concepts, with the additional complication that the terms "detention" (*detención*), "prison", "imprisonment", "retention" (*retención*), and others used throughout Article 7 of the Convention, have different meanings in the legal language of the different States Parties.[32] The variety of nomenclature makes any attempt to specify the meaning of the two concepts found in paragraph 4 useless. The addition of the word "retained" in this paragraph can only be understood as an attempt to broaden the protection to another form of deprivation of liberty, likely derived from the drafters' knowledge of the variety of nomenclature used in this field.[33]

This interpretation is backed by a request from the Panama delegation that the record show

> that it understands the word "detention" to be a synonym for *deprivation of liberty*; and finds that the remedy for demanding the right to freedom should include the case of those who have been *convicted* should that conviction have been illegal. Protection should also be given to those who have been *convicted* without the guarantee of due process.[34]

No one objected to Panama's position, meaning that it should be understood that all forms of deprivation of liberty, including deprivation of liberty through a domestic court judgment not compatible with the Convention (which was what seemed to have been that delegation's concern) is included in the concepts of detention and retention.

14. There are various procedural requirements. Although one could argue that conditions for arrest procedures are clearly established, careful examination shows that interpretive work in order to specify them point by point is indispensable. The purpose of these requirements is to protect individuals from

---

31 Specialized Conference, *supra* n. 9, p. 442.

32 For a comparison of legislation, see "Question of human rights of all persons under any form of detention or imprisonment. Report of Working Group on Arbitrary Detention", E/CN.4/1997/4, 17 December 1996, section 4.

33 See in *ibidem* the considerations of the Working Group on Arbitrary Detention addressing the problem of deciding on which elements could distinguish between the terms "detention" and "imprisonment".

34 Specialized Conference, *supra* n. 9, p. 443.

arrest and later illegal or arbitrary detention. Thus, their interpretation must take this idea as a guiding principle.

The importance of the right to personal freedom and the serious effects of deprivation of that personal freedom have led to the emergence of numerous declarations or resolutions from the United Nations developing the basic rights established in treaties. Among them are the Minimum Rules for the Treatment of Prisoners,[35] the Body of Principles for the Protection of All Persons under Any Form of Detention or Imprisonment,[36] and the Rules of the United Nations for the Protection of Minors Deprived of their Liberty.[37] These principles and rules attempt to construct with precision the rights and obligations arising from international treaties in this field and are being incorporated by international supervisory bodies as they interpret the corresponding provisions on deprivation of liberty.

3.2.1. Right to be informed of the reasons for arrest

15. The first requirement is the obligation for the person making the arrest to inform the person being arrested[38] of the reasons for the arrest. Even when the Convention is not specific, it seems obvious that this information must be provided immediately; any State interference with human rights requires an explanation of the action; this allows the person to have an opportunity to react with arguments that could perhaps lead the agent to desist.[39] At this stage, no charges have been made. This is simply a reasonable explanation of why the action is taking place that nevertheless cannot be limited to indicating, for example, the legal provision authorizing the arrest. Rather it must contain a summary description of the facts being invoked as grounds for the arrest.

The Court had the opportunity to examine this point in the case of Gangaram Panday. The case was related to several aspects of Article 7 of the Convention: the alleged failure to inform the victim of the reasons for the detention, the illegality of the detention and the detention's possible arbitrariness. Regarding the first point, which is the one at issue here, the Inter-

35 Adopted by the First United Nations Congress on the Prevention of Crime and the Treatment of Offenders, held at Geneva in 1955, and approved by the Economic and Social Council by its Resolutions 663 C (XXIV) of 31 July 1957 and 2076 (LXII) of 13 May 1977.

36 Adopted by the UN General Assembly in Resolution 43/173 of 9 December 1988.

37 Adopted by the UN General Assembly in Resolution 45/113 of 14 December 1990.

38 I use the expressions "the person making the arrest" and "the person arrested" to draw a distinction between the moment of the apprehension and the maintaining of the detention by a judge.

39 The Convention used both the European Convention and the International Covenant on Civil and Political Rights as precedents for its drafting, but Article 7 seems to have been guided principally by the latter. The Covenant explicitly establishes both moments in its Article 9(2), and there is no explanation of why the Convention formulates this paragraph incompletely.

American Court found that there was not sufficient evidence to conclude that the victim and the victim's family had been unaware of the reasons for the detention, as the case file showed that:

> the victim himself, when he was detained at the airport, said to his relatives: "I've got problems"; that in the early hours of the day following the above-mentioned detention, the victim's brother [...] was informed by the Military Police that the reason for the detention was the fact that [the victim] had been expelled from Holland and, furthermore, that the latter had told the guard at the shelter "that he had been expelled from Holland, even though he had of his own free will reported to the Immigration Police".[40]

Possibly because it ruled definitively that the detention was illegal, the Court did not elaborate further on this point, something that would have been very useful for elucidating its opinion on whether: (i) knowing that one "has problems" is sufficient to conclude that a person was informed "of the reason for his detention"; and (ii) reporting the reasons to the relatives can exempt the State from its obligation to inform the person being arrested at the time of his arrest.[41]

The Court has emphasized this obligation in later rulings and explained its objective by indicating that the information "is a mechanism to avoid illegal or arbitrary detentions, from the very moment when a person is deprived of his or her liberty. It also ensures the right to defense of the detainee."[42]

In the case of children and adolescents, the information must also be provided to those representing them, that is, their legal guardians.[43]

3.2.2. Right to be notified of the charges without delay

16. The wording of paragraph 4 of Article 7 of the Convention allows for the assumption that the requirement that a detainee be notified without delay of the charge or charges being brought against him or her comes at a stage that can be subsequent to the act of apprehension itself.[44] The content of this notification is more formal and will require a description of the legal charges for which a person has been detained, empowering that person to be able to eventually challenge the detention.[45]

---

40 *Case of Gangaram Panday*, para. 44.

41 Nor did the Court rule on the possible arbitrariness of the detention, and it would have been interesting to know its opinion on whether the fact of having been deported from the Netherlands is a legitimate ground for detention of a citizen of a State, compatible with the Convention.

42 *Case of Juan Humberto Sánchez*, para. 82; *Case of Bulacio*, para. 128.

43 *Case of Bulacio*, para. 128.

44 One reason for not immediately providing notification of the charges could be, for example, a lack of training of the person making the arrest on how to properly articulate the charges.

45 See in this regard a similar provision in the International Covenant on Civil and Political Rights, M. Nowak, *supra* n. 1, p. 175.

There is nothing to indicate the criteria that must be taken under consideration to decide whether this notification was made "without delay". As will also be seen in other situations, such as for example in the interpretation of Article 8(1) of the Convention, the Court must rule on each case on its individual merits, taking into consideration that according to the wording of the paragraph itself, the period of time must be very short.

3.2.3. Right to be brought promptly before a judicial authority

17. The third requirement is that all individuals deprived of liberty must be brought promptly before a judge or other officer authorized by law to exercise judicial power. This official may be the one who informs the detainee of the charges against him or her. This is the stage of the proceedings at which the individual ceases to be under police custody,[46] and if the person is not set free or released provisionally with precautionary measures, the person will be in detention or preventative detention pursuant to the orders of a court authority.

The involvement of a judge or official authorized to exercise judicial power ensures the rectitude and legality of the detention, considering that as the Court has found, this is a measure that prevents a detention from becoming arbitrary and illegal.[47]

It seems clear that the State official who does not have the title of judge must at least be a person holding a position that is independent of other State bodies, as independence is the minimum guarantee for protecting individuals' personal liberty and, eventually, personal integrity.

In the case of Cantoral Benavides, the Court moved the interpretation of the provision forward. The Court found that Peru had violated Article 8(1) of the Convention due to the fact that Mr Cantoral Benavides had been processed by a military criminal judge who was not the "competent, independent and impartial judge" required by that provision. As a consequence of this, Peru had also violated Article 7(5) of the Convention, as it had put the victim at the disposal of a military criminal judge.[48] With this, the Court seems to find that not just any authority has judicial power to examine the legality and reasonableness of a detention. Rather, only those who do not violate the principle of the judge with rightful jurisdiction (*juez natural*) can do so.[49]

18. The placing of the detainee at the disposal of the judicial authority must be carried out "promptly". The Court, in my opinion without fully realizing the

---

46 I use the expression "*custodia policial*" in the sense of the English term "custody" and the French expression "*garde à vue*".

47 *Case of Bulacio*, para. 129.

48 *Case of Cantoral Benavides*, paras. 75 and 76.

49 Regarding the "*juez natural*", which is the wording in Spanish, see Chapter 5 on due process, section 2.3.

meaning and consequences of the statement, has spoken in some judgments of "immediate judicial oversight",[50] which could lend itself to an erroneous interpretation of the Convention. Clearly this obligation cannot be imposed on the State, as it is often physically impossible to comply with it.

The term "promptly" must be interpreted on a case-by-case basis. Often, domestic legislation itself indicates the time periods for these purposes, which normally range between 24 and 48 hours; these time periods can serve as a basis for a ruling of the Court on a possible violation of the provision, but they are not decisive. The Inter-American Commission has opined that a tolerable delay is "that which is necessary for preparing the transfer", which seems to be a good standard for examining each situation.[51] The Court has found this provision to have been violated several times after States failed to put detainees at the disposal of a judicial authority, particularly but not exclusively[52] in the case of disappearances[53] and summary executions.[54]

19. The obligations established for States in Article 7 of the Convention can be suspended during an emergency, given that this provision is not included in Article 27(2) of the American Convention. Without prejudice to this, the Court has reiterated that with regard to this right, as with others, the suspension of obligations must not go beyond what is strictly necessary, given that:

> The limits imposed upon the actions of a State come from "the general requirement that in any state of emergency there be appropriate means to control the measures taken, so that they are proportionate to the needs and do not exceed the strict limits imposed by the Convention or derived from it."[55]

This means that although Article 7 of the Convention does not fully apply during an emergency, legislation must exist establishing a detainee's right to be put at the disposal of a judicial authority. The Court had an opportunity to rule on time periods in the context of an emergency in the case of Castillo Petruzzi. The arrests of Castillo Petruzzi and other accused individuals took place during a time of "great disturbance of the public peace". The emergency law in Peru allowed individuals presumably implicated in the crime of treason to be held in detention without judicial intervention for 15 days, extendable for another similar period of time. The State's defense in this case consisted of arguing that

---

50 *Case of Bulacio*, para. 129; *Case of Maritza Urrutia*, para. 66.

51 *Case of Castillo Petruzzi*, para. 105(a), citing the Commission.

52 In the *case of Suárez Rosero*, a detention that took place in the context of a proceeding related to drug trafficking, the Court found that the petitioner had never been brought before a judicial authority (*Case of Suárez Rosero*, para. 56). See also *Case of Maritza Urrutia*, para. 74.

53 *Case of Velásquez Rodríguez*, para. 155; *Case of Castillo Páez*, paras. 57–58; *Case of Bámaca Velásquez*, paras. 142–143.

54 *Case of the "White Van" (Paniagua Morales et al.)*, para. 166; *Case of the Street Children (Villagrán Morales et al.)*, paras. 133–135; *Case of Juan Humberto Sánchez*, para. 83.

55 *Case of Castillo Petruzzi*, para. 109.

Peru had adopted emergency measures that included the suspension of Article 7 of the Convention. In its judgment, the Court reminded Peru that no measures adopted during an emergency situation may go beyond what is strictly necessary and concluded that Peruvian law itself contradicts paragraph 5 of Article 7 of the Convention.[56] It ruled, moreover, that the facts had taken place during a period of time of approximately 36 days from the detention to the date on which the accused were put at the disposal of a judge, which was obviously excessive.[57]

3.2.4. *Right to be brought to trial within a reasonable time or to be released*

20. Paragraph 5 of Article 7 of the Convention grants protection to personal liberty on establishing that detention cannot exceed "a reasonable time", because detention while awaiting trial, or preventative detention, cannot be the general norm but rather must be the exception, as it is a restriction of a human right and restrictions are always exceptional.[58]

The right to be brought to trial within a reasonable time or to be released is the basis of frequent complaints before international supervisory bodies. It is regularly violated on the American continent; there is a clear tendency to transform pre-trial detention into the norm and freedom into the exception, with the resulting consequence that a significant number of those held in prison are accused but not convicted.[59] The subject raises certain problems that deserve to be examined independently of one another.

3.2.4.1. Reasons for keeping a person in detention

21. The reasons that can be invoked in order to keep a person in detention can be derived from the text itself of paragraph 5 of the article under analysis: liberty can "be subject to guarantees to assure his appearance for trial". Consequently, detention can be ordered when there is a risk that the person will not appear at the trial if released. Because the objective of criminal proceedings is to be able to investigate the facts without interference, it also seems possible to keep in detention a person who could be reasonably expected to go into hiding or alter the

---

56 *Ibidem*. However, this reasoning did not make it clear whether the Court felt that 15 days was an excessive period of time for the state of emergency or if the expression "promptly" found in Article 7(5) should always be applied, whether in normal times or in states of emergency. The Court reiterated this in the *case of Cantoral Benavides*, para. 73. In the same sense, see *case of Loayza Tamayo,* paras. 49–50.

57 *Case of Castillo Petruzzi*, para. 111.

58 The idea of the exceptionality of detention is explicitly included in the text of Article 9(3) of the International Covenant on Civil and Political Rights.

59 See A. Bovino, "El encarcelamiento preventivo en los tratados de derechos humanos", in M. Abregú and C. Courtis (eds.), *La aplicación de los tratados sobre derechos humanos por los tribunales locales,* Centro de Estudios Legales y Sociales, Buenos Aires, 1997, p. 430.

evidence of a crime if released, that is, generally block the judicial proceedings.[60] Pre-trial detention therefore cannot help but have procedural aims.[61]

Without prejudice to this, the European Court of Human Rights has accepted other reasons for keeping a person in detention, such as for example the necessity of preventing crime and preserving the public order.[62] This is highly doubtful as far as its compatibility with international law. At the time of writing there was no case law on this point in the inter-American system.

22. Given that liberty is the general rule, the risk of escape or alteration of evidence must be imminent and real. Elements for deciding whether there is a risk of escape can include, for example, whether the accused has a stable work relationship in the country, a family, or property; the accused's character; and other similar considerations. Should it be proven that the risk exists, it must also be proven that it is not possible to counteract that risk in any way other than deprivation of liberty. Therefore, the first alternative the judge must examine when assessing whether there is a risk of flight is the possibility of ensuring appearance at trial through another kind of guarantee, which could include bail or, for example, confining the person inside the country, which constitutes a limitation that is less burdensome than deprivation of liberty and that is permitted by Article 22(3) of the Convention. It is possible to require other elements in order to prevent manipulation of evidence. These other elements would depend on the type of evidence whose protection is sought.

3.2.4.2. Concept of a reasonable period of time

23. The American Convention, in the same way as other human rights treaties regulating the right to personal liberty, establishes the right of a detainee to be brought to trial within a reasonable period of time or to be released. The Convention does not establish the duration of the reasonable period of time, domestic legislation can (and often does) establish specific maximum time periods for detention or preventative detention. As with the time periods mentioned in the previous section, domestic time periods can be an element to take into consideration in cases in which a violation of this right found in the Convention is alleged, but they are not definitive for the international supervisory body's ruling.

---

60 Regarding interference with justice, see D.J. Harris et al., *supra* n. 5, p. 140. In the context of the International Covenant on Civil and Political Rights, see, *inter alia*, *A. v. Australia*, Communication 560/93, decision of 3 April 1997, A/52/40, Vol. II, Annex VI, sect. L (pp. 125–146), para. 9(2); *W.E.B. v. the Netherlands*, Communication 432/90, decision on inadmissibility of 23 October 1992, para. 6(3); and *Hill and Hill v. Spain*, Communication 526/93, decision of 2 April 1997, A/52/40, Vol. II, Annex VI, sect. B (pp. 5–21), para. 12(3).

61 A. Bovino, *supra* n. 59, pp. 442–445.

62 D.J. Harris et al., *supra* n. 5, p. 140–142.

24. It is important to indicate here that this right is different from the one established in Article 8(1) of the Convention, which establishes that a person has a right to a "hearing, with due guarantees and within a reasonable time [...] in the substantiation of any accusation of a criminal nature made against him." The time period found in Article 7 has to do with the duration of detention, while the time period found in Article 8 refers to the duration of a trial, whether or not those involved are subjected to pre-trial detention. A situation is possible in which the period of detention is not reasonable – in which circumstance the individual must be released under penalty of the State's action being found to be in violation of the Convention – while the duration of the trial is found to be reasonable, in which case no violation will have taken place on that point.

It should also be emphasized that this right is not equivalent to finding that an individual must be released due to lack of grounds for keeping the individual detained. In that case, the detention must cease immediately without taking its duration into consideration. In order to have any effect, Article 7(5) of the Convention must be interpreted in the sense that even though there may in principle be reasons for keeping an individual detained, that person must be released if the period of detention has exceeded a reasonable period of time.

25. The European Court of Human Rights has emphasized an interpretation according to which the key element for understanding Article 5(3) of the European Convention on Human Rights, the equivalent to Article 7(5) of the American Convention, is recalling that it forms part of the guarantee of personal liberty, for which reason "it is the provisional detention of accused persons which must not, according to Article 5(3), be prolonged beyond a reasonable time". The purpose of supervisory bodies is to determine

> whether the time that has elapsed, for whatever reason, before judgment is passed on the accused has at some stage exceeded a reasonable limit, that is to say imposed a greater sacrifice than could, in the circumstances of the case, reasonably be expected of a person presumed to be innocent.[63]

In the Stögmüller case,[64] the European Court of Human Rights indicated that it does not agree with a distinction proposed by the Austrian government that argues that on examining the duration of a detention, the reasons invoked for it need not be examined because they are irrelevant. The European Court of Human Rights finds that a *sine qua non* condition for the validity of

---

63 ECtHR, *Wemhoff v. Germany*, judgment of 27 June 1968, para 5; and *Matznetter v. Austria*, judgment of 10 November 1969, para. 12, reproduced in Council of Europe, *Digest of Strasbourg Case-Law relating to the European Convention on Human Rights*, Vol. 1 (Articles 1–5), Carl Heymanns-Verlag KG, Köln/Berlin/Bonn/München, 1984, p. 505. Also see *Letellier v. France*, judgment of 26 June 1991, para 35, cited by D.J. Harris et al., *supra* n. 5, p. 137.

64 ECtHR, *Stögmüller v. Austria*, judgment of 10 November 1969, para. 4, Publ. Court A, Vol. 9, pp. 39–40, reproduced in *ibidem*, pp. 505–506.

maintaining a detention is that reasonable suspicion persists with regard to whether the detainee has committed a crime, but that in order to decide on whether to prolong a detention, the reasonableness of the grounds that persuaded the judicial authority to decide to break so seriously from the rules on personal liberty and the presumption of innocence must be examined; the grounds must demonstrate that there are "good reasons in the public interest" for maintaining the detention.[65] By putting it this way, the European Court of Human Rights veered from its central objective to consider the reasons for the detention; this is correct, as if there are no reasons for keeping a person in detention that are compatible with the Convention, that person must be freed. What the European Court of Human Rights states is that in order to keep a person detained beyond a reasonable period of time, reasons are required that are more powerful than the ones that would allow the initial detention. However, this does not clarify the problem of deciding how to determine what that reasonable period of time is; in addition, the European Court of Human Rights' position seems to be contrary to the very idea of the right to not be detained "beyond a reasonable period of time" because it would suggest that if there are "good reasons in the public interest", the detention would be legitimate even if it were to last for many years, which would completely annul the right being interpreted.

In addition, the European Court of Human Rights has found that the European Convention on Human Rights would also be violated should the investigation and the trial itself be carried out over a longer period of time than what could be reasonably expected.[66] Under its second approach, the supervisory body's examination would be similar to the one made with regard to Article 6(1) (the equivalent to Article 8(1) of the American Convention).

The only criteria that seems salvageable from the European Court of Human Rights judgment under examination is the criteria that weighs whether prolonging the detention has "imposed a greater sacrifice than could, in the circumstances of the case, reasonably be expected of a person presumed to be innocent".

26. At the time of writing, the Inter-American Court had not had further opportunity to examine the problem of the reasonable period of time. The subject has been raised only in the case of Suárez Rosero and, in my opinion, in that judgment the Court was not careful about the distinction between the period of time mentioned in Article 7(5) and the one mentioned in Article 8(1), both from the American Convention. In part of its reasoning, the Inter-American Court indicated that the purpose of the reasonable period of time referred to in these two articles "is to prevent accused persons from remaining in

---

65 ECtHR, *Wemhoff v. Germany*, *supra* n. 63, paras. 16–17.

66 *Ibidem.*

that situation for a protracted period and to ensure that the charge is promptly disposed of."[67] This, however, is the purpose of the period of time mentioned in Article 8(1), not of that found in Article 7(5), whose objective is to protect the personal liberty of the accused.[68]

In the same case, the Inter-American Court examined a domestic law in Ecuador that ordered individuals be released who had remained in detention without their cases having received an order to dismiss or open a plenary action over a time period equal to or greater than a third of the length of the maximum punishment for the crime; this provision was not applicable to individuals charged with crimes punished under the Narcotic and Psychotropic Substances Act. Unfortunately, the Inter-American Court did not analyze the law itself but only the laws on equal protection of those being put on trial for consumption or distribution of drugs. A jurisdictional ruling on the compatibility of a provision that enshrines the idea that pre-trial detention should not exceed a reasonable period of time would have been interesting.[69]

27. The Inter-American Commission delves more deeply into the subject in its final report in the case of Giménez v. Argentina.[70] Its focus emphasizes that the basis of Article 7(5) of the American Convention is "that no person should be punished without a prior trial which includes a charge, the opportunity to defend oneself, and a sentence", all this within a reasonable period of time, "intended to protect the accused with respect to his or her fundamental right to personal liberty, as well as the accused's personal security against being the object of an unjustified procedural risk."[71] A failure to comply with this period of time would also violate the principle of presumption of innocence and could interfere with the right to defense.[72]

A factor in the Giménez case was the existence of a law establishing deadlines for the final judgment in criminal proceedings and allowing a judge to release the accused when this deadline expired unless "an objective assessment of the nature of the deed and the personal characteristics of the accused are grounds for presuming that he will attempt to escape the law".[73] Based on this, the Inter-American Commission first examined the role that national deadlines could play in a decision on a possible violation of Article 7(5) of the Convention, expressing that the reasonableness of a period of time in prison without

---

67 *Case of Suárez Rosero*, para. 70.

68 For the pertinent examination of the Court's position on the reasonable period of time found in Article 8, set forth in its judgment in *Suárez Rosero*, see Chapter 5, section 2.4.3.

69 *Case of Suárez Rosero*, paras. 95–99.

70 IACHR, *Giménez v. Argentina*, Case No. 11.245, Report No. 12/96, 1 March 1996, in *1995 Annual Report*.

71 *Ibidem*, para. 76.

72 *Ibidem*, paras. 78–81.

73 Articles 379(6) and 380 of the Criminal Procedural Code of Argentina, reproduced in *ibidem*, paras. 62, 63 and 64.

a conviction "cannot be established in the abstract",[74] for which reason reasonableness cannot be given a legal definition beforehand and "what is reasonable must be analyzed in light of the specific facts of each case".[75]

Without prejudice to this, the Commission argued it was possible to establish "a general term limit beyond which a detention is considered *prima facie* illegal no matter the crime charged or the complexity of the case". This would be consistent with the principle of presumption of innocence and with all the other rights associated with due process of the law.[76] Unfortunately, the Commission did not follow this line of thought by shedding light on which elements must be taken into consideration in order to estimate a period of time that would not be reasonable. Rather, it linked this idea with the deadlines established under Argentine domestic law, arguing that, as the maximum period of time established under Argentine law for the total length of the proceedings had passed without that proceedings concluding and without the accused being released, the pre-trial detention of Mr Giménez was to have been considered *prima facie* illegitimate, implying that it was the State's responsibility to demonstrate the existence of pertinent and sufficient reasons for justifying the detention, thus legitimizing it internationally.

The Commission later examined two other points, stating first that the possible existence of pertinent and sufficient reasons for keeping Mr Giménez imprisoned must be examined, and second analyzing whether the duration of the proceedings itself was reasonable.

Regarding the reasons, the criteria that the Argentine courts had followed in denying Mr Giménez's release were categorized by the Commission as follows: (i) danger of flight, seriousness of the act and possible severity of the judgment; (ii) risk of recidivism; and (iii) personal circumstances.[77]

The Argentine courts indicated that the gravity of the violation and severity of the punishment were elements to take into consideration when analyzing the risk of detainee flight. The Commission found these elements acceptable in principle, although it concluded by rejecting them because deprivation of liberty should not be based solely on the fact that an alleged crime is especially objectionable from a social point of view. Trying to make the duration of pre-trial detention proportionate to the possible duration of the crime can only be a justification for early punishment, which would violate the presumption of innocence. Another argument invoked by the Commission was that the threat of a future sentence for the detainee that could incite him or her to flee diminished if the detention continued, as the sentence that remained pending compliance would have also diminished considerably.[78]

---

74 *Ibidem*, para. 67.

75 *Ibidem*, para. 69.

76 *Ibidem*, para. 70.

77 *Ibidem*, para. 71.

78 *Ibidem*, paras. 86–89.

Regarding risk of recidivism as a criterion for keeping a person in pre-trial detention, the Argentine courts evaluated it based on the criminal history of the accused, who had been convicted for theft with aggravating circumstances and repeated theft of automobiles. The Commission rejected this criterion, arguing that the courts should have examined the individual's interest in rehabilitating and reinserting himself into society, reflected, *inter alia*, in the accused's response to the consequences of his crime, his desire or willingness to provide reparations, his willingness to adopt a conduct that was socially acceptable, and his social and family environment.[79] It seems clear that the risk of recidivism, however it is evaluated, is not a valid reason before international law to keep a person in detention, so the Commission should have had summarily rejected this justification.

As regards personal circumstances as a criterion for denying release, the Commission repeated the foregoing arguments, indicating that it violates the presumption of innocence and also constitutes a punishment imposed for prior conduct; the Commission argued that once a convict has served his or her sentence or probation, "the person is returned to his or her full civil status".[80]

In sum, the Commission rejected the criteria invoked by the Argentine courts for keeping Mr Giménez in detention.

This should have concluded the examination of the compatibility of the facts of the case with Article 7(5) of the Convention. Strictly according to law, the facts indicated that Mr Giménez's detention was arbitrary, independently of the period of time that may have passed, given that the reasons invoked to keep him in detention were not compatible with the cited article. However, the Inter-American Commission turned to considering the reasonableness of the period of time that the proceedings had lasted, presumably for greater justification, reaching the conclusion that given that the case was not complex and the conduct of the accused would not have been an obstacle for the investigation, the period of time that passed between the start of the investigation and the date of the communication – from 29 September 1989 to 17 November 1993, and extended until 1 December 1994, the date on which he was granted release – was excessive and imputable to the State's lack of diligence in pursuing the trial.[81]

The approach used by the Commission to analyze this case could perhaps lead to diminishing the effectiveness of the right enshrined in Article 7(5) of the Convention, as it tends in my opinion to inappropriately link the right to be released with the court's activity in the case, thus changing the object of the test from reasonableness of the period of detention to reasonableness of the period of the trial.

79 *Ibidem*, para. 92.
80 *Ibidem*, para. 97.
81 *Ibidem*, paras. 99–108.

28. From all that has been said, one can appreciate the difficulty of establishing the scope and content of this right to be judged within a reasonable period of time or to be released. Without presuming to solve the problem, but rather to contribute to shedding some light towards reasoning out this point, it seems useful and necessary to establish certain basic premises from which to start in order to attempt to find the meaning of paragraph 5 of Article 7 of the Convention.

The first is that the interpretation should give Article 7(5) content that is different from that of Article 8(1) of the Convention; otherwise, the right found in Article 7(5) is meaningless because it lacks its own content.

The second is that this differentiated content must come from the fact that this paragraph protects personal liberty, in contrast to Article 8(1), which protects the notion of "a due process" or a just process, with the purpose, for example, of preventing damage from being caused to a person as a result of spending a long time in a situation of uncertainty over his or her situation in criminal proceedings, or of seeing his or her right to defense damaged, among other things because the passage of time blurs the memories of witnesses or makes it difficult for them to appear at trial to testify. As a consequence of this, the time period indicated in Article 7 of the Convention must have to do with the duration of the period of detention, while the time period mentioned in Article 8 of the Convention refers to the duration of the trial, whether or not the persons on trial are in detention. It is thus possible to conceive of the existence of a violation of Article 7(5) of the Convention for an excessive period of detention without a violation of Article 8(1), because the time period of the trial is reasonable.

The third is that the need for its own content implies that the right established in Article 7(5) cannot be equivalent to finding that an individual must be released because the grounds for keeping the individual detained no longer apply. In that case, I would reiterate, the detention must cease immediately without taking its duration into consideration. Otherwise, it would be arbitrary and in violation of Article 7(3). In order to have any effect, Article 7(5) of the Convention must be interpreted in the sense that even when reasons exist in principle for keeping a person detained, that person must be released if the period of detention has exceeded a reasonable period of time.

The fourth is that this time period cannot be determined in the abstract, but rather on a case-by-case basis and according to the circumstances of each case. This raises the problem of determining what elements must be taken into consideration for deciding when a period of time ceases to be reasonable.

What are the possible options for interpretation? One, which seems to be the option pursued by both the European Court of Human Rights and the Inter-American Commission, is to argue that the right established in Article 7(5) of the Convention is related with the persistence of strong reasons for keeping a person in detention and that the reasonable period of time is, in reality, the period of the trial itself. Therefore, when strong reasons exist for depriving someone of liberty, one must examine whether the investigation and trial have been carried out with the necessary swiftness, taking into consideration that a person is involved who has been accused and is deprived of liberty. This would imply that Article 8(1) can be differentiated from Article 7(5) in that when there is an accused individual deprived of liberty, the period of time must be shorter than when not. This is despite the fact that in our examination of due process, we will see that an element to take into consideration when deciding whether the time period is reasonable or not is how much the duration of the trial affects the accused. For this reason, the same result can be obtained without the existence of Article 7(5) of the Convention. The only advantage of the existence of Article 7(5) would be that once this period of time has passed, the accused would have the right to be released whether or not the reasonable period of time established in Article 8(1) has also been violated.

The second option is perhaps to argue that what should be examined is only whether the duration of the detention is excessive, and that this examination must be carried out through an attempt to balance the public interest against the burden that the deprivation of liberty places on each accused individual. There has not yet been any case law that determines the elements that should be used in making this measurement. Could one of these elements be the seriousness of the crime or the dangerousness of the criminal? It does not seem possible, as the only reason for pre-trial detention is to protect the course of justice. It will be up to the Inter-American Court to make an authorized interpretation of this subject.

3.2.4.3. Period to be considered for the purposes of application of Article 7(5)

29. Another problem arises in determining how to measure the period of time that must be examined in order to decide whether Article 7(5) of the Convention has been violated. The start date is simple, as that is determined by the moment at which the individual was deprived of liberty. It is more difficult to decide on the date of conclusion, because there is a substantial difference between the Anglo-Saxon system and the Continental system. In the Anglo-Saxon system, pre-trial detention generally ends with the handing down of a judgment at the conclusion of an oral trial. If the ruling imposes a sentence of deprivation of liberty, the person begins serving that sentence as of that moment and is no longer considered to be in preventative detention, even if the ruling itself is not final and there are remedies pending. In contrast, in the civil law system, deprivation of liberty is considered preventative detention as long as a judgment is not final and there is no *res judicata*, although often the time during which the person is subjected to preventative detention is counted after sentencing as time served.

The job of the supervisory body, however, is to transcend specific legal systems and establish law that applies to all individuals alike. I would argue that if the reason for the existence of the right to be brought to trial within a reasonable period of time or to be released is to not cause harm unjustly by depriving a presumably innocent person of liberty, then that reasoning works as long as there is a possibility that the accused will be declared innocent.[82] Thus it would seem just to apply the civil legal system.

3.3. OTHER STATE OBLIGATIONS WITH REGARD TO THE DEPRIVATION OF LIBERTY

30. As stated previously, the provisions of Article 7 of the Convention have been complemented by other declarations or bodies of principles and by the development of international case law.[83]

31. One initial important development can be found in what is set forth in Advisory Opinion 16/99 with regard to the right to legal aid in the context of the Vienna Convention on Consular Relations, in which the Court ruled that in the case of deprivation of liberty of a foreign national, the receptor State must inform the detainee of his or her rights "without delay", understanding that this implies that the notification must be made "at the time the accused is deprived of his freedom, or at least before he makes his first statement before the authorities". The purpose of this is to guarantee due process, and particularly the right to defense.[84] Among the rights of detainees is the right to know that they can "notify a third party that he or she is in State custody". For example, the detainee could notify a relative, an attorney and/or legal counsel, as applicable at the time of deprivation of liberty.[85]

32. The mention of the right to notify an attorney is related to Principle 17 of the Body of Principles[86] which establishes that the individual must be informed of the right to assistance from an attorney "at the time the accused is imprisoned" and that the State must facilitate adequate means for exercising that right; it also establishes that should it be required in the interest of justice, the individual under arrest will have the right for a judge or authority to assign him or her an attorney, free of charge should that person lack sufficient means to pay the attorney.[87]

---

82 The European Court of Human Rights found a conflicting solution, but the provision of Article 5(1) on which the Court based its conclusion is different from that found in Article 7, such that it is not an appropriate reference (see D.J. Harris et al., *supra* n. 5, p. 137–138).

83 OC-16/99, para. 106.

84 *Ibidem*, paras. 86–87.

85 *Case of Bulacio*, para. 130.

86 See *supra* n. 36.

87 Also see Principle 18.

The Human Rights Committee has been clear in establishing that the presence of an attorney from the moment of the detention itself is a right held by the detainee.[88] In the European system, the Court has approached the subject from a different angle, indicating that if according to the domestic legal system consequences are attached to the attitude of an accused at the initial stages of police interrogation which are decisive for the prospects of the defense in any subsequent criminal proceedings, an attorney must be present in order to comply with the demands of due process.[89]

33. Another important State obligation arises from Advisory Opinion 16/99: the obligation to identify the detainee, which among other things allows for the detainee's age to be established and ensures treatment appropriate to his or her circumstances.[90] In one case, the Court ordered Honduras in the reparations section of a ruling to set up "a record of detainees to enable control of legality of the detentions, which must therefore include identification of the detainees, the reason for their detention, the competent authority, the day and time of admission and of release, and information on the arrest warrant".[91] A later judgment broadened this by ruling that:

> As this Court has recognized in previous cases, there must be a record of detainees to enable control of legality of detentions. This requires entry, among other data, of: identification of the detainees, cause for detention, notification to the competent authority, and to those representing them, exercising custody or acting as defense counsel, if applicable, and the visits they have paid to the detainee, the date and time of entry and release, information given to the minor and to other persons regarding the rights and guarantees of the detainee, record of signs of beating or mental illness, transfers of the detainee, and meal schedule. The detainee must also sign and, if he or she does not, there must be an explanation of the reason.[92]

34. Deprivation of liberty causes the arrestee or detainee to be vulnerable. Experience in the Latin American states of the treatment of those deprived of liberty bears this out,[93] and it is no coincidence that Article 5 of the American

---

88 See HRC, *Kelly v. Jamaica*, Communication 537/1993, decision dated 16 July 1993, A/51/40, (1996), Vol. II, Annex VIII, sect. O, (pp. 98–107), para. 9.2.

89 P. van Dijk, F. van Hoof, A. van Rijn and L. Zwaak (eds.), *Theory and Practice of the European Convention on Human Rights*, 4th edn, Intersentia, Antwerp/Oxford, 2006, p. 639, commenting on the Court's ruling in *John Murray*, of 8 February 1996 (Reports 1996-I, Vol. I, para. 63).

90 OC-16/99, para. 94.

91 *Case of Juan Humberto Sánchez*, para. 189.

92 *Case of Bulacio*, para. 132.

93 This has been a subject that has caught the attention of the Inter-American Commission on Human Rights, which in 1995 created a Working Group on the conditions of persons deprived of liberty (see IACHR, *1995 Annual Report*, OEA/Ser.L/V/II.91 Doc. 7 rev., 28 February 1996, pp. 233–235). In addition, it is a very current problem for non-

Convention requires States to treat persons deprived of liberty with the respect that is due based on the dignity inherent in the human being,[94] and that the Inter-American Court has linked the right to *habeas corpus* with the protection of physical integrity of persons.[95] Along with this, the Human Rights Committee indicated in its General Comment on Article 7 of the International Covenant that "the protection of the detainee [...] requires that prompt and regular access be given to doctors".[96] Principle 24 of the Body of Principles mentioned previously establishes that all persons imprisoned or under detention shall be provided with proper medical examinations within the shortest time possible following their entry into the place of detention.[97]

The Inter-American Court has ruled in the same vein, indicating that:

> The detainees must be examined and given medical care, preferably by a physician chosen by themselves or by those who have their legal custody or representation. Results of any medical examination ordered by the authorities – and which must not be conducted in the presence of the police authorities – must be delivered to the judge, the detainee and his attorney, or to him and whoever exercises custody or representation of the minor according to the law.[98]

3.4. EFFECTS OF DEPRIVATION OF LIBERTY ON OTHER HUMAN RIGHTS

35. Deprivation of liberty necessarily affects the enjoyment of other human rights. As the rule for every restriction is that it must lead to and be proportional for achieving its objective, it is important to try to limit as much as possible the effects, which we could perhaps call collateral, that deprivation of liberty has on other human rights. This is established in the Standard Minimum Rules for the Treatment of Prisoners.[99] A right that will necessarily be affected is the right to

---

governmental organizations in Latin America. See Human Rights Watch, *Annual Report 2002 (General Overview).*

94 On this, see Chapter 3.

95 OC-8/87, paras. 35–36.

96 HRC, General Comment No. 20, 44th Period of Sessions (1992), HRI/GEN/1/Rev.5, 26 April 2001, para. 11.

97 Also see Principles 25 and 26.

98 *Case of Bulacio,* para. 131.

99 "Imprisonment and other measures which result in cutting off an offender from the outside world are afflictive by the very fact of taking from the person the right of self-determination by depriving him of his liberty. Therefore the prison system shall not, except as incidental to justifiable segregation or the maintenance of discipline, aggravate the suffering inherent in such a situation." Standard Minimum Rules for the Treatment of Prisoners, adopted by the First United Nations Congress on the Prevention of Crime and the Treatment of Offenders, held at Geneva in 1955, and approved by the Economic and Social Council by its resolutions 663C (XXIV) of 31 July 1957 and 2076 (LXII) of 13 May 1977, *ibidem*, para. 57 citing para. 10 of the Rules.

privacy and non-interference with the family life of the detainee; another that could be affected would be freedom of expression, particularly with regard to the right to be informed by any medium and to communicate privately with persons. There is also a possibility that the right to participate in government will be affected, as well as the right to assembly.

However, the idea that deprivation necessarily brings with it restrictions that are implicit or inherent to it must be rejected.[100] It is essential that the eventual restriction of these rights be subject to an examination of their necessity in a democratic society according to the standards on restricting each one of the rights. From this point of view, detainee contact with family and with the world has tended to progressively broaden, and what seemed impossible before, such as for example conjugal visits, is now a right in a significant number of States. Nor does it seem to justify at all the elimination of the right to vote in some countries for people accused of crimes punishable by relatively harsh sentences, as this is done not in application of a sentence but as a consequence of the status of the accused.

The Inter-American Court ruled on the rights of persons deprived of liberty on the occasion of a provisional measure requested by the Commission with regard to inmates in the Urso Branco prison in Brazil. In that measure, handed down in August 2002, the Court found that the State had a special obligation to ensure the rights of inmates and, in particular, to make the Minimum Rules for the Treatment of Prisoners[101] applicable, rules which have in this way been incorporated into inter-American case law.

4. WRIT OF *HABEAS CORPUS*

36. Paragraph 6 of Article 7 of the Convention sets forth the right of all persons deprived of liberty to have "recourse to a competent court, in order that the court may decide without delay on the lawfulness of [their] arrest or detention and order [their] release if [an] arrest or detention is unlawful." This right to a remedy is violated if the remedy does not exist at all or if it exists but is not granted "without delay", even if the detention itself is legal. The Inter-American Court has connected *habeas corpus* with the general right found in Article 25 of the Convention to a simple and quick remedy for protecting rights recognized by that international instrument, as well as the rights recognized by the constitutions and domestic legislation of States Parties.[102] *Habeas corpus* is the

---

100 On this point in the European system, see P. van Dijk and G.J.H. van Hoof, *Theory and Practice of the European Convention on Human Rights,* 3rd edn, SIM, Kluwer Law International, The Hague/London/Boston, 1998, pp. 763–765.

101 *Provisional measures regarding the Federal Republic of Brazil, Urso Branco Prison*, decision of 29 August 2002, para 6.

102 *Case of Suárez Rosero*, para. 64.

way in which this right found in Article 25 of the Convention is expressed when protecting personal liberty.[103]

According to case law, *habeas corpus* is "the suitable means to ensure liberty, to control respect for life and the right to humane treatment [of the person], and to impede [...] their disappearance or non-determination of [...] their place of detention."[104]

As the remedy protects not only liberty but also personal integrity, the Court has found that *habeas corpus* requires that the detainee be brought before a judge or court that is competent to examine the legality of the detention.[105]

37. The remedy can be granted with regard to all deprivations of liberty and not only detentions carried out by the police or ordered by a court. It also applies to individuals in solitary confinement[106] and even during periods of constitutional emergency, as it is one of the guarantees that cannot be suspended pursuant to Article 27 of the Convention and the Court's interpretation of it.[107] The Convention is also violated when the suspension is not explicit but rather implicit.[108] This remedy cannot be eliminated based on the type of crime for which a person has been detained: in the case of Loayza Tamayo, the Inter-American Court ruled that Peru had violated Article 7(6) by establishing by law that actions for guaranteeing the rights of detainees could never be granted with regard to crimes of treason, those actions including *habeas corpus*.[109]

38. The Court has reiterated that the principles of due process of law cannot be suspended in a situation of emergency, particularly with regard to *habeas corpus*, as they are indispensable for the protection of human rights that cannot be suspended.[110]

Petitioners should be able to exercise the remedy at reasonable intervals, given that pre-trial detention requires the persistence of circumstances that make detention indispensable. It is also subject to the requirement that it must not exceed a reasonable period of time.[111] The remedy also must be fast, as it seeks

---

[103] OC-8/87, paras. 32 and 34.

[104] *Case of Juan Humberto Sánchez*, para. 122; *Case of Maritza Urrutia*, para. 111.

[105] OC-8/87, para. 35. On this point, see C. Riego, "El sistema procesal penal chileno frente a las normas internacionales de derechos humanos", in M. Abregú and C. Courtis (eds.), *supra* n. 59, pp. 296–299.

[106] *Case of Suárez Rosero*, para. 59; *Case of Cesti Hurtado*, para. 123.

[107] OC-8/87, paras. 35–36 and 42–43. Also see *Case of Castillo Petruzzi et al.*, paras. 109 and 186.

[108] *Case of Neira Alegría et al.* Therein, the Court found that the Armed Forces' control and jurisdiction over the San Juan Bautista Prison had the effect of implicitly suspending *habeas corpus*, in violation of the Convention (paras. 84–85).

[109] *Case of Loayza Tamayo*, paras. 51–55; *Case of Castillo Petruzzi et al.*, para. 182; *Case of Cantoral Benavides*, para. 165.

[110] OC-9/87, para. 30.

[111] The European Court of Human Rights ruled that 15 months was not a reasonable period of time and that one month could be reasonable (see ECtHR, *Herczegfalvy v. Austria*,

to review whether the legal provisions protecting liberty have been violated.[112] As far as the meaning of the expression "promptly" is concerned, the Court has not established general criteria for determining whether a remedy complies with Article 7(6) of the Convention; it only found that a period of 14 months for a *habeas corpus* ruling was obviously excessive.[113] Given that *habeas corpus* is one of the species of the general remedy created by Article 25 of the Convention, it must also be effective; remedies that turn out to be illusory because of the general conditions in a country or specific conditions of a case do not comply with the provision of Article 7(6) under analysis.[114]

Finally, the judge hearing a remedy must also have authority to address the jurisdiction of the official who has ordered the deprivation of liberty, as it is this judge's responsibility to consider not only whether the detention is illegal but also whether it is arbitrary. This could be related to the judicial authority handling the case.[115]

5. PROHIBITION OF DETENTION FOR DEBTS

39. The right to not be detained for debts, established in Article 7(7) of the Convention, is also set forth in Article 11 of the International Covenant. The Convention does not differentiate between the origins of the debt for the application of this provision. From this, one could argue that in principle, whatever the source of the debt, a failure to pay it cannot result in deprivation of liberty. In drafting this paragraph during the Specialized Conference, there was some debate over the concept of "debts" arising from the question of whether this would exclude deprivation of liberty for failing to pay support for a spouse and children. The delegate from Brazil indicated that the legal concept of debt in the civil law world was as broad as possible, for which reason he could not accept that wording. The delegate from Colombia clarified that he would understand the concept as it is understood in Colombia's constitution, which is to say that it refer to purely civil debts or obligations "save for a special judicial form of deprivation of liberty" (*arraigo judicial*).

The discussion did not conclude with a common interpretation of the concept, but rather with the addition of a sentence that left "orders of a competent judicial authority issued for non-fulfillment of duties of support"[116] out of the prohibition.

judgment of 24 September 1992, A.244, pp. 24–25; and ECtHR, *Bezicheri v. Italy*, judgment of 25 October 1989, A.164; both cited in P. van Dijk, F. van Hoof, A. van Rijn and L. Zwaak (eds.), *supra* n. 89, p. 502).

112 *Case of Suárez Rosero*, para. 63.

113 *Ibidem*, para. 64.

114 *Case of Cesti Hurtado*, para. 125.

115 *Ibidem*, para. 130.

116 Specialized Conference, n. 9, pp. 188–190.

At the time of writing, the Inter-American Court had not had any opportunity to rule on this prohibition.

6. FORCED DISAPPEARANCE OF PERSONS AND ARTICLE 7

40. In Chapter 2 on the right to life, an aspect of the American Convention was examined with regard to disappearance and its relationship with Article 4, as the Court constructed the phenomenon of disappearance as a combination of the violation of three rights, including the right to life.[117] The subject of disappearances was also addressed in the next chapter, as according to the Court's interpretation, disappearances also violate Article 5 of the Convention by causing injury to both the disappeared and, at times, the relatives of the disappeared.[118] This section will examine the Inter-American Convention on Forced Disappearance of Persons (hereinafter the "Convention on Disappearance") more generally, taking into consideration that it defines the phenomenon as an aggravated violation of the right to personal liberty.

41. As stated previously, the forced disappearance of persons constituted a systematic and regular practice in many countries on this continent. Its emergence put to the test the creativity of the Inter-American Court, which was faced with forced disappearance in its first case, that of Manfredo Velásquez Rodríguez. The case resulted in the legal construction of forced disappearance of persons as a type of violation normally prejudicial to three human rights: the right to life, the right personal integrity and the right to personal liberty.[119] Later, the occurrence of this phenomenon and the problem of impunity resulting from it led to a specific instrument for regulating it: the Convention on Disappearance was adopted in 1994.[120] The gravity of the violation was the main consideration taken into account for qualifying it as a "crime against humanity"[121] and for establishing a series of provisions whose purpose was to prevent forced disappearance by combatting the impunity of those involved in it in a variety of ways.

42. In contrast to the Inter-American Court's construction of the phenomenon, the Convention on Disappearance defines it as:

> the act of depriving a person or persons of his or their freedom, in whatever way, perpetrated by agents of the state or by persons or groups of persons acting with the

[117] See Chapter 2, section 6.

[118] See Chapter 3, section 3.4.

[119] *Case of Velásquez Rodríguez*, para. 155.

[120] Inter-American Convention on Forced Disappearance of Persons, adopted on 9 June 1994, in Belém do Pará. It entered into force on 29 March 1991. As of July 2003, it had 31 States Parties.

[121] Convention on Disappearance, Preamble.

authorization, support, or acquiescence of the state, followed by an absence of information or a refusal to acknowledge that deprivation of freedom or to give information on the whereabouts of that person, thereby impeding his or her recourse to the applicable legal remedies and procedural guarantees.[122]

43. As can be noted, the Convention on Disappearance placed the action in the field of personal liberty, with the violation constituting a deprivation of liberty that does not allow any of the safeguards established in the American Convention for protecting the right to personal liberty to be put into effect. This action violates (i) the obligation to bring a detainee promptly before a judge or other officer authorized by law to exercise judicial power; and (ii) the obligation to allow the detainee to solicit a remedy from a judge or court competent to examine the legality of the detention.

44. Without prejudice to this definition, the preamble of the Convention on Disappearance makes it clear that its drafters were aware that forced disappearance violates not only the right to personal liberty but also "multiple rights". It seems clear that the inability of the disappeared or their family members to have recourse to pertinent remedies results on one hand in a violation of what for all of them is a right that is just as important as personal liberty: the right to personal integrity, at the very least due to the anguish produced by the isolation and the uncertainty of their fate. It also seems clear that as the purpose of disappearance is the commission of human rights violations without evidence, deprivation of liberty that is not admitted often leads to a violation of the right to life.

45. In order to achieve its objectives, the Convention on Disappearance first regulates jurisdiction and the way in which the accused are processed. It starts by establishing an obligation for States Parties to establish forced disappearance as a crime associated with an appropriate penalty[123] as a way of deterring individuals from participating in these types of actions. Later, it establishes universal jurisdiction for pursuit of this crime, ordering States Parties to adopt measures to establish jurisdiction – considering the definition found in Article II of the Convention on Disappearance – in order to be able to pursue cases of disappearance.[124] To ensure that prosecutions are carried out, this jurisdiction is not voluntary but rather obligatory in the sense that if the State does not try the accused, it must extradite them.[125] Because the continent's experience shows that impunity is often the result of the investigation into these cases being assigned to military jurisdiction, Article IX of the Convention on Disappearance

122 Convention on Disappearance, Article II.
123 *Ibidem,* Article III.
124 *Ibidem,* Article IV.
125 *Ibidem,* Article VI.

establishes that cases of disappearance can only be brought to trial before the competent civilian jurisdiction and cannot be assigned to any special jurisdiction, principally military. Nor can the facts constituting a disappearance ever be found to have been committed in the exercise of military duties, nor are privileges, immunities, or special exemptions allowed. Article VIII of the Convention on Disappearance prohibits due obedience from being ruled to provide exemption from criminal responsibility.

46. As another way of preventing impunity, Article V of the Convention on Disappearance establishes that forced disappearance will not be considered a political crime for the purposes of extradition and will always be considered as included among crimes for which extradition is allowed, with the Convention able to serve as sufficient legal basis for it.[126]

The criminal action resulting from the disappearance, and the subsequent sentence itself, will not be subject to the statute of limitations unless it is established in a norm with the same hierarchy level as that of the Constitution, in which case the statute of limitations period shall be equal to that of the most serious crime in that State's legal system.[127]

47. Finally, the Convention establishes certain basic provisions for preventing forced disappearance. Persons deprived of liberty must be kept in places of detention that are officially recognized and brought without delay before the competent judicial authority. Updated official registries of detainees must be kept. Those registries must be made available to "any [...] person having a legitimate interest, as well as other authorities".[128] Judicial authorities must have free and immediate access to detention centers and any other place where they may have reason to believe that a disappeared person may be located, even under military jurisdiction.[129] Finally, as another form of prevention, States must provide "the education necessary" on the crime of disappearance as part of the training of the personnel in charge of applying the law.[130]

48. The Inter-American Court has not used the Convention on Disappearance as a principal source for ruling on a case. Thus, all its case law on disappearances was at the time of writing in reference to the right to life or the right to personal integrity.[131]

---

126 *Ibidem,* Article V.
127 *Ibidem,* Article VII.
128 *Ibidem,* Article XI.
129 *Ibidem,* Article X.
130 *Ibidem,* Article VIII.
131 For the examination of this case law, see Chapters 2 and 3 of this book.

7. DEPRIVATION OF LIBERTY AND CHILDREN AND ADOLESCENTS

49. The adoption and entry into force of the International Convention on the Rights of the Child has had important consequences for the interpretation of the American Convention as regards children. The Inter-American Court was consulted by the Inter-American Commission "with the aim of determining whether the special measures set forth in Article 19 of that same Convention establish 'limits to the good judgment and discretion of the States' with respect to children."[132]

Although the consultation was made with regard to Articles 8 and 25 of the American Convention, the opinion has important implications for the right to personal liberty that must be taken into consideration. For one thing, it uses the International Convention on the Rights of the Child, the United Nations Standard Minimum Rules for the Administration of Juvenile Justice (the "Beijing Rules"), the Directives of the United Nations for the Prevention of Juvenile Delinquency (the "Riad Directives"), and the Standard Minimum Rules for Non-custodial Measures (the "Tokyo Rules") as bases for its assertions, legitimating all these instruments for the interpretation of the provisions of the American Convention.

This Advisory Opinion is enriched by contributions made by Costa Rica and the United Mexican States, the Inter-American Children's Institute, the United Nations Latin American Institute for the Prevention of Crime and the Treatment of Offenders (ILANUD) and various non-governmental organizations, as one can derive a common vision from them of ways to protect children who are abandoned or who enter the justice system due to their actions.

50. The Court accepts in this consultation that it refers to individuals who have not reached 18 years of age[133] and, as expressed by Judge García Ramírez, this implies that:

> the age of 18 is a precise borderline between two ages that involve two distinctive situations in the ambit of this Opinion: one, regarding those who find themselves outside the subjective validity of normal criminal rules, and the other pertaining to those who are subject to them.[134]

It is therefore argued that children must have their own statute that is different in certain aspects from that of adults, although this does not mean that they do not enjoy the safeguards of international human rights law as regards their own human rights.

---

132 OC-17/2002, para. 1.

133 *Ibidem*, para. 42.

134 *Ibidem*, concurring opinion of Judge Sergio García Ramírez, para. 5.

51. The reason for the consultation is clear. At least in Latin America, the doctrine of the "irregular situation of minors"[135] is applied generally, with the result that children and adolescents are not recognized as rights holders and can be deprived of liberty without any kind of safeguards.[136] In addition, it also seems necessary to examine which additional safeguards children must have due to their situation of greater vulnerability compared to that of adults.[137] With regard to personal liberty, the Commission consulted the Court on the following hypothetical practice:

> b) deprivation of liberty of minors by internment in guardianship or custodial institutions on the basis of a determination that they have been abandoned or are prone to fall into situations of risk or illegality, motives which should not be considered of a criminal nature, but, rather, as the result of personal or circumstantial vicissitudes.[138]

52. The Court establishes the basic premise that the interpretation and application of the provisions of the Convention must be carried out taking "the best interests of the child" as a guide.[139] A logical consequence to this is that the institutions that protect children and take part in their care or protection must provide "appropriate staff, adequate facilities, suitable means and proven experience in this type of tasks".[140] This implies that places of detention and State agents that take part in depriving children of liberty must comply with these requirements.

53. The Advisory Opinion cited finds likewise with regard to jurisdictional bodies,[141] and refers to the impossibility of comparing the situation of children alleged to have broken criminal laws to

> minors who have not incurred in conduct defined by law as a crime, but who are at risk or endangered, due to destitution, abandonment, extreme poverty or disease, and even less so those others who simply behave differently from how the majority does, those who differ from the generally accepted patterns of behavior, who are involved in conflicts regarding adaptation to the family, school, or social milieu, generally, or who alienate themselves from the customs and values of their society. The concept of crime committed by children or juvenile crime can only be applied to

---

135 On this point, see E. García Méndez, *Derecho de la Infancia y Adolescencia en América Latina: de la situación irregular a la protección integral*, Forum Pacis, Bogotá, 1994. Also see Inter-American Children's Institute, OAS and Inter-American Court, *Juridical Condition and Human Rights of the Child*, Annex II, pp. 196–197.

136 OC-17/2002, para. 2.

137 An excellent explanation of this can be found in the concurring opinion of Judge García Ramírez with OC-17/2002.

138 OC-17/2002, para. 18.

139 *Ibidem*, paras. 56–61.

140 *Ibidem*, para. 78.

141 *Ibidem*, para. 109.

> those who fall under the first aforementioned situation, that is, those who incur in conduct legally defined as a crime, not to those who are in the other situations.[142]

As deprivation of liberty is only possible in general with the purpose of subjecting a person to criminal proceedings, this means that deprivation of liberty is not justified for the children to which this paragraph of the Opinion refers. In its conclusion, the Court found that the State can only intervene when the child's conduct is described in criminal law, and that cases of "abandonment, destitution, risk or disease, must be dealt with in a different manner from procedures applicable to those who commit criminal offenses."[143] With wording that is unmistakable, the Inter-American Children's Institute opined that:

> internment of youths who are in situations of social risk, applying the principles of the doctrine of the "irregular situation" that viewed them as objects of protection rather than subjects of rights, involves applying an undefined sanction, which breaches the principle of lawfulness of punishment, aggravated by the fact that generally this is ordered without defining its duration. It is also contrary to the rules of due process.[144]

---

142 *Ibidem*, para. 110.

143 *Ibidem*, para. 137, conclusion 12.

144 *Ibidem*, para. 15. In the same sense, see Costa Rica (*ibidem*).

CHAPTER 5
RIGHT TO DUE PROCESS

Article 8. Right to a Fair Trial

1. *Every person has the right to a hearing, with due guarantees and within a reasonable time, by a competent, independent, and impartial tribunal, previously established by law, in the substantiation of any accusation of a criminal nature made against him or for the determination of his rights and obligations of a civil, labor, fiscal, or any other nature.*
2. *Every person accused of a criminal offense has the right to be presumed innocent so long as his guilt has not been proven according to law. During the proceedings, every person is entitled, with full equality, to the following minimum guarantees:*
   a. *the right of the accused to be assisted without charge by a translator or interpreter, if he does not understand or does not speak the language of the tribunal or court;*
   b. *prior notification in detail to the accused of the charges against him;*
   c. *adequate time and means for the preparation of his defense;*
   d. *the right of the accused to defend himself personally or to be assisted by legal counsel of his own choosing, and to communicate freely and privately with his counsel;*
   e. *the inalienable right to be assisted by counsel provided by the state, paid or not as the domestic law provides, if the accused does not defend himself personally or engage his own counsel within the time period established by law;*
   f. *the right of the defense to examine witnesses present in the court and to obtain the appearance, as witnesses, of experts or other persons who may throw light on the facts;*
   g. *the right not to be compelled to be a witness against himself or to plead guilty; and*
   h. *the right to appeal the judgment to a higher court.*
3. *A confession of guilt by the accused shall be valid only if it is made without coercion of any kind.*
4. *An accused person acquitted by a non-appealable judgment shall not be subjected to a new trial for the same cause.*
5. *Criminal proceedings shall be public, except insofar as may be necessary to protect the interests of justice.*

1. INTRODUCTION

1. Article 8 of the Convention, which according to its heading enshrines the right to a "fair trial", establishes what is known in international human rights law as the right to "due process".[1] The Inter-American Court emphasizes this on finding that the application of Article 8 "is not limited strictly to judicial remedies, 'but to a series of requirements that must be observed by the procedural bodies' so that a person may defend himself adequately against any act of the State that could affect his rights."[2]

One can appreciate from the text of the article that due process is very broad, as it seeks to protect individuals' right for conflicts arising between two parties to be resolved in as just a manner possible, whether those conflicts are, on the one hand, between private parties or State bodies, whether or not dealing with issues of human rights; or, on the other, criminal proceedings for determining the guilt or innocence of a person.[3]

For this, the Convention establishes general requirements that must be met by all proceedings, and in addition – because the accused is particularly vulnerable to State power and because criminal proceedings always affect the reputation of persons and bring with them at least the risk that another human right (the right to personal liberty) will be limited – Article 8(2) of the Convention contains the minimum guarantees for ensuring due process for the accused. These guarantees are applied jointly with the general provisions established in that Article's paragraph 1. In criminal proceedings, paragraph 2 of Article 8 does not replace paragraph 1 but rather complements it; this means that guarantees additional to the minimum ones indicated therein may eventually be required in order for particular criminal proceedings to be compatible with the demands of due process, in accordance with the provisions of paragraph 1 of the Article.

2. Due process of law is the cornerstone of the human rights protection system; it is, *par excellence*, the guarantor of all human rights and a *sine qua non* requirement for the existence of the rule of law. It is enshrined both in Article 6 of the European Convention on Human Rights and in Article 14 of the International Covenant.

Together with its finding that the guarantees found in Articles 7(6) and 25(1) cannot be suspended in situations of emergency,

1 The title in Spanish is *garantías judiciales* (judicial guarantees).

2 *Case of Ivcher Bronstein*, para. 108.

3 See M. Melgar Adalid, "El derecho humano de acceso a la justicia", in Inter-American Court, *Liber Amicorum Héctor Fix-Zamudio*, Vol. I, San José, Costa Rica, 1998, pp. 1035–1048 (1045–1040).

> the importance of the right to a fair trial has led the Inter-American Court to indicate that the general principles of due process of law cannot be suspended in situations of emergency, as those principles establish the conditions necessary for the procedural instruments regulated by the Convention to be considered as judicial guarantees.[4]

As a result of this, the rules of due process apply to the remedies of *habeas corpus* and *amparo* enshrined respectively in the aforementioned articles.[5]

3. The fact that Article 8 of the Convention regulates judicial criminal proceedings with such precision can lead to problems due to the wide variety of different legal systems of the States Parties. On our continent, the civil law criminal system, found in the Spanish- and Portuguese-speaking countries, coexists with the Anglo-Saxon system that can be found in Caribbean countries, some of them parties to the American Convention. Thus, one of the things case law must do is interpret the due process provisions in a way that transcends particularities to establish a minimum standard applicable in all States Parties to the Convention.

4. Monitoring of States Parties' compliance with the rules of due process often places the Commission and the Court in the situation of ruling on matters on which one or more domestic courts have already ruled. A natural reaction to this among States Parties, and as a product of the incipient development of international human rights law in our countries, is based on the argument that once domestic courts have ruled definitively on a case, resulting in the corresponding *res judicata*, it is not up to an international body to alter that ruling, especially because the courts have heard the case and weighed the evidence at the time it was presented, and it would seem unlikely that an international body with *a posteriori* involvement and that did not participate directly and personally in collecting the evidence would be able to re-evaluate and judge the case anew. This is known as "the fourth instance doctrine".

The truth of it is that no international supervisory body – be it the European Court of Human Rights, the Human Rights Committee or Commission, or the Inter-American Court – has attempted to replace domestic courts with its rulings on cases. A proceeding pursued before an international body does not infringe on the principle of *res judicata* because a domestic proceeding that can lead to a violation of Article 8 of the Convention has different parties (*eadem personae*), the substance of the claim (*eadem res*) is different, and the reason of the claim (*eadem causa petendi*) is different. When a case of this kind reaches the supervisory body – in the case of the inter-American system, the Commission and eventually the Court – that body examines the judiciary's compliance with

---

4 OC/9/87, para. 30.

5 *Ibidem.*

the obligations imposed by Article 8 of the Convention; if it finds that all or any of the article's requirements have not been met, it will rule that the State has violated that international obligation and determine the way in which that violation shall be redressed. The Commission and the Court do not examine anew the evidence of the trial in question in order to find, for example, that a defendant in a criminal trial is innocent and not guilty. Instead, they examine whether domestic courts have respected the obligation, *inter alia*, to grant adequate time and opportunity for defense and give the party the chance to challenge the evidence presented against him or her. In sum, it weighs up whether there has been a violation of the basic procedural rules established in Article 8 of the Convention. If any of these requirements have not been met during the domestic trial, the supervisory body will find that this provision has been violated. Thus, none of these bodies exercises its authorities as if it were an appeals court of fourth instance. One must insist on this point, as it would not be appropriate for an international body to cease rigorously supervising compliance with the demands of due process – a pillar of human rights guarantees – due to a fear of becoming a "fourth instance" court.

5. The Court has addressed this problem. In the case of Villagrán Morales,[6] it found that Guatemala's courts had not carried out "an adequate investigation and judicial proceeding that would lead to the punishment of those responsible" given that it had completely failed to investigate the details of the kidnapping and torture of the victims (some of them minors) and to "order evidence gathering, carry it out, or examined the evidence, all of which would have been very important for solving the murders."[7] With regard to the weighing of the evidence, the Court expressed that: "Having examined the actions of those judges taken as a whole, it is clear that they fragmented the body of evidence and later attempted, case by case, to enervate the scope of each and every piece of evidence of the guilt of the accused."[8]

6. Examining the case law of the Court on this point, in which this case is absolutely not an exceptional example, a superficial analysis could lead one to think that the Court reaches quite far in its review of the establishment of the facts and the evidence by domestic courts, and in doing so, transforms itself into a "fourth instance" court. However, this is not so. It should be taken into

---

6 *Case of the Street Children (Villagrán Morales et al.)*, para. 229.

7 *Ibidem*, para. 230. Translator's own translation of the judgment. The official English version reads: "evidence that could have been very important for the due clarification of the homicides was not ordered, practiced or evaluated." This paragraph and those following it in the judgment include the details supporting this general assertion.

8 *Ibidem*, para. 233. Translator's own translation of the judgment. The official English version reads: "If we consider how those judges proceeded as a whole, it is evident that they fragmented the probative material and then endeavored to weaken the significance of each and every one of the elements that proved the responsibility of the defendants, item by item."

consideration that the case law on the Court's jurisdiction on the subject of facts and evidence is often established in cases of disappearance or summary executions at the hands of State agents. In those cases, domestic courts commonly do not wish or are not able to comply with any of the rules of due process.

The Inter-American Court has expressed this clearly. In the same case of Villagrán Morales, it stated that:

> In order to clarify whether the State has violated its international obligations owing to the acts of its judicial organs, the Court may have to examine the respective domestic proceedings.[9]

Later, citing the European Court of Human Rights, it stated that "the function of the international court is to determine if all the proceedings, and the way in which the evidence was produced, were fair."[10] Insisting on the scope of its jurisdiction, the Court added that it

> has attributions, not to investigate and punish individual conduct of State agents that may have participated in these violations, but to establish the international responsibility of States as a result of human rights violations.[11]

In the case of Genie Lacayo, it also indicated that:

> the Inter-American Court does not act as an appellate court or a court for judicial review of rulings handed down by the domestic courts. All it is empowered to do in this Case is call attention to the procedural violations of the rights enshrined in the Convention which have injured Mr Raymond Genie-Peñalba, the interested party in the matter; however, it lacks jurisdiction to remedy those violations in the domestic arena, a task, as has been pointed out before, that falls to the Supreme Court of Justice of Nicaragua.[12]

7. The case law of the inter-American system on this point is muddled by the ruling of the Court in the case of Las Palmeras. In that case, it was demonstrated before the Court that the Contentious Administrative Court of Nariña, Colombia, ruled in several judgments that the State was responsible for some of the deaths denounced in the case and sentenced it to pay damages for pain and suffering. Colombia – correctly in my opinion – acquiesced to the complaint before the Court, recognizing its partial responsibility for the facts alleged. However, the Court established in paragraph 34 of the judgment that "Colombia's responsibility was established by virtue of the principle of *res judicata*", which seems to contradict the arguments that it has so carefully developed with regard to this point.[13]

---

9 *Ibidem*, para. 222.

10 *Ibidem*.

11 *Ibidem*, para. 223.

12 *Case of Genie Lacayo*, para. 94.

13 In this sense, see *Case of Las Palmeras*, concurring separate opinion of Judges Cançado Trindade and Pacheco Gómez, para. 5.

2. GENERAL REQUIREMENTS OF DUE PROCESS

8. As already indicated, Article 8 of the Convention contains in paragraph 1 a general rule that applies to all proceedings, while paragraph 2 contains the minimum guarantees enjoyed by the accused. This section will analyze the first paragraph of that article, which establishes the due process requirements that are applicable to all cases, whether criminal or not. The Court has found consistently that this paragraph must be given a broad interpretation based on both the letter and the spirit of this provision, and must be appreciated in accordance with Article 29(c) of the Convention, whereby none of its provisions shall be interpreted as precluding other rights or guarantees that are inherent to human beings or derived from a representative, democratic form of government.[14]

2.1. RIGHT TO A HEARING

9. The obligation for the determination of rights or obligations and a ruling on the guilt or innocence of a person to be made in accordance with due process obviously implies that every individual has the right to appear before a court for such purposes. In order for the right to be exercised, this in turn implies a State obligation to establish agencies and proceedings that meet the requirements of Article 8, as well as to provide individuals with the minimum means for accessing them.

10. The existence of the courts and proceedings necessary for a State to be in compliance with due process must be accompanied by a real opportunity for the corresponding judges or courts to exercise the judicial authorities assigned to them. In the cases that have come before the Inter-American Court, situations are not uncommon in which a State has formally established agencies and authorities, and yet judges cannot materially exercise their authority due to obstacles put in place by other State agents. In the case of Genie Lacayo, the Court ruled it proven that certain military authorities had blocked the judge's work to the point "that the judge had to appeal to the President of the Republic [...] to intercede before military authorities in order for them to provide him with the opportunities necessary to inspect Unit 003, its weapons, its vehicles and its weapons logs."[15]

---

[14] *Case of Blake*, para. 96. Also see, for example, *Case of Durand and Ugarte*, para. 128.

[15] *Case of Genie Lacayo,* para. 76. Translator's own translation of the judgment. The official English version reads: "where that court was constrained to contact the President of the Republic [...] to intercede with the military authorities for them to afford the facilities needed for the inspection of Military Unit 003, and that unit's weapons, vehicles and weapons log." Also see *Case of Bámaca Velásquez*, para. 200, and *Case of Las Palmeras*, para. 57, in which the Court indicated, among other obstructive actions, the following: the changing of the

11. One case that is typical of violations of access to justice for these reasons is that of Myrna Mack Chang. The Court analyzed the alleged violation of Article 8 of the Convention, organizing its examination according to subjects that show the degree to which the obstruction of the exercise to the right to due process can reach. The Court ruled it proven: (i) that elements had been omitted that were fundamental to the proper course of the judicial investigation, including failures to take blood samples and to examine the victim's clothing;[16] (ii) that the highest police authority, at that time a member of the Army, covered up and manipulated the official version of the investigation;[17] (iii) that the President's staff and the National Ministry of Defense submitted "manipulated documents with the intention of concealing information that was important for elucidation of the facts";[18] (iv) that the National Ministry of Defense invoked secrecy in order to avoid turning over documents or in order to provide judicial authorities with only vague information;[19] and (v) that an investigator was murdered and that other police investigators, witnesses and several individuals connected with the investigation into the case were harassed.[20]

All these actions were classified by the Court as constituting a violation of Article 8 of the Convention.

The Court's resolution of the conflict of interest that can arise in a trial between the need for protecting State secrecy and the State's obligation to investigate human rights violations is an interesting one. The Court shares the Commission's opinion to the effect that "public authorities cannot shield themselves behind the protective cloak of official secret to avoid or obstruct the investigation of illegal acts ascribed to the members of its own bodies".[21] These types of actions constitute an obstacle to access to justice.

12. The Inter-American Court examined another method of hindering access to justice in the judgment in the case of Cantos. Some of the case's facts are important for the Court's ruling, for which reason they are explained briefly herein. (i) On July 15, 1982, prior to Argentina's ratification of the American Convention, Mr Cantos and the governor of the province of Santiago del Estero allegedly signed an agreement according to which the latter granted the former an indemnity for damages suffered as a result of confiscations made by the province. (ii) Mr Cantos began to demand that the province comply with this agreement on

garments the victims were wearing and their later destruction, the absence of an official document registering the collection of the bodies at the place of death, the failure to collect evidence, intimidation and threats toward relatives and witnesses, and the spread of distorted information about the activities of the victims.

16 *Case of Myrna Mack Chang*, paras. 166–167.

17 *Ibidem*, paras. 168–172.

18 *Ibidem*, para. 173.

19 *Ibidem*, paras. 175–182.

20 *Ibidem*, paras. 183–196.

21 *Ibidem*, para. 181.

March 24, 1986; in response to its silence, he brought a lawsuit against the province and the federal State before the Supreme Court of Justice. (iii) In order to pursue the litigation, the victim had to pay a "court filing fee", which he felt should be minimal as the amount of damages at issue in the trial had not been determined. (iv) After a series of procedural issues, the Court found that the amount of damages at issue in the trial was established, and that therefore a court fee in the amount of 83.4 million Argentine pesos (equivalent to the same amount in US dollars) had to be paid on pain of incurring a fine equivalent to 50% of the amount should the payment not be made within five days.[22] (v) Mr Cantos did not pay the filing fee in time and the aforementioned fine was thus levied.[23] (vi) The case was suspended due to the failure to pay the filing fee, but it apparently continued until the final judgment was handed down on 3 September 1996. (vii) As a result of the failure to pay the court filing fee, on 9 October 1996, the National First Instance Adversarial Administrative Court placed a "general injunction" on Mr Cantos to prevent him from carrying out his economic activity.[24]

The question brought before the Inter-American Court was whether a court filing fee of that amount was compatible with Articles 8 and 25 of the Convention. The Court found that the amount set in the form of filing fees and the corresponding fine were, in the view of this Court, an obstruction to access to the courts. They were unreasonable, even though in mathematical terms they were proportional to the amount being claimed.[25]

It also found that the limitations that the State places on access to justice must maintain a correlation between the means employed and the purpose sought and cannot themselves become a denial of the right.[26] Finally, the Court reasoned that:

> The fact that a proceeding concludes with a definitive court ruling is not sufficient to satisfy the right of access to the courts. Those participating in the proceeding must be able to do so without fear of being forced to pay disproportionate or excessive sums because they turned to the courts. The problem of excessive or disproportionate filing fees is compounded when, in order to force payment, the authorities attach the debtor's property or deny him the opportunity to do business.[27]

The Court also found that the fact that the Argentine Supreme Court ordered Mr Cantos to pay the amount of 6.4 million Argentine pesos in honoraria to the attorneys representing Mr Cantos, the State and the Province, the State's technical advisor, and the expert witnesses was an obstruction to access to justice.[28]

---

22 Mr Cantos' claim was for the amount of 2,780,015,303.44 Argentine pesos, and the court filing fee was equivalent to 3% of the total value of the suit, with no cap (see *Case of Cantos*, para. 53).

23 *Ibidem*, para. 43(k) to (n).

24 *Ibidem*, para. 43(t).

25 *Ibidem*, para. 54. The English version has been corrected to match the Spanish one.

26 *Ibidem*.

27 *Ibidem*, para. 55. Also see paras. 56, 60 and 62.

28 *Ibidem*, paras. 43(q) to (s), and 56.

13. The right to a hearing has been broadly interpreted by the Inter-American Court. In Advisory Opinion 18/03 on the human rights of migrants and particularly on the right to due process – likely based on the universality of human rights and the State obligation to respect and ensure human rights for "all persons subject to [its] jurisdiction", established in Article 1 of the Convention – the Court concluded:

> That the general obligation to respect and guarantee human rights binds States, regardless of any circumstance or consideration, including the migratory status of a person.[29]

Likewise,

> That the right to due process of law must be recognized as one of the minimum guarantees that should be offered to any migrant, irrespective of his migratory status. The broad scope of the preservation of due process encompasses all matters and all persons, without any discrimination.[30]

14. In the case of Hilaire, Constantine and Benjamin, *et al.*,[31] the Court found that the individual clemency petitions provided for in the Constitution of Trinidad and Tobago have been characterized by "a lack of transparency, lack of available information and lack of participation by the victims", and that this was a violation of the Convention, as those petitions "should be exercised through fair and adequate procedures, in conformity with Article 4(6) of the Convention and in conjunction with the relevant due process guarantees established in Article 8".[32] In this way, the Court broadened the scope of the right to a hearing to include this type of proceedings.

15. In criminal trials, the accused has the right to a hearing. In the inter-American system, this right has been extended not only to the accused but also to the victim or the relatives of the victim. Taking into consideration that, as mentioned previously, the case law of the Inter-American Court has been built mainly with cases of disappearance or summary execution, it is not surprising that the Court has been generous with its position. In the case of Blake, the Court indicated the need to interpret Article 8(1) broadly, basing its argument – in addition to the letter and spirit of the provision – on Article 29(c) of the Convention, "whereby none of its provisions shall be interpreted as precluding other rights or guarantees that are inherent in the human personality or derived from representative, democratic form of government."[33] It continued:

---

29 OC-18/03, para. 173.

30 *Ibidem.* Also see separate concurring opinion of Judge Sergio García Ramírez, particularly paras. 35–39.

31 *Case of Hilaire, Constantine and Benjamin, et al.*, para. 189.

32 *Ibidem*, paras. 186 and 188.

33 *Case of Blake*, para. 96.

> Thus interpreted, the aforementioned Article 8(1) of the Convention also includes the rights of the victim's relatives to judicial guarantees, whereby '[a]ny act of forced disappearance places the victim outside the protection of the law and causes grave suffering to him *and to his family*' (United Nations Declaration on the Protection of All Persons Against Enforced Disappearance, Article 1(2)). Consequently, Article 8(1) of the American Convention recognizes the right of Mr Nicholas Blake's relatives to have his disappearance and death effectively investigated by the Guatemalan authorities to have those responsible prosecuted for committing said unlawful acts; to have the relevant punishment, where appropriate, meted out; and to be compensated for the damages and injuries they sustained."[34]

With this interpretation, the Court establishes that the victim or the victim's relatives have the right to a hearing in a criminal trial, along with the right to demand that criminal proceedings be pursued. This includes actors in the criminal proceeding that would not seem *prima facie* to have been included in the provision.

In the case of Villagrán Morales, the Court reiterated this position, indicating that "it is evident from Article 8 of the Convention that the victims of human rights violations or their next of kin should have substantial possibilities of being heard and acting in the respective proceedings, both in order to clarify the facts and punish those responsible, and to seek due reparation."[35] In the case of Las Palmeras, the Court concluded that "the use of the military courts in this case did not guarantee due process in the meaning of Article 8(1) of the American Convention, which recognizes the right of the victims' next of kin to a hearing by a competent, impartial and independent court."[36]

In the case of Juan Humberto Sánchez, the Court established in its judgment that:

> The next of kin of the victim must have full access and the capacity to act, at all stages and levels of said investigations [referring to investigations into the extrajudicial execution of the victim], in accordance with domestic laws and the provisions of the American Convention.[37]

In the case of Bulacio, in considering forms of reparation for the violations that Argentina was responsible for, the Court found that the situation was one of grave impunity. Thus, the State must pursue and conclude the investigation into the facts and punish those responsible, specifying that the relatives of the victim must have full access and capacity to take action at all stages of the investigation and trial.[38]

16. This subject is closely related to the concept of "the right to truth", which I have already addressed in the chapter on the right to life. It is also closely related

---

34 *Ibidem*, para. 97 (emphasis added).

35 *Case of the Street Children (Villagrán Morales et al.)*, para. 227. It ruled likewise in the *Case of Durand and Ugarte*, paras. 128–130.

36 *Case of Las Palmeras*, para. 54.

37 *Case of Juan Humberto Sánchez*, para. 186.

38 *Case of Bulacio*, paras. 121 and 137, No. 5.

with the problem raised therein of distinguishing whether the State obligation to investigate, prosecute and punish those guilty of specific human rights violations is based on the obligation to guarantee the protected right – whether that right be the right to life or to humane treatment – and/or on Article 25 granting the right to simple and prompt recourse, or any other effective recourse, to a competent court or tribunal in order to protect persons from violations of their human rights. The Court seems to have reached the conclusion that individuals have a right to demand that a criminal proceeding be brought against those allegedly responsible for a crime prejudicial to a human right (possibly life and humane treatment and other forms of violation of the right to personal liberty) and uses Article 8 as a basis for this. The subject has already been addressed with regard to the right to life,[39] but I review it again in this chapter because the Court's position implies the use of Article 8 as the basis for the right of the victim and the victim's relatives to a hearing in a criminal trial, and more directly, their right to press criminal charges or demand that the State do so. Making an argument to support this is difficult, as in reality Article 8 starts with the assumption that a right or obligation already exists that must be ruled upon. What Article 8 enshrines is the way in which this ruling must be made and the body that must make it.

17. The issue of the position of the victim in a criminal proceeding and of the victim's right to demand a criminal trial is currently under debate in Latin America and there is still no consensus.[40] The increase in everyday crime has meant that significant emphasis is beginning to be placed on the protection of victims, and many of the criminal procedural reforms of the last decade have granted them one or another right during criminal proceedings. I do not intend to enter into this debate, as it more appropriately falls to legal specialists in criminal and procedural law. I would only like to call attention to the impact of all this on the interpretation of Article 8 and the need for this point to be reviewed in order to fine tune the solutions.

The position taken by Judge García Ramírez in his concurring opinion in the judgment in the case of Myrna Mack Chang presents a novel point of view. Therein, he argues that on the one hand:

> This access implies both the ability and the possibility of having recourse to bodies that provide justice independently, impartially and competently, of formulating claims, contributing or requesting evidence and arguing in favor of interests and rights (procedural justice), and also of obtaining a final judgment that satisfies the substantive requirements of justice (substantive justice). Without the latter, justice

---

39 See Chapter 2, section 4.3.

40 See M.I. Horvitz and J. López, *Derecho Procesal Penal Chileno. Principios. Sujetos procesales. Medidas cautelares. Etapa de investigación*, Volume I, Editorial Jurídica de Chile, Santiago, 2002, pp. 281–310.

> would be sterile: the simple appearance of justice, an ineffective instrument that does not produce the result for which it was conceived,[41]

and on the other hand, that:

> Access to justice, one of the outstanding issues of contemporary life, presumes the clarification of unlawful facts, the timely correction and reparation of the violations committed, the re-establishment of conditions of peace with justice, and the appeasement of the public conscience, troubled by the fact that the law has been broken, as a general control of conduct and the subjective rights recognized to individuals, and as a measure for all individuals to achieve their potential. This case, as others which have been heard by the Court, provides a dramatic example of the harm to which effective judicial protection is subjected in conditions that also have singular characteristics.[42]

It will be interesting to see how the Court articulates these two ideas in light of the consequences they could have for the procedural law of member States and the interpretation of Article 8.

18. Without prejudice to an exploration of this route, it seems to me that the right in question arises from the State's obligation to ensure human rights: in this case, the rights that have been affected by the commission of a crime. As already mentioned in Chapter 1, on the obligation to ensure, and in Chapter 2, on the protection of the right to life through monitoring of compliance with preventative regulations, protection is not complete solely with the existence of provisions that could become useless if not applied consistently and without discrimination.

The State has an obligation to establish procedural regulations that are adequate for controlling its agents, as well as to establish independent and impartial agencies to carry out that oversight and apply the regulations without discrimination in order to deter possible offenders. This conduct forms part of the obligation that the State assumes with regard to the rights that the Convention recognizes and gives expression to in Article 1(1).

2.2. CRIMINAL CHARGES AND DETERMINATION OF RIGHTS AND OBLIGATIONS

19. The right to be heard raises the question of what kind of proceedings it applies to. Article 8(1) of the Convention answers this question in principle in its own wording, where it indicates that every person has the right to a hearing for "the determination of his rights and obligations of a civil, labor, fiscal, or any

41 *Case of Myrna Mack Chang*, concurring separate opinion of Judge Sergio García Ramírez, para. 5.

42 *Ibidem*, para. 6.

other nature" and in "the substantiation of any accusation of a criminal nature made against him". As has already been noted, for this latter case, the Convention adds another special provision to this general one with the article's second paragraph, establishing what are known as "minimum guarantees for the accused".

20. Regarding the determination of rights or obligations of any kind, the broad wording of the American Convention's provision almost makes it unnecessary to examine the nature and characteristics of required noncriminal due process, given that in principle, practically all determinations of rights and obligations are covered by the guarantees. This is different from what happens in the European system, where given the restrictive wording of Article 6 of the European Convention that only enshrines the existence of due process for the determination of civil rights and obligations, the idea of an autonomous concept of "civil rights and obligations" had to be developed, determinable by the international supervisory body. The development of this concept was crucial for preventing legal systems from avoiding the requirements of due process by transferring matters to administrative venues.

21. The concept of "criminal charges" does not appear in the Convention, and neither does the Inter-American Court seem to have had a chance to examine the subject in cases that have come before it. Nevertheless, it would be worthwhile to use the case law of the European Court of Human Rights for interpreting these terms. The European Court of Human Rights found first of all that the concept of "criminal offense" was, like all civil rights and obligations, an autonomous concept that transcended domestic legal systems. It thus falls to the international supervisory body to rule on whether a criminal offense is involved in each specific case that it hears.[43] Second, it found that the concept should be interpreted broadly, arguing that a restrictive interpretation does not fit with the objective and purpose of Article 6 of the European Convention on Human Rights establishing the right to due process.[44] Next, the European Court of Human Rights addressed what should be understood by the term "charge" and from what point charges can be considered to exist. It defined charge as "the official notification given to an individual by the competent authority of an allegation that he has committed a criminal offence", but added that it could also refer to criminal charges that are at the stage in which the prosecutor makes a proposal for settlement even "if there is no notification of impending

---

43 ECtHR, *Deweer v. Belgium*, judgment of 27 February 1980, cited in P. van Dijk, F. van Hoof, A. van Rijn, and L. Zwaak (eds), *Theory and Practice of the European Convention on Human Rights*, 4th edn, Intersentia, Antwerp/Oxford, 2006, p. 540.

44 ECtHR, *Delcourt v. Belgium*, judgment of 17 January 1970, cited in P. van Dijk, F. van Hoof, A. van Rijn and L. Zwaak (eds), *supra* n. 43, p. 540.

prosecution".[45] Finally, in the case of Engel v. the Netherlands, the European Court of Human Rights established three criteria for determining whether a charge was criminal in the sense of Article 6 of the European Convention on Human Rights: the classification of the offense by domestic law; the nature of the offense; and the level of severity of its possible punishment. If the State itself classifies the offense as criminal, that is sufficient for the Court to consider it so; if the State does not place the offense in the category of criminal offenses, the two other criteria come into play.[46]

22. Given that Article 8 of the American Convention regulates due process in general and the guarantees of the accused in a criminal trial differently, it is important to draw a distinction between criminal and other proceedings. In my opinion, the case law of the Inter-American Court has not been clear in making this distinction and has unnecessarily broadened the scope of the application of Article 8(2). Some cases before the Court have raised the issue of the scope of the application of Article 8, illustrating this tendency.

23. One was that of the three members of the Constitutional Tribunal of Peru who were dismissed during the government of Alberto Fujimori in the context of an impeachment proceeding that took place in the Congress of Peru. The dismissal was in response to a statement made by the Constitutional Tribunal in which it ruled Law 26.657, which apparently interpreted the law to allow Mr Fujimori to be re-elected president, inapplicable. The Inter-American Commission, the body that brought the case before the Court, did not address the problem from the point of view of whether this proceeding determined civil, labor, economic or any other kinds of rights or obligations, but rather argued that the magistrates of the Constitutional Tribunal should enjoy the guarantees of independence and impartiality enjoyed by all judges, adding that Article 8(1) of the Convention implicitly guarantees the permanence of judges. For this reason, the removal of judges must be carried out through a proceeding established in the Constitution or that enjoys "all due judicial guarantees", a requirement that had not been met in this case.[47] For its part, the Court began its examination by indicating: (i) that a political trial constitutes an exercise of the State's power to impose sanctions; (ii) that this power not only presupposes that authorities act with total respect for the legal order, but also implies that the *minimum guarantees* of due process will be granted to all persons subject to its jurisdiction under the requirements established in the Convention;[48] and (iii) that therefore, every individual subject to a trial before any kind of State

---

[45] *Ibidem*.

[46] D.J. Harris, M. O'Boyle and C. Warbrick, *Law of the European Convention on Human Rights*, Butterworths, London/Dublin/Edinburgh, 1995, p. 167.

[47] *Case of the Constitutional Court*, para. 64.

[48] *Ibidem*, para. 68.

body must be provided with the guarantee that the body is competent, independent and impartial and acting pursuant to procedures established in law for hearing and ruling on cases brought before it. The Court then reiterated that "although [... Article 8] does not establish minimum guarantees in matters relating to the determination of rights and obligations of a civil, labor, fiscal or any other nature, the full range of minimum guarantees stipulated in the second paragraph of this article are also applicable in those areas and, therefore, in this type of matter, the individual also has the overall right to the due process applicable in criminal matters."[49]

24. The second case in which the subject of the type of proceedings that must be subjected to the requirements of Article 8 was examined was that of Baena Ricardo *et al.*, a case on the dismissal of 270 state employees through an improper proceeding. The workers were fired by the executive branch, which used the powers granted to it by Law 25 to dismiss public servants who participated in various types of action that threatened democracy and constitutional order. The law authorized the Cabinet Council to determine which actions would be placed in that category. The State argued that Article 8 of the Convention was not applicable to this case because dismissals are administrative sanctions, not criminal.[50]

First, the Court clarified for the State that there is a difference between exercising administrative discretion that allows for freely naming and removing public officials, and removing a worker through administrative sanction. Discretionary removal of an official is obviously not subject to due process; removal as a result of a sanction, in contrast, does require due process.[51] The Court introduces a certain amount of doubt with this seemingly categorical argument on considering in its ruling the fact that the dismissals in the Baena case "had serious socioeconomic consequences". Therefore, "in applying a sanction with such serious consequences, the State should have ensured to the worker a due process with the guarantees provided for in the American Convention".[52] It can be understood, however, that the circumstance of the dismissal having "serious economic consequences" is only one more argument, not a *sine qua non* requirement for the application of Article 8(1) to administrative disciplinary proceedings.

The second argument, which is the specific reason for analyzing these paragraphs, has to do with the nature of the administrative disciplinary proceeding. The Court was in agreement with the State in that the case involved an administrative or labor issue, stating that it was clear that Law 25

---

49 *Ibidem*, paras 69–70. The Court has said this in the *case of the "White Van" (Paniagua Morales et al.)* and in Advisory Opinion 11.

50 *Case of Baena Ricardo et al.*, para. 129.

51 *Ibidem*, para. 131.

52 *Ibidem*, para. 134.

did not refer to a criminal subject matter "since it does not characterise an offence nor does it sanction through the imposition of a punishment". Still, the Court argued that "the determination of the realm of influence of Article 8 of the Convention, in particular whether or not it is applied only to penal proceedings, corresponds to this Court".[53] Starting with the presentation of the problem, the Court is not precise: it is obvious that Article 8 does not apply only to criminal proceedings. This reference should have only been made with regard to paragraph 2. Examining this point, the Court made the following argument:

> Justice, done through the due process of law, as a legally protected true value, must be ensured in all disciplinary proceedings, and the States cannot evade such obligation based on the argument that the due guarantees of Article 8 of the American Convention do not apply in the case of disciplinary and not penal sanctions. Allowing the States to make such interpretation would be equivalent to leaving up to their free will the decision of whether or not to observe the right of all persons to a due process.[54]

It could be argued that the conclusion reached by the Court is that, as Article 8 contains the collection of requirements that must be met by procedural instances "in order for all persons to be able to defend their rights adequately vis-à-vis any type of State action that could affect them", it follows that "the due process of law must be respected in any act or omission on the part of the State bodies in a proceeding, whether of a punitive, administrative, or of a judicial nature".[55] The wording of this argument seems to indicate that the Court was considering Article 8(1) insofar as it enshrines due process for the determination of rights or obligations of any kind, and it was not attempting to classify the administrative disciplinary proceeding as a criminal proceeding. However, the Court cited for support the ruling of the European Court of Human Rights to the effect that:

> the principles stipulated in paragraph 2 (art. 6.2) and 3 (to whit, sections a, b and d) [... of the European Convention on Human Rights] are applied *mutatis mutandis* to the disciplinary proceedings to which section 1 refers (art. 6-1), in the same manner in which they are applied to cases where a person is charged with an offence of a penal nature.[56]

This latter point seems to indicate that the administrative disciplinary proceedings were examined as if they were penal, something that is coherent with the European Court of Human Rights' judgment, given that the criteria developed by the European Court of Human Rights in the Engels case are being applied. The Inter-American Court used this differently, finding that, given that Article 8(1) applies in the determination of civil, labor, economic or any other

53 *Ibidem*, para. 123.
54 *Ibidem*, para. 129.
55 *Ibidem*, para. 124.
56 *Ibidem*, para. 128.

rights and obligations, it is broad in scope, and consequently, "the individual has the right to the due process *as construed under the terms of Articles 8(1) and 8(2) in both, penal matters, as in all of these other domains*",[57] repeating in the subsequent considering paragraph that "minimum guarantees must be observed in the administrative process and in any other procedure whose decisions may affect the rights of persons".[58] Curiously, when the Court examined the possible violation of Article 9 of the Convention, it compared administrative sanctions to penal ones, stating that at times they can be "similar in nature".[59]

25. The third case in which the Court ruled in the area of the application of Article 8 is that of Ivcher Bronstein. That case addressed the problem of proceedings to nullify the Peruvian nationality acquired by the victims. Peru's General Directorate of Immigration and Naturalization was the authority that handed down the resolution in question. In the judgment handed down in that case, while at the same time insisting that Article 8 is applicable "in situations in which a public rather than a judicial authority issues resolutions that affect the determination of such rights",[60] the Court indicated that:

> although this article does not stipulate minimum guarantees in matters which concern the determination of the rights and obligations of a civil, labor, fiscal or any other nature, the minimum guarantees established in paragraph 2 of the article should also apply to those categories and, therefore, in that respect, a person has the right to due process in the terms recognized for criminal matters, to the extent that it is applicable to the respective procedure.[61]

The Court had already held that same position in its Advisory Opinion 11/90, which said:

> For cases which concern the determination of a person's rights and obligations of a civil, labor, fiscal, or any other nature, Article 8 does not specify any minimum guarantees similar to those provided in Article 8(2) for criminal proceedings. It does, however, provide for due guarantees; consequently, the individual here also has the right to the fair hearing provided for in criminal cases.[62]

In this way, instead of ruling that there are types of proceedings that the international body can consider criminal proceedings despite having a different classification domestically and using, for example, the European standards in the Engels case to differentiate between them, the Court establishes that the

57 *Ibidem*, para. 125 (emphasis added).

58 *Ibidem*, para. 127.

59 *Ibidem*, para. 106.

60 *Case of Ivcher Bronstein*, para. 105.

61 *Ibidem*, para. 103.

62 OC-11/90, para. 28. The Court also repeated this in the *case of the "White Van" (Paniagua Morales et al.)*, para. 148. Para. 70 of the judgment in the *case of the Constitutional Court* reiterated this, but clarified it with the idea that "in this type of matter, the individual also has the *overall* right to the due process applicable in criminal matters" (emphasis added).

minimum guarantees of the accused apply to all proceedings. Thus the Court finds it unnecessary to differentiate between the different natures of the proceedings, given that the same rules apply to all types of proceedings.

26. At the risk of getting off track, I must comment on the Court's somewhat unfortunate position. It seems erroneous – inconveniently so – to derive guarantees for all proceedings by making paragraph 2 of Article 8 applicable to all non-criminal cases. An interpretation of this nature reads too much into the wording and, in addition, requires States to establish all minimum guarantees for all types of proceedings. This would at times appear to be excessive. I believe that the requirements that should inform all proceedings can and should be derived from Article 8(1), given that Article 8(1) is the generic rule. Paragraph 1 establishes that persons shall be heard "with due guarantees", an expression that can be interpreted in the sense that it at least includes the application of the principle of equality and the adversarial principle,[63] and that this in turn allows for the establishment of the need for equality of arms, the right to defense, and other rights without the need to turn to paragraph 2 of the article. If the Court finds that in some particular proceedings, all the minimum guarantees found in the second paragraph must be granted to the person affected, then instead of extending paragraph 2 to proceedings of any and all nature, it should develop criteria for making the expression "accusation of a criminal nature" an autonomous concept, thus allowing the Court to decide when an "accusation of a criminal nature" is at issue and legitimately apply the specific guarantees found in Article 8(2). This, as mentioned before, is what the Court did in the Baena case, although not through analyzing the violation of Article 8, but rather the violation of Article 9 of the Convention.[64]

27. In the case of Maritza Urrutia, the Court broadened the minimum guarantees of the accused to cover another area. Maritza Urrutia was kidnapped in Guatemala at a time when the country was facing a domestic armed conflict and had begun a peace negotiation process. During that time, the military was conducting psychological operations, during which they presented alleged members of the URNG (Unidad Revolucionaria Nacional Guatemalteca) to the media, where they were forced to say that they wished to leave the rebel groups and requested the help of the Armed Forces to do so.[65]

---

63 See in this sense, HRC, *Yves Morael v. France*, decision of 28 July 1989, para. 9.3, in A/44/40 (1989) Annex X, sect. E (pp. 210–221).

64 On this point, see Chapter 6, where the Court's examination of the violation of Article 9 in this case is addressed in detail.

65 *Case of Maritza Urrutia*, para. 58.1–2.

The statements were obtained by capturing the individuals and keeping them in secret detention, where they were subjected to physical and psychological torture.[66]

Maritza Urrutia was subjected to that treatment, and as a result gave forced on-camera testimony in which she referred to, among other things, her participation and that of her ex-husband and her brother in the Ejército Guerrillero de los Pobres.[67] The Court ruled that these facts were covered by the guarantees found in Article 8(2) and by Article 8(3), indicating that these provisions must be respected in proceedings or procedures before or accompanying the judicial proceedings, which, should these guarantees not be respected, could have an unfavorable and unjustified impact on the juridical status of the person in question.

Based on this, it concluded that "in this case, the said Articles 8(2) and 8(3) of the Convention have been violated because the victim was obliged to incriminate herself in the context of procedures that might have entailed unfavorable procedural consequences."[68]

I find the Court's position doubtful because I believe the violation of Article 8 could have only taken place if Maritza Urrutia's statements could have been used later in criminal proceedings, which does not seem to have been the case.

2.3. COMPETENT, INDEPENDENT AND IMPARTIAL TRIBUNAL, PREVIOUSLY ESTABLISHED BY LAW

2.3.1. Concept of a tribunal

28. The right to a hearing requires that the determination of rights or of a person's guilt or innocence be made by a competent, independent and impartial tribunal, previously established by law. Inter-American case law clearly indicates that for the Court, a body is classified as a "tribunal" based on the type of functions it carries out and not on the name assigned to it: if its function allows it to make decisive rulings that affect the rights of persons, Article 8 will be applicable. Once its function has been established, the body must comply with the requirements of competence, independence and impartiality even if national legislation does not classify that body as a "judge or tribunal". The Court's position on this subject has been consistent. In the case of the Constitutional Court, it indicated that when the Convention refers to the right of everyone to be heard by a competent judge or court to "determine his rights", this expression

66 *Ibidem*, para. 58.3.

67 *Ibidem*, para. 58.8.

68 *Ibidem*, paras. 120–121.

refers to any public authority, whether administrative, legislative or judicial, which, through its decisions determines individual rights and obligations.[69]

It complemented this position by adding that therefore, "any State organ that exercises functions of a materially jurisdictional nature has the obligation to adopt decisions that are in consonance with the guarantees of due legal process in the terms of Article 8 of the American Convention."[70] In the Baena case, the Court insisted – in my opinion correctly – that the titles of those who make the determination of a right are not important. It is, however, essential that the rulings they make affect the rights of persons.[71]

2.3.2. The establishment of the tribunal previously by law

29. An essential requirement is that the tribunal must be established by law in order to ensure that the legislature is the body that decides on the organization and jurisdiction of a State's tribunals, all prior to the date on which the facts being judged took place. The purpose of the provision is to ensure the independence and impartiality of the body making the determination and to prevent *ad hoc* tribunals, which distort these qualities essential for and inherent to all bodies that hold court.

30. The Inter-American Court makes reference to this due process requirement in the case of Ivcher Bronstein. In that case, a few weeks before issuing a resolution to take away Mr Bronstein's naturalized Peruvian nationality, the Executive Commission of the Peruvian Judicial Branch changed the composition of the chamber of the Supreme Court and gave that chamber the authority to create temporary Superior Chambers and Specialized Public Law Courts, as well as to appoint and/or ratify their members. The chamber created the First Specialized Temporary Corporate Public Law Court and named its judge. That judge heard several of the remedies sought by Mr Bronstein in his defense. The Inter-American Court found that these facts did not guarantee the petitioner his "right to be heard by judges or courts 'previously established by law'".[72]

In the case of Castillo Petruzzi *et al.*, the Court also made reference to the same point, adding the need for the law to establish a tribunal's jurisdiction, as this was an element that would ensure independence. Thus it held that "[a] basic principle of the independence of the judiciary is that every person has the right to be heard by regular courts, following procedures previously established by law", adding that "States are not to create '[t]ribunals that do not use the duly

69 *Case of the Constitutional Court*, para. 71.

70 *Ibidem*.

71 *Case of Baena Ricardo et al.*, para. 130. The authorities who had ordered the dismissals were general directors and the boards of directors of the State enterprises.

72 *Case of Ivcher Bronstein*, paras. 113–114.

established procedures of the legal process [...] to displace the jurisdiction belonging to the ordinary courts or judicial tribunals'".[73]

31. As a logical consequence of the importance that the Convention assigns to the body hearing the case, the trial must be carried out before the person or body with these qualifications. That is, the "principle of immediacy" (judges must have direct apprehension of the evidence), as it is known in procedural law, must be applied.[74] Procedural practices in which criminal trials take place mostly before court employees who do not meet these requirements – starting with the lack of jurisdiction granted by law – infringe on Article 8 of the Convention,[75] as they clearly threaten the requirements of independence and impartiality that a judge or a tribunal must meet.

2.3.3. Competent tribunal

32. The requirement that the court providing the hearing be competent is intimately related with the previously addressed requirement. The spatial, temporal, material and personal areas in which a court can exercise its jurisdictional authority must be established by law broadly and independent of the specific case, a requirement whose purpose is also to ensure the independence and impartiality of the judge. This means that on establishing the court and assigning it jurisdiction, the State must respect the ban in Article 1(1) on discrimination. This idea is behind the concept of the "judge with rightful jurisdiction" (*juez natural*), which is a very well-developed doctrine in Latin America.[76] This concept requires not only that courts be established by statute, but that on assigning competence, the statute must respect certain principles.

33. The Court has made reference to this point in its analysis of military jurisdiction. The Court's case law was doubtful at the beginning, finding as it did

73 *Case of Castillo Petruzzi et al.*, para. 129. The citation in the considering paragraph is from the Basic Principles on the Independence of the Judiciary, adopted in the seventh United Nations Congress on the Prevention of Crime and the Treatment of Offenders (Milan, Italy, from 26 August to 6 September 1985) and confirmed by the General Assembly in its resolutions 40/32 of 29 November 1985, and 40/146 of 13 December 1985.

74 On the principle of immediacy, see M.I. Horvitz and J. López, *supra* n. 40, pp. 96–98.

75 Regarding the principle of immediacy and Chilean legislation, see C. Riego, "El sistema procesal penal chileno frente a las normas internacionales de derechos humanos", in C. Medina and J. Mera, *Sistema Jurídico y Derechos Humanos. El derecho nacional y las obligaciones internacionales de Chile en materia de derechos humanos,* Universidad Diego Portales, special publications series no. 6, Santiago, 1996, pp. 256–258.

76 On the concept of the *juez natural* in criminal proceedings, see A. Binder, *Introducción al derecho procesal penal*, 2nd updated and expanded edition, Ad-Hoc Publishing, Buenos Aires, 2000, pp. 141–148; J. Maier, *Derecho procesal penal argentino, Fundamentos,* Editorial Hammurabi S.R.L., 1989, pp. 487–497.

in the case of Genie Lacayo that military jurisdiction did not *per se* mean "that the human rights guaranteed the accusing party by the Convention are being violated".[77] But it did not respond to the Commission's argument – not based on competence but with a bearing on it – that "to prosecute ordinary crimes as though they were military crimes simply because they had been committed by members of the military breached the guarantee of an independent and impartial tribunal."[78] But the Court's case law has since evolved to the point of concluding in the case of Castillo Petruzzi *et al.* that Peru had violated Article 8 and that "[t]ransferring jurisdiction from civilian courts to military courts, thus allowing military courts to try civilians accused of treason, means that the competent, independent and impartial tribunal previously established by law is precluded from hearing these cases", given that the military courts were created to maintain order and discipline within the armed forces and civilians "cannot engage in behaviors that violate military duties".[79]

In the case of Durand and Ugarte, it found that:

> In a democratic State governed by the rule of law, criminal military jurisdiction must have a restrictive and exceptional scope and be directed toward protecting special juridical interests related to the functions assigned by law to the armed forces. Consequently, civilians must be excluded from military jurisdiction and only military personnel shall be judged for the commission of crimes or offenses that by nature threaten the legal rights of the military.[80]

This therefore prohibits not only the processing of civilians but the assignation of military jurisdiction to try the commission of ordinary crimes committed by members of the armed forces even if those crimes were committed while the perpetrators were exercising their duties.[81]

A different argument for concluding that the obligation for the court to be competent had been violated was put forward in the case of Loayza Tamayo, in which the Court reached the conclusion that the military courts lacked jurisdiction to determine an acquittal and then remit the action to an ordinary criminal court and place the victim at the disposal of the competent authority, thereby keeping that victim in detention. The court ruled that the military court had acted *ultra vires*, exceeding its jurisdiction. In addition, it had invaded the authority of civilian judicial bodies, given that in Peruvian law the National Police and the Public Prosecutor are responsible for investigating this particular crime, with the authority to order an arrest belonging to civilian judges.[82]

---

77 *Case of Genie Lacayo,* para. 84.

78 *Ibidem*, para. 53.

79 *Case of Castillo Petruzzi et al.*, paras. 128 and 132. The Court reiterated this in the *Case of Cantoral Benavides*, para. 112, and in the *Case of Las Palmeras,* para. 51.

80 *Case of Durand and Ugarte*, para. 117. In the same sense, *Case of Cesti Hurtado,* para. 151.

81 *Case of Durand and Ugarte*, para. 118.

82 *Case of Loayza Tamayo,* para. 61. The Court, however, did not mention violation of Article 7 on this point.

2.3.4. Independent and impartial tribunal

34. As a result of the application of the doctrine of separation of powers, the foundation of a democratic system, a tribunal's independence is related with its autonomy from any other State agency to exercise its jurisdictional functions. Impartiality, for is part, means that in order to be able to make a fair ruling in a particular case, a court must be free from prejudice or bias as regards the court's relationship with the parties in a given proceeding. While a lack of independence also frequently means a lack of impartiality, it is useful to maintain a distinction between the two concepts.[83] Both independence and impartiality are requirements that apply to the structure of the judicial branch. For this reason, in principle these requirements cannot be waived by a directly affected individual.[84]

35. Independence requires the application of certain principles as regards the appointment of judges, the duration of their terms, the conditions governing their promotions, transfers and removal from duties, and even their remuneration.[85]

There is no one single solution for designing a system of appointments, promotions and transfers of judges that fully ensures their independence. There are States in which the appointment is left exclusively up to the executive branch; in others, the system involves a second body that could be the judicial branch or Congress; further developed models create an independent body to handle these tasks; finally, there are States in which judges are elected by popular vote.

Regarding appointments, popular election clearly raises the risk of politicization and can therefore have a considerable impact on independence. It could be argued that mechanisms that involve more than one agency ensure independence better than other mechanisms. In addition, it should be taken into consideration that the participation of political bodies such as Congress would tend to politicize judicial appointments. Also, if we look at the duration of the term to be served, a short term certainly makes it difficult for judges to interpret the law and apply it to the facts of a case under the scrutiny of the body that decides their re-appointments. Therefore, should the appointments not be for life, ending only under certain circumstances such as misconduct, illness, etc., it

---

83 For an analysis of different aspects of judicial independence, see L.P. Mora Mora, "La independencia del Juez como derecho humano", in Inter-American Court, *Liber Amicorum Héctor Fix-Zamudio*, Vol. I, *supra* n. 3, pp. 1079–1096.

84 D.J. Harris, M. O'Boyle and C. Warbrick, *supra* n. 46, p. 239.

85 On the independence of courts in the European system, see *ibidem*, pp. 231–234, and P. van Dijk, F. van Hoof, A. van Rijn and L. Zwaak (eds), *supra* n. 43, pp. 613–614. For the system under the International Covenant on Civil and Political Rights, see S. Joseph, J. Schulz and M. Castan, *The International Covenant on Civil and Political Rights, Cases, Materials, and Commentary*, Oxford University Press, Oxford, 2000, pp. 287–288.

is advisable that the term at least be a long one. There is also an argument that independence can only be achieved when a judicial system controls its own finances (as opposed to having the executive or Congress controlling its budget), and when remuneration of judges allows them a standard of living similar to that of other professionals.

In sum, it is vital that extreme care be taken in designing the mechanism, and possibly a combination of a good appointment system together with systems that ensure other aspects related to independence is the most appropriate.

36. As far as impartiality is concerned, the case law is persistent in holding that it must be both subjective and objective.[86] The European Court of Human Rights has used this wording in many cases, establishing that subjective impartiality has to do with the personal convictions of a particular judge in a particular case, while objective impartiality means that an individual being judged would have a reasonable impression of impartiality that would preempt legitimate doubts.[87] The European Court of Human Rights has found that "[w]hat is at stake is the confidence which the courts in a democratic society must inspire in the public and, above all, as far as criminal proceedings are concerned, in the accused."[88] The importance of impartiality can be observed in numerous cases heard by the European system in which the Court held, for example, that a judge that ruled on the pre-trial detention of an accused person based on his conviction that there is a reasonable suspicion of the accused's guilt could not later form part of the tribunal that would rule on that person's innocence or guilt.[89]

37. The Inter-American Court has on several occasions made reference to the requirements of independence and impartiality of courts, but generally does not differentiate between the concepts. A case in which it referred only to independence was that of the Constitutional Court, in which it found a need for strict proceedings in both the appointment and dismissal of judges, ruling that the separation of powers was a guarantee for the independence of judges.[90]

38. The majority of the judgments of the Court analyze the problem of independence and/or impartiality as regards military courts, closely related with the requirement that the tribunal be "competent". Case law has varied. As

---

86 See S. Stavoros, *The Guarantees for Accused Persons under Article 6 of the European Convention on Human Rights*, Martinus Nijhoff, London, 1993.

87 The first judgment establishing this distinction was ECtHR, *Piersack v. Belgium*, judgment of 1 October 1982, paras. 30–32, reproduced in Council of Europe, *Digest of Strasbourg Case-Law relating to the European Convention on Human Rights*, Vol. 2 (Article 6), Carl Heymanns-Verlag KG, Köln/Berlin/Bonn/München, 1984, pp. 672–674.

88 D.J. Harris, M. O'Boyle and C. Warbrick, *supra* n. 46, p. 235, citing *Fey v. Austria*, judgment of 24 February 1993, para. 30.

89 See *ibidem*, p. 237.

90 *Case of the Constitutional Court*, para. 73. Also see paras. 74 and 75.

previously noted, in the case of Genie Lacayo, the Court found that "the fact that it involves a military court does not *per se* signify that the human rights guaranteed the accusing party by the Convention are being violated."[91] However, the Court did not move to examine the elements previously indicated as decisive for determining whether a tribunal is independent and impartial. Although it made reference to the pleadings found in the application to the extent that the impartiality and independence of military courts are not assured both because of their members and because of "the possible use of ideological elements such as that of the 'Sandinista juridical conscience'", it examined only the latter, deciding that as the provision mentioning "Sandinista conscience" had not been applied in the case, there was no violation.[92] The Court also found that using a provision that called for the application of "Sandinista's legality" in the proceedings was not a violation of independence and impartiality, deriving from the context of the provision that the expression made reference to guidelines that "are common to general military criminal law regardless of the political orientation of the State in question".[93]

Later, however, the Court ruled that the military courts that tried the petitioners in the case of Castillo Petruzzi *et al.* did not comply with the requirement of independence (because "members of the Supreme Court of Military Justice, the highest body in the military judiciary, are appointed by the minister of the pertinent sector" and because the members of that Council "also decide who among their subordinates will be promoted and what incentives will be offered to whom"), nor did they comply with the requirement of impartiality because it was "the armed forces, fully engaged in the counter-insurgency struggle", who were in charge of trying the persons connected to those groups.[94]

39. Without prejudice to this, the argument that the Court uses to examine these tribunals – leading the Court to conclude that given particular circumstances, Article 8(1) of the Convention has been violated – is still not clear. For example, in the case of Loayza Tamayo, the Court found that it was not necessary to rule on the alleged lack of independence, nor on the alleged lack of impartiality of military courts "as Ms María Elena Loayza Tamayo was acquitted by that military court and, therefore, the possible failure to meet those requirements did not cause her legal injury in that regard."[95] This appears to establish that as far as this subject is concerned, the result of the trial is what is important, and it fails to take into consideration that the rules of due process must be in place regardless of whether they affect the outcome of a trial. Nor

---

91 *Case of Genie Lacayo*, para. 84.

92 *Ibidem*, para. 86.

93 *Ibidem*, para. 87.

94 *Case of Castillo Petruzzi et al.*, para. 130. In the same sense, *Case of Durand and Ugarte*, para. 126, *Case of Cantoral Benavides*, para. 114, and *Case of Las Palmeras*, para. 53.

95 *Case of Loayza Tamayo*, para. 60.

does it take into account aspects such as the difference in treatment of a case before these courts and the consequences resulting from it, for example, in order to protect the rights set forth in Article 7 of the Convention.

40. Another grounds for the violation of impartiality examined by the Court is the existence of "faceless" judges who prevent the accused from learning their identities "and thus assessing their competence".[96] Although the Court asserts this as a violation of the competence requirement, I find it obvious that this situation is more precisely a violation of the impartiality requirement given that if the identity of the judge is not known, it is impossible to know whether the judge is in compliance with this requirement. This also prevents the judge from being challenged, given that grounds for doing so cannot be brought against an anonymous judge.

2.4. DUE GUARANTEES

41. The expression "due guarantees" alludes to the Anglo-Saxon legal concept of a "fair trial". Both concepts are undefined as they do not determine the elements comprising them, for which reason it is necessary to examine each individual trial in order to assess whether it is in general a "due or just process".[97] One could say *grosso modo* that due guarantees have to do with certain minimum requirements for conducting a trial. It is not enough for the trial to be carried out by a competent, independent and impartial tribunal; it is also necessary for the tribunal to give the parties the opportunity to present their cases without obstacles. This means the presence of a defense attorney in all types of trials should the defendant so wish; time and opportunity to present the evidence in support of their pleadings; a reasonable evaluation of the evidence; and reasoned rulings from the tribunal, all based on the principle of equality.

2.4.1. Principles of audi alteram partem *and of equality in a proceeding*

42. Due guarantees include the idea of the principle of *audi alteram partem*. In a proceeding, there are two parties who must have the right to take part in a dispute. The rules of procedure must be drafted in such a way as to allow this.

As with every human right, the right to due process must be enjoyed by all, without discrimination; the principle of equality therefore underlies this, as it does all other human rights found in the Convention, and must be reflected in the principle of *audi alteram partem*. In terms of a proceeding, this means that

96 *Case of Castillo Petruzzi et al.*, para. 133, *Case of Cantoral Benavides*, para. 127(c).

97 On "fair hearings", see D.J. Harris, M. O'Boyle and C. Warbrick, *supra* n. 46, pp. 202–203.

the court must behave similarly toward all parties to a proceeding and that the parties must have the same rights, both to present petitions, pleadings and evidence and to challenge the petitions and evidence presented by the other party. This also includes the notion that the rules of procedure must be worded in such a way that they do not place one party at a disadvantage compared to the other.

In criminal proceedings, the principle of *audi alteram partem* "consists of a real opportunity for the defense for maximum rebuttal of the accusations"[98] and constitutes a guarantee for the accused. As far as the principle of equality, during the debate over the draft Convention, the inclusion of subparagraph (b) under paragraph 2 of Article 7 (today 8) was suggested, establishing that "due process in criminal proceedings will include the following minimum guarantees: [...] b) Equality of rights and duties of the parties during the trial." The suggestion was rejected and replaced with the current wording of paragraph 2, which grants minimum guarantees only to the accused, in full equality, abandoning the idea of equality of the parties.[99] It seems clear that due process is a right of individuals before the State and cannot be invoked by the State before itself. As Maier says, criminal procedural law can grant authority to the Public Prosecutor's Office with which it can exercise the State's power of criminal prosecution. However, it cannot provide guarantees to that office.[100] It seems clear that when the American Convention was adopted, there was no trace of the idea that "bilateralness of the hearing" between the accused and the victim applied in criminal proceedings, although this could be in the process of changing.

43. The Court made reference to both principles in a case that is not recent – that of Genie Lacayo – applying not Article 8 but rather Article 24 of the Convention, and ruling that:

> it has not been proven that Mr Raymond Genie-Peñalba [father of the victim] found himself in a *clear situation of inferiority* in relation to the defendants or the military judges when he appeared as the accusing party before the military courts; consequently, there was no violation of the right to equal protection of the law.[101]

The judgment speaks here of the right of the victim or the victim's relatives and seems to use European case law on requiring the possible situation of inferiority to be clear. In the case of Kaufman v. Belgium, the European Commission found that "everyone who is a party to such proceedings [referring to both criminal and

98 M.I. Horvitz and J. López, *Derecho Procesal Penal Chileno*, Vol. II, Chapter X, section 3.3.

99 Specialized Conference, San Jose, Costa Rica, 7–22 November 1969, *Minutes and Documents,* General Secretariat, OAS, Washington DC, OEA/Ser.K/XVI/1.2, pp. 59, 105 and 190.

100 J. Maier, *Derecho Procesal Penal*, pp. 543–44, cited in M.I. Horvitz, "Estatus de la Víctima en el Proceso Penal. Comentario a dos fallos de la Corte Suprema", in (2003) 3 *Revista de Estudios de la Justicia* 135.

101 *Case of Genie Lacayo,* para. 88 (emphasis added).

non-criminal cases] shall have a reasonable opportunity of presenting his case to the court under conditions which do not place him at *substantial* disadvantage vis-à-vis his opponent" (emphasis added).[102] The adjective "clear", which could be understood, in this case, as equivalent to the word "substantial" as used in European case law, could in my opinion provide space for excessive discretion in its interpretation. Apart from this, the situations considered by the European Commission and the Court are different because the European body is in this case considering the rights of the accused and not of the relatives of the victim.

2.4.2. Right to be represented by an attorney

44. An important guarantee is the opportunity to have legal assistance in court. Article 8 does not establish a State obligation to provide this legal assistance for free to people without means to pay for it, neither for criminal nor for non-criminal proceedings. According to the American Convention, due process can be complied with simply by allowing the person without means to present his or her case before the court personally. However, an individual's lack of sufficient education together with a lack of means can be a greater obstacle to serving justice. Although the Convention does not make this obligation for the State explicit, the principle of due process could at some point require the State to provide this kind of assistance in certain criminal or even non-criminal trials, for example when the proceedings are not simple enough to make having or not having legal assistance irrelevant.[103] Of course, if the domestic legal system does not allow a person to litigate on his or her own behalf, it seems evident that the State is required to provide free legal assistance to persons lacking sufficient financial means.

The Inter-American Court has established the groundwork for developing this idea, both in an advisory opinion and in several judgments. In response to a consultation from the Inter-American Commission on exceptions to exhaustion of domestic remedies, the Court opined that, "[e]ven in those cases in which the accused is forced to defend him or herself because he or she cannot afford legal counsel,[104] a violation of Article 8 of the Convention could be said to exist if it can be proved that the lack of legal counsel affected the right to a fair hearing to which the person is entitled under that Article",[105] adding that in non-criminal cases, the concept of "due guarantees" applies also to these orders; consequently, on these issues the individual also has the right to the due process that applies in

---

102 D.J. Harris, M. O'Boyle and C. Warbrick, *supra* n. 46, p. 207, citing the judgment of the European Court of Human Rights in the case of *Kaufman v. Belgium* No. 10938/84, 50 DR 98 at 115 (1986).

103 The problem was examined by the European Court of Human Rights in *Airey v. Ireland*, judgment of 9 October 1979, A.32 (1980).

104 See the debate on the interpretation of Article 8 with regard to free legal assistance, *infra* section 3.2.5.

105 OC-11/90 of 10 August 1990, para. 27.

criminal cases. It is important to note here that the circumstances of a particular case or proceeding – its significance, its legal character, and its context in a particular legal system – are among the factors that bear on the determination of whether legal representation is or is not necessary for a fair hearing.[106]

2.4.3. *Reasonable time*

2.4.3.1. Criteria for determining reasonableness

45. Article 8(1) establishes a person's right to a hearing "within a reasonable time". The notion of a reasonable time was examined in some detail in the prior chapter in regard to the provision contained in Article 7(5) of the Convention.[107] In Article 8(1) of the Convention, the purpose of the requirement of a reasonable time for the completion of the proceedings is clear. In criminal proceedings, it seeks to prevent the accused from remaining in a situation of uncertainty for a long time, given that such situations undoubtedly affect the enjoyment of certain of their human rights. In civil proceedings, the purpose is the quick determination of rights or obligations in order for the one whose right is recognized to be able to begin to enjoy it, and the one whose obligation is established to be relieved of the uncertainty of not knowing whether he or she has an obligation to fulfil. As will be seen further on, the Inter-American Court has broadened the purpose of the reasonable time, finding that victims of human rights violations also have a right to know the truth about the facts leading to violations and for the guilty parties to be tried and convicted within a reasonable period.[108]

46. The Convention does not set forth criteria for guiding those who apply these provisions in establishing this reasonable period, but there is enough case law, particularly European, developing said criteria. The Inter-American Court used them in resolving the case of Genie Lacayo, in which it examined a criminal proceeding. In its judgment, it ruled that in order to decide on the reasonableness of the period of time in a proceeding, the following three elements must be taken into account: "a) the complexity of the matter; b) the judicial activity of the interested party; and c) the behavior of the judicial authorities."[109] The complexity of the matter could, for example, arise from the fact that a proceeding has many parties, or the fact that many difficult expert witness reports must be prepared, or the fact that part of the investigation must be carried out through requests for judicial assistance from other courts.[110] The procedural activity of

---

106 *Ibidem*, para. 28.
107 See Chapter 4, section 3.2.4.
108 See *supra*, paras. 14 and 15.
109 *Case of Genie Lacayo*, para. 77; *Case of Juan Humberto Sánchez*, para. 129.
110 In the *Case of Genie Lacayo*, para. 78, the "great impact of the death of young Genie Lacayo" is mentioned, in my opinion erroneously, as an element for determining complexity.

the interested party is analyzed from the point of view of the good faith with which the actions are carried out; the use of all remedies that the law itself provides for cannot, in principle, cause a delay; on the contrary, it is the State's responsibility to prevent the rules of procedure themselves from causing the delay.[111] The conduct of judicial authorities is a particularly important factor:[112] any delay must have a justification, and an excessive amount of work faced by the court cannot be one of them. This, I would reiterate, is because the responsibility for due process "within a reasonable time" fully belongs to the State, and it is the State that has the obligation to organize a justice system that functions.

In the case of Juan Humberto Sánchez, which also examined a criminal proceeding, the Court found that the case had no complexity that could justify a preliminary investigation stage that was still pending ten years after being opened.[113] The Court did not spell out its reasoning, noting in an examination of the case file that the delays were clearly attributable to State agencies. First, there was evidence that the judicial authorities had not been diligent in processing the case; an example of this was the fact that the collection of evidence had been carried out between 1992 and 1998, with long periods of inactivity. Second, other State authorities had been negligent in carrying out their duties, such as, for example, the Armed Forces, which did not respond to the courts' requests for several years.[114] Nor did the Court accept the State's defense that the relatives were responsible for taking action to move the proceedings forward. The Court reiterated here that it is the State's responsibility to investigate, and that it must act *ex officio*.[115] For this reason, one must conclude that the criteria for assessing a party's activity in criminal proceedings must refer to the accused and not to the victim or the victim's relatives. This shows the complexity of the Court's position granting the relatives of a victim a role in criminal proceedings.

In the case of Bulacio, the Court referred to the subject of judicial neglect and abuse of procedural remedies – this latter in direct reference to the activities of the accused – as a basis for finding the time period to have been unreasonable. It argued that in the domestic proceedings, "the defense counsel for the accused filed a large number of diverse legal questions and remedies [...] which have not allowed the proceedings to progress toward their natural culmination",[116] something that has been tolerated by acting judicial bodies "forgetting that their function is not exhausted by enabling due process that guarantees defence at a trial, but that they must also ensure, within a reasonable time, the right of the

111 *Ibidem*, para. 79.
112 *Ibidem*, para. 80.
113 *Case of Juan Humberto Sánchez*, para. 130.
114 *Ibidem*, paras. 130–131.
115 *Ibidem*, para. 132.
116 *Case of Bulacio*, para. 113.

victim or his or her next of kin to learn the truth about what happened and for those responsible to be punished."[117] The consequence of these delays in the proceedings, which can allow the accused to object to the criminal action on the grounds of prescription, was rejected by the Court in this type of criminal proceedings.[118]

In the case of Myrna Mack Chang, the Court did an examination of the collection of judicial actions and reached the conclusion that a "lack of diligence and of willingness of the courts was demonstrated, as regards moving the criminal proceeding forward to elucidate all the facts pertaining to the death of Myrna Mack Chang and to punish all those responsible."[119] Although it admitted that one reason for the delay was the existence of rules of procedure that required writs of *amparo* requested by the accused to be processed even when they were manifestly inadmissible, it found that the judges had exceeded legal deadlines, paralyzing the criminal proceedings. As it did in the Bulacio case, the Court warned the State that a court must balance the guarantee of defense in the trial with the right of the victim or the victim's relatives to know the truth within a reasonable time, stating that: "The right to effective judicial protection therefore requires that the judges direct the proceeding in such a way as to avoid undue delays and obstructions that lead to impunity, thus frustrating due judicial protection of human rights."[120]

47. To these three criteria that we have examined, a fourth criteria should be added that, in fact, the case law takes into account:[121] the seriousness of the consequences of the procedural delay for the party. It seems reasonable to think that in general, criminal proceedings must be resolved in less time than non-criminal proceedings. In criminal cases, the accused being held in detention is an important element to consider for increasing the swiftness of the case, but there can be other factors, such as for example an accused person in a state of mental health that means that the burden of waiting for a ruling on guilt or innocence would be greater for that person than for an average person. In non-criminal cases, a trial in which alimony is sought for a minor could in principle be a proceeding that must always be resolved urgently; in other trials, it would depend on the particular circumstances. This type of reasoning constitutes a legitimate argument that the defense attorney of an affected party would have the right to raise under Article 8(1) of the Convention.

117 *Ibidem*, para. 114. In the same sense, separate opinion of *Ad Hoc* Judge Ricardo Gil, para. 4, where he contrasts the guarantees found in Article 8 with Article 25's protection of the victim.
118 *Ibidem*, para. 116. This position that argument expressed in the *case of Barrios Altos*, para. 41.
119 *Case of Myrna Mack Chang*, para. 203.
120 *Ibidem*, para. 210.
121 D.J. Harris, M. O'Boyle and C. Warbrick, *supra* n. 46, p. 226.

48. Although most of the case law and scholarship refer to a maximum period of time when examining the State's obligation to conclude proceedings "within a reasonable time", the idea of reasonableness of time period must also apply when determining a minimum time period, given that the proceedings must give the parties opportunity to present their evidence and to contest the evidence of the opposing party, as well as give the judge the opportunity to be able to study the case and offer support for his or her ruling. In non-criminal cases, the problem is closely related with the concept of "due guarantees" and the principle of *audi alteram partem*: in criminal cases, it has to do with one of the minimum guarantees of the accused, that of adequate time and means for defense.[122] The Inter-American Court made reference to the brevity of the period of time in the case of Las Palmeras, in which it analyzed the possible violations of rights found in the Convention perpetrated during an operation that had resulted in the deaths of several people. The proceeding that was the subject of study was an investigation into the responsibility of police officers in that operation, but the ruling that the time period was not reasonable because of its brevity attempted to safeguard the right of the relatives of the dead individuals to a serious investigation. In that judgment, the Court ruled that a disciplinary proceeding that lasted only five days "prevented the presentation of evidence"[123] without making it clear if that consideration in itself was enough for finding a violation of Article 8(1) of the Convention.

49. It is clear from this that reasonable time is an open and indeterminate concept and that a specific period of time to be applied generally in all cases of a similar nature cannot be established because only on a case-by-case basis can the delicate equilibrium that must exist between the quickness of the ruling, the opportunity for the parties to develop their defenses, and the chance for the judge to have the necessary time to carefully examine the pleadings and evidence be assessed. Domestically, rules of procedure often exist that establish a standard time period for the different types of proceedings. This is positive in principle, but normally the rules also allow a court to justify having missed the deadline. These time periods in domestic legal systems can serve as a reference for international bodies when deciding on reasonability, but for the reasons already stated, they are not definitive.

2.4.3.2. Burden of proof

50. The right to proceedings within a reasonable time raises the problem of determining to whom the burden of proof belongs: should the affected party prove that the period of time was not reasonable, or should the State prove that

---

122 See *infra*, 3.2.3.

123 *Case of Las Palmeras*, para. 49.

the period of time was reasonable? In order to answer the question, however, a supervisory body needs an initial baseline, which appears principally in the case law and practice of the Human Rights Committee: it is important to have a rough idea of the minimum time generally needed for proceedings to be carried out adequately. If at the time the lack of reasonableness of the time period is alleged, this minimum, abstract and general period of time has not passed, the supervisory body shall rule immediately that there has been no violation unless the petitioner making the complaint provides pleadings as to why that period of time, although brief, is not reasonable. On the other hand, if the period of time presumed theoretically reasonable has passed, a violation will have taken place unless the State justifies, based on the aforementioned criteria, that the time period is reasonable, despite being long. Of course, this abstract period of time will vary depending on the type of proceedings under examination, and the decision of what that period is will be made based on the experience of the members of the supervisory body.[124]

The Inter-American Commission used this reasoning in its pleadings in the case of Hilaire, Constantine and Benjamin, *et al.*, arguing that "in cases of unacceptable delay, the burden of proof falls on the State to justify the delay".[125] The Inter-American Court has also placed the burden of proof on the State when the time period clearly appears to be excessive. The Court ruled thusly in the case of Las Palmeras, in which it rejected an objection raised by the State of a failure to exhaust domestic remedies, finding that the facts of the case originated in January 1991 and the State had not given "a satisfactory explanation regarding the procedural measures between that date and the beginning of 1998". During that period of time, the case had not gone beyond the preliminary investigation stage.[126] The Court reiterated its position in the judgment on the merits on finding a violation of Article 8(1) for the same reason.[127] It did the same in the case of Hilaire, Constantine and Benjamin, *et al.*[128] However, in the case of Genie Lacayo, the Court ruled that a period of five years from the moment the court order was issued to open the proceedings with no final judgment was not reasonable, yet it did not address whether the State had provided any explanation.[129]

---

124 For example, see HRC, *Allen v. Jamaica,* Communication 332/1988, decision of 31 March 1994, in which the duration of a criminal trial seem to be brief and the petitioner did not provide evidence of negligence, and *Fillastre and Bizouarn v. Bolivia,* Communication 336/1988, decision of 5 November 1991, in which the duration of a criminal trial was four years (para. 6.6).

125 *Case of Hilaire, Constantine and Benjamin, et al.*, para. 122.

126 *Case of Las Palmeras, preliminary objections*, para. 38.

127 *Case of Las Palmeras,* para. 62.

128 *Case of Hilaire, Constantine and Benjamin, et al.*, para. 145.

129 *Case of Genie Lacayo,* para. 81.

2.4.3.3. How to measure the time period

51. For the purposes of Article 8(1), the moment from which one begins counting the time period depends on the type of trial. In criminal matters, the time period must be counted from the point at which an individual first comes in contact with the criminal court system as a suspect. In the case of Suárez Rosero, for example, the Inter-American Court found that "the first act of the proceeding was Mr Suárez Rosero's arrest on 23 June 1992, and, therefore, the time must be calculated from that moment."[130] On the other hand, in the case of Genie Lacayo, as the claimant was the father of the victim and not the accused, the Court found that the time period must be counted from the date on which the first instance judge issued the order to open the proceedings.[131]

In non-criminal proceedings, the time period must be counted from the first action taken to initiate it; the standards that are often applied in domestic procedural law to decide when a lawsuit is in place cannot be used here. For the complainant, for example, it is his or her complaint that puts the legal system in motion and it is at that moment that the State is called on to act.

As far as the moment up to which the time period is counted, the general rule is to count until there is a final judgment in the proceedings. This is what the Inter-American Court found in the case of Genie Lacayo[132] and in the case of Suárez Rosero. In this latter case, the Court clearly expressed that "the time must cover the entire proceeding, including any appeals that may be filed".[133]

2.4.3.4. Which periods count? Is the trial one entity?

52. Finally, it is important to determine which periods are relevant in deciding whether a process's duration is reasonable, and if that decision is to be made by taking into consideration the trial as a whole or by examining a trial's proceedings individually. In regard to the former, the task of the supervisory body is to add up the time that the court has spent on the case – subtracting possible unjustified delays that are the responsibility of the party in question – in order to be able to conclude whether the State has violated the obligation found in Article 8(1) of the Convention.

With regard to the second point, one possibility is to follow European case law as set forth as follows in Harris *et al.*: the European Court of Human Rights first examines the total duration of the case. If it seems excessive on its face, the proceedings are then examined in detail and the burden of proof falls on the State. The authors, with whom I agree, argue that this method can be detrimental

---

130 *Case of Suárez Rosero*, para. 70.

131 *Case of Genie Lacayo*, para. 81.

132 *Ibidem*.

133 *Case of Suárez Rosero*, para. 71. In the same sense, *Case of Hilaire, Constantine and Benjamin, et al.*, para. 142.

to the injured party, as there is a possibility the European Court of Human Rights would overlook unnecessary delays should it find that as a whole, the proceedings had concluded within a reasonable period of time, thus basing its ruling on an abstract criterion of how long a trial of a particular nature should last and not on the specific characteristics of the case under examination.[134] Thus the focus of the Human Rights Committee, explained above in relation to the burden of proof, seems more appropriate, as it combines an examination of the period of time as a whole with an examination of each individual delay.

53. In the case of Genie Lacayo, the Court decided to carry out an analysis of the overall proceedings, using the European Court of Human Rights' focus.[135] It repeated this approach in the Cantos case, allowing us to observe the problem raised previously, although the judgment on this point also inter-mixes other elements.[136] In this latter case, it was shown that a period of ten years had passed between the moment Mr Cantos filed his complaint before the Supreme Court of Justice and the moment that court issued its judgment. Based on this, the victim argued that the time period was not reasonable. The Inter-American Court agreed that ten years was in principle excessive, but nevertheless found that "a careful examination of the history of the case, shows that both the State and the plaintiff engaged in behaviors that, either by action or omission, served to prolong the proceedings in the domestic courts. If the plaintiff's own conduct somehow helped to prolong the proceedings, then it is hard to make the case that it is the State that has violated the "reasonable time" clause.[137]

Without commenting on the final result, I would argue that this reasoning may be the subject of criticism as while the problem of the delays that may arise in the proceedings due to the actions or omissions of a plaintiff is related with the time periods that can be added up to decide whether the period was reasonable – periods of delay attributable to actions of the plaintiff must be subtracted from the final total – they should not serve to cancel out the State's neglect. Also, a reading of the judgment in this specific case indicates that it is probable that many of the applicant's actions that delayed the proceedings had to do with the fact that the Argentine courts were requiring him to pay an exorbitant court filing fee that he was not able to pay.[138]

Nevertheless, the Court ruled in the end that "taking into account the complexity of the matter and the lack of interest on the part of the plaintiff, among other factors, the total duration of the litigation is not sufficiently significant for declaring a violation" of the requirement for a reasonable period

---

134 D.J. Harris, M. O'Boyle and C. Warbrick, *supra* n. 46, p. 229.

135 *Case of Genie Lacayo*, para. 81.

136 See *infra*, para. 12.

137 *Case of Cantos*, para. 57.

138 See *infra*, para. 12.

of time found in Article 8(1) of the Convention.[139] Thus it is not precisely known whether the ruling was based solely on the neglect of the plaintiff or if considerations of the complexity of the matter had an influence.

2.4.4. Right to a reasoned ruling

54. Article 8(1) does not establish that a ruling in a case must be accompanied by the reasoning for it, but it is evident that due process guarantees could be annulled if a court is not required to offer a basis for its rulings – both legal and regarding a case's proven facts – and to set forth that basis explicitly. In addition, the absence of reasoning blocks the parties' right to formulate their own reasoned appeal, as appropriate.

2.4.5. Right for a ruling to be enforced

55. Although this right is not explicitly set forth in Article 8 of the Convention, clearly if individuals can demand that their civil rights and obligations – or their guilt or innocence – be determined by a court that meets a series of requirements in a proceeding that also meets international standards, the State will not have complied with its obligations regarding the rights at issue until the ruling made by the courts in a case reaches its conclusion – that is, until the final judgment is carried out. For me, a failure to comply with a final judgment clearly constitutes a violation of due process, as the ultimate purpose of due process is the clear resolution of a problem.

56. The Inter-American Court does not seem to have had the same opinion when it declined to rule on the possible violation of Article 8 of the Convention in the case of the Five Pensioners despite the fact that the State administration's failure to execute a court ruling was an important part of the basis for the claim. Although this was in reference to Article 25, the Commission argued that the principal purpose of the instant case is for the Court to decide on the State's international responsibility for non-compliance with the firm and executable judgments in favor of the alleged victims delivered by the highest Peruvian courts, the Supreme Court of Justice of Peru and the Peruvian Constitutional Court.[140]

In the judgment handed down in that case, the Court reaffirmed its jurisdiction to rule on Article 8 of the Convention even when it has not been invoked by the victim in the proceeding before the Inter-American Commission. However, it did not rule definitively because it failed to find sufficient evidence in

139 *Case of Cantos*, para. 57.

140 *Case of the "Five Pensioners"*, para. 122(i).

the case file to rule one way or the other.[141] In its ruling on the claim related to Article 25, the Court found that the State's position constituted a violation of that provision.[142] However, it added that the State could not separate itself from court rulings "at the risk of incurring in violations of the right to property and to judicial protection",[143] which could be understood as a reference to Article 8. In this judgment, therefore, the Court extended the provisions of Article 25(2)(c) to all court rulings, although from a strict perspective, Article 25 refers only to a ruling on a "remedy".

3. SPECIAL GUARANTEES FOR THE ACCUSED

57. As stated previously, Article 8(2) of the Convention establishes certain special guarantees for the accused. These guarantees coexist with the general guarantees found in the first paragraph of that article and are intended to set forth specific protection for people subjected to a criminal trial given the effect that this type of trial can have on certain human rights, such as the right to personal freedom and the honor of the person subjected to the proceedings.[144]

3.1. PRESUMPTION OF INNOCENCE

58. The second paragraph of Article 8 guarantees that any person accused of a crime has "the right to be presumed innocent so long as his guilt has not been proven according to law". The presumption of innocence establishes explicitly that the State cannot affect any human right without a justification for doing so. Given that one consequence of a criminal conviction is a significant diminishing of a person's capacity to exercise and enjoy a number of human rights, it seems appropriate that as long as a person's guilt has not been demonstrated, that person should not suffer the consequences. Next, on initial approach, the principle seems to mean both that the person must be treated as innocent until found guilty in a court ruling, and that nobody can be convicted unless the State proves to the reasonable satisfaction of the court that the person is guilty of what he or she is accused of. The judge hearing the matter is the one directly and most fundamentally bound to the presumption of innocence.

---

141 *Ibidem*, paras. 149–157.

142 *Ibidem*, para. 141.

143 *Ibidem*, para. 138.

144 In general, with regard to criminal due process, see V.M. Rodríguez Rescia, "El debido proceso legal y la Convención Americana sobre Derechos Humanos", in Inter-American Court, *Liber Amicorum Héctor Fix-Zamudio*, Vol. I, 1998, San Jose, Costa Rica, pp. 1295–1328 (1306 ff).

59. Because of the position it takes with regard to several of these points, one interesting ruling is the judgment on the merits in the case of Cantoral Benavides, in which the Court ruled that this presumption had been violated. The apparent basis for the Court's ruling was that the decision to convict had been handed down before any clear evidence had been established of the guilt of the accused. This was demonstrated by the existence of a pardon benefiting the accused, granted "to persons who have been convicted of terrorism or treason against the fatherland on the basis of insufficient evidence".[145] This consideration was in itself sufficient for finding a violation of the presumption of innocence. However, the Court added another consideration in the section examining the violation of the principle, a consideration that is worth analyzing even though it is not clear that it was decisive for finding a violation. The Court indicates in the judgment that the petitioner was "paraded before the media, dressed in defamatory clothing, as the perpetrator of the crime of treason against the fatherland, before he had been legally tried or convicted."[146] The Court's consideration that Mr Cantoral Benavides had been paraded before the media before he was brought to trial or convicted broadens the principle's field of action and removes it from the narrow realm of the procedural. In reality, it could be argued that this minimum guarantee, along with others, must be respected from the moment a person comes in contact with the justice system. This interpretation also takes into consideration the fact that the term "accused" can have different meanings in the different legal systems of the States parties to the Convention and that in order to properly read the guarantee, its objective and purpose have to be taken into account.

60. Another point that should be noted is that parading Mr Cantoral Benavides before the media was not ordered by the judge in the case but rather by the government of Peru. One could thus wonder whether the principle goes beyond the framework of the actions of the court during a criminal proceeding and is also binding for other State bodies aside from the court hearing the matter. This would seem to be the Court's position, and it coincides with that of the United Nations Human Rights Committee, which has ruled as much by stating in its General Comment on Article 14 of the International Covenant that "the presumption of innocence implies a right to be treated in accordance with this principle. It is, therefore, a duty for all public authorities to refrain from prejudging the outcome of a trial."[147]

145 *Case of Cantoral Benavides*, paras. 120–122.

146 *Ibidem*, para. 119.

147 Human Rights Committee, General Comment No. 13 (1984) in A/39/40 (1984) Annex VI, pp. 143–147.

61. From another perspective, the Court also established that the treatment of a person as innocent also applied to infractions of personal freedom when it ruled that the principle of the presumption of innocence is violated when a person remains in detention for an extended period of time,[148] and when it ruled that *razzias* (mass detentions carried out by the police in Argentina) were not compatible with respect for fundamental rights, the presumption of innocence among them.[149]

62. The Court has also made reference to the presumption of innocence in the case of Loayza Tamayo. In that judgment, it established that the principle had been violated because military courts had ascribed to Ms Loayza "a different crime to the one for which she was prosecuted and convicted, without having jurisdiction to do so". The basis for this ruling is difficult to understand. Notwithstanding the fact that in this case, Peru clearly violated several rights set forth in the Convention – among them the right to personal freedom by detaining Ms Loayza after a ruling to acquit was handed down – with regard to the presumption of innocence, the military courts do not seem to have done anything but file a complaint over the commission of a crime before a civilian court. It would be difficult to argue that this action in and of itself constitutes a violation of the principle.[150]

3.2. OTHER MINIMUM GUARANTEES

63. Article 8(2) of the Convention also takes pains to establish certain rights that would seem to be essential for people to be able to defend themselves from the charges against them. Although it is up to the State to prove the guilt of the accused, the accused must enjoy the appropriate conditions to be able to contest the evidence on which the State bases its accusation.

64. The Inter-American Court has heard cases in which possible violations of these guarantees were alleged, but an examination of its case law reveals the precarious situation that the accused have faced on the issue of guarantees of their rights and how much further there is to go to make this continent's legislation and judicial practices compatible with its international obligations. In general, the kinds of violations that have been brought before the Court with

---

148 *Case of Suárez Rosero*, paras. 77–78. In that case, detention pending resolution of the case had lasted for almost four years.

149 *Case of Bulacio*, para. 137.

150 *Case of Loayza Tamayo*, para. 63. Similarly to Mr Cantoral Benavides, Ms Loayza was also paraded before the media as a terrorist. However, this fact was not taken into consideration by the Court in her case for the purposes of ruling on the existence of a violation of the presumption of innocence.

regard to these guarantees are so flagrant that the Court has not been able to bring the content of these rights into sharp focus. We must await progress in this area and hope that other types of cases begin arriving to the system that allow for the development, through international case law, of these guarantees that are so important for the defense of persons subjected to criminal proceedings.

3.2.1. Right to a translator or interpreter

65. It seems obvious that "the right of the accused to be assisted without charge by a translator or interpreter, if he does not understand or does not speak the language of the tribunal or court", contained in Article 8(2)(a) of the Convention, must exist given that in order to defend themselves, the accused must be able to understand what they are accused of. Possibly the problem of how much an accused person must understand in order to make an interpreter unnecessary will arise in the future. For example, I would point to the continent's indigenous populations and the difficulty that many of their members may have in fully expressing their thoughts, despite the fact that they speak Spanish. Inadequate language skills is a significant disadvantage, particularly in trials that must be oral.

66. Interpretation of the text suggests at least one question that the Court must eventually resolve: Article 8(2) refers to the "proceedings", a term that can include both oral and written actions. This raises the question of whether assistance for the accused refers only to that person's ability to communicate orally with the court or if it extends to the reading of trial documents. A restrictive interpretation could be based on the use of the conjunction "or", which perhaps indicates that the drafters of the Convention felt that the words were synonyms. A broad interpretation could be based on the meaning assigned to these words, given that in Spanish the word "translator" (*traductor*) applies to a person who puts something written in one language into another language, while an "interpreter" (*intérprete*) is a person who explains to others, in a language that they understand, what is being said in another language which is unknown to them.[151] In support of the broader interpretation, it could be argued that in addition to the interpretation of the literal meaning of the provision, it must be taken into consideration that the objective and purpose of the right is to allow people to understand the charges and the evidence brought against them. The financial costs that this could have for the State make it advisable that the domestic court be the one to decide which instruments of the proceedings in each case the accused needs to be able to understand in order to mount an adequate defense, or if on the contrary it is enough that the accused's defense

[151] In Spanish: *traductor* applies to someone who "traduce una obra o escrito" and *intérprete* is used to mean a "persona que explica a otras, en lengua que entienden, lo dicho en otra que les es desconocida". *Diccionario de la Lengua Española*, Real Academia Española, vigésima segunda edición, 2001, Tomo II, pp. 2205 and 1293, respectively.

attorney understands their content. Naturally, an oversight body would have jurisdiction to review whether this obligation has been fully complied with.

67. The word "accused" in this provision must also be understood broadly, as the right must exist from the moment it becomes necessary for the person who has come in contact with the justice system to communicate with the authority in question. For example, even though Article 7(4) does not establish the right for persons to be informed of the reasons for their detention and of the charge or charges brought against them in a language that they understand, it is clear that the State must provide an interpreter should it become aware that a detainee does not understand what is being said.

3.2.2. Right to be informed of the accusation

68. According to Article 8(2)(b), once formal charges have been filed, a "prior and detailed" notification of them must be made to the accused. The word "prior" would indicate a moment preceding the beginning of the oral trial and has to do with the idea that the accused must have the information available for an amount of time sufficient for preparing a defense. This is closely related with the guarantees found in subparagraph (c). The word "detailed" seems to indicate the difference between this communication and communication with the detainee that is intended to comply with the obligations of Article 7(4) of the Convention. The latter communication can be more general, given that the obligation must be complied with "without delay", preventing the kind of exhaustive analysis that would allow for the formulation of precise charges. The other goal here is to provide the accused with all the elements of fact and law on which the charges are based so that he or she might defend him or herself properly.

3.2.3. Granting the accused adequate time and means to prepare a defense

69. In subparagraph (c), Article 8(2) establishes that the accused has a right to adequate time and means to prepare a defense. Decisions regarding adequate time and means must be made on case-by-case basis. In the case of Castillo Petruzzi *et al.*, the court ruled that Peru had violated this right, as in accordance with the Code of Military Justice applied by the Peruvian military court in this case, once charges have been filed, the defense was given 12 hours to study the court documents, a period of time that was clearly not sufficient to prepare adequately.[152] In addition, there were numerous restrictions on work that the defense attorneys could do to prepare the defense.[153]

---

152 *Case of Castillo Petruzzi et al.*, paras. 138 and 141.

153 See, for example, *ibidem*, para. 86.16.

3.2.4. Right of the accused to defend himself personally or to have a lawyer with whom he may communicate freely and privately

70. Subparagraph (d) of Article 8(2) allows the accused to either defend himself personally or be assisted by legal counsel of his own choosing, and to communicate with that legal counsel freely and privately.

This right has also been examined by the Court. It was somewhat limited in Peru in proceedings on terrorism, as Decree Law 25.475 on the crime of terrorism contained a provision banning one defense attorney from assisting more than one accused individual simultaneously, even when they were not co-defendants.[154] The Court found that although this limited choice, it was not *per se* a violation of Article 8(2)(d) of the Convention.[155] It is understandable that a defense attorney cannot represent more than one defendant when there is a possibility of conflict of interest, and in such cases, the provision is justified. But a prohibition without any justification is in itself incompatible with Article 8. The ruling of the Court does not appear to me to have examined the reasoning behind that prohibition, nor does it take into consideration the situation of those accused of terrorism and Peru. During the time at which these trials were carried out, obtaining legal assistance for the accused was difficult: on the one hand, attorneys feared consequences for defending one of these people; on the other, the accused were normally individuals without money who could not hire private attorneys. For this reason, they often turned to *pro bono* services, which were always scarce and almost non-existent if an attorney could only defend one client at a time. Consequently, the prohibition seriously affected an accused person's ability to obtain a defender not named by the military court itself – as that court was frequently the one with jurisdiction in these cases.

Naturally, this brought with it a serious risk that the accused would be provided with a poor defense.

71. The right of the accused to communicate freely and privately with his or her defender has also been examined by the Court. In the case of Castillo Petruzzi *et al.*, the Court used clause 8 of the Basic Principles on the Role of Lawyers[156] as a parameter for measuring compliance with this provision. That clause establishes that "All arrested, detained or imprisoned persons shall be provided with adequate opportunities, time and facilities to be visited by and to communicate and consult with a lawyer, without delay, interception or censorship and in full confidentiality", with only visual supervision being allowed during attorney–

---

154 See expert witness report from attorney Bazán Chacón in the judgment in the *case of Loayza Tamayo,* para. 45(g).

155 *Case of Castillo Petruzzi et al.*, para. 147.

156 Basic Principles on the Role of Lawyers, adopted by the Eighth Congress of the United Nations Congress on the Prevention of Crime and the Treatment of Offenders, Havana, Cuba, 27 August to 7 September 1990.

client meetings.[157] The Court found that in this case, "by virtue of laws currently in effect in Peru, the victims were not allowed legal counsel between the time of their detention and the time they gave their statements to DINCOTE. Only then were they assigned court-appointed attorneys." Thus, Article 8(2)(d) had been violated.[158] In the case of Cantoral Benavides, the Court also found a violation of this provision because the State had impeded the victim from communicating freely and privately with his defense attorney.[159]

3.2.5. Right to counsel provided by the state, according to domestic law

72. Article 8(2)(e) establishes the right to legal counsel as an inalienable right, although it could be debated, from the point of view of human rights, whether it is appropriate for a court to always have the authority to name a defense attorney for an accused individual who refuses to have one, or whether it is required to appoint one in the interest of justice, as suggested in Article 14 of the International Covenant. The *travaux préparatoires* of the Convention do not shed much light on this point. The delegate from the United States called attention to this provision, arguing that it conflicted with the article's previous paragraph. However, the Presidency clarified that "according to the legislation of Latin American countries, the accused must always receive counsel even if he or she does not wish to mount a defense. Should he or she not wish to mount a defense, the State places an attorney at the disposal of the accused, even if the accused does not want one."[160] The rule therefore intends to maintain this aspect of the region's civil legal system. Nevertheless, one might wonder what reasoning could be invoked to, for example, give a court that the accused considers to be incompetent and biased the authority to assign an attorney, thereby blocking the accused from expressing repudiation by refusing to defend him- or herself and entering into the public record that he or she did not defend him- or herself, nor was he or she defended. This latter issue deserves more reflection.

The expression "paid or not as the domestic law provides" also led to a discussion during the Specialized Conference, a discussion that did not reach a clear conclusion: the delegate from Trinidad and Tobago argued that it was not possible to impose such a financial burden on the State, while the delegate from Uruguay suggested that the Convention state expressly that legal counsel would be free for the accused. A workgroup was set up to settle the dispute. However, the minutes of its meetings are not on the record, and the only fact on the record is the approval of the paragraph as it is found in the Convention along with a comment from the delegate from Uruguay to the effect that:

---

157 *Case of Castillo Petruzzi et al.*, para. 139.

158 *Ibidem*, para. 146.

159 *Case of Cantoral Benavides*, para. 127.

160 Specialized Conference, *supra* n. 99, p. 201.

> This paragraph was subjected to very careful consideration and [...] the fact that a final text has been produced speaks very favorably of the goodwill of the delegations from the representatives of the Anglo-Saxon legal system, who with spirit of conciliation sought to understand our reasoning, as we did theirs.[161]

It could be understood from this quote that the Convention allows for the possibility that States can decide on remuneration. The report from the Rapporteur of Commission I, in which this part of the Convention was discussed, indicates: "the advisability of specifying terminology with regard to the courts, legal defense for the accused, and providing those legal defense services for free was considered."[162] Barbados and Dominica seem to have understood the provisions of Article 8(2)(e) to mean that the State is required to provide free legal defense, as both of them made a reservation on this provision.[163]

In its Advisory Opinion 11/90 in response to the Commission's petition for interpretation of Article 46(2) of the Convention containing exceptions to the obligation to exhaust domestic remedies, the Court took a position on this point, stating:

> To that extent the Convention guarantees the right to counsel in criminal proceedings. But since it does not stipulate that legal counsel be provided free of charge when required, an indigent would suffer discrimination for reason of his economic status if, when in need of legal counsel, the state were not to provide it to him free of charge.[164]

Nevertheless, the Advisory Opinion found that although the Convention did not require the legal counsel to be provided for free, the necessity of legal counsel for ensuring due process took precedence. The Court stated this by arguing that:

> Even in those cases in which the accused is forced to defend himself because he cannot afford legal counsel, a violation of Article 8 of the Convention could be said to exist if it can be proved that the lack of legal counsel affected the right to a fair hearing to which he is entitled under that Article.

It added that this situation can also arise in matters concerning the determination of civil, labor and other rights and obligations.[165]

While I am in agreement with this latter argument, I would argue that the Court's interpretation is not correct with regard to criminal trials. Human rights must be interpreted *pro persona*, and grounds can be found in the preparatory work to resolve the unclear points of the provision in a different way.

---

161 *Ibidem*, p. 224.

162 *Ibidem*, p. 297.

163 Barbados submitted its reservation on ratifying the Convention on 5 November 1981; Dominica submitted its reservation on ratifying the Convention on 3 June 1993.

164 OC-11/90, para. 25.

165 *Ibidem*, paras. 27 and 28.

Additionally, one should always remember that for the reasons stated previously, Article 8(2) always establishes greater guarantees for criminal trials.[166]

3.2.6. Right of the defense to examine witnesses or to obtain the appearance of experts or other persons

73. Article 8(2)(f) establishes the principle of *audi alteram partem* – to which I have already made reference – which involves the idea that the accused has the right to use all evidentiary measures at his or her disposal and can object to all the evidentiary measures brought before the court by the State. However, its wording is unfortunate as it does not allude to all the aspects of the principle. However, regardless of the wording, there is no doubt that, they can clearly be derived from a correct reading of Article 8(1) of the Convention.

The Court has found violations of this provision on several occasions. In the case of Castillo Petruzzi, it found that the defense had not been able to interrogate the DINCOTE agents – the police officers who participated in the investigation phase of the case and on the basis of whose testimony the accused were convicted. In addition, one of the accused had been convicted by the highest court "based on new evidence that his defense attorney had not seen and consequently could not rebut".[167] As found by the Court, the fact that a defense attorney was not involved in the Castillo Petruzzi case from the time the accused came in contact with the justice system up to the moment in which he was allowed to testify meant, according to the court, that it was impossible to challenge the evidence collected and placed in the police affidavit, resulting in a violation of Article 8(2)(f). The same violation resulted from "restrictions imposed on the victims' defense attorneys", restrictions that came, *inter alia*, from the laws governing the proceeding, as attorneys were given 12 hours to examine the case file and the ruling was issued the following day.[168] In the case of Cantoral Benavides, the Court found that the violation had been proven based on the fact that "the victim's lawyer was unsuccessful in presenting certain evidence crucial to the defense". These procedures included interrogation of DINCOTE members and the cross-examining of an expert witness.[169]

3.2.7. Right to be present at the trial

74. The minimum guarantees contained in Article 8(2) do not expressly provide for the right to be present at the trial. However, this right undoubtedly

---

[166] In the *case of Loayza Tamayo*, the Court found a clear violation of the principle of *audi alteram partem*, as "the defendants were not allowed [by law] to challenge or examine the evidence" (para. 62).

[167] *Case of Castillo Petruzzi*, paras. 138 and 140.

[168] *Ibidem*, paras. 138, 140–141, 153 and 155.

[169] *Case of Cantoral Benavides*, para. 127.

derives from – among other rights – the right of the accused to defend themselves personally and to object to evidence submitted against them.

The right to defense and to be present at the trial mean that in principle, *in absentia* trials are not compatible with international law. However, there can be exceptions to this rule. The purpose of a trial is to determine the guilt or innocence of a person, but also, if the court finds that the accused is guilty, to apply the criminal punishment deserved. Therefore, it does not seem fair for the accused to be able to prevent justice from being done by choosing not to appear at trial. However, nor does it seem fair that a person who is not attempting to evade justice be tried *in absentia*. Additionally, waiting for the accused to appear can harm the process of collecting evidence for the case. One solution to this problem is to allow an *in absentia* trial once all possible actions have been taken to inform an individual that he or she will be subject to the proceedings, as long as the person in question is given the opportunity to defend him or herself should he or she later appear.[170]

The Court has not ruled on this point, but Venezuela made a reservation to Article 8(1) because *in absentia* trials are practiced in that country.[171] This reinforces the idea that this in principle is not compatible with the Convention.

3.3. POSSIBILITY OF OTHER GUARANTEES

75. The thrust of minimum guarantees for the accused and due process guarantees in general is to subject the process to rules that ensure that the individuals affected are able to mount a good defense. It is therefore possible that other guarantees are necessary that are not expressed in the Convention but that must nonetheless be respected. These unexpressed guarantees are normally implicit in the correct interpretation of the general provision. For example, one is that a person can only be brought to trial if he or she has the mental capacity to understand the charges and provide the background information necessary for mounting a defense. If this is not the case, the trial cannot take place on pain of violating Article 8, as it would be impossible in such a case for the accused to be able to make use of the rights granted him or her by this provision.

76. In order to answer a consultation submitted by Mexico on the individual's right to information on consular assistance established in Article 36(1)(b) of the Vienna Convention on Consular Relations, the Court made an important ruling on the minimum guarantees of the accused, broadening on the previously

170 In the European system, a new trial is often not allowed if the accused has fled to escape justice (D.J. Harris, M. O'Boyle and C. Warbrick, *supra* n. 46, p. 205).

171 Venezuela made its reservation on ratifying the Convention on 9 August 1977.

mentioned approaches on finding that these guarantees evolve and, like all international human rights law, are progressive in nature.[172] To reach this conclusion, the Court reasoned that one objective of due process is "to protect, to ensure, or to assert the entitlement to a right or the exercise thereof" and indicates that its requirements are "the prerequisites necessary to ensure the adequate protection of those persons whose rights or obligations are pending judicial determination".[173] With this being the general principle, all other guarantees required for responding to needs arising from special circumstances or that are the result of greater development and refinement of the idea of due process must be added to the minimum guarantees set forth in Article 8.

This idea of special circumstances leads the Court to advance the interpretation of the principle of equality that informs due process, arguing that "to accomplish its objectives, the judicial process must recognize and correct any real disadvantages that those brought before the bar might have."[174] In doing this, the Court indicates that the State must adopt "countervailing measures that help to reduce or eliminate the obstacles and deficiencies that impair or diminish an effective defense of one's interests."[175] In the case of this Advisory Opinion, which addresses the right of a foreign national being subjected to legal proceeding to information on consular assistance, the Court indicates that "the real situation of the foreign nationals facing criminal proceedings must be considered".[176]

Taking all these ideas into consideration, and in order to establish its jurisdiction pursuant to Article 64 of the Convention, the Court found that Article 36 of the Convention enshrines a true individual right to information on consular assistance that "concerns the protection of the rights of a national of the sending State and is part of the body of international human rights law",[177] law that includes Article 14 of the International Covenant, which for its part addresses the protection of human rights "in the American States".[178]

Next, the Court added that this right to be informed "allows the right to the due process of law recognized in Article 14 of the International Covenant on Civil and Political Rights to have practical effects in concrete cases", and that this provision "establishes minimum guarantees that can be amplified in the light of other international instruments such as the Vienna Convention on Consular Relations, which expand the scope of the protection afforded to the accused."[179] A logical consequence of all this is that the State has the obligation to provide that information, and a failure to comply with that obligation would

[172] OC-16/99, para. 117.
[173] *Ibidem*, paras. 117 and 118.
[174] *Ibidem*, para. 119.
[175] *Ibidem*.
[176] *Ibidem*, para. 121.
[177] *Ibidem*, paras. 141(1) and (2).
[178] *Ibidem*, paras. 141(4) and (5).
[179] *Ibidem*, para. 141(6).

constitute a violation of due process leading to international State responsibility, for which reparations must be provided.[180] Regarding the specific consultation, a failure to comply with this obligation led the Court to hold that, as the situation serving as context for this consultation involved proceedings that concluded with a death sentence for the accused, the failure to comply would, in addition to a violation of due process, be a violation of Article 4 of the American Convention and Article 6 of the International Covenant.[181]

3.4. PUBLIC TRIAL, ORAL TRIALS, AND RULINGS OPEN TO THE PUBLIC

77. Article 8(5) establishes that "criminal proceedings shall be public, except insofar as may be necessary to protect the interests of justice". In contrast to the provisions of Article 14(1) of the International Covenant, the Convention's requirement that proceedings be public only applies to criminal proceedings.[182] This is a formal requirement intending to ensure transparency in the justice system by allowing the presence of third parties when the trial takes place. The State therefore has an obligation to make it possible in fact and law for the public to have access to the trial. In addition to attempting to protect the accused, requiring a trial to be public is also a community right, as everyone should be able to supervise, through their own presence, the way in which justice is served in a democratic society.

The right to a public trial means that it must be oral, as a written proceeding does not allow for this sort of democratic supervision.[183] The Human Rights Committee has already addressed this to the effect that the requirement for a public trial implies that its oral nature forms part of the concept of "due process" in international law.[184] In principle, it does not seem necessary for everything that takes place during the proceedings to do so orally given that the purpose of this requirement is for the accused and the judge to be able to get a direct impression of the evidence, and for the accused to be able to hear that evidence

180 *Ibidem*, para. 141(7).

181 *Ibidem*.

182 Without prejudice to this, given that all States Parties to the Convention are also parties to the International Covenant on Civil and Political Rights, non-criminal proceedings are also required to be public in all these countries.

183 In addition, it does not seem possible to ensure the accused's minimum guarantees or the principle of immediacy in a written trial.

184 Article 14(3)(d) of the International Covenant on Civil and Political Rights does not call for proceedings to be oral, but there is consensus that this is implicit in the requirement found in Article 14(1) that all trials, whether criminal or not, must be public (See M. Nowak, *UN Covenant on Civil and Political Rights. CCPR Commentary*, N.P. Engel Publisher, Kehl/Strasbourg/Arlington, 1993, p. 249). For oral proceedings in the European system, see P. van Dijk, F. van Hoof, A. van Rijn and L. Zwaak (eds.), *supra* n. 43, p. 589.

directly and contest it. For example, a cassation proceeding, in which only questions of law are discussed, would not need to be carried out orally.

The public nature of the proceeding also covers the reading of the ruling, as the American Convention states that the "proceedings" must be public, and the ruling is the culmination of the proceedings.

78. The Convention authorizes closing proceedings to the public. However, it does not specify the cases in which this is allowed, thus giving the judge a great degree of discretion to decide when the need to preserve the interests of justice require closed proceedings. The expression "the interests of justice" does not clearly refer to certain situations in which closing proceedings to the public is intended rather to protect the parties, such as, for example, in criminal cases in which the accused is a child or an adolescent. However, it seems clear that the Court would consider this type of reasoning to be compatible with the Convention.

79. The Inter-American Court has found violations of the requirement that proceedings must be public in the case of Castillo Petruzzi *et al.*, because the proceedings were carried out by anonymous military judges and prosecutors, in secret and in isolation;[185] and in the case of Cantoral Benavides, whose trial proceedings before civilian courts included several hearings that took place inside prison facilities.[186]

3.5. RIGHT NOT TO BE COMPELLED TO BE A WITNESS AGAINST ONESELF OR TO PLEAD GUILTY

80. This guarantee emphasizes the idea that it is the State that must demonstrate the guilt of the person subject to proceedings, and it is fundamentally associated with the prohibition of torture and cruel, inhuman or degrading treatment.[187] This being the case, it leads to the necessary conclusion that a confession dragged out of a person using this type of treatment is not valid as evidence. The Convention reiterates this by establishing in Article 8(3) that: "A confession of guilt by the accused shall be valid only if it is made without coercion of any kind." I would refer there reader here to Chapter 3 of this book on Article 5 of the Convention in the sense that it is the State's responsibility to investigate all allegations of this type of treatment. The person making the allegations has neither the responsibility to take the initiative nor

185 *Case of Castillo Petruzzi et al.*, paras. 172–173.

186 *Case of Cantoral Benavides*, paras. 146–147.

187 This guarantee was added to the text of the Convention at the last minute, as a similar prior provision had not been approved. See Specialized Conference, *supra* n. 99, pp. 203 (motion of Paraguay) and 443.

the burden of proof of the existence of the torture or cruel, inhuman or degrading treatment being alleged.

81. The Court found a violation of Articles 8(2)(g) and 8(3) of the Convention in the case of Cantoral Benavides on finding it proven that the victim was subjected to torture and forced to confess to certain criminal conduct.[188] In contrast, in the case of Castillo Petruzzi *et al.*, the Court found that merely demanding that the accused tell the truth did not constitute a violation of Article 8(3), as "nothing in the record suggests that any punishment or other adverse legal consequence was threatened if they did not tell the truth." Nor was there evidence that the accused had been asked to give a sworn statement or make any promises to tell the truth. The Court found that should this have been the case, it would have been a violation of "their right to choose between testifying and not testifying".[189]

3.6. RIGHT TO APPEAL THE JUDGMENT TO A HIGHER COURT

82. In criminal trials, the accused have the right to appeal the ruling to a higher court. This guarantee applies equally to all criminal trials. Thus the provision requires domestic legal systems to allow the first instance rulings to be appealed, and that appeal must be heard by a higher court. The provision is also applicable with regard to criminal trials with special proceedings, such as, for example, trials in which a higher court acts as the first instance court due to the privileged forum assigned to the accused.

Of course, the process of reviewing the ruling enjoys all the guarantees mentioned thus far, given that only when a final judgment has been issued can it be said that the guilt or innocence of the accused has been decided. In the case of Castillo Petruzzi *et al.*, the Court found that the right to appeal the ruling required the Superior Court to "have the jurisdictional authority to take up the particular case in question". This requirement was not fulfilled in the case because the court in question was a second instance court that was part of the military, and therefore it did not have the necessary independence nor constitute the "natural judge" (*juez natural*) required to hear the appeal.[190] The Court's case law on "reasonable time" must also be recalled. Therein, the Court has found that in calculating this period of time, the whole appeals process must be included.[191]

188 *Case of Cantoral Benavides*, paras. 132–133.
189 *Case of Castillo Petruzzi et al.*, para. 167.
190 *Ibidem*, para. 161.
191 *Case of Genie Lacayo*, para. 81; *Case of Suárez Rosero*, para. 71.

83. For the Convention, the nomenclature of the domestic legal system used to identify the remedy is irrelevant; what does matter is that the appeal be adequate, meaning that the authority of the Superior Court to review the ruling in order to satisfy this provision's requirements must be decided on. A remedy could include a full review of fact and law or a review of the way in which the laws for the evaluation of the evidence and substantive laws were applied. It could also be a review of the law that is limited to certain aspects of the proceedings. The Human Rights Committee established in the case of Gómez v. Spain that the State had violated Article 14(5) of the International Covenant – similar to the provision in question of the American Convention – because, as recognized in the cassation judgment handed down in the trial before the Supreme Tribunal of Spain, the cassation Court cannot review the evaluation of evidence because evaluation is the exclusive function of the *a quo* tribunal.[192] This is a difficult point to resolve, as one must take into consideration that one of the guarantees made to the accused is that the evidence shall be presented in a public trial in the presence of a judge. In addition, the principle of immediacy, which allows judges to form their own impressions of evidence, is an important aspect of the trustworthiness of the factual basis of a judgment.

The *travaux préparatoires* of the Convention do not contain any discussion on subparagraph (h) of Article 8(2), nor at the time of writing had the Inter-American Court heard cases in which it has been invoked, aside from the cases already mentioned.

3.7. PRINCIPLE OF *NE BIS IN IDEM*

84. Article 8(4) of the Convention holds that "An accused person acquitted by a nonappealable judgment shall not be subjected to a new trial for the same cause." The principle does not apply in the case of a possible review of the conviction based on the appearance of new facts indicating the person's innocence.[193]

The wording of the Convention differs from that of the International Covenant, which does not refer to "the same cause". Rather, it refers to the "same crime", something that has moved the Inter-American Court to indicate that the Convention is more favorable to the victim than the Covenant.[194]

---

192 HRC, *Gómez v. Spain*, Communication 701/1996, decision of 20 July 2000, paras. 3(2) and 11(1). Published in A/55/40, Vol. II (2000), Annex IX, sec. I (p. 102–110).

193 See *infra*, Chapter 6.

194 *Case of Loayza Tamayo*, para. 66. In reality, I would argue that notwithstanding the wording of Article 14(7) of the Covenant, an interpretation that allows someone to be tried again based on the same facts but changing the type of crime would not be acceptable, as this would make the provision irrelevant.

85. In the case of Loayza Tamayo,[195] the victim was brought to trial and acquitted for the crime of treason (also called aggravated terrorism). However, the victim was subjected to a second criminal proceeding for the crime of terrorism. The Court found that this violated Article 8(4) of the Convention. This case clearly constituted a violation of the principle: On one hand, the definitions of crimes contained in various decree laws "refer to actions not strictly defined, so that they may be interpreted similarly within both crimes, in the view of the Ministry of the Interior and the corresponding judges and, as in the case under consideration, of the 'Police (DINCOTE) itself'";[196] on the other hand, meanwhile, the case constitutes a violation because the second proceeding was based on the same expanded police report used before the Special Navy Court that had acquitted Ms Loayza Tamayo.[197]

In the case of Cantoral Benavides, the Court took a completely different position. The facts of the case are similar, as Cantoral Benavides was put on trial for treason before a military court and was acquitted. All the trial material was then forwarded to a civilian court for a new trial, and this second proceeding culminated in a conviction and a sentence of 20 years in prison. Later, the victim submitted a request for a pardon, which was granted.[198] However, the Court, taking a dubious position from a technical point of view, ruled that based on the fact that the first trial was carried out before a military court that did not meet the requirements that it be competent, that it be independent, and that it be impartial, "the actions and decisions taken by the authorities of the exclusive military jurisdiction in the matter of [the victim] do not constitute the type of proceeding called for in Article 8(4) of the Convention."[199] Thus, "the alleged infraction of Article 8(4) of the Convention is included in the violation of Article 8(1) of same."[200]

---

195 On the principle of *ne bis in idem* in the *case of Loayza Tamayo*, see D. Acevedo, "La decisión de la Corte Interamericana de Derechos Humanos sobre enjuiciamiento penal múltiple (*non bis in idem*) en el caso Loayza Tamayo", in Inter-American Court, *Liber Amicorum Héctor Fix Zamudio*, Vol. I, San José, Costa Rica, 1998, pp. 279–300.

196 *Case of Loayza Tamayo*, para. 68.

197 *Ibidem*, paras. 74–75.

198 *Case of Cantoral Benavides*, para. 63(ll),(ñ), (o) and (r).

199 *Ibidem*, paras. 137–138.

200 *Ibidem*, para. 140.

CHAPTER 6
PRINCIPLE OF LEGALITY, FREEDOM FROM *EX POST FACTO* LAWS AND RIGHT TO COMPENSATION FOR MISCARRIAGE OF JUSTICE

Article 9

Freedom from Ex Post Facto Laws

> *No one shall be convicted of any act or omission that did not constitute a criminal offense, under the applicable law, at the time it was committed. A heavier penalty shall not be imposed than the one that was applicable at the time the criminal offense was committed. If subsequent to the commission of the offense the law provides for the imposition of a lighter punishment, the guilty person shall benefit therefrom.*

Article 10

Right to Compensation

> *Every person has the right to be compensated in accordance with the law in the event that he has been sentenced by a final judgment through a miscarriage of justice.*

1. PRINCIPLE OF LEGALITY

1. Article 9 of the American Convention enshrines a basic principle of criminal law whose Latin wording is as follows: *nullum crimen et nulla poena sine lege*. The principle is fundamentally important for the protection of several human rights, leading the Convention to establish it as an international State obligation that cannot be suspended, even in an emergency situation.[1] This provision also enshrines the principle according to which a convict must benefit from a lesser punishment when a lesser punishment is established by law after the commission of a crime.

Article 9 of the Convention applies to all criminal convictions, regardless of significance or scope.[2] The Inter-American Court made reference to the scope of

---

1 ACHR, Article 27.

2 See Chapter 5, section 2.2, on the meaning of "criminal charges".

the article in question in the case of Baena Ricardo *et al.*, which addressed the application of judicial guarantees in the area of administrative sanctions. The Court found that administrative sanctions, "as well as penal sanctions, constitute an expression of the State's punitive power and that, on occasions, the nature of the former is similar to that of the latter".[3] It found that the principle of legality and freedom from *ex post facto* criminal laws

> govern the actions of all bodies of the State in their respective fields of competence, particularly when the exercise of that punitive power where the State manifests with the maximum strength, one of its most serious and intense functions vis-à-vis human beings – repression [–] applies.[4]

2. *NULLUM CRIMEN SINE LEGE*: FREEDOM FROM *EX POST FACTO* CRIMINAL LAWS

2. The first aspect of this principle involves prohibiting the recognition of a crime having occurred without a law in place prior to the commission of the act established as criminal; a person cannot be convicted for conduct that was not at the moment of its execution classified as a crime under the law. It is in this sense that criminal law cannot be applied retroactively.

The law must be a law both formally and materially.[5] In civil law countries, it is easy to verify that a requirement for laws to be formally in place has been met, given that those countries have constitutions that precisely establish the steps that must be taken in order for a law to take effect. This ensures that the decision on what constitutes a criminal act is made by the legislative organ, which represents the sovereign, who has the final power to make the law.[6] In countries with a common law system, on the other hand, a law can be contained in a legal precedent that has emerged from practice. It would be the responsibility of the courts to apply it and often to develop the law through specific cases.

The requirement that a law should exist establishing an act as criminal has another purpose: that of informing people that the commission of a certain act would violate the country's criminal laws. From this, it follows that the definition of criminal conduct must contain all the elements necessary for a person to be able to know with precision what is prohibited; vague descriptions do not satisfy the requirements of Article 9 of the Convention. In defining the prohibited conduct, the law must therefore take this into consideration. The European

---

3 *Case of Baena Ricardo et al.*, para. 106.

4 *Ibidem*, para 107.

5 Formal" refers to a law having been issued following the proceedings establish in the domestic legal system; "material" has to do with the content of the law, which must be general and thus not discriminatory. See Chapter 1, para. 40.

6 In this sense, see OC-6/86, which interpreted the expression "laws" found in Article 30 of the Convention.

Court of Human Rights has developed case law in this respect, indicating that the law must be accessible to individuals and must describe conducts that are foreseeable.[7] In contrast to a written law, the specific terms of a law established through precedent are harder to establish, as it is possible for such laws to be developed gradually through case law. This can cause problems for the application of the principle in question. The European Court of Human Rights has placed a limit on this, on finding that the clarification by a judge of the existence and provisions of a law is permissible "provided that the resultant development is consistent with the essence of the offense and could reasonably be foreseen".[8]

Given that there can be no crime without a specific law defining the conduct, it is clear that the law must be interpreted restrictively: there can be no crime by analogy. Consequently, international oversight can and should review the application of domestic law if an accusation of a violation of Article 9 invokes the application of a crime as defined by analogy.[9]

3. In contrast to Article 15(1) of the International Covenant and Article 7(1) of the European Convention, Article 9 of the Convention does not specify that actions or omissions can be classified as criminal by both domestic and international law. Rather, it uses the expression "according to applicable law". During the drafting of the Convention, this was criticized by the delegate from Colombia, who proposed placing a reference to international law in the text; the president of the Commission replied that the reference was not necessary given that the expression "applicable law" covered both domestic and international law. However, the delegate from Argentina argued that "the suggestion from the delegate from Colombia would be an interesting aspiration for the future, but the approval of a minimum number of acceptable articles must be achieved".[10] For this reason, one could assume that he felt that "applicable law" meant only domestic law. Colombia's suggestion was not brought to a vote, and there was no more debate on the subject. Given the prior examples of the International Covenant and the European Convention, as well as the wording of the provision itself, it seems reasonable to conclude that despite what the delegate from Argentina had said, the expression "applicable law" includes both domestic and international law. This then raises the possibility that a crime not defined by

---

7 P. van Dijk, F. van Hoof, A. van Rijn and L. Zwaak (eds.), *Theory and Practice of the European Convention on Human Rights*, 4th edn, Intersentia, Antwerp/Oxford, 2006, pp. 653-654.

8 *Ibidem*, pp. 654-655, citing the cases *S.W. v. United Kingdom* and *C.R. v. United Kingdom*, judgment of 22 November 1995 (A-355-B and A-335-C, respectively).

9 For European case law on this point, see P. van Dijk and G.J.H. van Hoof, *Theory and Practice of the European Convention on Human Rights*, 3rd edn, SIM, Kluwer Law International, The Hague/London/Boston, 1998, p. 482, n. 1123.

10 Specialized Conference, *Minutes and Documents*, San José, Costa Rica, 7–22 November 1969, p. 206.

domestic laws can be punished if it exists as a crime under international law, making use of universal jurisdiction.[11]

4. The Inter-American Court has addressed the requirement that criminal activity be specifically defined in judgments handed down in cases against Peru over the application of the Decree Laws on treason and terrorism. In the case of Loayza Tamayo – and without alluding to Article 9 of the Convention – the Court criticized the fact that Peru's Decree Laws 25.659 and 25.475 "refer to conduct not strictly delineated, meaning that they could be understood just as easily to be part of one crime as another according to the standards of the Ministry of the Public Prosecutor and the corresponding judges and, as in the case in question, of the 'police themselves (DINCOTE).'"[12] In the case of Castillo Petruzzi *et al.*, the Inter-American Court introduced on its own initiative an examination of a possible violation of Article 9 of the Convention, indicating that the crime of treason was recognized by the parties as "aggravated terrorism", adding that in drafting definitions of crimes, strict and unambiguous terms must be used that clearly define criminal conduct, giving full range to the principle of criminal legality. This means a clear definition of the conduct in question that establishes its elements and allows for it to be differentiated from activity that is not punishable or from noncriminal illegal activity.[13]

In the case of Cantoral Benavides, the Court reiterated this position, again clarifying that Article 2 of Decree Law 25.475 and Article 1(a) of Decree Law 25.659 contained definitions of the crimes of terrorism and treason that "do not clearly describe the criminal acts in question, the elements used in their commission, the objects or assets against which they are directed, and the impact they have on society". The Court added that "the inclusion of such broad methods of participation in the commission of the corresponding crime [established in Article 2...] alters the definition of the perpetrator of treason against the fatherland, bringing this crime and the crime of terrorism so close together that they become one."[14]

Consequently, the Court found that in this case, Article 9 of the Convention had been violated.[15]

5. In the case of Baena Ricardo *et al.*, the Court also found that a violation of the principle of legality had taken place because "Law 25 [which was applied to the petitioners] contained only a very broad and imprecise concept of possible unlawful conduct", characterizing the crime as "participation in acts

---

[11] See M. Nowak, *UN Covenant on Civil and Political Rights. CCPR Commentary,* N.P. Engel Publisher, Kehl/Strasbourg/Arlington, 1993, p. 276.

[12] *Case of Loayza Tamayo,* para. 68.

[13] *Case of Castillo Petruzzi et al.*, paras. 118 and 121.

[14] *Case of Cantoral Benavides,* para. 155.

[15] *Ibidem,* paras. 157–158.

contrary to democracy and the constitutional order".[16] Article 2 of that law established that the executive, via the Cabinet Counsel, would be the one to determine "which actions would be considered attacks on democracy and constitutional order for the purposes of 'applying the administrative punishments of dismissal'". The Inter-American Court did not comment on the fact that the law would allow a non-legislative body to define the criminality of an act. Rather, it found a violation of the principle of non-retroactivity, both because the ruling that found that the abrupt collective public labor strikes were an attack on the aforementioned values was made long after the facts that were punished took place,[17] and because Decree Law 25 itself had entered into force on 14 December 1990, although the facts took place on the fourth of that month, and established that it would apply not only to "those who *participate* in 'actions against Democracy and the Constitutional Order,' but also to those who *participated* in those actions",[18] thus clearly making it retroactive.

3. *NULLUM POENA SINE LEGE*

6. A punishment[19] cannot exist without a law that establishes it. In the European system, Van Dijk and Van Hoof argue that it is not necessary for a law to define a punishment with exactitude. Rather, they argue that it is enough for it to indicate, for example, a maximum punishment, or the nature of the punishment without specifying a maximum; if there is no maximum punishment, in order to prohibit the application of a sentence that is stricter than the punishment allowed for at the time a crime is committed, it should be understood that what must be applied "is the penalty which is usually inflicted within the legal system concerned, or which in any event was reasonable to be expected for the offender".[20] The Inter-American Court addressed punishment in the case of Baena Ricardo *et al.*, in which it said that "the categorization of an act as unlawful and the establishment of the subsequent juridical consequences must pre-date the conduct of the individual considered to be in violation".[21] There is still no case law on whether a law must establish something beyond the mere nature of the punishment.[22]

---

16 *Case of Baena Ricardo et al.*, para. 108.
17 *Ibidem*, para. 114.
18 *Ibidem*, paras. 109–110.
19 With regard to what constitutes a "punishment", I refer the reader to the explanation of "criminal charges" in the previous chapter, section 2.2.
20 P. van Dijk and G.H.J. van Hoof, *supra* n. 9, p. 484.
21 *Case of Baena Ricardo et al.*, para. 106.
22 On this, see J. Mera, "Adecuación del Derecho Penal chileno a las exigencias de los derechos humanos", in C. Medina and J. Mera (eds.), *Sistema jurídico y derechos humanos. El derecho*

7. International law establishes certain rules with regard to the establishment of punishments. To start with, it bans cruel, inhuman or degrading punishments[23] and imprisonment due to debts.[24] In addition, it should not be forgotten that a punishment always constitutes a restriction of a human right: normally, the right to personal freedom (although it can also affect the right to free movement should certain kinds of punishments that provide alternatives to imprisonment be imposed) or the right to property if fines are applied. The State thus does not have absolute discretion to establish a punishment, as it must abide by the requirement of proportionality.[25] This is indicated explicitly in Article 4 of the Convention, which, for the application of the death penalty, requires that a crime be among "the most serious of crimes". Although strictly speaking this is not yet reality, punishments must be regulated based on all the existing limitations on restrictions on human rights.

It must, for example, be determined whether the punishment is appropriate for achieving its objective. In the case of deprivation of liberty, this objective includes not only the protection of the rights of victims but also the "reform and social readaptation of the prisoners".[26] One could expect this to develop further in the future, in parallel with research into the effects of punishments on criminals, especially imprisonment. This could lead to a change in culture and legal perspective.

8. In addition to prohibiting the imposition of a punishment that is more serious than the one allowed at the time a crime is committed, the American Convention also establishes that "[i]f subsequent to the commission of the offense the law provides for the imposition of a lighter punishment, the guilty person shall benefit therefrom." When the change in the punishment is one not only of severity but also of nature, such as for example from deprivation of liberty to a fine, the problem arises of deciding which punishment is harsher. At this point, with the advanced development of the idea that certain punishments can replace deprivation of liberty, the problem can take on new dimensions. The Inter-American Court has not yet had any opportunity to rule on this. Nor has the Court had an opportunity to rule on the problem of whether the retroactivity of a lighter punishment has a time limit or if it should apply even after a sentence is final and becomes subject to the principle of *res judicata*.[27] One question that

---

nacional y las obligaciones internacionales de Chile en materia de derechos humanos, Universidad Diego Portales, special publications series No. L, Santiago, Chile, 1996, pp. 343–475 (389).

23 ACHR, Article 5(2). On this point, see Chapter 3, section 2.

24 ACHR, Article 7(7).

25 On proportionality of punishments, see J. Mera, *supra* n. 22, p. 394.

26 ACHR, Article 5(6).

27 For the discussion on this point in the International Covenant of Civil and Political Rights, see M. Nowak, *supra* n. 11, pp. 278–280.

the Court must ask in this regard is whether it would be possible to continue with the execution of a more severe punishment for an action that society has decided no longer deserves that punishment.

4. RIGHT TO COMPENSATION FOR MISCARRIAGE OF JUSTICE

9. Article 10 of the Convention presents us with problems of interpretation, as it is particularly cryptic. The *travaux préparatoires* could be useful for clarifying the meaning of the provision. In reality, however, they do not contribute much. Originally, the wording of Article 10 was very confusing, as it stated that:

> All persons who have been deprived of liberty illegally or due to a miscarriage of justice will receive indemnity for the losses suffered as a result of the conviction and the deprivation of liberty except in the cases in which the convicted individual contributed to making the miscarriage of justice possible.[28]

In its comments on the draft, the Argentine government did not criticize the wording but rather recommended that it should be eliminated completely, arguing that the provision represented "an aspiration for the future".[29] The comments of the Dominican Republic focused more on the content, indicating that it would be in agreement "with this type of liability as long as it is understood that the error must be equivalent to an abusive application of the law, gross error, or an act of authority exercised in bad faith or with reprehensible negligence". It added that "the term 'miscarriage of justice' could include any case overturned on appeal, including cases in which the guilt of the accused is overturned for procedural or technical reasons".[30] For its part, Ecuador suggested replacing the text with the text found in Article 14(6) of the International Covenant,[31] which would have broken the link that up to that point existed between miscarriage of justice and deprivation of liberty.

---

28 Specialized Conference, *supra* n. 10, p. 17.

29 *Ibidem*, p. 46.

30 *Ibidem*, p. 50. In the comments, it also proposed an alternative text: "All persons who have been unjustly convicted and imprisoned will have the right to appeal to a court and another authority and to receive an indemnity as long as their convictions have been annulled and none of the actions for which they were effectively accused were committed, or the actions related to the accusation did not constitute a criminal offense and the individual in question did not cause or contribute to making the prosecution possible due to misconduct or negligence." (*Ibidem*, p. 60.)

31 *Ibidem*, p. 105. The text is as follows: "When a final judgment to convict has been subsequently overturned or when the convicted individual has been pardoned based on the production or discovery of evidence demonstrating a miscarriage of justice, the person who has suffered from a punishment as a result of the judgment shall be indemnified in keeping with the law unless it is demonstrated that the failure to reveal the unknown fact was in whole or in part attributable to that person."

During the discussion of the text, the Venezuelan delegate stated that his country would not accept granting an indemnity for miscarriages of justice, while the delegates from Honduras, Argentina, Nicaragua, Mexico and Chile expressed opposition to the approval of the text on indemnities. The delegate from the United States also expressed concern at the wording of the provision, concern which Guatemala shared. As a result of the discussion, a working group was formed to study the article.[32] That working group later submitted a new text, which itself was replaced during the discussion (the content of which was not placed on the record) by another text submitted by Mexico. In the end, that was the text that was approved.[33]

In sum, one can conclude from the debate that the majority of the delegates who took part in drawing up Article 10 of the draft Convention sought to limit indemnity requirements in order to prevent abuse and an enormous financial cost to the State. However, they were not sufficiently explicit in making this clear.

10. In order to aid in the interpretation of the provision, it is also useful to take into consideration that similar rules can be found in Article 14(6) of the International Covenant[34] and in Article 3 of the Seventh Protocol to the European Convention on Human Rights.[35] Both are drawn up in more detail; the text from the European system is also accompanied by an explanatory memorandum to help resolve possible problems of interpretation. For example, the memorandum indicates that Article 3 does not apply when an accusation has been dismissed or when the accused has been declared innocent, whether by a first instance court or an appeals court; the provision only applies when the conviction has been overturned or a pardon has been granted because *new or recently discovered facts* demonstrate conclusively that a miscarriage of justice has taken place, meaning "some serious failure in the judicial process involving grave prejudice to the convicted person". Domestic law is responsible for establishing the proceedings for determining whether a miscarriage of justice has taken place.[36]

---

32 The discussion indicates that the United States submitted written comments on the provision, but those comments are not included in the *Minutes and Documents*, Specialized Conference, *supra* n. 10, pp. 207–209.

33 *Ibidem*, p. 250.

34 For the text, see n. 31.

35 The text of Article 3 reads as follows: "When a person has by a final decision been convicted of a criminal offence and when subsequently his conviction has been reversed, or he has been pardoned, on the ground that a new or a newly discovered fact shows conclusively that there has been a miscarriage of justice, the person who has suffered punishment as a result of such conviction shall be compensated according to the law or the practice of the state concerned, unless it proved that the non-disclosure of the unknown fact in time is wholly or partly attributable to him."

36 The Memorandum (Doc. H(84)5) is cited in D.J. Harris, M. O'Boyle and C. Warbrick, *Law of the European Convention on Human Rights*, Butterworths, London/Dublin/Edinburgh, 1995, p. 568.

11. The first requirement for applying Article 10 is that a final judgment to convict must have been issued, meaning a sentence has been handed down with regard to which no recourse remains for the convicted individual.[37] However, the provision says nothing about how an individual convicted in a final judgment can appeal and before which authorities, when seeking a decision as to whether the conviction was the result of a "miscarriage of justice". The discussion and the precedent of the similar provision found in the Covenant lead to the conclusion that the "judicial error" must have been made in an authorized State ruling. Thus in order for the right enshrined in Article 10 of the Convention to function, national legal systems must establish the right to a remedy that allows for the individual convicted due to an error to file a related claim. This is the first State obligation arising from the article.

The International Covenant and the European Convention provide that the error may also be identified as such in a pardon, a power that always falls to the executive branch. A pardon, however, is an act of grace that does not revoke the ruling to convict. Should there have been an error in a ruling on the guilt of a person, it does not seem appropriate for the ruling to maintain any sort of validity. It therefore seems more appropriate to require a remedy that allows for the erroneous judgment to be revoked.

12. Article 10 of the American Convention appears to be broader than Article 14(6) of the International Covenant and Article 3 of the Seventh Protocol to the European Convention, as it does not establish that in order for an indemnity to be required, the revocation of a judgment or the pardon must have been based on new facts or facts that were discovered after the judgment. It is likely, however, that this is how the article would be interpreted should it be raised for the Court's consideration, as it seems to be the most reasonable interpretation. As already mentioned, it is the responsibility of the domestic legal system to decide on how the right is to function. In many legal systems, there is a judicial review remedy that establishes the circumstances that can be invoked in order to access it. The circumstances generally follow the provisions of the International Covenant and the European Convention, as they refer to the existence of a fact that is decisive for proving the error and that has taken place or come to light following the conviction.[38]

37 This coincides with the European system's provision. The European system's Protocol 7 explanatory memorandum indicates that the judgment must be irrevocable, that is, there must not be any ordinary remedy available, whether because the party has exhausted all remedies or because the time period for accessing the remedies has expired (see *ibidem*).

38 The remedy of review is obviously compatible with the provisions of Article 8(4) (enshrining the principle of *ne bis in idem*) given that its purpose is to correct a situation to the benefit of the convicted individual.

13. Finally, the second obligation that arises from Article 10 of the Convention is the obligation to establish laws setting forth the right to an indemnity once it has been determined that a miscarriage of justice has taken place.

14. As can be noted, space for interpreting and clarifying the provisions contained in Article 10 is vast and the work of the body that applies it will have to make use of international case law in order to give it content that is reasonable and favorable to persons.

CHAPTER 7
RIGHT TO JUDICIAL PROTECTION

Article 25. Right to Judicial Protection

1. *Everyone has the right to simple and prompt recourse, or any other effective recourse, to a competent court or tribunal for protection against acts that violate his fundamental rights recognized by the constitution or laws of the state concerned or by this Convention, even though such violation may have been committed by persons acting in the course of their official duties.*
2. *The States Parties undertake:*
   a. *to ensure that any person claiming such remedy shall have his rights determined by the competent authority provided for by the legal system of the state;*
   b. *to develop the possibilities of judicial remedy; and*
   c. *to ensure that the competent authorities shall enforce such remedies when granted.*

1. INTRODUCTION

1. The existence of human rights enshrined in the American Convention, constituting a minimum standard that State Parties must respect and ensure, requires that mechanisms be established for the supervision and protection of those rights. As the primary responsibility for complying with international obligations falls to the State, it is the State that must establish effective domestic remedies for protecting rights, without prejudice to the existence of subsidiary international supervisory mechanisms. Human rights are to be enjoyed and respected at all times and in all places, and in the event they are violated, there must be a rapid response to protect them; this response can only come from the State in question, given that international monitoring is by necessity slow and late, and it would be completely impossible for such monitoring to replace domestic protection with any sort of efficiency. These are the fundamentals on which Article 25 of the American Convention is based. This Article enshrines the individual's right to have his or her human rights protected efficiently by domestic authorities via judicial remedy. On the American continent, this right is known as the right to an *amparo* remedy.

The importance of this remedy is evident and has been recognized by the Inter-American Court, which has found that Article 25 "is one of the fundamental pillars not only of the American Convention, but of the very rule of law in a democratic society in the terms of the Convention."[1]

2. Article 25 – the writ of *amparo* – has its origins in Latin America. It was established in the Mexican Constitution of 1857 and from there spread to other countries in the region from early on.[2] Its purpose is to provide domestic protection for the fundamental rights established in the constitutions of the countries on the continent. The Court has recognized this origin, indicating that Article 25(1) is "a general provision that gives expression to the procedural institution known as *amparo*, which is a simple and prompt remedy designed for the protection of all of the rights recognized by the constitutions and laws of the States Parties and by the Convention."[3] It is no surprise, therefore, that the American Convention enshrines in Article 25 every individual's right to a domestic remedy to protect not only the rights established in the Convention but also the human rights recognized by the constitution and laws of each State.

3. It should be noted that the writ of *amparo* found in Article 25 is not the only remedy that must be established in States' domestic legal systems. This can be derived indirectly from the requirement established in Article 46(1)(8) of the Convention that victims must exhaust "the remedies under domestic law" before they can turn to the inter-American supervisory mechanisms with an individual complaint.[4] In contrast to the remedy found in Article 25 of the Convention, the domestic remedies that must be exhausted can require longer proceedings and may be various in nature. They run the gamut from providing for an action for putting a judicial proceeding in motion to remedies that normally form part of a proceeding itself, such as appeal, for example. Naturally, all the remedies would be required to be effective and adequate, with effectiveness including the requirement that they do not take longer than necessary to reach a solution.[5]

---

1 *Case of Castillo Páez*, para. 82; *Case of Suárez Rosero*, para. 65; and *Case of Blake*, para. 102.

2 See C.M. Ayala, "Del amparo constitucional al amparo interamericano como institutos para la protección de los derechos humanos", in Inter-American Court, *Liber Amicorum Héctor Fix-Zamudio*, Vol. I, 1998, San Jose, Costa Rica, pp. 341–373 (342–344).

3 OC-8/87, para. 32.

4 The exhaustion of domestic remedies is a standard of admissibility that comes from international public law and applies in cases of diplomatic protection. Its purpose is to give the State the chance to resolve an alleged violation of international obligations and avoid the matter having to come before an international jurisdiction. The exhaustion requirement is established to the benefit of the State, although it can obviously hold benefits for the offended individual if the remedies are effective. See I. Brownlie, *Principles of Public International Law*, 5th edn, Clarendon Press, Oxford, 1998, pp. 496–506.

5 *Case of Velásquez Rodríguez*, paras. 64 and 66–68.

2. ARTICLE 25 AND ITS CONNECTION WITH OTHER PROVISIONS OF THE CONVENTION

2.1. ARTICLE 25 AND ARTICLES 1(1) AND 8

4. The right to judicial protection is intimately connected with Article 1(1) and Article 8 of the Convention. The existence of a protective remedy is, on the one hand, a way of complying with the obligation to guarantee derived from Article 1(1) of the Convention and, on the other, connected with the right to a hearing contained in Article 8(1) of the Convention, as Article 25 requires that the remedy be judicial.

The majority of the case law on Article 25 of the Convention was already analyzed in the examination of Article 1(1) and Article 8.[6] As far as the connection between Article 25 and Article 1(1), for the purposes of this chapter, it is sufficient to cite what seems to be the most suitable interpretation given by the Court:

> This Court has established that "Article 25 is closely linked to the general obligation in Article 1.1 of the American Convention, in that it assigns duties of protection to the States Parties through their domestic legislation" [...], from which it is clear that the State has the obligation to design and embody in legislation an effective recourse, and also to ensure the due application of the said recourse by its judicial authorities.[7]

As regards its relationship with Article 8, the clear explanation given by the Inter-American Court in Advisory Opinion 9 is sufficient, wherein it indicates that Article 25 enshrines the right to certain remedies – *amparo* and *habeas corpus* – while Article 8 enshrines the way in which it should be made effective, as the remedies must be processed in accordance with "due process".[8] This position is reiterated in the judgment of Hilaire, Constantine and Benjamin, *et al.*, in which the Court noted that:

> In order to protect the right to effective recourse, established in Article 25 of the Convention, it is crucial that the recourse be exercised in conformity with the rules of due process, protected in Article 8 of the Convention, which include access to legal aid.[9]

Without prejudice to this, this chapter will show that the dividing line drawn by the Court's case law between Article 25 and the other two provisions cited is often tenuous or, in certain cases, invisible.

---

6 In the chapters on the right to life and the right to humane treatment, see the corresponding sections on the duty to investigate. Also see the chapter on due process, principally the section on the right to a hearing (Chapter 5, section 2.1).

7 *Case of the Street Children (Villagran Morales et al.),* para. 237.

8 OC-9/87, para. 24.

9 *Case of Hilaire, Constantine and Benjamin, et al.*, para. 148. 148.

5. Given the settled case law of the Court to the effect that the violation of any rights in the Convention leads automatically to a violation of Article 1(1) – case law that has been objected to with some justification in a dissenting vote in the case of Cantos[10] – it is no surprise that when the Court finds that Article 25 has been violated, it also finds a violation of Article 1(1). Curiously enough, sometimes a violation of Article 1 is found due to the absence of remedies, yet no violation of Article 25 is declared. This was the case, for example, in the Court's first judgment, preliminary objections in the case of Velásquez Rodríguez, in which Honduras alleged the lack of exhaustion of domestic remedies. There, the Court recalled Article 25 and held that:

> When certain exceptions to the rule of non-exhaustion of domestic remedies are invoked, such as the ineffectiveness of such remedies or the lack of due process of law, not only is it contended that the victim is under no obligation to pursue such remedies, but, indirectly, the State in question is also charged with a new violation of the obligations assumed under the Convention.[11]

This reasoning appears to anticipate a final ruling of a violation of Article 25 should the ineffectiveness or nonexistence of remedies be proven. However, in the judgment on the merits, although the Court found that the inefficiency of the remedies had been proven, it limited itself to rejecting the preliminary objection, which it had left pending resolution,[12] and declared a violation of Article 1 of the Convention. Perhaps this could be explained if the Court was in reality not examining the Article 25 remedy, but rather other domestic remedies according to admissibility rules. However, that explanation does not appear in the text of the judgment.

Furthermore, in the case of Neira Alegría *et al.*, although the Commission alleged a violation of Articles 1(1) and 25,[13] and the State made reference to the same articles,[14] the Court refrained from ruling on Article 25 and only ruled that Article 1(1) had been violated.[15]

6. When we examine the relationship between Article 25 and Article 8, we also note that the Court often finds that the absence of remedies or their lack of effectiveness leads to a violation of Article 8 of the Convention, or that the absence of one of the elements of due process indicated in Article 8 leads to a violation of Article 25 of the Convention. Normally, the Court examines the violation of both articles in the same section of the judgment and combines

10 *Case of Cantos*, separate opinion of Judge Julio Barberis. I would note that I do not share some of the arguments expressed therein: Article 1(1) clarifies the content of the obligations of the States parties with regard to each human right.

11 *Case of Velásquez Rodríguez,* para. 91.

12 *Ibidem*, para. 81.

13 *Case of Neira Alegría et al.*, paras. 2, 8, 58 and 73.

14 *Ibidem*, para. 59.

15 *Ibidem*, paras. 85 and 91.

them, like in the judgment handed down in the Cantos case: "Article 25 of the Convention also upholds the right of access to the courts".[16]

If we take the judgment in the recent Myrna Mack Chang case as an example, we will be able to note the not very advantageous symbiosis resulting from the simultaneous application of both articles. In that judgment, the Court ruled that:

> In view of what the Court has deemed proven with respect to the right to fair trial and judicial protection, the analysis of Articles 8 and 25 will address the following topics: a) gathering of evidence at the scene of the crime; b) alteration and concealment of the report on the police investigation; c) manipulation of the evidence supplied by the Presidential General Staff and the Ministry of National Defense; d) official secret; e) murder of a police investigator; harassment and threats against legal operators, police investigators, members of the Myrna Mack Foundation and of AVANCSO and the next of kin of Myrna Mack Chang; f) lack of diligence of the judges in the criminal proceedings; and g) reasonable term.[17]

This method of applying Article 25 is different from what the Court expressed in Advisory Opinion 9, as in the latter the relationship between the articles allowed for their differentiation. With this interpretation, both Article 8 and Article 25 enshrine the "right to a hearing," which does not contribute to the development and expansion of human rights through interpretation. Rather, it leads to a confusing situation, as will be seen in detail subsequently.

A confusion of the two articles can also be observed in the opinion of *Ad Hoc* Judge Ricardo Gil in the Bulacio case, in which he said that judges must ensure compliance with the rules of due process, enabling unrestricted exercise of the guarantees set forth in Article 8 of the American Convention, but on the other hand that they must also protect the victim's right to justice (Article 25 of the Convention), the concrete expression of which is delivery of a judgment on the facts and responsibilities.[18]

7. This position parallels the Court's position that was addressed during the examination of the issue of the "right to the truth" in the chapters on the right to life and the right to due process. It seems to illustrate that the Court finds that Article 25 not only enshrines the right to a simple, rapid and effective remedy, but also to other remedies, among them a victim's right to a criminal investigation into crimes that would be in violation of human rights to be launched and pursued to its conclusion in a final judgment. This has probably – and I say probably because it has not been addressed directly in the case law – been the case because, as noted earlier, the State has an obligation to provide other remedies additional to the writ of *amparo* to guarantee human rights, and the Court has wanted to identify this provision as the source of all those

16 *Case of Cantos,* para. 52.

17 *Case of Myrna Mack Chang,* para. 164.

18 *Case of Bulacio,* separate opinion of Judge Ricardo Gil Lavedra.

remedies. In my opinion, based on several of the Court's judgments that I have mentioned previously, this obligation instead derives from Article 1(1), interpreted jointly with the substantive right to which the guarantee must apply.

I think this is a crucial point in the interpretation of this provision. The position that Article 25 includes the right to all types of remedies distorts its original purpose of establishing the right to a fast and simple remedy and is to the detriment of the victims. Upon further study, one will note that the Court's case law has not developed the scope and content of this right in the sense that it establishes the Latin American remedy of *amparo*, thus depriving *amparo* of the prominent position that it should hold. I would argue that beginning the task of identifying which particular prompt, simple and effective remedies must be included in the legal systems of States Parties in order to be in compliance with the obligations of this provision would represent a great step forward for the interpretation of the Convention

2.2. ARTICLE 25 AND ARTICLE 7(6)

8. Article 25 is not the only one with provisions enshrining the right to a remedy for the protection of human rights. Article 7(6) of the Convention establishes a remedy specifically for protecting the right to personal freedom (*habeas corpus*) with its own requirements, and that remedy takes priority over the general remedy found in Article 25. In an advisory opinion, the Court clarified that the relationship between the two was one of genus to species,[19] with *habeas corpus* as established in Article 7(6) being the species. Without prejudice to this, the Court often finds that a fact has caused a violation of Article 7(6) and Article 25 at the same time. For example, this happened in the cases of Caballero Delgado and Santana,[20] Suárez Rosero,[21] and Castillo Páez.[22] The Court has also found that Article 25 has the same purpose as Article 7(6): in the case of Blake, it found that Article 25 "is an important means of determining the whereabouts of persons deprived of their liberty and of preventing forced disappearance in any circumstances".[23]

It seems curious that a fact would be considered simultaneously as a violation of genus (Article 25) and species (Article 7(6)); it would be more appropriate to rule simply that there has been a violation of species. In addition, it should be noted that the wording of these two remedies is different: Article 7(6) establishes that the remedy must be resolved "without delay", while Article 25 requires the remedy be "prompt". The difference in wording means that we must decide

19 On this point, see OC-8/87, paras. 33–34.

20 *Case of Caballero Delgado and Santana*, para. 66.

21 *Case of Suárez Rosero*, paras. 64–66.

22 *Case of Castillo Páez*, paras. 81–84.

23 *Case of Blake*, para. 103. In the same sense, see the *case of Bámaca Velásquez*, para. 192.

whether the two provisions differ substantively, and if so, in what way. For example, one could reasonably lean toward an interpretation according to which the time period granted by Article 7(6) is shorter than the one allowed for by Article 25. If the concepts are different, it is even more reasonable to draw a distinction between them when making a ruling. It would therefore be extremely useful if the Inter-American Court would begin to differentiate between the different elements it takes into consideration in deciding whether a violation has taken place, as this would help develop the scope and content of each right more clearly.

3. CHARACTERISTICS OF THE REMEDY

9. One cannot help but notice that an examination of the characteristics that the remedy outlined in Article 25 must have often used standards similar to the ones used for analyzing other domestic remedies. I have made the decision in this chapter not to elaborate further on this point. Still, a full examination must be carried out of the differences between the writ of *amparo* and the other remedies that must exist in a State in order to ensure human rights. As stated previously, all remedies must be adequate and effective, and the evaluation of those characteristics requires that parameters be established that are pertinent to the objectives of each one of those remedies. This task falls to the regional oversight bodies.

3.1. JUDICIAL REMEDY

10. Article 25 is innovative as compared to the international law in existence prior to the adoption of the American Convention in the sense that it establishes a remedy that must be judicial. This is in contrast with the provisions of Article 2(3) of the International Covenant on Civil and Political Rights (the Covenant) and Article 13 of the European Convention on Human Rights, which only require the State to provide an effective remedy.

The assertion that Article 25 demands a judicial remedy must be backed up, particularly because paragraph 2(b) of that article requires the State to commit to "develop the possibilities of judicial remedy". This can lead to the assumption that there is no direct and immediate obligation for States parties to have the remedy in place from the moment the obligations of the Convention took effect. Such an interpretation can be dismissed out of hand based on the title that the Convention itself gives to this right, which is precisely "judicial protection". However, the preparatory work of the Convention also disqualifies this interpretation.

11. The Article's original text establishes the right to an "effective, simple and prompt remedy before competent domestic judges and courts that protects against acts that violate fundamental rights recognized by the Constitution or by law".[24] This wording was rejected because it did not make reference to the human rights set forth in the Convention. In order to fix this omission, two governments proposed inserting a provision similar to Article 2(3) of the Covenant into the Article, whose subparagraph (a) would contain the State obligation to ensure an individual's right to access an "effective" remedy, and not necessarily a judicial one; subparagraph (b), the obligation for the competent authority to rule on the rights and develop "the potential judicial remedy"; and subparagraph (c), the obligation to comply with all rulings arising from the remedy.[25] The logic of Article 2(3) was impeccable, but it had to be taken up in its entirety in order to avoid contradictions. The suggestion, however, was to add it to the original text, where the right to a "judicial" remedy had already been established. Noting this, the Colombian delegate objected to the proposal, stating that the commitment to adjust the domestic legal system to the Convention was already enshrined in Article 1. For this reason, he suggested what seemed to be the obvious solution: simply add a reference to the Convention's rights to the text under discussion. Following a short debate in which Chile explained that the purpose of its proposal was "to establish clearly that the Governments were committed to adopting the proper measures for making the rights effective", the suggestion to reproduce Article 2(3) of the Covenant was passed.[26]

Regardless of the fact that from a technical legal point of view, the passage of the proposal was a mistake, it is clear that the purpose of paragraph 2(b) of Article 25 of the Convention is identical to that of the addition of Article 2 of the Convention, that being to reinforce the State's obligation to adjust its legal system to the treaty's obligations. The intention is not to change the State obligation set forth in paragraph 1.

3.2. SIMPLE, PROMPT AND EFFECTIVE REMEDY

12. The Convention establishes the right to a "simple and prompt" remedy, although it adds "or any other effective recourse", raising doubts over whether the State's obligation is fulfilled with the establishment of an "effective" remedy, even if it is not simple or prompt. Study of the origins of this proposal only deepens the doubt. The original wording read: "Every person has the right to an

24 Specialized Conference, *Minutes and Documents*, San Jose, Costa Rica, 7–22 November 1969, (OEA/Ser.K/XVI/1.2), p. 22.

25 *Ibidem*, p. 41 (comments from the government of Chile) and pp. 55–56 (comments from the government of the Dominican Republic).

26 *Ibidem*, pp. 261–263.

effective, simple and prompt remedy".[27] In its comments on the draft, the Government of the Dominican Republic stated that cases may arise in which protection was "effective" even when it was not "simple and prompt", and argued that the only criteria necessary for a remedy to be legitimate was that it be "effective". It then proposed a new text in which this part was identical to that of the final version.[28] During discussion of the article, the Mexican delegate asked that the text be amended, again suggesting the original wording of a "simple, prompt and effective remedy". The American delegate had a different proposal – a return to the Dominican Republic's text without stating as much. He added, along with the proposal, that he "did not believe that [the words] changed the meaning". The discussion then moved on to the problem of the rights that must be protected by the remedy (as commented on previously) and discussion on this particular subject concluded.[29] The Report of the Rapporteur of Commission I clarified that the article contains the right to "a simple, prompt and effective remedy" and that the purpose of the amendments was to add a second subparagraph setting forth the States' commitments as regards this remedy.[30] There is no other background information in the preparatory work.

13. For its part, the Court has taken the sensible position of holding that all three conditions must be in place at the same time. So for example, in Advisory Opinion 9/87, the Court states that Article 25(1) "gives expression to the procedural institution known as *amparo*, which is a simple and prompt remedy designed for the protection of all the fundamental rights". The opinion adds that, "This article also establishes in broad terms the obligation of the States to provide an effective judicial remedy to violations of fundamental rights to all persons within their jurisdiction". The Court's conclusion is that Article 25(1) of the American Convention incorporates the principle of the effectiveness of procedural instruments or measures designed to guarantee human rights, as recognized in international human rights law.[31] The Court can be observed to have taken the same position in the judgment in the case of Suárez Rosero, in which it found that Mr Suárez had been denied access to "a simple, prompt *and* effective judicial remedy."[32]

3.2.1. Simple and prompt remedy

14. The Court's case law still does not provide a guide for deciding when the remedy enshrined in Article 25 is "simple and prompt". As far as simplicity is

27 See text of Article 23 in *ibidem*, p. 22.

28 *Ibidem*, p. 66.

29 *Ibidem*, pp. 261–263.

30 *Ibidem*, pp. 302–303.

31 OC-9/87, paras. 23 and 24.

32 *Case of Suárez Rosero*, para. 66 (emphasis added).

concerned, there has been no ruling describing it in the terms of Article 25. Regarding the promptness of the remedy, the Court frequently analyzes it in connection with the parameters of reasonable period of time as established in Article 8 of the Convention. In the case of Ivcher Bronstein, it addressed the subject by stating that:

> Likewise, the general circumstances of this case indicate that the judicial recourses filed by Mr Ivcher to defend his shareholder's rights were not simple and prompt; to the contrary, as the witness Emilio Rodríguez Larraín declared during the public hearing, "they were only resolved after a long time", which contrasts with the process given to the actions filed by the minority shareholders of the Company, which were resolved promptly.[33]

In the case of Cantos, the Court found that:

> considering, *inter alia*, the complexity of the case and the plaintiff's failure to take action to move the case forward, the overall duration of the litigious proceedings would not be significant enough for a finding that the articles that protect access to the courts and judicial guarantees have been violated.[34]

This argument by the Court has already been criticized for other reasons in Chapter 5 of this book on Article 8 of the Convention.[35] Regarding Article 25 (even though the Court did not find that there had not been a violation, but rather that there was insufficient evidence to rule on that point) the criticism is more severe, as it does not seem possible to argue that the simplicity and promptness of an *amparo* remedy can be measured with the same standard as that of a reasonable period of time for concluding the trial, and one clearly cannot argue that a ruling on such a remedy can last many years, even if there has been a "lack of interest on the part of the plaintiff."

In the case of Suárez Rosero, connecting the right to a writ of *habeas corpus* as established in Article 7(6) of the Convention with the rights established in Article 25, the Court found that 14 months was an excessive period of time for ruling on the request for a remedy, and that therefore Articles 7(6) and 25 of the Convention had been violated.[36]

In the case of the Constitutional Court, the Inter-American Court based its ruling in part on the time period given in Peru's own legal system for processing *amparo* remedies, in order to argue that a remedy that had been ruled on more than six months after it was invoked in a situation in which Peruvian law gave a maximum and final deadline of 20 days for doing so violated Article 25 of the American Convention.[37]

---

33 *Case of Ivcher Bronstein*, para. 140.

34 *Case of Cantos*, para. 57.

35 See Chapter 5, section 2.4.3.

36 *Case of Suárez Rosero*, paras. 64–66.

37 *Case of the Constitutional Court*, para. 91.

15. From another angle, in the case of Myrna Mack Chang, the Court used the absence of quickness in the processing of *amparos* brought by the plaintiff as a basis for finding a violation of Articles 8 and 25 to the detriment of the relatives of the victim: *amparo* remedies could be ruled on in up to four different instances and paralyzed the main criminal trial where the facts of a violation of human rights were being investigated; they were therefore remedies that delayed the proceedings,[38] not to the detriment of the individual submitting them, but to the detriment of those who sought to hold the perpetrators of human rights violations criminally responsible for their actions.[39]

3.2.2. Effective remedy

16. The Court's case law on the requirement of the existence of an "effective" remedy is abundant.[40] In the judgment on the merits in the case of Velásquez Rodríguez, the Court explained the meaning of the word "effective", indicating that the remedy must be "capable of producing the result for which it was designed".[41] It added that this did not mean that all remedies must necessarily be granted, but rather that there must be at least a serious possibility that they will be.[42]

Advisory Opinion 9/87 expanded on this argument, finding that:

> for such a remedy to exist, it is not sufficient that it be provided for by the Constitution or by law or that it be formally recognized, but rather it must be truly effective in establishing whether there has been a violation of human rights and in providing redress. A remedy which proves illusory because of the general conditions prevailing in the country, or even in the particular circumstances of a given case, cannot be considered effective. That could be the case, for example, when practice has shown its ineffectiveness; when the Judicial Power lacks the necessary independence to render impartial decisions or the means to carry out its judgments; or in any other situation that constitutes a denial of justice, as when there is an unjustified delay in the decision; or when, for any reason, the alleged victim is denied access to a judicial remedy.[43]

---

38 *Case of Myrna Mack Chang*, paras. 204–205.

39 On this point, I refer the reader to the discussion of the role of the victim in a criminal proceeding: see Chapter 5, section 2.1.

40 I would add the caveat that much of this case law involves rulings on Article 7(6) and Article 8.

41 *Case of Velásquez Rodríguez*, para. 66.

42 *Ibidem*, paras. 67 and 68. Also see, *inter alia*, OC-9/87, para. 24; *Case of the Mayagna (Sumo) Awas Tingni Community*, paras. 111–113; *Case of the Constitutional Court*, para. 90; *Case of Bámaca Velásquez*, para. 191; *Case of Cesti Hurtado*, para. 125; *Case of the "White Van" (Paniagua Morales et al.)*, para. 164; and *Case of Suárez Rosero*, para. 63.

43 OC-9/87, para. 24. Also see, *inter alia*, *Case of the "White Van" (Paniagua Morales et al.)*, para. 164; *Case of Suárez Rosero*, para. 63; *Case of Ivcher Bronstein*, paras. 136–137; and *Case of Cantos*, para. 52.

17. It thus seems that for the Court, effectiveness has to do with a remedy's potential capacity in fact and law to produce the result necessary to protect the right. However, it is also related to due process, as the Court tends to find that Article 25 of the Convention has been violated when one or more of the elements set forth in Article 8 of the Convention is absent.

This latter point is clearly illustrated in the case of Ivcher Bronstein, in which the Court found that because the requirements that the court be independent and impartial as established in Article 8(1) of the Convention had not been met in the domestic proceedings, the remedies available to the petitioner had not been effective.[44] The Court ruled likewise in the case of Durand and Ugarte, where it examined the problem of bias and lack of independence of military courts and the absence of an effective remedy for investigating the facts and trying and punishing those responsible, as well as failure to provide reparations for the damages, all according to the provisions of Articles 25 and 8(1). It reached the conclusion that both articles had been violated.[45] Here once again one notes the broadness of the interpretation, as it makes Articles 25 and 8 almost indistinguishable.

18. The lack of effectiveness of remedies is often the result of a situation and not the facts of a specific case. As a general rule, States in situations of massive and systematic violations are understood to not be providing effective remedies, as the ineffectiveness of the remedies is in reality an aspect of the situation.[46] An early judgment assessing the effectiveness of remedies was handed down in the case of Gangaram Panday (which took place during the Bouterse dictatorship in Suriname), in which the Court used an argument contrary to the one just described: in response to the Commission's allegation that Article 25 had been violated, the Court observed that:

> in principle, the confirmation of a single case of violation of human rights by the authorities of a State is not in itself sufficient grounds to presume or infer the existence in that State of widespread, large-scale practices to the detriment of the rights of other citizens.[47]

In the case of Bámaca Velásquez, who disappeared after being apprehended by State agents, the Court found that the lack of effectiveness of *habeas corpus* in Guatemala had been demonstrated by, among other things, the statements of the president of the Guatemalan Supreme Court himself to the effect that the "mechanisms that currently exist for *habeas corpus* procedures are inadequate to carry out an effective investigation under petitions for *habeas corpus*."[48]

---

44 *Case of Ivcher Bronstein*, para. 139.

45 *Case of Durand and Ugarte*, paras. 125–127 and 130.

46 On this point, see C. Medina, *The Battle of Human Rights. Gross, Systematic Violations and the Inter-American System*, Martinus Nijhoff, Dordrecht/Boston/London, 1988, pp. 15–16.

47 *Case of Gangaram Panday*, para. 64.

48 *Case of Bámaca Velásquez*, para. 193.

19. The Court has also found remedies to be ineffective because the individuals affected were prevented from exercising the remedies in practice. This is the case when individuals are secretly detained, secret detention being common in situations of massive and systematic violations. The Court's case law on this issue has not been consistent.

In the case of the Street Children, in which the victims were detained for several hours before being executed, the Court ruled that Article 25 had been violated because the victims – both adults and minors – and the third parties representing them were prevented from exercising the right to seek an effective remedy before domestic courts, presumably *habeas corpus*.[49] In contrast, in the case of Caballero Delgado and Santana, the Court did not find that the Convention – Article 8, which the Court often applies jointly with Article 25 – had been violated "[g]iven the short time that transpired between the capture of the persons [...] and their presumed death[s]"[50] under circumstances in which the victims would not have been able to make use of the remedy. In both cases, the relatives would have been able to request a remedy, but only the mother of the victim in the second case did so, and without result.

In the case of Paniagua Morales, the basis of the violation with regard to several of the murder victims was that prior to their deaths, they had been in the hands of State agents and it had not been proven that they had access in any way "to the judicial remedy that would have guaranteed both their freedom and their lives".[51] With regard to Ms Paniagua Morales, the *habeas corpus* writ sought by her relatives had no result "because from the time she was detained by members of the Treasury Police her whereabouts were unknown and she was subsequently found dead", thus proving "the ineffectiveness of the remedy of *habeas corpus*".[52] However, in the case of Caballero Delgado and Santana, similar circumstances led to a different ruling: in that case, the writ of *habeas corpus* sought by the relatives brought no results either because the commander of the Fifth Brigade of Bucaramanga, the director of the Bucaramanga Model Prison, the Administrative Security Department and the Judicial Police, all State bodies, replied to the judge that Caballero Delgado was not being held in any of their agencies, and that there were no warrants out for his arrest, nor had he been convicted of anything. The Court found that this did not constitute a violation of Article 25 of the Convention.[53]

Finally, in the case of Bámaca Velásquez, the lack of results from a *habeas corpus* writ sought for the benefit of Mr Bámaca led the Court to find that there had been a violation of Article 25.[54]

---

49 *Case of the Street Children (Villagrán Morales et al.),* para. 236.
50 *Case of Caballero Delgado and Santana,* para. 64.
51 *Case of the "White Van" (Paniagua Morales et al.),* para. 167.
52 *Ibidem,* para. 166.
53 *Case of Caballero Delgado and Santana,* para. 66.
54 *Case of Bámaca Velásquez,* para. 193.

20. There have been cases in which the basis of a violation of Article 25 has been that State agents blocked the processing of a writ of *habeas corpus*, as for example in the case of Castillo Páez. In its judgment, the Court found "that the remedy filed by Mr Castillo Páez's next of kin against his detention (*habeas corpus*) was obstructed by State agents through the adulteration of the logs of entry of detainees, which made it impossible to locate the victim". For this reason, the writ of *habeas corpus* was ineffective and Article 25 of the Convention had been violated.[55] However, in the case of Génie Lacayo, in which the Commission argued that Articles 8, 25 and 24 had been violated, and in which the Court found that it had been proven that Nicaragua's military authorities had obstructed or failed to collaborate adequately with the preliminary investigations and the judge hearing the case, the Court found that Article 8(1) had been violated, but not Article 25, because "the Commission has indicated the possible violation of [...] procedural rights protected under Article 8(1) of the Convention [...] but not the non-existence or ineffectiveness of this remedy, nor even that it was applied".[56] It seems that the Court found that the obstruction was not enough to rule that Article 25 had been violated because the father of the victim had been able to take part in the military proceedings, offer evidence, execute the corresponding remedies, and bring a cassation appeal before the Supreme Court.[57]

A similar case is that of Blake. Therein, the Court ruled that Article 25 had not been violated because the father of Blake, whose body had been missing for several years, had not specifically sought a writ of *habeas corpus,* even though one of Blake's relatives stated in the hearing before the Court that they "had never met with or talked to a representative of the Judiciary about this case, because the State alleged that the area in question was controlled by the army and that it was better to deal directly with the military officials".[58] The State agents' obstruction of the criminal proceedings which occurred in this case was not enough for the Court to find that Article 25 of the American Convention had been violated.[59]

21. The lack of effectiveness can be specific to a single case. The Court has found that when a court sets court or legal fees that are very high, this is "an obstruction to effective administration of justice" and a violation of Article 25 and Article 8 of the Convention.[60] In the case of the Constitutional Court, the lack of impartiality of the members of the Constitutional Court was basis enough to find that Article 25 had been violated.[61] Evidently, the Inter-American Court also ruled that the remedies were not effective when they did not resolve the situation for which they were sought.[62]

---

55 *Case of Castillo Páez,* paras. 81–83. In the same sense, see *Case of Suárez Rosero,* para. 65.

56 *Case of Genie Lacayo,* paras. 68, 76 and 89.

57 *Ibidem,* para. 85.

58 *Case of Blake,* paras. 100 and 104.

59 *Ibidem,* paras. 89, 92 and 93.

60 *Case of Cantos,* para. 54–56.

61 *Case of the Constitutional Court,* para. 96.

62 *Case of Baena Ricardo et al.,* paras. 138 and 141.

22. Of course, if the law itself does not grant the remedy, the violation is a general and clear one. In two cases against Peru whose victims were individuals being tried for terrorism, the Court ruled that the fact that Peruvian law did not admit the remedy of *habeas corpus* for the plaintiffs constituted a violation of Article 25 of the American Convention.[63] The Court has also connected applying the statute of limitations to a pending trial with the right set forth in Article 25, indicating that the general obligations enshrined in Articles 1(1) and 2 of the American Convention require that the States Party adopt timely provisions of all types so that no one is denied the right to judicial protection, enshrined in Article 25 of the American Convention.[64]

4. STATE OBLIGATIONS

23. Paragraph 2 of Article 25 sets forth States' obligations as regards the right of every individual to a simple, prompt and effective remedy. This is nothing new; the obligations set forth here are necessary for the right recognized in the first paragraph. Subparagraph (b) of paragraph 2 of this article has already been discussed. With regard to subparagraphs (a) and (c), clearly if there is a right to a remedy, it must be granted to "any person" and in connection with all rights, even if this last point is not explicit; the decision regarding the remedy must be made by the competent authority; and once the decision is made, it must be complied with and respected by the corresponding State bodies, given that compliance with court orders is part of the due process enshrined in Article 8.

24. In the case of the Five Pensioners, the Court examined the petitioners' allegation that Peru failed to comply with the final judgments of both the Supreme Court of Peru and the Peruvian Constitutional Court. It concluded that since some of the rulings had not been complied with and orders had been issued "resulting from the applications for protective measures, which protect the status quo, the State cannot fail to comply with such decisions, at the risk of incurring in violations of the right to property and to judicial protection".[65] Notwithstanding this conclusion, the Court seems to ascribe the violation to the fact that the remedies were not effective. It does not mention a failure to comply with Article 25(2)(c),[66] nor does it mention the argument that, as stated in the previous paragraph, the obligation to comply with court orders in any kind of proceeding or remedy emanates from Article 8 of the Convention.

---

63 *Case of Loayza Tamayo*, paras. 52–55; *Case of Castillo Petruzzi et al.*, paras. 180–181.

64 *Case of Bulacio*, para. 116.

65 *Case of the "Five Pensioners"*, paras. 138 and 141. On this, see Chapter 5, section 2.4.5.

66 *Ibidem*, para. 136.

25. On examination of the case law, one can conclude that this provision is in need of further development, both from the Court and in the academic discussion, particularly because of its enormous importance for protecting the human rights set forth in the Convention and enshrined domestically. Article 25 deserves to be interpreted and applied in a way that provides it with its rightful autonomy.

5. RIGHT TO A REMEDY AND EMERGENCY SITUATIONS

26. Article 27 of the Convention, which limits the way in which States can suspend the obligations implicit in the Convention in an emergency situation, includes among its limitations a list of rights whose obligations may never be suspended. That list concludes with a ban on the suspension of the judicial guarantees that are indispensable for protecting the rights contained in the Convention.[67]

27. As Article 27(2) does not link the guarantees to any specific provision of the Convention, it is the responsibility of the body applying the Convention to decide which provisions the article applies to. The Court moved to interpret the wording in two advisory opinions. In the first, at the request of the Inter-American Commission, it addressed the matter of *habeas corpus* in the case of an emergency situation, a remedy provided for in Article 7(6) of the Convention, and the right to a simple and prompt remedy for preventing human rights violations, as established in Article 25.[68] In the second advisory opinion, this time requested by the government of Uruguay, it interpreted Articles 8 and 25.[69]

28. Regarding Article 25(1), the Court based its opinion on two basic suppositions: first, the need to examine which proceedings "will effectively guarantee the full exercise of the rights and freedoms protected by" Article 27 in order to advise or give an opinion on which guarantees may not be suspended;[70] and second, the need to be aware that the non-derogable guarantees are different depending on the rights affected. As examples, the Court pointed to the guarantees of the rights protecting personal integrity and name.[71]

The Court began its analysis of the suspension of guarantees regime in general terms, indicating that the abuses that could arise from the State authority

---

67 While this was already discussed in Chapter 1, section 7, this is a more appropriate place to develop the subject.

68 OC-8/87.

69 OC-9/87.

70 OC-8/87, paras. 27 and 29.

71 *Ibidem*, para. 28.

to suspend obligations as set forth in the Convention cannot be ignored or set aside, and therefore, the Court must emphasize that the suspension of guarantees cannot be disassociated from the "effective exercise of representative democracy" referred to in Article 3 of the OAS Charter.[72]

Thus it established the condition for the regulation of suspensions of guarantees that they may not affect representative democracy.

Next, it stated that the suspension of guarantees does not entail "a temporary suspension of the rule of law", nor does it authorize a government "to act in disregard of the principle of legality by which they are bound at all times", as "the principle of legality, democratic institutions and the rule of law" are inseparable.[73]

The Court structured its opinion based on this, placing special emphasis on the fact that the guarantees referred to in Article 27 are "judicial", stating that:

> The expression "judicial" can only refer to those judicial remedies that are truly capable of protecting these rights.
>
> Implicit in this conception is the active involvement of an *independent and impartial* judicial body having the power to pass on the lawfulness of measures adopted in a state of emergency.[74]

This statement is important if one considers that in the countries on this continent, authority in a state of emergency is often given to military courts that do not meet the required conditions of independence and impartiality.

Using these ideas as a basis, the Court found that: (i) as regards the rights set forth in Article 27(2), both Article 25(1) (genus) and Article 7(6) (species) represent judicial guarantees that cannot be suspended, arguing additionally that they also serve "to preserve legality in a democratic society";[75] and (ii) legal provisions in States parties that "authorize, expressly or by implication, the suspension of the legal remedies of *habeas corpus* or of *amparo* in emergency situations cannot be deemed to be compatible with the international obligations imposed on these States by the Convention."[76]

Of course, remedies that protect rights that are not suspended during a state of emergency cannot be suspended either.[77]

The second advisory opinion repeats these arguments with regard to Article 25(1) and examines Article 8 in detail, concluding that, as examined previously, Article 8 contains the requirements necessary to give substance to the remedies set forth in Article 25(1).[78]

---

72 *Ibidem*, para. 20.
73 *Ibidem*, para. 24.
74 *Ibidem*, para. 30 (emphasis added).
75 *Ibidem*, paras. 44 and 42.
76 *Ibidem*, para. 43.
77 OC-9/87, para. 46.
78 See Chapter 1, section 7.2, and in this chapter, section 2, para. 3.

29. The Court has applied this interpretation in several contentious cases. In the case of Durand and Ugarte, the problem arose of ruling on the limitations that the application of certain decrees declaring an emergency in Peru had imposed on judges hearing *amparo* pleas. Those limitations prevented judges from entering the prisons because they were located in restricted military zones. Here the Court found that:

> The limitations imposed on the obligations of the State respond to 'the general requirement that in any state of emergency there be appropriate means to control the measures taken, so that they are proportionate to the needs and do not exceed to strict limits imposed by the Convention or derived from it'.[79]

Taking this into consideration, the Court found that this limitation on the judges made the writ of *habeas corpus* – the appropriate remedy for establishing the whereabouts of victims – useless, and that therefore, the limitations were not permissible during a state of emergency.[80]

Similar arguments and conclusions can be found in the judgment in the case of Cantoral Benavides.[81]

30. The case law of the Court on this point is of great value and has undoubtedly served as inspiration for other international supervisory bodies for the broadening of their interpretations of the rules they apply toward consolidating the need for the right to a simple, prompt and effective remedy to remain in force during periods of emergency.

---

79 *Case of Durand and Ugarte*, para. 99.

80 *Ibidem*, paras. 100, 103, 108 and 109.

81 *Case of Cantoral Benavides*, paras. 165–166.